W9-BCR-783

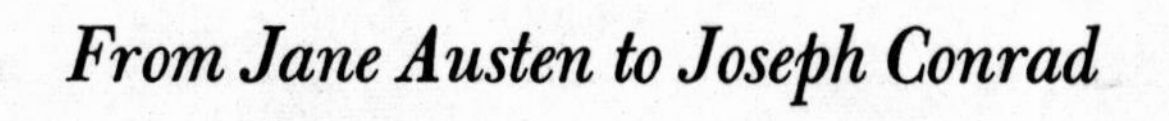
From Jane Austen to Joseph Conrad

From Jane Austen to Joseph Conrad

ESSAYS COLLECTED IN MEMORY OF

James T. Hillhouse

EDITED BY

Robert C. Rathburn

AND

Martin Steinmann, Jr.

UNIVERSITY OF MINNESOTA PRESS · MINNEAPOLIS

PRINTED IN THE UNITED STATES OF AMERICA AT THE
NORTH CENTRAL PUBLISHING COMPANY, ST. PAUL

 3

Library of Congress Catalog Card Number: 58-59589

Second printing 1967

PUBLISHED IN GREAT BRITAIN, INDIA, AND PAKISTAN BY THE OXFORD
UNIVERSITY PRESS, LONDON, BOMBAY, AND KARACHI, AND IN CANADA
BY THE COPP CLARK PUBLISHING CO. LIMITED, TORONTO

ACKNOWLEDGMENTS

CERTAIN contributors wish to thank individuals and institutions that have been especially helpful to them as they prepared their contributions to this book.

Mr. Steinmann thanks the American Philosophical Society, of Philadelphia, and the Louis W. and Maud Hill Family Foundation, of St. Paul, for their generous grants of funds; and the University of Minnesota for the sabbatical leave which allowed him to complete his contribution to this volume.

Mr. Murrah thanks the Oxford University Press, of New York, for permission to quote from its edition of *Mansfield Park*, edited by R. W. Chapman.

Mr. McKillop thanks the Clarendon Press for permission to quote from its editions of Jane Austen's *Minor Works* and *Letters*, edited by R. W. Chapman.

Mr. Haight thanks the Yale University Press for permission to quote from *The George Eliot Letters*.

Mr. Korg thanks Mr. Alfred C. Gissing for permission to quote from unpublished letters of George Gissing; Miss Marjorie G. Wynne of the Yale University Library for permission to quote from the letters from George Gissing to Eduard Bertz; and Mr. Rutherford D. Rogers, chief of the reference department of the New York Public Library, for permission to quote from the Gissing letters in the Berg collection.

PREFACE

WE UNDERTOOK the production of the present volume with two purposes in mind. First, we wished to honor Professor James T. Hillhouse, whose more than forty years of teaching at the University of Minnesota were then about to draw to a close. Second, we wished to produce a volume valuable as a contribution to literary criticism and history.

Anxious to avoid the usual collection of papers by divers hands on a variety of subjects, we chose as our theme the nineteenth-century British novel. That choice was especially fitting because of Professor Hillhouse's interest in the novel, demonstrated throughout his years of teaching and by his *The Waverley Novels and Their Critics*, a work called "indispensable" by J. C. Corson in his definitive modern bibliography of Scott. Critics and scholars were asked to write essays on the various novelists within the period marked off by Jane Austen and Joseph Conrad. As requested, each has focused his attention on some one novel or aspect of an author's work and yet, while being particular, has endeavored to give the reader a sense of the author's whole achievement. We are grateful to our contributors for accepting the invitation to write and, moreover, are pleased with their demonstrated ability to take our suggested assignment and make it their own. As complements to the particular pieces, the general essays outline the development of the British novel before and after the nineteenth century. All the major nineteenth-century novelists are represented by essays and some of the minor novelists as well. In selecting the latter, we have been guided in part by the contributors' own interest in the minor figures. All essays were written expressly for this volume, and none has previously appeared elsewhere. We hope that the book is representative of the best contemporary critical judgment of the nineteenth-century British novel.

One hope for the book will not be fulfilled. Professor Hillhouse died suddenly during the course of the preparation of the volume; hence, instead of its serving as a gift upon his retirement, it will have to stand as a memorial to his teaching and scholarship.

We wish to thank Professor Theodore Hornberger, chairman of the Department of English at the University of Minnesota, for his constant encouragement and aid to this project. We are also thankful to Professor William Van O'Connor for his helpful advice at many points during the volume's preparation. To Dean Errett W. McDiarmid and other members of the University Press advisory committee go our thanks for their approval of the book. We are particularly indebted to Miss Helen Clapesattle (now Mrs. Roger W. Shugg), former director of the University of Minnesota Press, for her original blessing of the volume. We also wish to thank Mr. John Ervin, Jr., present director of the Press, and his staff, who carried the book through to publication. For their advice at critical editorial moments we are grateful to Professor Edgar F. Shannon, Jr., of the University of Virginia; Dr. Julian H. Markels, of The Ohio State University; and Mr. John D. Kendall, of Bowdoin College. Further, we wish to acknowledge generally the helpful inquiries and suggestions made by other members of the academic community at Minnesota and elsewhere. We thank especially Mrs. Jane Tyack Steinmann and Mrs. Louise Jones Rathburn for their help in the preparing of copy and the reading of proof.

Finally — and once again — we thank our contributors. Without their willing cooperation and splendid work this Hillhouse memorial volume could not have been produced.

ROBERT C. RATHBURN
MARTIN STEINMANN, JR.

Minneapolis, Minnesota
November, 1957

JAMES THEODORE HILLHOUSE

JAMES THEODORE HILLHOUSE was born on February 17, 1890, in Willamantic, Connecticut. He was a graduate of Yale College in the class of 1911. After advanced study leading to the Ph.D. degree in 1914, he joined the staff of the University of Minnesota, maintaining that connection without break, other than for sabbatical leaves, for more than forty-two years. From 1948 until his death on December 10, 1956, he was associate chairman of the Department of English.

Three books by Professor Hillhouse are to be found in every respectable library of English literary history: an admirable critical edition of Henry Fielding's *The Tragedy of Tragedies, or, The Life and Death of Tom Thumb the Great* (Yale University Press, 1918); *The Grub-street Journal* (Duke University Press, 1928); and *The Waverley Novels and Their Critics* (University of Minnesota Press, 1936). His last scholarly work was his contribution of the chapter on Scott to *The English Romantic Poets and Essayists* (Modern Language Association, 1957).

His teaching paralleled his research interests. Many generations of students, often in large numbers, surveyed British drama since 1660 under his direction, and numerous dissertations originated in his sequence of seminars on the British novel. He commanded the respect, and to an extraordinary degree the affection, of undergraduate and graduate students alike.

To his colleagues, he was a tower of strength in all the crises, great or small, with which an academic community can be afflicted. Well-mannered, conscientious, generous of his time and good sense, utterly honest in indicating where he stood, and meticulous in meeting every obligation, he was a man long to be remembered by those fortunate enough to be associated with him.

THEODORE HORNBERGER
University of Minnesota

TABLE OF CONTENTS

From Jane Austen to Joseph Conrad

From Jane Austen to Joseph Conrad

THE MAKERS OF THE BRITISH NOVEL

Robert C. Rathburn
UNIVERSITY OF MINNESOTA

ALTHOUGH something approaching the modern novel had been written in England and elsewhere before the eighteenth century, it was not until that time that the novel can be said to have been invented, formed, and sent on its way to dominance over all other genres. By the time the century closed, the technical devices of the novel had been invented. Later novelists would perfect them but would not add to them. Many themes for the novel had been set forth, and sub-classes or types of novels had been begun.

The rise of the novel in the eighteenth century coincided with the rise of prose to respectability and the emergence of a middle-class reading public ready for prose fiction. Although earlier prose has its admirers, its ornate and periphrastic qualities mark it off sharply from the clear, simple prose that began perhaps with Dryden and was perfected by Addison, Steele, and Swift — and by Defoe, the writer of the first British novels. That prose, devoted to clarity and simplicity, was addressed to a widening public, readers of periodicals and of political pamphlets. To the periodical writers' purpose of informing and persuading the public was soon added the purpose of entertaining through prose fiction.

The Elizabethans had almost invented the novel, but the form was not quite a serious matter with them. They were much too interested in "higher" genres — poetry and the drama — to do more than experiment with the long prose tale. Sir Philip Sidney's *Arcadia* (published 1590) is but an idealized pastoral romance. Its emphasis on the deeds of romance and chivalry cut it off from realistic life; its lack of unified action estranges it from our idea of the novel. John Lyly in *Euphues* (1578) anticipated the later novel of manners, but the book's *préciosité* and the artificiality of the story distinguish it from the modern novel. Thomas Lodge's *Rosalynde* (1590) was another Arcadian romance, but it owed something to Lyly's example too, as the sub-title *Euphues' Golden Legacie* demonstrated. Robert Greene and Thomas Nashe wrote more realistic prose tales of London low life and a rogue's adventures. In *The Unfortunate Traveller* (1594), Nashe imitated the picaresque adventure story of Spain, like the *Lazarillo* attributed to Mendoza and translated into English in 1576. But Nashe's story of the adventures of Jack Wilton is a sequence of loosely connected episodes, not a unified novel. The Elizabethans anticipated the structure and the diverse purposes of the novel, but they left for later writers the task of combining the entertaining qualities of romance and the depiction of real life so as to serve a social purpose.

Daniel Defoe combined these elements successfully in *Robinson Crusoe* (1719). The charm of Defoe's tale still is the blend of realism and romance: granted the romantic situation of the island castaway, a real man might well act as Crusoe does. The effect of the experience on the hero — his change from a harum-scarum youth to a serious, God-fearing man as he meets the natural challenges of his isolated existence — provides Defoe with a social message and the reader with a character who "develops" as a result of the action. The three levels of interest — action, character, and idea — are all served in Defoe's novel.

Defoe's contribution to the structure of the novel, great as it was, must be considered to be limited to one book, *Crusoe*. Therein the unity of the action is plain: we have a unit of a man's experience and its effects upon him, not merely a succession of episodes. True, Defoe has difficulty in beginning and ending, but we partially excuse that ineptness by realizing that the author had to get Crusoe on his island and then off. The framework for the island story may mar the unity, but the central action on the island consists of a series of scenes which lead up to the point of the action (Crusoe's conquering of the environment) and to the development of the character (Crusoe's change to a mature outlook). This in turn develops the idea (moral, if one prefers the old-fashioned term) that anyone so beset as Crusoe might well reassess his relationship to God and his purpose in the world.

Defoe's later novels have not so neat a structure. *Moll Flanders* (1722) pretends to similar unity, but Moll's moral renunciation of her past life is marred by strings of episodes from her evil days seemingly told for their own sake. *Captain Singleton* (1720) and *Colonel Jacque* (1722) are throwbacks to the old picaresque series of adventures, and *Roxana* (1724) is merely a Moll Flanders in higher life. The narrator of the incidents of the plague year is limited by the time of the historical event, and the action dominates other levels of interest; the same is true of the Cavalier's account of the campaigns of Gustavus Adolphus and of Charles I. For concentrated attention to unity of action, the novel had to wait for Fielding; nevertheless Defoe, perhaps by happy choice of subject, succeeded in *Crusoe* in being more than anecdotal. In his first novel he told a unified tale, complete in theme and not arbitrarily limited by historical time and circumstance.

In addition to forming the novel into a coherent whole, Defoe made two other contributions to its stock of technical devices. To twentieth-century readers, the more important contribution is Defoe's handling of point of view, or focus of narration. Although his immediate successors ignored his example, we with our concern for technique can see how skillfully Defoe created his personae who tell their own stories. Some readers may object that Defoe was not nearly so conscious in the management of point of view as was, say, Henry James, but the aim of both — and indeed of all writers careful of the view from which the story is given to the reader — is verisimilitude. The modern novelist wishes, by presenting his tale through the eyes of one of his characters, to create the illusion of reality. Defoe's desire for verisimilitude was even greater; he wanted his fictions to be accepted as fact.

Defoe's previous experience as a pamphleteer, journalist, and counter-spy led him, accidentally if you will, to write his novels from the first-person point of view, with the narrator as the leading participant in the action. In an early piece of propaganda, *The Shortest Way with Dissenters* (1702), Defoe used the device of a persona so well that his satire had a doubly ironic effect in that the persons satirized took him seriously. The "high-flying" Tory who presumably wrote *The Shortest Way* suggested the alternatives of the gallows or full conformity for dissenters. This supposed revelation of the extreme Tory view was at first taken by both Anglican and dissenting readers as a proposition made seriously, not satirically for the purpose of shaming the Tories out of their wish to repress dissent at any cost. The pamphlet brought Defoe to the pillory, but it also showed his skill in writing from an assumed point of view. Later he exploited that talent by infiltrating the ranks of extreme Tory journalists and writing for their periodicals while secretly in the pay of the Whig government. This journalistic experience made it only natural that he should continue the device of writing through a persona when he came to write his novels.

Thus Robinson Crusoe tells his own story, and Moll Flanders tells hers. Indeed, all of Defoe's novels including those which James Sutherland, in a recent bibliography of Defoe (*Writers and Their Work: No. 51*), chooses to call "narratives" were written from the first-person point of view. Defoe had another reason besides habit for continuing the device. The reading public to which he appealed could not be bothered with mere fiction; when it read, it wished to read of what was true, what had actually happened. The low status of prose fiction in the early eighteenth century is aptly demonstrated by Addison's *Spectator* paper in which he chides ladies for the novels hidden in their libraries behind more solid, imposing volumes. Defoe was working against the bad name given the novel by *Le Grand Cyrus* (1649–53) and *Clèlie* (1654–61) of Madeleine de Scudéry; therefore he wished that his works not be identified as frivolous novels at all but as true accounts. In his turn, Fielding tried to dignify the novel, but he chose to draw a distinction between his kind of novel and the French romances; he did not pass off his work as fact but only insisted that it was representative of fact.

Defoe's success at creating a persona can be seen from Crusoe's reactions. Whenever Crusoe discovers something dangerous — the footprint in the sand, for instance — he hastens to his stockade, locks himself in, and sits down to think over what he should do. Crusoe is not a daring adventurer, intrepid to the point of being foolhardy; he is an average middle-class man in the abnormal circumstance of a castaway on a desert island. He acts normally; he is afraid and a bit slow about taking aggressive action. Likewise he is no mechanical genius. The mistakes which he makes in fabricating his boats, his crockery, his clothing, and other things necessary to hewing out a tolerable living in his isolated wild make credible his otherwise rather astonishing achievements. His turning to the Bible and to God for consolation is a reaction normal enough to the eighteenth century (if not to ours); hence his development as a character is realistic. In the case of Moll Flanders, the moral reform is not quite so convincing, but it has its credible touches.

Defoe's other contribution to the novel is related to his use of the first-person view. The wealth of realistic detail that supports the persona's story is a hallmark of the novel. Defoe used factual detail to reinforce the illusion of reality; later writers seeking to make the same impression have followed suit. Defoe's detail is so profuse, in fact, that one caught up in a first reading of a story is apt to miss contradictions that he would consider blemishes in a modern writer. For instance, so powerful is Crusoe's reaction to the footprint on the beach that the reader does not stop to wonder until later, if at all, about its singularity. Why not a succession of prints? The reader may never ask himself that, caught up in the excitement and circumstantiality of Crusoe's reaction. Similarly, in *Memoirs of a Cavalier* (1720) the reader may not, until a second reading, ask why the Cavalier deplores the fact that the English did not help the French Protestants, though this seems an odd reaction from a man who was later to fight for Charles I in the English revolution. Other details — the battle plans and the disturbed condition of continental Europe — overwhelm the reader so that he misses the intrusion of Defoe's own sentiment into a persona so unlike him. In *A Journal of the Plague Year* (1722) the detail is encyclopedic to the extent that statistical tables of the day's dead are given. The reader is not upset by the persona's omniscience and omnipresence, for the narrator is, like Crusoe, an average man so beset by the duty of survival that he naturally concerns himself with all the details of the plague's progress. In short, Defoe settled once and for all the literary convention according to which an observer in fiction may be much more acute than an observer in life. He fixed on the novel its circumstantiality: no detail is too slight, no reaction too trivial to escape recording. The emphasis upon realism released the novel from the bonds of the fabulous, the allegorical, and the impossibly romantic strains of earlier English prose fiction — say, *Morte d'Arthur*, *Pilgrim's Progress*, and the *Arcadia*. While Defoe retained the romance of the unusual — the adventures of a castaway, or a prostitute, or a pirate — he so founded the unusual on realistic detail that thereafter a novel was to be a story of real life.

Defoe's influence on later writers must be taken as general rather than specific. He is part of the picaresque, realistic tradition. The nineteenth-century novelists harked back to Fielding, more than to Defoe — or Richardson or Smollett — as the inventor of the novel whose art they practiced. For instance, that Fielding was the founder of the novel was said jokingly by Sir Walter Scott in the spoofing Introductory Epistle to *The Fortunes of Nigel* and repeated seriously in the Introduction to *The Monastery*. Scott praised Fielding for the unity of *Tom Jones* and *Amelia*, wherein "every step brings us a point nearer to the final catastrophe" (*The Fortunes of Nigel*). He probably cast Defoe's novels among those stories of "an unconnected course of adventures" (*The Monastery*). Scott's opinion was typical of his century. Fielding's achievement was so great and so consciously intended that nineteenth-century writers slighted or ignored the work of other eighteenth-century novelists. Only Dickens, whose childhood reading of *Crusoe* left him enthralled ever after, spoke much of Defoe's power as a novelist. In a *Household Words* paper "Where We Stopped Growing" (January 1, 1853), Dickens wrote: "We have never grown the thousandth part of an inch out of Robinson Crusoe. He fits us just as well, and in exactly the same way, as when we were among the smallest of the small. We have never grown out of his parrot, or his dog, or his fowling-piece, or the horrible old staring goat he came upon in the cave, or his rusty money, or his cap, or umbrella." As this passage and the rest of the essay show, Dickens found in Defoe that quality he liked to call "fancy," a quality which, says F. R. Leavis in *The Great Tradition*, Dickens pled for in *Hard Times* (1854) and tried to sustain in his other works. Dickens caught the blend of romantic situation and realistic detail in *Crusoe*; his own novels frequently show the same mixture of appeals. Although speculating about literary influences is chancy business, one can see that Dickens liked Defoe's circumstantiality, his romance, and his scenic power and — perhaps, though the influence of Dickens' childhood reading has never been properly assessed and probably could not be — unconsciously imitated those things in his own novels.

Defoe's device of the first-person narrator was followed by Smollett in *Roderick Random* and by Sterne in *Tristram Shandy*. In the next century, Fielding's example of the omniscient author had much greater force, although some novels — and great ones — were written in the first-person limited view. Dickens in *David Copperfield* (1849–50) and *Great Expectations* (1860–61) had his protagonist tell his own story, but he was not so successful in turning over half of *Bleak House* (1852–53) to Esther Summerson to tell. Thackeray tried the limited first-person view by giving over *The Newcomes* (1853–55) to Arthur Pendennis to narrate as first-person observer, in conscious imitation of Bulwer-Lytton's narrative device in *My Novel* (1853). Such disguise of the old omniscient Thackeray was easily penetrated and was often an awkward impediment whenever Pendennis had to explain his knowledge of events which he did not witness. In *The Way of All Flesh* (written 1873–84; published 1903), Samuel Butler curiously mixed the first-person observer and the omniscient author with the third-person limited point of view, forecasting by the latter what Defoe's first-person participant was to become. Broadly speaking, refinement of Defoe's point of view had to wait upon Henry

James's recasting of the device into the now ubiquitous third-person limited narration. In this he was anticipated, claim the Janeites, by Miss Austen's *Emma* (1816); Meredithians make a similar claim for their favorite. The important point, however, is that Defoe's limited point of view was so overshadowed by Fielding's omniscient author that the limited view (first- or third-person) waited a century and more to be taken up seriously by writers seeking greater reality than the omniscient view afforded.

Despite all these qualifications, even from this distance we can see that Defoe, at one moment at least, had hold of the novel form entire. Whether *Robinson Crusoe* was an accidental creation of a busy journalist or no, it remains the first British novel. The unity of its action coupled with the immediacy of its point of view makes it more readable today than some of the novels that immediately followed it.

Samuel Richardson was the next writer of a novel, and he too entered upon its composition by accident. Defoe had turned his hand to fictitious narrative because, as a former businessman turned professional writer, he wrote anything which promised to pay well. Richardson, a London printer, produced his novel from a similar commercial motive. He was asked by friends in the publishing business to write a volume of letters for the instruction of country people unversed in the art of letter writing. Once started on his project to turn out a manual of letter forms, Richardson's moralistic bent induced him to write something quite different. The result was *Pamela, or Virtue Rewarded* (1740)—a volume of letters, surely, but one which told a story of a young servingmaid as a moral lesson for both servants and masters.

The letter form of narration which Richardson adopted saddled the novel with a cumbersome device that was first imitated and later forsaken, but it had certain advantages that Richardson exploited well. First, the letter provided Richardson with a ready-made point of view that limited the story. Pamela tells the whole tale save for one or two interpolations by the omniscient "editor" of her correspondence with her parents. This limitation also allowed for much analysis of the characters. Pamela tries to assess her own feelings and to judge the changing motives of Mr. B. as they move from the positions of resister and would-be seducer to lovers who finally marry. This analysis of motivation, albeit often awkward, made Richardson the first writer of a psychological novel. When Pamela recounts her own virtues, her priggishness in paying herself compliments is thereafter equaled only by Esther Summerson's smug joy over her keeping of Bleak House. When Pamela analyzes the other characters, however, her presentation of Mr. B., his sister Lady Davers, the housekeeper Mrs. Jewkes, and others of Mr. B.'s circle is often acute. Furthermore, Pamela develops as a character; her original naïveté, before it becomes utterly cloying, is sharpened by her experience so that her later assessment of her situation shows her not without perception and even some humor.

The very strength of the letter form led to those excrescences now recognized as its essential weakness. Credibility is first enhanced by the first-person letters, then is strained by the length of the scenes and conversations that Pamela reports. Waggish persons have said that Pamela could not have done all the things that she reported because she was too busy writing letters. Even a serious reader may wonder that Pamela is still writing a half hour before her wedding and be perplexed by the clumsy artifice which allows her to write again the afternoon of her marriage day, and again at ten and again at eleven that evening. Furthermore, the minuteness of Pamela's reportage runs into tedium. Unfortunately for Richardson's fame, he continued his habit of chronicling everything in *Clarissa* (1747–48) and *Sir Charles Grandison* (1753–54). Those novels reach such a length that they are now more often commented upon than read. In them, Richardson improved the characterization by having the letters written by several persons; thus no single letter writer need report his own good character but may leave that task to another. But the introduction of more than one correspondent lengthened the novels and hampered continuity of the story by the repetitions of the various writers.

Still, Richardson's example induced later writers to take up the letter form. Smollett used letters from several correspondents in *Humphry Clinker* (1771), and Fanny Burney let Evelina tell her own story with some help from Mr. Villars and Lady Howard. Scott began to tell *Redgauntlet* (1824) via the correspondence of Alan Fairford and Darsie Latimer, but he gave up part way through the tale with the remark that the omniscient author must take over in the interest of economically forwarding the story. The inserted letter (there are letters within letters in *Pamela*) is still a device used for its immediate revelations of a character's reactions.

Pamela has unfortunately, like Jarndyce and Jarndyce, "passed into a joke." Hence it is difficult to view Richardson's moral purpose with the seriousness that he intended it to be taken. Yet it was for this that he was immediately admired, even though Fielding and others found Pamela's "virtue" too strictly defined and too commercially exploited. Jolly readers have since suggested that Mr. B.'s stratagems to seduce Pamela led Richardson unwittingly close to prurience; however, the seduction scenes are not a patch on the diagrammed love-play of a twentieth-century novel which such jocular ones do not mock. A more sympathetic reader may find Pamela appealing despite her "miss-ish" qualities, as she struggles to serve her conscience not only in opposition to Mr. B. but to her dawning love for him. In portraying Clarissa, Richardson did better. Even Fielding admired the honorable Clarissa villainously ravished, however much he disliked the designing Pamela who tricked her would-be seducer into becoming her husband.

Tedious or limited as Richardson's moral preachment may now seem, it must be admitted that he dealt with serious moral and social problems. Sometimes he is surprisingly modern and penetrating in his analysis, as when he has Mr. B. tell Lady Davers that her marrying her groom is not at all the same thing as his marrying Pamela, for the woman takes on the status of her husband. Although Richardson perhaps forgot that he himself had succeeded partly by the time-honored device of marrying the boss's daughter, yet one would agree generally with the shrewdness of his observation. Richardson's moral emphasis stressed the *utile* of Horace as Fielding was to stress the *dulce*. Moreover, Richardson's single-mindedness is kin to the general British (and American) demand that art exhibit a moral or social purpose. The most titillating of modern novelists will claim that their work serves a social purpose, as Richardson claimed morality for *Pamela* and Defoe for *Moll Flanders*, or, for that matter, Congreve and Wycherley claimed it for their dramas despite their ribaldry. After Richardson, the novel had to have a professed moral purpose.

Richardson's choice of female characters and his protracted analysis of them heightened a pathetic note sounded earlier in the "she-tragedies" of Nicholas Rowe. The pathos was admired on the continent as well as in Britain; the descent from high to middle life and from the tragic to the pathetic was a forecast of that atmospheric change, the Romantic movement. Richardson's portrayal of the tender emotions greatly influenced Diderot and Rousseau, and later Goethe as well. In England the most notable reaction to Richardson was Fielding's denial that Richardson's picture was true to life, a denial spelled out with only partial success in his novels. Rousseau might not have written *La Nouvelle Héloïse* without the stimulus of Richardson, nor Werther sorrowed had not Goethe been moved by *Clarissa*, nor—to take an opposite example—would the British novel have been enriched by a classic of anti-sentiment had not Fielding been irritated into answering Pamela's morality. Finally, as Alan D. McKillop has said (*The Early Masters of English Fiction*), Richardson's influence on the development of the novel of manners, notably with regard to Jane Austen for whom *Sir Charles Grandison* was favorite reading, was considerable. Richardson's introspective analysis of motives and feelings, McKillop adds, showed later writers that the struggles of ordinary persons to live within social codes frequently set up a crisis of human importance.

The entrance of Henry Fielding into novel writing brought a conscious literary craftsman to experiment with and perfect the genre. Accident yet attended this advance of the novel, on two counts: Fielding produced *Joseph Andrews* (1742) as a comic answer to Richardson's portrait of Pamela Andrews; further, Fielding's answer was in novel form perhaps because the stage was closed to him as a result of the Licensing Act of 1737, which caused him to abandon the production of satiric plays. In his dramatic work, Fielding had specialized in farce and burlesque. Behind his stage comedy was the long tradition of the comedy of manners, which itself looked back to Ben Jonson's comedy of humours, and, through Jonson, to the Terentian comedy of Rome and the New Comedy of Menander. In depicting comic persons, Fielding thus worked in a well established mode of presenting types. He said in *Joseph Andrews* (Bk. III, Ch. I), "I describe not men, but manners; not an individual, but a species." For this purpose he "copied from the Book of Nature," as he avers in the Preface when saying that the characters and events are "taken from my own observations and experiences." That famous Preface set forth Fielding's distinctions between his kind of novel and the French romances (his is realistic; the French are not, and are silly into the bargain) and between burlesque and comedy or, to use his analogy, between caricature and realistic painting. He cited Jonson as his authority for considering the source of comedy to be the ridiculous arising from affectation. Fielding's claim that he presented persons from life, not caricatures, sets him somewhat apart from the Jonsonian humours; yet Lady Booby and Mrs. Slipslop of *Joseph Andrews* have humour names that suggest their roles. In *Tom Jones* Fielding better fulfilled his promise; Allworthy and Western start out as humour characters who become more "rounded" or developed as the action proceeds. The grandest claim in the Preface to *Joseph Andrews* is Fielding's announcement that his novel was written after the manner of Homer, differing only in that it was in prose; hence he classifies it as a comic epic.

Although one could suppose that the preface to a comic epic might itself contain some spoofing, Fielding's remarks have been taken seriously, sometimes more sober-sidedly than they deserve. No doubt Fielding used his prefaces to puff his work, much as Bernard Shaw later did. But the critical theory which Fielding expounded he made good in *Joseph Andrews* and later sustained more thoroughly in *Tom Jones* (1749). While one must be careful to observe Fielding's own admonition not to take as serious dicta of a classic author's practice "little circumstances" that one finds in his work (*Tom Jones*, Bk. v, Ch. i), the prefatory remarks to *Joseph Andrews* are certainly borne out in the novel. With Fielding, the novel found an artist of wide reading, well grounded in literary theory and practice, who knew what he was about to invent.

Fielding wrote in another tradition besides the Homeric and the Jonsonian. His full title for *Joseph Andrews* acknowledged his imitation of Cervantes' *Don Quixote* (1605, 1615), and certainly Parson Abraham Adams is an English version of the idealistic Spanish don. In fact, Fielding's prefatory claim of creating a comic epic in prose echoes Cervantes' remark in *Don Quixote* (Pt. i, Bk. iv, Ch. xx) that epics may be written in prose as well as in verse. The mock-heroic style and the epical treatment of humorous incidents Fielding took from Cervantes, though he may also have been led to these devices by Scarron's *Roman Comique* (1651, 1657), as Scott suggested in his life of Fielding written for *Ballantyne's Novelist's Library*. In the matter of the picaresque, Fielding had before him a nearer example than Cervantes in Le Sage's *Gil Blas* (1715–35). He was also intentionally inventing a novel distinct from the Scudéry *romans* of the seventeenth century, just as Cervantes earlier created *Quixote* partly in reaction against the chivalric novels that his book ridicules. It is no wonder that one may ignore earlier English attempts at the novel when speaking of the eighteenth-century novelists, for they ignored their native predecessors in favor of foreign models. At least Defoe and Fielding followed picaresque, anti-romantic models, if we allow that Richardson hewed out his own form. Smollett, who translated *Gil Blas* in 1749 and *Don Quixote* in 1755, followed their picaresque lead.

Fortunately, Fielding had expended his talent for burlesque in the parody *Shamela* (1741) before he wrote *Joseph Andrews*. Hence, although Joseph is the male counterpart of Pamela in that he guards his chastity against the assaults of Lady Booby, Fielding was able to break loose from the narrow confines of strict ridicule of Richardson's novel and instead to expose the affectations of the world through its reactions to the quixotic Adams and his companion Joseph. The novel thus becomes independent of its genesis; only a relatively small part of its humor is dependent upon a knowledge of *Pamela*.

In following both his epic plan and his model Cervantes, Fielding made the heart of the book a journey. The ideal Adams does not tilt at windmills, but he fights epical combats with footpads. Fielding as omniscient author writes an invocation to Vanity, and in epic manner inserts stories extraneous to the main action, turning over to characters the narration of the history of Leonora the jilt and Wilson's life story. Except for these inserted stories, the omniscient author tells the action, frequently intruding with a general observation and writing introductory essays to the reader for the first three of the four books. This narrative pattern Fielding pursued again in a more thoroughgoing way in *Tom Jones*. There each of the eighteen books begins with an essay; the appearance of Sophia is heralded in the "sublime" style; the fight between Molly and Bess is "sung by the muse in the Homerican style"; and the Man on the Hill tells a long story aside from the main plot. The flash backs in both novels are Fielding's sop to the classical beginning *in medias res*. In addition, Fielding shows his stage training by the opening chapters introducing the cast of characters, the conclusions wherein all the characters come back on stage, and his power to create scenes. His fondness for the essay chapters one may trace not only to Scarron but to his own earlier journalistic writing.

Most of these devices were widely copied by later novelists. Fielding's example fastened upon the nineteenth-century novel the omniscient point of view, with or without the direct address to the reader. Thackeray is the example that springs readiest to mind, not only for his lavish use of the device but also for his frank admission of his admiration for Fielding, recorded in the preface to *Pendennis* (1848–50) and elsewhere. The panoramic view of the eighteenth century that we get in Fielding's novels is duplicated for the nineteenth century by *Vanity Fair* (1847–48). Trollope, who loved to talk to his readers, carried on the Fielding manner indirectly, for he got the habit from his hero Thackeray. Dickens did not "dear-reader" his public, but he grew fond of the omniscient apostrophe, as the "Dead, my lords and gentlemen" passage commenting on Jo's death (*Bleak House*, Ch. XLVII) shows. Not only Thackeray and Trollope, but Scott, Dickens, Eliot, Meredith, and Hardy gave a picture of society as broad as each knew or could draw. After Fielding, the novel was epic in scope if not always in devices. Fielding's essay chapters (always excepting Thackeray and Trollope) disappeared save for an occasional indulgence like that of George Eliot in *Adam Bede* (1859), whose second book opened with a chapter "In Which the Story Pauses a Little" while the author defended her characters as realistic. Yet her Mrs. Poyser and Bartle Massey of that novel are in the Fielding tradition of humours. Dickens, following both Fielding and Smollett, probably did the most to keep the humour tradition alive. It died hard, reappearing in unlikely authors such as Meredith with his Mrs. Berry of *The Ordeal of Richard Feverel* (1859). Extraneous tales, another Fielding trick, are found in Scott and Dickens, but "Wandering Willie's Tale" bears upon the main story of *Redgauntlet*; whereas the inserted stories in *Pickwick Papers* (1836–37), *Nicholas Nickleby* (1838–39), and *Little Dorrit* (1855–57) bear only symbolic relation, if that, to the main action.

Fielding's last novel, *Amelia* (1751), is something apart from the earlier comic epics. Indeed, except that it ends happily, the novel is not comic but rather a pathetic tragedy for most of its length. It is a realistic novel of domestic life, a lesson, Fielding said in his first and only essay chapter, in the "art of life." In this story of Captain William Booth and his wife Amelia, Fielding came close to the sentiment that he had earlier mocked. The comedy that appears is more satirically bitter and more touched with social reformism than that of the earlier novels; the scenes in the prison and the doings of characters about London — lawyers, landladies, and persons in high life — carry some of the old humor, reinforced with social criticism. The clergyman Dr. Harrison is a *deus ex machina*; only once does he remind us of the comic Parson Adams, in a scene where he is taken in by the flattery of a designing friend. The only purely funny character is a humour character, Colonel Bath, who will take offense at anything in order to gratify his humour for dueling. Fielding, beginning *in medias res*, turns over a good bit of the novel to first-person narrators — Captain Booth, Miss Matthews, and others — but their stories are relevant to the main drift. When one compares Fielding's treatment of Amelia with Richardson's treatment of his heroines, Fielding, interestingly enough, comes off badly. At a moment of crisis, where Richardson would have analyzed minutely the heroine's reaction, Fielding too often says that Amelia was thrown into a state beyond description. The handling of the action, however, is as compact as the plotting in *Tom Jones* or *Joseph Andrews* — tighter, if one views the inserted stories of the earlier novels as blemishes. Fielding's systematic plotting was a great advance in the novel; his example remained a mark for later writers to aim at. *Amelia*'s serious subject is the same as that treated comically through Parson Adams, namely, the role of the passions in human life. Booth's sin is that he believes every man to be actuated by self-interest; when he becomes "purged" of this "humour," chiefly because of the goodness of his wife and the unselfishness of Dr. Harrison, the novel ends happily with the Booths restored to good fortune. On the level of idea, Fielding is not so effective here as he was when showing Parson Adams, who denied the role of the passions, getting angry while arguing for the brotherhood of man or stricken by grief at the news of a drowned child immediately after having asserted the supremacy of reason — nor as he was in picturing Tom Jones and Mr. Allworthy as prototypes of the good-natured man. Fielding's attempt to demonstrate philosophic concepts in his novels affected the practice of later writers. Thackeray ruefully managed to make his good characters "twaddling" persons (his own phrase), while he pictured most of the world as evil and self-seeking. Dickens, on the other hand, sought out the innate goodness in man — in children and among the poor especially — while he satirized evils in the social structure. After Fielding, social comment in the novel could pertain to public as well as private virtues.

The last great innovator among eighteenth-century novelists was so original that his contribution remained unique until the twentieth century. Laurence Sterne, following Locke's doctrine of "associated ideas," in *The Life and Opinions of Tristram Shandy* (1759–67) anticipated by almost a century and a half the stream-of-consciousness technique pioneered by James Joyce in *A Portrait of the Artist as a Young Man* (1914–15). The resemblance between the two works is striking; in each, the persona tells his life as he remembers it or as he looks at it. (Sterne uses the first-person, Joyce the third-person limited point of view.) To Sterne, the important thing is not the "life" of Tristram but the "opinions" — the thoughts that the events of life give rise to. Sterne wrote of the mental life of his persona, whose physical adventures — really, the adventures of others — serve only to give him material to recall for speculation and digression. Sterne "identified" with his first-person narrator in an autobiographic way different in intent and manner from that of Defoe. Tristram was a vehicle for expressing Sterne's personality; whereas Defoe became Robinson Crusoe.

Sterne's manner was purposely whimsical in both a superficial and a profound way. The surface eccentricities — his punctuation, his breaking off in the middle of sentences, his blank pages, marbled pages, black pages — are obvious whimsey, but, we ask, for what? Sterne himself tells us in the course of his recollections of Tristram's life. Walter Shandy and Uncle Toby talk about the "succession of our ideas," and thereby unfold Locke's theory that ideational patterns result from habitual associations of various ideas in the mind and thus create our sensation of the duration of time. Sterne — or Tristram — tells us that when he puts down one word he is not certain what the next word will be. The curved and involuted diagram of the "plot" is just another invitation from Sterne's mind to the reader's: follow me, see how I work. Amid the welter of asterisks, misplaced dedicatory and prefatory chapters, sermons, and digressions, the characters of the story emerge. Tristram himself exists via his recollections of "my mother, my father, my Uncle Toby." Those personages are humour characters, each on a hobbyhorse, but Sterne is a new-fashioned writer of humours. He delights in the eccentricity of his characters and does not wish to purge them of their oddities. He thus brings a new kind of laughter to comedy — a sympathetic laughter that views quaintness and individuality with pleasure, distinct from the older-fashioned laughter intended to ridicule oddity in order to reform it.

Sterne's sympathetic laughter is, however, close to pathos. Some modern readers of Sterne assert that he saw the tragic fact behind the oddity of each human being: namely, that each is isolated from the other because each person's peculiar complex of associated ideas bars communication with another whose set of associations is equally his own. While it is true that Sterne's novel of human isolation and separateness, comically worked out, is close to the modern theme of mental isolation and the discontinuity of human experience, yet to draw the parallel too strictly is to make Sterne tragic instead of comic and to represent him as a more serious, systematic thinker than he was.

Sterne's sympathy led him to dwell upon tender emotion, expended upon slight objects, for the deliciousness of the tender feeling itself. Sterne extracts sensation out of slight stimuli — Uncle Toby's catching of the fly, for instance, or the manner in which Walter Shandy lies grief-stricken on his bed. In these and like cases, the gesture, the posture, the slightest word or the significant pause in a speech — all evoke sensation in appreciation of the whole incident, often greater emotion than we would expect from such slight things. This "sentimental" (a word that Sterne popularized if he did not coin) emphasis on feeling for its own sake prefigured the emotional outburst of the Romantic movement which was to close the Age of Reason; it was also Sterne's answer to the eighteenth century's continual questioning about the role of the passions with respect to reason. Although Sterne's narrative structure lay fallow until Joyce refined it for his purposes, Sterne's sentiment was widely imitated, the most ridiculous extreme being Henry Mackenzie's *The Man of Feeling* (1771). Some have argued that Sterne's pattern of narration was no pattern at all, and his novel no novel, since its nine volumes, appearing serially and ending only at Sterne's death, could have been added to indefinitely. Probably so, but the result would have been further demonstration of Sterne's Lockean thesis and reiterated invitation to the readers to follow the associations of Sterne's mind.

With Sterne's achievement, the British novel had been invented insofar as its devices of narration were concerned. Later novelists added to the scope of the novel by suggesting new themes or devising sub-genres, but no new artistic devices were added. It is customary to think of Tobias Smollett as one of the founders of the British novel; so he was, if one considers that Smollett wrote novels contemporary with those of Fielding and Sterne, novels of popularity and influence. But Smollett added little to the technique of the novel. *Roderick Random* (1748) was a picaresque novel in a fashion already established, and *Peregrine Pickle* (1751) was a series of incidents about humour characters, together with a long digression, "The Memoirs of a Lady of Quality," included to ensure sale of the book. *Humphry Clinker* adapted the epistolary mode of Richardson to comic purposes. Smollett added to the store of characters for the novel, chiefly by his sailors, and he followed Fielding in characterizing his comic figures by their prevailing humour or trait. Smollett's humour characters, however, come closer to caricature as Fielding defined it than Fielding's characters, after *Joseph Andrews*, did. Smollett's characterization greatly affected Dickens' practice, particularly at one point. For instance, Lismahago of *Humphry Clinker* is made to appear all kinds of fool; then, just as the reader has written off the character as hopelessly ridiculous, Lismahago tells of his poor lot as a soldier. As a mouthpiece for Smollett's social satire, he becomes respectable if not quasi-heroic. Dickens also redeemed his comic figures, as, for example, Micawber by his exposure of Uriah Heep, or Joe Gargery by his telling Pip that he is better at home in the forge than in London in fine clothes that don't suit him. Such revelation of the other facets of a comic character, said G. K. Chesterton (*Charles Dickens*), was Dickens' way of displaying the "natural dignity" of his lower-class, predominantly comic figures. Scott's humour characters likewise show this Smollett touch, from Jonathan Oldbuck the antiquarian and Major Dugald Dalgetty of *A Legend of Montrose* (1819) to Sir Roger Wildrake of *Woodstock* (1826) and Sigismund Biederman of *Anne of Geierstein* (1829). In such cases, the comic character is not purged of his humour in the Jonsonian sense but instead reveals a side of his personality unsuspected because of the author's previous harping upon the prevailing trait. If this trick of characterization be a substantial addition to the devices of the novel, then Smollett too ranks among the contributors to its technique.

The Gothic novel was more an extension of the novel's material than an addition to its technique. It sprang from writers unwilling to heed Fielding's rationalistic advice in *Tom Jones* (Bk. VIII, Ch. I) to eschew the marvelous and be sparing of ghosts. Horace Walpole's *The Castle of Otranto* (1765) exhibited the romantic stream running submerged beneath the rationalistic main current of the century. His medieval scene provided a haunted castle wherein the marvelous, the terrible, and the supernatural could have play. Such confused echoes of French romantic fiction became increasingly popular and were brought to a high pitch by Mrs. Ann Radcliffe in the last decade of the century. Mrs. Radcliffe, however, was careful to provide rational explanations for her supernatural effects.

The original Gothic productions are not so important as the reactions that they provoked in later, greater writers. Scott's debt to the Gothic is a commonplace: the interest in architecture and scenery — the picturesque of places remote in distance or time — aroused by the Gothic novels established an atmosphere conducive to acceptance of the romantic in Scott's novels. Scott played with the supernatural element of the Gothic novel as well as its picturesque. In the Introduction to *The Monastery* written for the collected novels, he had to apologize for the White Lady of Avenel, the familiar family spirit which he had put into the novel as consistent with the superstitious time of the tale. Another nineteenth-century name frequently coupled with the Gothic is that of the Brontës. (In the present volume, Robert B. Heilman discusses what Charlotte Brontë took from and did to the Gothic, and Alan D. McKillop comments on Jane Austen's negative reaction to the Gothic novel in *Northanger Abbey.*) Dickens also has been said to show Gothic traces in his work, especially in the fabulous inserted tales in the early novels and in his Christmas books. His interest in these fancies, however, was inspired by his childhood reading of *Arabian Nights* and the *Tales of the Genii*, not by the Gothic novelists of the preceding century.

In so strict a limitation of inventors of the British novel as has been made, some reader will certainly ask whether Scott ought not be named as inventor of the historical novel. Again, this is more a matter of theme than form, as much so as Fanny Burney's "invention" of the society novel in *Evelina* (1778). Scott "invented" the formula for the historical novel by placing fictitious personages to roam at will among historical characters whose movements had previously been tied down by historians. At that, Scott took outrageous liberties with history, such as making the Countess of Derby in *Peveril of the Peak* (1823) a Catholic instead of the stout French Protestant that she was. In his jocular Prefatory Letter to *Peveril*, the "Author of Waverley" defended his historical inaccuracies against the censure of "Doctor Dryasdust" by saying that dramatized inaccurate history was better than no history at all, citing Shakespeare's memorable plays as precedent. Scott's historical fiction is a sub-genre of the novel, a new theme, not an innovation in form. Furthermore, in the use of historical events for fictional purposes he had been anticipated at least as early as Defoe's *Memoirs of a Cavalier* and *A Journal of the Plague Year*. Structurally, Scott followed Fielding's omniscient-author point of view and tried with varying success to imitate his tight plotting. As for the better half of the Waverley novels — the Scottish novels — these are not historical in quite the sense in which we now use the term, any more than William Faulkner's remembrance of the Southern past is historical fiction. To Scott, the Scottish novels were so much remembered lore from childhood, and their times a part of his life as if he had lived them. As James Ballantyne remarked after seeing the original manuscript of *Waverley* in 1810, nothing in Scotland had changed from Jacobite times to Scott's day save the cut of a coat (James T. Hillhouse, *The Waverley Novels and Their Critics*).

There remains one kind of novel that is so out of the common as to be considered as not properly a novel, but some unclassifiable something-else. This is the so-called novel of ideas, which the French developed during the eighteenth century as *le conte philosophique*. Jonathan Swift's *Gulliver's Travels* (1726) is an early British example, and Samuel Johnson's *Rasselas* (1759) a later one. Fielding wrote such a philosophic novel in *Jonathan Wild* (1753), wherein he concocted a life for a notorious real rogue and with sustained irony insisted that Wild was a study of greatness in men. Oliver Goldsmith in *The Vicar of Wakefield* (1766) tried to write a philosophic tale in the quixotic vein, but his sentimental Irish streak betrayed him into producing a pastoral idyl instead. If one compares these British productions with Voltaire's *Candide* (1759), he will see telling similarities. In *Gulliver* and *Rasselas* the settings if not always the characters are fabulous, as are those of *Candide*; chiefly, however, the idea level rules supreme over the levels of action and character. Similarly, Fielding's satiric idea that the villainy of Wild equals true greatness is paramount, although his protagonist is a real person. In Goldsmith's case, his intention of showing the quixotic Primroses living in a paradise invaded by the evil of the outside world became mixed with his desire to rescue the good family. Hence his eighteenth-century version of *Pilgrim's Progress* stepped down from the level of idea to that of melodrama. Such use of the novel as a vehicle for ideas continued in the didactic and revolutionary novels of the last two decades of the century. The genre of the philosophic tale has persisted in isolated examples such as Samuel Butler's *Erewhon* (1872) and *Erewhon Revisited* (1902) and William Morris's *News from Nowhere* (1891). Aldous Huxley in *Brave New World* (1932) and *Ape and Essence* (1948) has brought *le conte philosophique* up to date, as has George Orwell with his philosophic fictions.

This brief review of a century of novels can only point out a few obvious things about the makers of the British novel. First, the invention of the novel seemed more accidental than designed, at least until Fielding turned his talents to the task. With Defoe and Richardson, the novel was a commercial by-product of their respective writing and publishing endeavors. It is noteworthy that Defoe, Fielding, Smollett, and Goldsmith were active writers in several genres besides the novel, notably in journalism. This journalistic training led Defoe to a clear, nervous prose and gave him his point of view for the novels. With the others, journalism led them to emphasize the idea level of the novel and to use it as a vehicle of social criticism. The novel demonstrates a certain hybrid character, perhaps as a result of the mixed literary experience of its inventors. It is realistic, or at least pretends to be a story of real life, even in *les contes philosophiques*. At the same time, it has the fictitious, arranged quality of art; the action is best if tied up in a neat package with nothing or no one mentioned left unaccounted for. This dramatic quality stems from the playwriting of Fielding and from the general influence of the drama. Fielding's claim that the novel was epic in scope has been realized, especially in the sprawling naturalistic novels of our own day. The novel has assumed the position of the highest genre in popular and critical esteem. It has taken up the position that the epic once held partly because it does what the epic did—namely, represent the national life and embody the national myths. The novel is more than epic in its moral purpose, however; it must be reforming and critical of manners and social institutions. These criteria for the novel were developed in the eighteenth century, as were the technical devices of the novel: handling of the action, development of characters, presentation of ideas, and focus of narration. The refinement of the novel, the perfection of its form and technique has been achieved by later writers, but none has added to the narrative devices invented by Defoe, Richardson, Fielding, and Sterne.

THE BACKGROUND OF *MANSFIELD PARK*

Charles Murrah
UNIVERSITY OF VIRGINIA

IN COMMENTING on the background of Jane Austen's novels—what might be called in theatrical terms their sets and props—critics have put heaviest stress on her strict economy in the use of descriptive details, sometimes with regret and apology, sometimes with true Janeite determination to make her reticence in this matter an essential element of all timeless fiction or all great comedy. Those who have offered something more, by way of qualification, have usually been content to point out and overpraise the description of Lyme Regis and its environs in *Persuasion* or, more recently, to join E. M. Forster (*Abinger Harvest*) in speculations about the descriptive mode of *Sanditon*, Jane Austen's last, unfinished draft, in which she may have been attempting something new.

Among the critics of the last twenty years Mary Lascelles, for one, takes us a bit farther in the direction of formal analysis by including in her interesting book *Jane Austen and Her Art* several astute observations on background. But only Samuel Kliger and Edgar F. Shannon, it seems to me, show real critical awareness of how carefully and unobtrusively Jane Austen relates her descriptions of scenes and objects to the other elements of her fiction; i.e., plot, character, style, and "thought." Kliger's study of the philosophical framework of *Pride and Prejudice* (*University of Toronto Quarterly*, XVI [1947]) and Shannon's new and valuable article on *Emma* (*PMLA*, LXXI [1956]) are almost certainly the most enlightening contributions to this field of Austenian criticism. No critic has discussed adequately the background of *Mansfield Park*.

On the other hand, certain puzzling aspects of this great but uneven work have received elaborate treatment, notably the surprising priggishness of its hero and heroine, the disarming charm of its two young villains, and what seems to be a curious inconsistency of attitude in the author, who has often but not always replaced her usual satiric irony with a heavy moral didacticism. Mrs. Q. D. Leavis, whose analysis (*Scrutiny*, X [1941–

42]) of these characteristics of the novel is the most ambitious we have, attempts to account for them with an elaborate genetic hypothesis involving Jane Austen's family, her *juvenilia* and *Lady Susan*, her religious opinions between 1809 and 1813, and a highly dubious conjecture that an earlier version of the novel was epistolary. Angrily rejecting most of Mrs. Leavis's conclusions, Marvin Mudrick in *Jane Austen: Irony as Defense and Discovery* insists on his own, morally uncommitted Jane Austen, here defending herself against her emotions with false conventions.

Without adopting Mrs. Leavis's doctrinaire approach or Mudrick's unfortunate tone many critics have also suggested that something goes wrong with Fanny, Edmund, and the Crawfords. Elizabeth Bowen calls the heroine a failure, an "unvital" character, and takes her to task for her refusal of Henry Crawford, who "was her one chance of growing up" (*Saturday Review of Literature*, xiv, August 15, 1936). Similarly, Lord David Cecil in his Leslie Stephen lecture on Jane Austen decides that the novelist fails with Fanny, not conveying successfully "the innocent romantic sweetness, the lovely youthful austerity, which should have been her charm." Fanny should have married Crawford, he thinks, whom Jane Austen has made to "act in a manner wholly inconsistent with the rest of his character." G. B. Stern goes even farther, defending both Crawfords strongly, dealing harshly with Fanny, and calling Edmund "a solemn, pompous, intolerant ass" ("The *Mansfield Park* Quartette," *Speaking of Jane Austen*). Even R. W. Chapman, the most learned and devoted of Jane Austen's admirers, cannot accept the moral of the novel, "that education, religious and moral, is omnipotent over character," and does not offer a complete defense of Fanny and Edmund, though he considers the Crawfords consistently reprehensible (*Jane Austen: Facts and Problems*). Lionel Trilling, unique among the critics in this regard, expresses an almost unqualified admiration for *Mansfield Park*. Though his brilliant and stimulating essay (in *The Opposing Self*) contains too little stylistic analysis, it nevertheless offers for the first time an acceptable explanation of the moral context of the novel — the contemporary religious concepts and ideals of duty that motivate Edmund and Fanny, the inadequacy of Henry Crawford's merely natural goodness, and the profound insincerity of his sister.

The account of the background of *Mansfield Park* presented here will not solve all these critical problems, but it will, I think, shed some light on them, as well as reveal in the novel a kind of artistry that even Jane

Austen's most generous critics have usually failed to recognize or appreciate.

Let us consider, first of all, the importance of the general setting. Other readers have noticed that in *Mansfield Park*, more nearly than in any of her other novels, Jane Austen has confined the principal action to a single place. Furthermore, this place, the country estate of Sir Thomas Bertram, beloved by Fanny and Edmund, becomes a symbol for all the elegance, refinement, order, and decorum that these two chief characters prize, as well as for the soul's calm sunshine and the heartfelt joy with which their virtue is rewarded. Drawing on a popular idea of her own time, expressed in the most familiar line of her favorite poet, that "God made the country, and man made the town," Jane Austen constantly associates good of all kinds with the rural environment of Mansfield and evil with London.

From the moment of their arrival at the parsonage at Mansfield the two Crawfords — and especially Mary — are set in opposition to the country and its ways. Mrs. Grant, their hostess, feels some "anxiety . . . lest Mansfield should not satisfy the habits of a young woman who had been mostly used to London." And "Miss Crawford was not entirely free from similar apprehensions, though they arose principally from doubts of her sister's style of living and tone of society." At first all goes well. "Miss Crawford found a sister without preciseness and rusticity — a sister's husband who looked the gentleman, and a house commodious and well fitted up . . ." But difficulties and conflicts of opinion soon arise. Mrs. Grant thinks her guests take a frivolous and cynical attitude toward marriage. "You are as bad as your brother, Mary; but we will cure you both. Mansfield shall cure you both — and without any taking in. Stay with us and we will cure you." And in this manner the issue is joined: will the Crawfords change Mansfield, or will Mansfield change the Crawfords?

A little later we hear of Mary's efforts to have her harp brought from Mansfield during the hay harvest, when all the wagons are in use. "I was astonished to find what a piece of work was made of it!" "I shall understand all your ways in time; but coming down with the true London maxim, that every thing is to be got with money, I was a little embarrassed at first by the sturdy independence of your country customs." Fanny and Edmund attribute the mercenary and irreverent side of her character to improper upbringing in the city. She, on the other hand, decides that Tom

Bertram has more liveliness and gallantry than Edmund because he has "been more in London."

Eventually the situation becomes more serious. Edmund falls in love with Miss Crawford, and she to some extent with him, but they cannot agree on the future. Edmund wishes to settle down at Thornton Lacey as a country clergyman, and Mary has only amused contempt for "the sweets of house-keeping in a country village." Furthermore, to her, "a clergyman is nothing." He has no "influence and importance in society." Edmund remonstrates, and Fanny, of course, shares his feelings. She shakes her head at Henry Crawford's notion of the clerical life.

When Mary leaves the country, she and Edmund have still not decided whether they can ever reconcile enough of their differences to become husband and wife. On the other hand, both Mary and Henry have been touched by the spirit of the country. She admits, "You all have so much more *heart* among you, than one finds in the world at large. You all give me a feeling of being able to trust and confide in you; which, in common intercourse, one knows nothing of." But when she attempts to pass over lightly her brother's gross misconduct with Maria Bertram, which occurs in London, Edmund realizes that she is also unregenerate. "This is what the world does. For where, Fanny, shall we find a woman whom nature had so richly endowed?—Spoilt, spoilt!—"

In her attempts to present dramatically her heroine's love of nature and other romantic feelings, which she contrasts with Mary Crawford's contrary attitudes, Jane Austen does not always succeed. Fanny's rhapsody on the stars falls very flat, and the style of her later apostrophe to Sir Thomas's evergreens makes Mary Crawford's unsympathetic response seem almost justified. "'To say the truth,' replied Miss Crawford, 'I am something like the famous Doge at the court of Lewis XIV; and may declare that I see no wonder in this shrubbery equal to seeing myself in it.'" In these passages Fanny's mode of expression becomes just as conventional and hackneyed as the jargon of the picturesque school used by Marianne Dashwood in *Sense and Sensibility* that Edward Ferrars criticizes so severely. Furthermore, when Fanny gives vent to her longing for Gothic atmosphere in the chapel at Sotherton, she sounds remarkably like the still unreformed Catherine Morland of *Northanger Abbey*; in this case Edmund assumes Henry Tilney's role of mentor.

During the course of the novel Mansfield Park is also set in opposition to a provincial city, the Portsmouth where Fanny was born and where her parents still live. Here, in the Portsmouth scenes, Jane Austen is at her best. With great skill, she uses descriptive detail to emphasize the contrast in Fanny's mind between the sordid dreariness of her father's house and the elegance and natural beauty of her uncle's estate. Critics have often noted and admired the striking naturalism of certain passages in this section of the novel; less obvious but just as noteworthy is Jane Austen's masterful treatment of light and shade.

Fanny's uncle sends her home, it will be remembered, to think over her refusal of Mr. Crawford, hoping that a taste of something like poverty will change her mind. He is seriously displeased with his niece. Nevertheless, on the very day of their last interview, at a time when she fears she has lost his love forever, Sir Thomas remembers to order a fire in Fanny's hitherto unheated room. "She was struck, quite struck, when on returning from her walk, and going into the east room again, the first thing which caught her eye was a fire lighted and burning. A fire! it seemed too much; just at that time to be giving her such an indulgence, was exciting even painful gratitude." A little later she muses once again on "the too great indulgence and luxury of a fire upstairs." In Portsmouth, on the other hand, she finds neither warmth nor light to comfort her. She and William arrive "before the door of a small house now inhabited by Mr. Price" just as the light is "beginning to fail." Mrs. Price apologizes for the poor state of the fire in the drawing-room.

> . . . And lastly in walked Mr. Price himself, his own loud voice preceding him, as with something of the oath kind he kicked away his son's portmanteau, and his daughter's band-box in the passage, and called out for a candle; no candle was brought, however, and he walked into the room.
>
> Fanny, with doubting feelings, had risen to meet him, but sank down again on finding herself undistinguished in the dusk, and unthought of.

When the "solitary candle" finally arrives, Fanny's father holds it "between himself and the paper, without any reference to her possible convenience; but she had nothing to do, and was glad to have the light screened from her aching head, as she sat in bewildered, broken, sorrowful contemplation." When Susan puts the teakettle on the fire and shows her some attention, Fanny feels a little better, but, all in all, it is a sorry homecoming.

To avoid the noise and bustle of the main part of the house Susan and Fanny stay in their room upstairs. "They sat without a fire; but *that* was a privation familiar even to Fanny, and she suffered the less because reminded by it of the east-room. It was the only point of resemblance. In space, light, furniture, and prospect, there was nothing alike in the two apartments . . ." When Henry Crawford comes to Portsmouth for the express purpose of seeing her, Fanny experiences mixed emotions. She does not wish for the return of his addresses, and she is ashamed that he should see her *en famille*, but she does find him improved, and she enjoys talking to him about people and places that are unknown to the Price family. Jane Austen puts considerable stress on the point that Henry's visit does not distress Fanny nearly so much as she feared it might. It is appropriate, therefore, that the day of their walk together should be half cloudy and half sunny. "The day was uncommonly lovely," and so is the passage, too long to quote, in which Jane Austen describes it. Indeed, the walk on the ramparts is the high point of Fanny's relationship with Crawford. Common "sentiment and taste" draw the two together here, just as Crawford's "moral taste" first made him think seriously of Fanny.

Henry tells Susan that Fanny "requires constant air and exercise . . . that she ought never to be long banished from the free air, and the liberty of the country." Fanny herself obviously associates the love and emotional security of Mansfield Park with its natural beauties, remembering fondly, as spring approaches, "the animation both of body and mind, she had derived . . . from the earliest flowers, in the warmest divisions of her aunt's garden, to the opening of leaves of her uncle's plantations, and the glory of his woods." For the joys of spring in the country with the adopted parents who love her, Fanny has no more adequate substitute than the misery of her real parents' Portsmouth drawing-room. Here are warmth and light enough; Jane Austen has varied her symbols; but the warmth and light merely give an edge of irony to the usual contrast of country and town.

She felt that she had, indeed, been three months there; and the sun's rays falling strongly into the parlour, instead of cheering, made her still more melancholy; for sun-shine appeared to her a totally different thing in a town and in the country. Here, its power was only a glare, a stifling, sickly glare, serving but to bring forward stains and dirt that might otherwise have slept. There was neither health nor gaiety in sun-shine in a town. She sat in a blaze of oppressive heat, in a cloud of moving dust . . .

A short time after Henry's elopement with Maria, Edmund arrives at Portsmouth to fetch Fanny and Susan. Her return to Mansfield Park makes Fanny conscious of time once again, but now she welcomes the signs of its advance with delight. Jane Austen's mention of "the trees . . . in that delightful state, when farther beauty is known to be at hand, and when, while much is actually given to the sight, more yet remains for the imagination" forms a wonderfully appropriate background for Fanny's arrival with Edmund, whom she is shortly to marry, and for her glad reception by the usually languid mistress of Mansfield Park.

The slight foreshadowing here becomes deeper and more obvious in other passages of the novel. In every such case Jane Austen uses details of the setting to clarify the issues and values of her plot, and those who have eyes to see may see. Readers who find the denouement unbelievably sudden and forced, would do well to consider the careful preparation for it that may be found in the writer's descriptions of background.

Without exploring the hints supplied by *Lovers' Vows*, the play rehearsed at Mansfield Park in the first volume of the novel, we may note, as Miss Elizabeth Jenkins in her book on Jane Austen has done, that Mary Crawford is doomed from the start by her tactics in the game of Speculation at Mansfield Parsonage, which "did not pay her for what she had given to secure it." Much more fully developed as symbols are William Price's amber cross, Edmund's gold chain, and Henry Crawford's necklace, the three pieces of jewelry that Fanny wears to her social debut at the Christmas ball. Jane Austen has contrived things so well that the ornaments on Fanny's breast represent perfectly the emotions of the heart within—her gratitude to the Crawfords, her unwilling recognition of Henry's attentions, and her tender affection for William and Edmund. Furthermore, the relative positions of necklace, cross, and chain suggest, symbolically, the relationship of the characters to each other at the end of the story. The chain, not the necklace, goes through the ring of the cross; thus Edmund, not Henry, will marry Fanny and complete the emotional life of the devoted sister. But at the time of the ball we are not to reject Mr. Crawford entirely, even if Fanny thinks she does; Jane Austen tells us later that if he had "persevered, and uprightly, Fanny must have been his reward—and a reward very voluntarily bestowed—within a reasonable period from Edmund's marrying Mary." Thus Fanny wears the necklace, as well as the cross and chain.

Jane Austen's most extensive and most interesting use of background in *Mansfield Park* occurs in the chapters that she devotes to the expedition to Sotherton. Many details appear here, none of them superfluous, and the whole section of the novel deserves the closest reading. The author describes the seat of the Rushworths much more minutely than the principal house in the novel; indeed, one might think it surprising that so many readers have sought so fruitlessly among the country houses of Northamptonshire for an original of Mansfield Park rather than for an original of Sotherton. But the house of Sir Thomas is the larger, more meaningful symbol; we *care* about it, even if we cannot visualize it. Sotherton, and particular aspects of Sotherton, mean many things to many people; thus our interest in the place as a whole is dissipated. Nevertheless the symbolism becomes so clear and specific that one cannot doubt a conscious intention on the part of the writer. Even more than Pemberley in *Pride and Prejudice*, Sotherton focuses the rays of thought and feeling that criss-cross through the novel.

We first hear of Sotherton in a discussion of improvements that takes place during dinner at Mansfield Park. Here and later Jane Austen lays special emphasis on the fact that Mr. Rushworth's imposing estate has not been improved according to picturesque principles of gardening and architecture. These principles, which, in their various forms, George Sherburn says, "dominated the literary use of landscape for two-thirds of a century" (*A Literary History of England*), are frequently alluded to in Jane Austen's works, where she seems to give them a cautious and qualified approval. Since the school of the picturesque advocated the newer, less formal, more romantic approach to the arts, it formed a convenient topic of conversation through which she could define both character and thought. By the time he reaches the conclusion of the discussion mentioned above, the reader of *Mansfield Park* has been told a great deal about the several participants, enough to gain some hint of the symbolic importance that the Sotherton improvements will acquire later on.

Mr. Rushworth, we gather from his inanities, is as much in need of improvement as his estate. Even though his wealth and position suffice to recommend him to Mrs. Norris and Sir Thomas, Edmund cannot "refrain from often saying to himself, in Mr. Rushworth's company, 'If this man had not twelve thousand a year, he would be a very stupid fellow.' " After meeting Henry Crawford, Maria also begins to feel that her future husband has unfortunate deficiencies. Not insensitive to the attractions of money and respectability, she nonetheless longs for something more — stimulating companionship and emotional fulfillment — that Mr. Rushworth seems quite unable to provide. Henry, with his natural advantages and his knowledge of how to "improve" various situations, may offer an exciting alternative to Maria's uninviting prospects. Mary Crawford likes to see people happy and contented, but her familiarity with domestic strife and marital infidelity has weakened her sense of right and wrong in such matters. Fanny and Edmund, on the other hand, believe that every person must work out his own happiness with fear and trembling, paying the strictest attention to means and methods; they will not be tempted away from traditional morality by newfangled wit and charm. The languid Lady Bertram concerns herself only with her own little comforts, and Mrs. Norris has the soul of a miser.

Having established the general character of Sotherton and defined various attitudes toward the place, Jane Austen can give to the trivial occurrences there a special emotional and moral significance. In the chapter devoted to the ten-mile journey from Mansfield to Sotherton she makes much of the desire of both Bertram sisters to sit on the barouche box with Henry Crawford. Besides the pleasure of the gentleman's company the occupant of this seat gets a better view of the landscape and a freer, more exhilarating contact with nature. "Happy Julia! Unhappy Maria!" From her lower position in the main part of the carriage Fanny can find entertainment "in observing the appearance of the country, the bearings of the roads, the difference of soil, the state of the harvest, the cottages, the cattle, the children," but Maria has "very little real comfort" until she can proudly call attention to the grandeur and importance of the "capital freehold mansion, and ancient manorial residence of the family, with all its rights of Court-Leet and Court-Baron." Maria's description, which suggests the shifting view from the moving carriage, also indicates the strength of her "Rushworth feelings." Fanny observes that the manor house is "a sort of building which she could not look at but with respect" and eagerly strains for a glimpse of the avenue, an unpicturesque feature that she and Edmund feel should be spared from the improver's hand.

Once the characters have arrived at Sotherton, Jane Austen emphasizes more strongly the dull, confining aspect of the place. First of all, the lengthy tour of the house bores every one but Fanny, and even she is disappointed in the chapel, as we have seen. Moreover,

The situation of the house excluded the possibility of much prospect from any of the rooms, and while Fanny and some of the others were attending Mrs. Rushworth, Henry Crawford was looking grave and shaking his head at the windows. Every room on the west front looked across a lawn to the beginning of the avenue immediately beyond tall iron palisades and gates.

Fences and gates, besides being unpicturesque, suggest confinement of natural impulses. Finally, "the young people, meeting with an outward door, temptingly open on a flight of steps which led immediately to turf and shrubs, and all the sweets of pleasure-grounds, as by one impulse, one wish for air and liberty, all walked out."

But even outside, all is not well. Mrs. Rushworth does not add to the liveliness of the party by her prosaic comments: "Here are the greatest number of our plants, and here are the curious pheasants." "James . . . I believe the wilderness will be new to all the party. The Miss Bertrams have not seen the wilderness yet." And Jane Austen takes pains to point out the lack of wildness and openness in the grounds.

Mr. Crawford was the first to move forward, to examine the capabilities of that end of the house. The lawn, bounded on each side by a high wall, contained beyond the first planted aerea, a bowling-green, and beyond the bowling-green a long terrace walk, backed by iron palisades, and commanding a view over them into the tops of the trees of the wilderness immediately adjoining. It was a good spot for fault-finding.

Leaving the rest of the party behind, Edmund, Fanny, and Miss Crawford turn through a door fortunately unlocked, and descend "a considerable flight of steps" into the wilderness, "which was a planted wood of about two acres, and though chiefly of larch and laurel, and beech cut down, and though laid out with too much regularity, was darkness and shade, and natural beauty, compared with the bowling green and the terrace." Here is a proper setting for feelings of escape.

They wander about until Fanny grows tired, and Edmund and Mary begin to dispute the length of their walk. "A few steps farther brought them out at the bottom of the very walk they had been talking of; and standing back, well shaded and sheltered, and looking over a ha-ha into the park, was a comfortable-sized bench, on which they all sat down." Fanny is content; she declares that "to sit in the shade on a fine day, and look upon verdure, is the most perfect refreshment." But "after sitting a little while, Miss Crawford was up again. 'I must move,' said she, 'resting fatigues me.—I have looked across the ha-ha till I am weary. I must go and look through that iron gate at the same view, without being able to see it so well." (The ha-ha is apparently filled in at the point where the gate has been set up; Jane Austen does not always make details of this sort completely clear to the modern reader.) Having communicated some of her restlessness to Edmund, Mary walks off with him, leaving Fanny alone on the bench.

In the next chapter the heroine witnesses a little comedy of manners from her seat in the shade, and the setting becomes a significant element in the drama. First Maria Bertram enters, escorted by Mr. Rushworth and Mr. Crawford, and "seating herself with a gentleman on each side, she resumed the conversation which had engaged them before, and discussed the possibility of improvements with much animation. Nothing was fixed on — but Henry Crawford was full of ideas and projects," and, of course, Mr. Rushworth has nothing to say.

After some minutes spent in this way, Miss Bertram observing the iron gate, expressed a wish of passing through it into the park, that their views and their plans might be more comprehensive. It was the very thing of all others to be wished, it was the best, it was the only way of proceeding with any advantage, in Henry Crawford's opinion; and he directly saw a knoll not half a mile off, which would give them exactly the requisite command of the house. Go therefore they must to that knoll, and through that gate; but the gate was locked.

Mr. Rushworth must go for the key. After his departure a dialogue ensues between Henry and Maria that contains enough *double entendre* and deliberate ambiguity about the word "improve" to make the symbolic meaning of the background perfectly clear. Maria asks him, "But now, sincerely, do not you find the place altogether worse than you expected?"

"No, indeed, far otherwise. I find it better, grander, more complete in its style, though that style may not be the best. And to tell you the truth," speaking rather lower, "I do not think that *I* shall ever see Sotherton again with so much pleasure as I do now. Another summer will hardly improve it to me."

After a moment's embarrassment the lady replied, "You are too much a man of the world not to see with the eyes of the world. If other people think Sotherton improved, I have no doubt that you will."

A little later Henry counters with, "Your prospects . . . are too fair to justify want of spirits. You have a very smiling scene before you." And then the central incident of the drama occurs.

"Do you mean literally or figuratively? Literally I conclude. Yes, certainly, the sun shines and the park looks very cheerful. But unluckily that iron gate, that ha-ha, give me a feeling of restraint and hardship. I cannot get out, as the starling said." As she spoke, and it was with expression, she walked to the gate; he followed her. "Mr. Rushworth is so long fetching this key!"

"And for the world you would not get out without the key and without Mr. Rushworth's authority and protection, or I think you might with little difficulty pass round the edge of the gate, here, with my assistance; I think it might be done, if you really wished to be more at large, and could allow yourself to think it not prohibited."

. . . Fanny, feeling all this to be wrong, could not help making an effort to prevent it. "You will hurt yourself, Miss Bertram," she cried, "you will certainly hurt yourself against those spikes — you will tear your gown — you will be in danger of slipping into the ha-ha. You had better not go."

But Maria laughs her cousin's objections aside, as she and Henry execute their dexterous maneuver.

Some time later Miss Crawford jokes about her brother's behavior at Sotherton, and Henry says to Fanny: "I should be sorry to have my powers of *planning* judged of by the day at Sotherton. I see things differently now." But we *can* judge both him and Maria by their behavior at Sotherton, for Jane Austen skillfully blends background and action here to portray character and foreshadow coming events. Maria will continue to feel galling restraints, even as the wife of Mr. Rushworth and the mistress of his town house in London. Her sensibility and need for self-expression, suggested by the reference to Sterne's starling, will require that Crawford "improve" her situation. And her honor will fare worse than her fine brocade. Then, as now, Fanny will regard the proceedings with horrified amazement. And, in the meantime, Edmund will have been distracted by Miss Crawford, only to suffer a bitter disillusionment, when he learns that she countenances her brother's evil-doing. Thus Jane Austen relates the description of Sotherton very closely to the plot and characters of *Mansfield Park*. She apparently recognized, in her later career, that background could be used for symbolic suggestion, as well as for ordinary emotional heightening. Those who find inconsistencies and faulty construction in *Mansfield Park* cannot, I think, accuse the author of misunderstanding her own intentions and design.

CRITICAL REALISM IN *NORTHANGER ABBEY*

Alan D. McKillop
THE RICE INSTITUTE

For the purposes of this discussion we may disregard the fact that Jane Austen's *Susan* (the original *Northanger Abbey*) came after *First Impressions* (the original *Pride and Prejudice*) and after both *Elinor and Marianne* and its revision as *Sense and Sensibility*. As it stands *Northanger Abbey* must contain more untouched early work than either *Pride and Prejudice* or *Sense and Sensibility*. The present study considers *Northanger Abbey* as the comprehensive result of Jane Austen's early reactions to and exercises in prose fiction.

At the beginning of her career Jane Austen could easily have drawn up an elaborate burlesque "Plan of a Novel" of the kind she actually wrote in 1814. Such a program underlies *Love and Freindship*, dated at the end June 13, 1790. This piece caricatures what Jane Austen later calls the "desultory novel," with rapid changes of place, sudden introduction of new characters, accidents, recognitions, and reversals. "My Father was a native of Ireland and an inhabitant of Wales; my Mother was the natural Daughter of a Scotch Peer by an Italian Opera-girl—I was born in Spain and received my Education at a Convent in France. When I had reached my eighteenth Year I was recalled by my Parents to my paternal roof in Wales." The heroine is excessively accomplished, learns everything without effort, and shows extreme sensibility at every turn. The prominence given to the theme of instantaneous love and friendship explains the title: "We flew into each others arms and after having exchanged vows of mutual Freindship for the rest of our Lives, instantly unfolded to each other the most inward secrets of our Hearts." The sentimental novel had already reduced to absurdity the principle set forth in one of Richardson's favorite quotations:

> Great souls by instinct to each other turn,
> Demand alliance, and in friendship burn.

With the first appearance of the young man Edward we have another cluster of novelistic devices, beginning with the knocking at the door and the appearance of the interesting stranger (as, for example, at the opening of Mrs. Helme's *Louisa; or, The Cottage on the Moor*). The actual presentation of the incident, with the knocking twice repeated and the situation prolonged by Father's deliberate comment, is probably a little independent exercise in the manner of Sterne. Then follow the instantaneous friendship and prompt rehearsal of previous history, introducing a *non sequitur* which delightfully hits off the emergence of such situations in the "desultory novel": "My Father's house is situated in Bedfordshire, my Aunt's in Middlesex, and tho' I flatter myself with being a tolerable proficient in Geography, I know not how it happened, but I found myself entering this beautifull Vale which I find is in South Wales, when I had expected to have reached my Aunts."

The basic method of the early burlesques is the direct inflation of the novel style, together with the *non sequitur*. It would be useless to list many instances of such mockery, but especially significant is the burlesque of didactic comment: after a phaeton is upset, "what an ample subject for reflection on the uncertain Enjoyments of this World, would not that Phaeton and the Life of Cardinal Wolsey afford a thinking Mind!" But there is also the deflationary comment, by writer or characters, to point up the absurdity: thus when Edward, in the scene just mentioned, makes a high-flown speech his father replies: "Where, Edward in the name of wonder did you pick up this unmeaning gibberish? You have been studying Novels I suspect." Or again, inflation and deflation appear together in such a passage as this:

> Isabel had seen the World. She had passed 2 Years at one of the first Boarding-schools in London; had spent a fortnight in Bath and had supped one night in Southampton.
>
> "Beware my Laura (she would often say) Beware of the insipid Vanities and idle Dissipations of the Metropolis of England; Beware of the unmeaning Luxuries of Bath and of the stinking fish of Southampton."
>
> "Alas! (exclaimed I) how am I to avoid those evils I shall never be exposed to? What probability is there of my ever tasting the Dissipations of London, the Luxuries of Bath, or the stinking Fish of Southampton? I who am doomed to waste my Days of Youth and Beauty in an humble Cottage in the Vale of Uske."

Here is the theme of seeing the world later to be developed in *Northanger Abbey*, "all the difficulties and dangers of a six weeks' residence in Bath," treated with mock-didacticism and a mock-heroic attitude toward adventure. Similarly in the first of *A Collection of Letters* an anxious mother supervises her girls' "*entrée* into Life" by taking them out to pay visits and drink tea; the girls return "in raptures with the World, its Inhabitants, and Manners." This is the lighter side of the *Grandison* tradition as transmitted by Fanny Burney and now treated playfully, though not with utter contempt. *A Collection* and *The Three Sisters* begin to give something like Richardson's long reports of dialogue and social detail, and present situations in which young girls display their patience, folly, disappointment, or impudence. The point of view of the girl is sometimes used to provide irresponsible humor, but the dialogue lends some social credibility to the extravagance. Playful exaggeration remains, but irony and deflation tend to become central, and the more extravagant burlesque devices tend to become marginal or incidental. We are at the beginning of a development which will assign the pompous didactic comment to a Mary Bennet, or the utterly preposterous letter to a Mr. Collins.

The heroine may be said to emerge in *Catharine, or the Bower*, dated August 1792. "Catharine had the misfortune, as many heroines have had before her, of losing her Parents when she was very young, and of being brought up under the care of a Maiden Aunt, who while she tenderly loved her, watched over her conduct with so scrutinizing a severity, as to make it very doubtful to many people, and to Catharine amongst the rest, whether she loved her or not." This is the moderated isolation and persecution of the heroine as it derived from the patterns of Richardson and Burney. We learn that "Kitty," as she is called henceforth, is an heiress, the daughter of a merchant; this too connects with the Burney pattern, but might raise the issue of social distinctions too sharply to fit Jane Austen's maturer plots. The opening immediately refers to characters to be introduced later: the friend who was sent to the East Indies to find a husband (a contemporary real-life situation never used elsewhere by Jane Austen); this friend's sister, serving as companion to the daughters of the Dowager Lady Halifax; the haughty Dudley family, who look down on Kitty. This cast might have proved to be unmanageable, but with the actual entrance of the Stanley family we find ourselves perhaps for the first time established in Jane Austen's social milieu. Kitty's opening conversation with Camilla Stanley uses the stock device of discussing novels in a fresh and effective way:

You have read Mrs. Smith's Novels, I suppose?" said she to her Companion—. "Oh! Yes, replied the other, and I am quite delighted with them—They are the sweetest things in the world—" "And which do you prefer of them?" "Oh! dear, I think there is no comparison between them—Emmeline is *so much* better than any of the others—" "Many people think so, I know; but there does not appear so great a disproportion in their Merits to *me*; do you think it is better written?" "Oh! I do not know anything about *that*—but it is better in *everything*—Besides, Ethelinde is so long—" "That is a very common Objection I believe, said Kitty, but for my own part, if a book is well written, I always find it too short." "So do I, only I get tired of it before it is finished." "But did not you find the story of Ethelinde very interesting? And the Descriptions of Grasmere, are not the[y] Beautiful?" "Oh! I missed them all, because I was in such a hurry to know the end of it—Then from an easy transition she added, We are going to the Lakes this Autumn, and I am quite Mad with Joy."

In 1792 Jane Austen is evidently taking the novels of Charlotte Smith seriously, and we may bear in mind the manifest connection of this little scene with the dialogue between Catherine Morland and Isabella Thorpe in *Northanger Abbey* concerning "horrid books." (See Alan D. McKillop, "Allusions to Prose Fiction in Jane Austen's 'Volume the Third,'" *Notes and Queries*, CXCVI [1951], 428–9.) The appearance of Camilla's brother Edward leads to episodes in which his "address and Vivacity" appeal to "the good natured lively Girl," but arouse the distrust of her aunt; his sudden departure troubles Kitty, though she still has hopes of gaining his affection. The fragment breaks off with the young novelist evidently perplexed about her next move. The heroine is still at her aunt's house near Exeter, corresponding with various friends, some of whom have not yet been brought on stage; evidently, it appears, she is to go to London, where Edward may disappoint her still further. We can find in *Catharine* some analogies with *Northanger Abbey*, though the earlier Kitty is more vivacious and independent than Catherine Morland in *Northanger Abbey*. Kitty talks of novels and other feminine concerns with a more sophisticated but silly acquaintance who no doubt turns out to be no true friend (Camilla Stanley = Isabella Thorpe); the brother of this girl appears as a possible suitor, though the gay Edward is otherwise utterly unlike the boorish John Thorpe; and the sister reports on the supposed state of this brother's mind. In their quick acquaintance and separation Kitty and Edward may remind us of Marianne Dashwood and Willoughby in *Sense and Sensibility*, though they are much gayer.

Alan D. McKillop

Northanger Abbey develops from the deflationary vein in the early writings and begins on the plan of introducing into a novel frequent references belittling the conventions of novels. In a crude and sporadic form this device was quite common: "Let it be remembered that our heroine has neither been in sea-storms nor land storms; she has never been interred in caverns, nor bewildered in the corridors of a haunted castle; no assassin has lifted his dagger against her innocent bosom; no ravisher has hung on her peaceful walks" (Mrs. Rachel Hunter, *Letitia: or, The Castle without a Spectre*, 1801). Maria Edgeworth's *Belinda* (1801) must have been read by Jane Austen about the time when she finished *Northanger Abbey* in its original form, and is mentioned with praise in the defense of novels and novelists as we now have it (I, V). (References to *Northanger Abbey* are to volume and chapter in R. W. Chapman's Oxford Edition.) In Miss Edgeworth's story Lady Delacour offers comments of this kind: "My dear, you will be woefully disappointed, if in my story you expect any thing like a novel. I once heard a general say, that nothing was less like a review than a battle; and I can tell you, that nothing is more unlike a novel than real life." In *Northanger Abbey* Jane Austen keeps saying in effect, "Catherine is not a story-book heroine, and things do not happen to her as they do in novels," and alternately, "Nevertheless she must be a heroine, and this *is* a novel after all."

In dwelling on these points the novelist interposes herself as in no other of her works. The scope of her satire appears in a mere listing of the conventions and formulas glanced at in the first few chapters: Catherine Morland's father was not a victim of misfortune or a domestic tyrant; her mother did not die at her birth; she was not a beautiful girl, versatile and prodigiously accomplished. Miss Lascelles aptly points out the contrast with Charlotte Smith's Emmeline, and though the theme was common—many a heroine brought up in obscurity astonishes fashionable people by her skill in music, embroidery, and languages—it is very likely that Jane Austen did have Charlotte Smith's heroine in mind here. No amiable youth appears in the neighborhood for Catherine to fall in love with—no young lord, foundling, squire's son, or ward brought up in her family. The "difficulties and dangers of a six weeks' residence in Bath," into which she is launched, call forth no presentiments, lengthened good advice, or warnings about the danger of abduction by some nobleman. Catherine did not promise to send her sister long letters from Bath full of characters and conversation. There was no tearful parting, no generous gift from her father, no storm, robbery, or carriage accident "to introduce them to the hero." The passage in *Northanger Abbey* on the uneventful journey to Bath may be compared with Jane Austen's account of her own journey to Bath in 1801:

Our journey here was perfectly free from accident or event; we changed horses at the end of every stage, and paid at almost every turnpike. We had charming weather, hardly any dust, and were exceedingly agreeable, as we did not speak above once in three miles. Between Luggershall and Everley we made our grand meal, and then with admiring astonishment perceived in what a magnificent manner our support had been provided for. We could not with the utmost exertion consume above the twentieth part of the beef.

According to rule, Catherine's companion Mrs. Allen should prove to be an imprudent, vulgar, or jealous guardian, and thus "promote the general distress of the work." But she is merely passive and colorless. Catherine at first made no impression in the public rooms at Bath; no young man "started with rapturous wonder on beholding her, no whisper of eager inquiry ran round the room, nor was she once called a divinity by any body" (I, ii). This sustained satire of novelistic formulas comes to a close when Jane Austen says of the Thorpes:

This brief account of the family is intended to supersede the necessity of a long and minute detail from Mrs. Thorpe herself, of her past adventures and sufferings, which might otherwise be expected to occupy the three or four following chapters; in which the worthlessness of lords and attornies might be set forth, and conversations which had passed twenty years before, be minutely repeated (I, iv).

In the preceding chapter the criticism had been lightly varied by playful slurs on the Richardson tradition, to be detected in Henry Tilney's remarks on young ladies' "delightful habit of journalizing" and their "talent of writing agreeable letters," and in Jane Austen's own reference to Richardson's severe standards of propriety. Throughout the early part of the story Jane Austen is careful to point out that Catherine has nothing of the conscious correctness and sententiousness to be found in the ideal heroine of a didactic novel. After some playful remarks on the vanity of dress, the novelist adds, "But not one of these grave reflections troubled the tranquillity of Catherine" (I, x). The device of rejecting the novel formula continues to be used now and then, as in the long passage at the end on the heroine's return. "A heroine in a hack post-chaise, is such a blow upon sentiment, as no attempt at grandeur or pathos can withstand" (II, xiv).

Thus the novelist conducts the story by acknowledging the defeat of the heroic and the ideally correct. Less frequently she professes to be keeping up the novel formula: "Monday, Tuesday, Wednesday, Thursday, Friday and Saturday have now passed in review before the reader; the events of each day, its hopes and fears, mortifications and pleasures have been separately stated, and the pangs of Sunday only now remain to be described, and close the week" (I, xiii). This mocks the day by day and hour by hour chronicle of Richardson's important sequences, with an echo perhaps of Fanny Burney's solemn indications of time in *Camilla*: "Thus passed the first eight days of the Tunbridge excursion, and another week succeeded without any varying event." "Thus again lived and died another week."

So far Catherine has been only *a* heroine or anti-heroine, not *the* heroine; Jane Austen has spoken not so much about her as about her role. But when Catherine develops as an individual two possibilities appear, and Jane Austen's difficulties come from trying to develop both possibilities at the same time. In a sharp opposition between fiction and ordinary life, common sense should have the upper hand, and Catherine by virtue of being commonplace is on the side of common sense. But in the quixotic mode Catherine is to illustrate, not merely to negate, romantic folly. The reader might expect to find her carried away from the outset by poetry and romance, well versed in the literature of the subject, and eager to find a romantic lover and to meet him more than halfway. We are told in the first chapter, "But from fifteen to seventeen she was in training for a heroine; she read all such works as heroines must read to supply their memories with quotations which are so serviceable and so soothing in the vicissitudes of their eventful lives." Yet Catherine does not oblige us with a single quotation, and her romantic dreaming is but slightly touched on, as when Henry Tilney's disappearance from Bath is translated into novelistic terms: "This sort of mysteriousness, which is always so becoming in a hero, threw a fresh grace in Catherine's imagination around his person and manners, and increased her anxiety to know more of him" (I, v).

Though it is playfully assumed that the novelist and the reader expect romance in Catherine's adventures at Bath, Catherine herself looks for nothing of the kind; her expectations are so inarticulate that they can hardly be put into words; she is denied a vocabulary even of "novel slang." She is docile and receptive, but unassuming good sense keeps her from a prompt and extreme adoption of romantic follies. For her, as for many young people, the value of a suggestion must depend on the value of the person who offers it, and she is chiefly susceptible to suggestions from people of her own age. But though she accepts to a degree the instantaneous friendship offered by Isabella Thorpe, she is never completely duped by it. This friendship leads directly to the introduction of novel-reading as part of the action of the story. Henceforth we are to have the characters talking, not too seriously and not always very sensibly, about novels. But before Jane Austen hands over the subject to her characters, she tries to make her own position clear. The passage (I, v) is too familiar for quotation, but we may note that Jane Austen wishes to suggest that her satire is directed not against the novel as such, but against silly novelists and novel-readers. She singles out the absurdity of complete condemnation of the novel in a novel, but even here she presents the theme lightly. Why shouldn't the heroine of one novel patronize another? We novelists must stick together. The defense is serious, but we still have the playful assumption, almost in the spirit of the *juvenilia*, that writing and reading novels is a kind of game.

What follows is an informal survey of novel-readers, whether silly, stupid, naïve, affected, or, as we now say, "sophisticated." The famous conversation about "horrid books" (I, vi) is perhaps the best remembered passage in *Northanger Abbey*. Its relation to the conversation in *Catharine* has been noted above. But the earlier passage contrasted the sensible Kitty with the foolish Camilla, whereas we now have the active folly of Isabella Thorpe and the naïve docility of Catherine. Isabella is twenty-two to Catherine's eighteen, more knowing in the ways of the world. She takes the initiative in reading and planning to read the Gothic novels; for Catherine such reading is part of her new social experiences, and the playful anti-Gothic satire is thus connected with and subordinated to the Burney theme. The ordinary didactic novelist of the time would have built up Catherine's reference to *Sir Charles Grandison* into a contrast between sensible and silly readers, and good and bad books; but though *Grandison* was one of Jane Austen's favorite novels, she is here interested in using the references to novels for purposes of characterization, rather than in building up a case against Mrs. Radcliffe and in favor of Richardson.

Talk about novels is less successfully used in Catherine's discussion with John Thorpe, who seems to refer to *Tom Jones* and *Camilla* chiefly because Jane Austen wants him to do so (I, vii). Catherine is soon comparing the uncertain weather at Bath with the beautiful weather at Udolpho, and thinks of Mrs. Radcliffe's towers and galleries as they plan a visit to Blaize Castle (I, xi). A little later *Udolpho* is wittily put in its place by Henry Tilney in the long discussion of Mrs. Radcliffe, the reading of history, and the principles of the picturesque (I, xiv). Here again Catherine is completely docile, accepting ideas from the Tilneys. Jane Austen takes occasion to comment that whereas "a sister author" (Fanny Burney in *Camilla*?) has praised "the advantages of natural folly in a beautiful girl," there are some people, among them Henry, who prefer simple ignorance to imbecility. Thus far Catherine's education at Bath, conducted without the solemnity of the didactic novelist, has gone well. Neither novelist nor heroine has been forced into absurdity or extravagance. Though Catherine has gone along with Isabella's reading of Gothic novels, she is carefully dissociated from Isabella's use of sentimental and romantic clichés. " 'Had I the command of millions, were I mistress of the whole world, your brother would be my only choice.' This charming sentiment, recommended as much by sense as novelty, gave Catherine a most pleasing remembrance of all the heroines of her acquaintance" (I, xv). Isabella, professing to be all for female friendship, sublime disregard of money, and love in a cottage, usually betrays her insincerity before she reaches the end of a sentence.

In all this Jane Austen certainly has in mind routine performances on the Richardson pattern, inferior imitations of Fanny Burney, current effusions of sensibility, the staple wares of the circulating library. But she names only Gothic novels, and this has obscured the actual relation of the story to contemporary fiction. As Catherine and the Tilneys approach the Abbey we have the last of the light conversations about fiction, in which Henry outlines to Catherine the supposed adventures of the Radcliffian kind that will befall her there. Henry playfully imputes Gothic quixotism to Catherine; her fantasies have at first to be devised for her, and even so she knows that Henry, as we say, is "kidding" her. No one is as yet seriously mixing up romance and real life. The approach to the Abbey, we are told, offers no landscapes in the manner of Mrs. Radcliffe, and Catherine enters without foreboding or suspicion. Things are still as they were at Bath. "Her passion for ancient edifices was next in degree to her passion for Henry Tilney—and castles and abbies made usually the charm of those reveries which his image did not fill" (II, ii). There is a nice hint here, a possible connection between her growing affection for

Henry and her Gothic fixation, but I am not sure that we can emphasize this without reading too much into the story.

But once Catherine's quixotism becomes so active that she suspects General Tilney of being a Montoni, and tries to ferret out dark family secrets, the tone of the story changes for a time. In the Bath chapters it was the novelist who was pointing out the disparities between literature and life; now it is Catherine herself who is illustrating these disparities by trying to find Gothic romance in the Midlands. The narrative is still interesting, and remarkably documentary; Jane Austen is more explicit than usual in her descriptions of the Abbey and the details of life there; her plan requires her to match in a way Mrs. Radcliffe's elaborate descriptions. But Catherine's active pursuit of Gothic illusions, culminating in Henry's gentle rebuke, jolts the story rather violently and for a time takes us back to the earlier mode of crude burlesque in which heroines were made to behave outrageously in order to reduce romance to absurdity. By 1800 Gothic burlesque had become commonplace, though it was still felt to be timely. As early as 1785 we can find in Elizabeth Blower's *Maria* a fair reader of *The Castle of Otranto* who anticipates "delightful horrors" in a Gothic castle. Jane Austen herself certainly enjoyed both the absurdities of Gothic fiction and, some fifteen years later, a burlesque like Eaton Stannard Barrett's *Heroine*, which is too broad and obvious for our taste. It is true that one of her favorite themes continues to be the illusions of her heroine; in *Emma*, more truly than in *Northanger Abbey*, the story turns on the heroine's eagerness to misunderstand, but such illusions are more natural in a spirited and eager girl (in Marianne Dashwood, Elizabeth Bennet, and Emma Woodhouse, rather than in Catherine Morland, Fanny Price, or Anne Elliot), and even when they are obstinately cherished they never, save in the Abbey sequence, pass the bounds of social probability. (For a brief comparison of the quixotism of Catherine and Marianne, see Alan D. McKillop, "The Context of *Sense and Sensibility*," *Rice Institute Pamphlet*, XLIV [1957], 67, 72.)

Though this breach in the imaginative continuity of *Northanger Abbey* is never fully repaired, another change in the conduct of the story goes some way toward mending the flaw. We now get, instead of a blank opposition between romance and real life, a kind of surrogate romance in real life. After all, there is no fixed rule that things should never happen as they do in novels. Eleanor Tilney has already proved herself a true friend, who more than makes up for the loss of the pseudo-romantic Isabella.

Henry at last appears as a lover in good earnest, and indeed the very qualities of docility and ignorance that had led to Catherine's quixotic reveries were the substantial ground of her attraction for him. Thus a reversal is brought about. "I must confess that his affection originated in nothing better than gratitude, or, in other words, that a persuasion of her partiality for him had been the only cause of giving her a serious thought. It is a new circumstance in romance, I acknowledge, and dreadfully derogatory of an heroine's dignity; but if it be as new in common life, the credit of a wild imagination will at least be all my own" (II, xv). If Catherine had dreamed of being a charmer, she could not have done better. When General Tilney abruptly and rudely sends Catherine home, he gives a pretty good imitation of Montoni in real life, the British domestic sub-variety of the Gothic tyrant. Catherine's intuitions about Henry and his father are confirmed. At the same time, Jane Austen concedes that she is writing a novel, and the pretense that Catherine is a heroine is more than mere pretense. "The anxiety, which in this state of their attachment must be the portion of Henry and Catherine, and of all who loved either, as to its final event, can hardly extend, I fear, to the bosom of my readers, who will see in the tell-tale compression of the pages before them, that we are all hastening together to perfect felicity." "To begin perfect happiness at the respective ages of twenty-six and eighteen, is to do pretty well" (II, xvi). Maria Edgeworth at the conclusion of *Belinda* likewise gives us a playful but more elaborate acceptance of novel conventions after having been at some pains to repudiate those conventions. "'And now, my good friends,' continued lady Delamere, 'shall I finish the novel for you?'" Jane Austen's conclusion may appear to be the light dismissal of the ending which is characteristic of the tradition of comedy; but taken in relation to the rest of the story, it implies also that one can come to terms with real life and still play the novel-writing game, still enjoy the heightened consciousness of making up a story which is so prominent in the *juvenilia*. Jane Austen even offers in the last sentence of the book to make a playful truce with the strictly didactic novel: "I leave it to be settled by whomsoever it may concern, whether the tendency of this work be altogether to recommend parental tyranny, or reward filial disobedience."

SCOTT'S *REDGAUNTLET*

David Daiches
CAMBRIDGE UNIVERSITY

Redgauntlet is the novel in which Scott found the most adequate "objective correlative" for his feelings about Scottish history and for that complex attitude toward the relation between tradition and progress which explains so much of the workings of his mind and imagination. In his earlier novels dealing with Scottish history he had explored the relation between heroism and prudence in periods of civil and religious conflict in which noble fanaticism or anachronistic romantic loyalties were challenged by a prudence which sympathized with, yet in the end rejected, outdated patterns of heroic action. His gaze was on the great transitional period in Scottish history, the seventeenth and eighteenth centuries, when, against a background of violence and extremist views, there quietly emerged an unromantic commercial Scotland committed to the Hanoverian succession, to ever closer ties with England, to a "British" rather than a "Scottish" point of view. This for Scott was the wave of the future; this was where Scotland's material interests lay. Yet the appeal of Scotland's stormy and romantic past was insistent. Could one reconcile a passion for the picturesque violence of Scottish history and the traditions and rituals associated with Scotland's former existence as an independent kingdom with a sober appraisal of the realities of the present situation? Scott's best novels are projections of the dilemma involved in endeavoring to answer this question. All of them end with the reluctant victory of prudence over the seductive but in the last analysis anachronistic claims of romantic action. Thus Edward Waverley withdraws from his brief association with the Jacobites to become a respectable subject of King George; Francis Osbaldistone in *Rob Roy* returns in the end to his father's countinghouse after it has been shown that in the modern age the romantic hero is simply a shabby bandit and the future resides with the prudent Glasgow merchant, Bailie Nicol Jarvie; and in *The Heart of Midlothian* the spectacular heroics are left to criminals and desperadoes while the real heroine, a humble

Scottish lass involved in a sordid family scandal, works her way out by quiet determination to find peace at last in facing the practical and economic problems of agricultural management.

Scott's imagination was kindled most effectively not by the contemplation of life in distant times and lands—his novels of medieval life are cardboard affairs compared with those dealing with recent Scottish history—but by observing the immediate past of his own country and chronicling, with deliberate ambiguity of feeling, the transition from the age of heroic violence to the age of prudence. He is concerned with the mutations of heroism. When, in *Redgauntlet*, Darsie Latimer impugns (though good-naturedly enough) the courage of his friend Alan Fairford's father, Alan replies by contrasting useless military adventures with useful civil courage. "This is civil courage, Darsie; and it is of little consequence to most men in this age and country, whether they ever possess military courage or no." Military courage was once a useful virtue, but "in this age and country" it is no longer so. The modern world is a world of businessmen and lawyers, and modern battles are fought in the law courts.

But it is not quite as simple as this. Scots law retained its independence—in content, in ritual, in procedure, and in vocabulary—after Scotland had lost its political independence and become part of Great Britain, and in lingering over Scottish legal customs and terms Scott was emphasizing a *national* aspect of his country's life. This was one area where the old Scotland survived. Yet the dusty arguments of lawyers were a poor substitute for the lost heroic way of life. The legal profession in eighteenth-century Scotland was in large measure the guardian of Scottish antiquities. It was the lawyers who wrote monographs on ancient Scottish customs and argued about the origin of the Picts or the nicer points of heraldry. Lawyers and antiquaries were the new kind of Scottish patriots, and the part played by both these professions (often combined, as in Scott's own case, in a single person) in Scott's novels of Scottish life is highly significant. *The Antiquary* provides the most specific example of the movement from heroism to antiquarian study; the old heroic way of life is, by the latter part of the eighteenth century, only something to be argued over and written about. Scott himself—lawyer, antiquary, historian, novelist—is the perfect example of the shift from participation in the life of heroic adventure to nostalgic scholarship about it, and Abbotsford, that museum of Scottish antiquities, is the perfect symbol of Scott's dilemma.

Redgauntlet opens with a series of letters between Darsie Latimer and his friend Alan Fairford. Both are young men not yet twenty-one. Alan, son of an Edinburgh lawyer, lives at home with his widowed father who keeps him rigorously at his legal studies, for he is at the point of being called to the bar and his father, desperately anxious that Alan should become a legal luminary, combines paternal strictness with deep devotion to his only son. Darsie, a high-spirited, romantic youth, has lived with the Fairfords since early childhood; he is an orphan whose parentage is mysterious, but we do know that he is kept supplied with money by an agent of his deceased parents and that he has prospects of entering into a fortune at the age of twenty-one. The mystery of Darsie's parentage is a conventional plot device which Scott used also in *The Antiquary* and which belongs to those outward trappings of fictional technique which he borrowed from the tradition of the novel as he found it. The important thing is the difference in character between the irresponsible, adventurous Darsie and his hard-working and conscientious friend. Darsie, who has given up his legal studies since he will have no need to enter a profession in order to support himself, has gone on a jaunt to the southwest of Scotland, while his friend remains working for his bar examination at home. The time is the middle or late 1760's—just over twenty years after the failure of the 1745 rebellion and a few years before Scott's own birth, in 1771. It is the time when the active heroics of the Jacobite rebellion were rapidly fading into sentimental antiquarianism, a time which Scott knew about at first hand through conversations with his parents and with his older friends.

Alan Fairford is said to be a portrait of the young Scott himself, and there is no doubt that the portrait of his father, Saunders Fairford, is in all essential respects that of Scott's own father. Darsie Latimer is said by Lockhart to be based on Scott's friend William Clerk, but though there is clear evidence that Scott had Clerk in mind in a few scenes there can be little doubt that fundamentally Darsie represents another side of his creator. Scott was both Alan and Darsie, both the prudent loyalist and the romantic seeker of the "crowded hour of glorious life," just as he was both the modern man of business and the celebrator of Scotland's lost glories, sensible Hanoverian and nostalgic sentimental Jacobite (the term "sentimental Jacobitism" was coined by Burns to denote those who, while recognizing the anachronistic folly of the '45 rebellion, had a nationalistic emotional sympathy with it after it became a lost cause). The liveliness, the immediacy, the vivid sense of character and of place, displayed in the opening of the novel, are matched in no other of Scott's openings, which are notoriously slow and even labored. The epistolary method enables Scott to plunge *in medias res* in a way he never does elsewhere. He is personally involved here, to a degree and in a way that we never find again in his novels. It is almost as though the epistolary method was forced on him by his sense of participation and involvement in the scenes he is describing.

It is not only in the portrait of Darsie and the two Fairfords that Scott draws on his autobiographical experiences. There are many other echoes of Scott's own early life in the novel, including, in the portrait of Green Mantle, a reminiscence of his early, unsuccessful love affair, an experience which left a deep and permanent mark on him. In Andrew Lang's words, "*Redgauntlet* is, in part, a memory of first love, first friendship, and of filial affection." It is significant that Scott should employ an unwonted directness of style and draw to an unusual degree on his own autobiography in the novel in which he faces most directly the theme which lay at the center of his imaginative life.

Darsie, as the letters reveal, becomes gradually involved in adventures in the southwest of Scotland near the Solway Firth, which divides Scotland from England on the west side. In spite of warnings not to go to England, he hangs about near the English border and is eventually kidnapped by a mysterious man of noble bearing and stern demeanor. The story of his kidnapping and his treatment by his captor is told in a journal which Darsie keeps during his captivity. He is puzzled to determine the reason for his kidnapping and the intentions of his captor, who is melodramatically stern yet not unkind; but he is cheered by the intermittent appearances of a fair young lady in a green mantle. Meanwhile, Alan, at home in Edinburgh, receives and answers Darsie's letters while preparing for the great day (especially great for his proud and anxious father) when he is called to the Scottish bar. Alan is continuously surrounded by the language and the atmosphere of Scots law, while Darsie finds himself among a variety of picturesque characters—Wandering Willie the blind fiddler, Joshua Geddes the Quaker, and eventually the strange and exciting characters who preside over his captivity. Alan lives very much in the present, in the Edinburgh of 1766; Darsie gets drawn more and more into the past. Eventually Alan discovers his friend's plight and leaves his first case—the cause of an impoverished and crazy litigant, poor Peter Peebles, who has lost his substance and his reason in almost a lifetime of vain litigation

—to hasten southwest in search of his friend. The novel now continues as straight narrative, with both the epistolary technique and the journal device abandoned. Scott had achieved his purpose in bringing the reader with force and immediacy into the action of the novel; now he continues more conventionally to unfold the remainder of the story.

Redgauntlet is in a sense the story of two worlds: the world of Alan Fairford and his father, which is the realistic, unromantic, modern world; and the world into which Darsie stumbles, a world of wild, romantic anachronism. For eventually Darsie discovers that his captor is his uncle, younger brother of Sir Henry Darsie Redgauntlet who was executed at Carlisle in 1746 for his part in the '45, and that he himself is Sir Henry's only son, Sir Arthur Darsie Redgauntlet. His uncle, who calls himself by a variety of names as well as by his real name of Redgauntlet, has ever since his brother's execution brooded fiercely over the injustices suffered by his country and his family, and has devoted himself to the ultimate restoration of the Stuart line. This is more than a matter of family pride or even of loyalty to a royal house: its basis is Scottish nationalism, a profound and even fanatical feeling for Scottish nationhood, which he identifies with the Stuart cause. When Redgauntlet finally tells his nephew something of the reasons for his kidnapping and of his family history, he opens like this:

> It was not of late years that the English nation learned that their best chance of conquering their independent neighbours must be by introducing amongst them division and civil war. You need not be reminded of the state of thraldom to which Scotland was reduced by the unhappy wars betwixt the domestic factions of Bruce and Baliol; nor how, after Scotland had been emancipated from the foreign yoke, by the conduct and valour of the immortal Bruce, the whole fruits of the triumphs of Bannockburn were lost in the dreadful defeats of Dupplin and Halidon; and Edward Baliol, the minion and feudatory of his namesake of England, seemed, for a brief season, in safe and uncontested possession of the throne so lately occupied by the greatest general and wisest prince in Europe [Robert the Bruce]. But the experience of Bruce did not die with him. There were many who had shared his martial labours, and all remembered the successful efforts by which, under circumstances as disadvantageous as those of his son, he had achieved the liberation of Scotland.

Eighteenth-century Jacobitism is equated with fifteenth-century Scottish nationalism, and support of the Stuart cause is linked with the name of Robert the Bruce and the heroic actions of those who fought in the Scottish War of Independence against Edward I and Edward II of England to restore the independence and integrity of the Scottish nation and kingdom. The aftermath of the Union of Parliaments of 1707, which finally merged England and Scotland politically, was an increasing consciousness among Scotsmen of the lost glories of their once independent country — glories which appeared ever more glorious as time removed them further and further and they could be looked at with an emotion of romantic nostalgia. This emotion merged with Jacobitism after the final defeat of the Stuart cause at Culloden in 1746, and sentimental Jacobitism remained for generations a form of Scottish nationalist feeling even among those whose family traditions were Whig and Presbyterian. But it remained a feeling only; the cause was well and truly lost at Culloden, and though the consequences were disastrous to the cultural life and economy of the Highlands most Scotsmen, particularly urban Scotsmen in the Lowlands, who cherished vague Jacobite sentiments, were content to let them remain mere sentiments and bent their practical activities toward means of prospering under the by now thoroughly established House of Hanover. Scott himself is a perfect example of this. He sighed after Scotland's lost independence, exerted himself (with success) to discover and exhibit to the public Scotland's lost regalia, zealously collected and displayed at Abbotsford every Jacobite relic he could lay his hands on, and at the same time worked hard to make George IV popular in Scotland and in many other ways showed how committed he was to the modern view of Scotland as the north part of Great Britain. Beside Redgauntlet's reference to Bruce we can put a remark about the same king made by Darsie Latimer in a letter from Dumfries to Alan Fairford: "Neither will I take the traveller's privilege of inflicting upon you the whole history of Bruce poinarding the Red Comyn in the Church of the Dominicans at this place, and becoming a king and patriot, because he had been a church-breaker and a murderer." But the anti-romantic view is more often represented by Alan, who writes to his friend:

> View things as they are, and not as they may be magnified by thy teeming fancy. I have seen thee look at an old gravel-pit till thou madest out capes, and bays, and inlets, crags and precipices, and the whole stupendous scenery of the isle of Feroe, in what was to all ordinary eyes a mere horsepond. Besides, did I not once find thee gazing with respect at a lizard, in the attitude of one who looks upon a crocodile?

Redgauntlet, in his recital of Scottish history to his nephew, is taking literally and seriously what to most eighteenth-century Scotsmen had become only a piece of emotional self-indulgence which had no relation to their practical lives. In showing this, and in modulating views of Scotland and Scottish history from Saunders Fairford through Alan Fairford and thence through Darsie Latimer to Redgauntlet, Scott is running the gamut of Scottish attitudes toward Scotland that were possible in the eighteenth century. And in bringing Darsie Latimer into the company of the last forlorn group of belated Jacobites, Scott is testing historical emotion by present fact. Redgauntlet's purpose in kidnapping his nephew was the quixotic one of persuading him to join the Jacobite cause, for his position as the head of the Redgauntlet family and the son of his father would, his uncle believed, bring hundreds of loyal Jacobites rallying to the cause. It eventually emerges that an actual conspiracy is under way, and that the Pretender himself has come over from France in the expectation of heading a new rebellion.

In describing the last Jacobite gathering Scott relentlessly exposes the widening gap between sentimental Jacobitism and active rebellion. The group of reluctant conspirators assembled at a shabby inn on the Solway Firth, brought there, as Charles Edward himself is brought there, only by the fanatical energy of Redgauntlet, are acutely embarrassed at having their professions put to the test so many years after the last fatal attempt at rebellion. Redgauntlet himself is the only one who unites theory with practice, sentiment with action, and it is his almost desperate activity in cajoling, flattering, urging, exhorting, that keeps the group together at all. None of the others — not even Charles Edward himself — believe any more in the practicability of rebellion. The picture of the slow disintegration of the meeting, of the embarrassment of the Jacobites when faced with the problem of reconciling their fierce protestations of loyalty to the House of Stuart with the realities of their present situation, is brilliantly done. The scene is one of the finest in Scott. The two worlds are finally brought together, and the romantic one disintegrates. The most poignant moment of all occurs when, as the result of betrayal by an informer, the Hanoverian General Campbell arrives, walking unnoticed into the midst of the wrangling assembly. He has, as they all know, troops to support him, and many in the Jacobite group, in a last surge of heroic action, are prepared to die fighting to cover the retreat of him whom they regard as their legitimate King. Death in this last desperate battle, or execution as traitors, seems now the only alternative. But these heroics prove unnecessary — worse than unnecessary, irrelevant. General Campbell calmly and politely informs them that they had better break up the party, since a gathering of people whose loyalty to the reigning house was suspect might be open to misunderstanding. Redgauntlet proudly asserts that "we are not men to be penned up like sheep for the slaughter," to which the general replies with a good-natured "Pshaw!" It takes him some time to convince them that his only objective is to persuade them to go peaceably home. There is going to be no battle. Nobody is going to be arrested or executed. They had presumably assembled here "for a bear-bait or a cock-fight" but it was really more sensible now for them to "return quietly home to their own houses." All were free to go. The dialogue continues:

> "What! — all?" exclaimed Sir Richard Glendale — "all, without exception?"
>
> "ALL, without one single exception," said the General; "such are my orders. If you accept my terms, say so, and make haste; for things may happen to interfere with his Majesty's kind purposes towards you all."
>
> "His Majesty's kind purposes!" said the Wanderer [Charles Edward Stuart]. "Do I hear you aright, sir?"
>
> "I speak the King's very words, from his very lips," replied the General. "'I will,' said his Majesty, 'deserve the confidence of my subjects by reposing my security in the fidelity of the millions who acknowledge my title — in the good sense and prudence of the few who continue, from the errors of education, to disown it.' — His Majesty will not even believe that the most zealous Jacobites who yet remain can nourish a thought of exciting a civil war, which must be fatal to their families and themselves, besides spreading bloodshed and ruin through a peaceful land. He cannot even believe of his kinsman, that he would engage brave and generous, though mistaken men, in an attempt which must ruin all who have escaped former calamities; . . ."
>
> "Is this real?" said Redgauntlet. "Can you mean this? — Am I — are all, are any of these gentlemen at liberty, without interruption, to embark in yonder brig . . . ?"
>
> "You, sir — all — any of the gentlemen present," said the General, — "all whom the vessel can contain, are at liberty to embark uninterrupted by me; but I advise none to go off who have not powerful reasons, unconnected with the present meeting, for this will be remembered against no one."
>
> "Then, gentlemen," said Redgauntlet, clasping his hands together as the words burst from him, "the cause is lost for ever!"

The heroic gesture cannot survive in the face of cool, good-humored, modern common sense. The Jacobite movement dissolves in the end because it is an unreal anachronism in the modern world. It does not really exist except as a sentiment. The victory lies with prudence and modernity.

Scott showed both courage and imagination in setting his novel in a period when the Jacobite movement was dwindling down to a trickle. Twenty years after the '45 rebellion Jacobitism had become, except for a tiny minority of die-hards, the merest emotional self-indulgence. It had produced a fine crop of songs, which showed Bonnie Prince Charlie's immense appeal to the folk (and not only the folk) mind and cast a fine romantic glow over the whole doomed enterprise; but in itself it was now more a matter of literature than politics. In *Waverley* Scott had brought his English hero into sympathetic contact with a group of Jacobites of the '45, who were shown in the end to be noble and heroic but at the same time histrionic and rather silly. Now, twenty years later, the essence of the movement was symbolized by its ultimate fate. It had been a foolish anachronism all along. And though a character like Redgauntlet arouses our admiration, his melodramatic posturings (which are not defects in the novel; Scott introduced them deliberately) reveal the essential unreality of the world he lives in. Like Helen MacGregor in *Rob Roy* he is not wholly real, and just as in the earlier novel Scott revealed this unreality by bringing the shrewd and realistic Bailie Nicol Jarvie into conversation with Helen, so in *Redgauntlet* Scott, in one of the master strokes of the novel, brings the half-crazed Peter Peebles, with his legal jargon and his utter indifference to anything except his own needs and problems, into conversation with Redgauntlet himself. Peter's brash accosting of the fanatical Jacobite (who at this stage is trying to keep himself anonymous, and who had been known in Edinburgh to Peter and others as Herries of Birrenswork) is true comedy—*critical* comedy, which both amuses and exposes:

"Ay, ay, Mr. Herries of Birrenswork, is this your ainsell in blood and bane? I thought ye had been hanged at Kennington Common, or Hairiebie, or some of these places, after the bonny ploy ye made in the forty-five."

"I believe you are mistaken, friend," said Herries, sternly, . . .

"The deil a bit," answered the undaunted Peter Peebles; "I mind ye weel, for ye lodged in my house the great year of forty-five, for a great year it was; the Grand Rebellion broke out, and my cause—the great cause—Peebles against Plainstanes, *et per contra*—was called in the beginning of the winter Session, and would have been heard, but that there was a surcease of justice, with your plaids, and your piping, and your nonsense."

"I tell you, fellow," said Herries, yet more fiercely, "you have confused me with some of the other furniture of your crazy pate."

"Speak like a gentleman, sir," answered Peebles; "these are not legal phrases, Mr. Herries of Birrenswork. Speak in form of law, or I sall bid ye gude day, sir. I have nae pleasure in speaking to proud folk, though I am willing to answer ony thing in a legal way; so if you are for a crack about auld langsyne, and the splores that you and Captain Redgimlet used to breed in my house, and the girded cask of brandy that ye drank and ne'er thought of paying for it, (not that I minded it muckle in thae days, though I have felt a lack of it sin syne), why, I will waste an hour on ye at ony time.—And where is Captain Redgimlet now? he was a wild chap, like yoursell, though they are nae sae keen after you poor bodies for these some years bygane; the heading and hanging is weel ower now—awful job—awful job—will ye try my sneeshing [snuff]?"

He concluded his desultory speech by thrusting out his large bony paw, filled with a Scottish mull of huge dimensions, which Herries, who had been standing like one petrified by the assurance of this unexpected address, rejected with a contemptuous motion of his hand, which spilled some of the contents of the box.

"Aweel, aweel," said Peter Peebles, totally unabashed by the repulse, "e'en as ye like, a wilful man maun hae his way; but," he added, stooping down and endeavouring to gather the spilled snuff from the polished floor, "I canna afford to lose my sneeshing for a' that ye are gumple-foisted wi' me."

Peter Peebles, on his first appearance in the novel, is an almost Dickensian figure, exemplifying the results of the law's delays. But he has other functions in the book. Scots law, which claims the attention of sober modern Scotsmen as the worthiest expression of Scottish nationhood after the Union, can also destroy and corrupt, and the legal language which comes with such force and dignity from the lips of Saunders Fairford trips crazily off the tongue of the obsessed Peter. If national feeling in an earlier, heroic age could break out into meaningless violence and cruelty, so in modern eighteenth-century Scotland the great national institution of Scots law could be used for destructive purposes. The realistic and critical mind is always necessary if national feeling and national institutions are to be properly guided. Though Peter Peebles is used in this scene to exhibit the melodramatic unreality of Redgauntlet, there is a sense in which Peter and Redgauntlet are the same character: Peter has long been obsessed with the unending legal case of Peebles against Plainstanes and can think and talk of nothing else, hoping still for a victory against Plainstanes, while Redgauntlet is similarly obsessed with the case of the House of Stuart against the House of Hanover and can think and talk of nothing else, hoping still for a victory against the Hanoverians. Here again the contrast between the older Scottish nationalism manifesting itself in military action and the modern Scottish nationalism represented by Scots law is clear.

Scott takes pains throughout the novel to remind his readers that this is a story of the *recent* past, dealing with the transition to the modern world of his own day. And the backward glances which he keeps sending to that past, the frequent references to dying customs and fashions which his older readers may remember, show with what reluctance he casts his vote for modernity and the wave of the future. And sometimes a Jacobite nationalist speaks for Scott himself, as when Pate-in-Peril declaims against modern female fashions:

"Can they not busk the plaid over their heads, as their mothers did? A tartan screen, and once a-year a new cockernony from Paris, should serve a Countess. But ye have not many of them left, I think — Mareschal, Airley, Winton, Wemyss, Balmerino, all passed and gone — ay, ay, the countesses and ladies of quality will scarce take up too much of your ball-room floor with their quality hoops now-a-days."

The ambivalence of feeling even touches his handling of the Jacobite rebellion itself. He is of course against it, as prudence and realism and the whole theme of the novel is to show Jacobitism up as an unreal and sentimental anachronism; yet once the cause is totally lost, and the last Jacobite conspiracy evaporates, he allows some of his patriotic admiration for the cause to emerge. He even, most improbably, has General Campbell call the man who betrayed the conspiracy to him a "traitor." But it is in the character of Provost Crosbie that the ambiguities of Scott's attitude are most adequately reflected. Crosbie acts like a loyalist but has a strong tinge of rebellious feeling; prudence and generosity, a sense of the duties and responsibilities of his office and a desire not to offend or distress the dispersed Jacobites, fight within him. His wife is the true sentimental Jacobite with some touches of the active one too. Altogether the Crosbie family is an important link in that modulation from Saunders Fairford, Protestant, Whig, Hanoverian, lawyer, to Redgauntlet, Catholic, Tory, Jacobite, rebel.

Redgauntlet is perhaps best known to the general reader for the inset "Wandering Willie's Tale." Wandering Willie himself represents the fate of the old feudal retainer in the modern world. In the days when the Redgauntlets were feudal lairds, Willie had his function, his social position, and his economic security. Now he is a wandering beggar. The violent breakup of Scotland's long-lingering feudal pattern after the '45 was in most ways a good thing, yet it broke down that paternal relation between master and vassal which Scott could not help sighing after and which in some degree he tried to re-create between himself and his servants at Abbotsford. Darsie Latimer, discussing with his sister the unlikelihood of Redgauntlet's former tenants rallying to his cause at this late period, significantly remarks: "Whatever these people may pretend, to evade your uncle's importunities, they cannot, at this time of day, think of subjecting their necks again to the feudal yoke, which was effectually broken by the Act of 1748, abolishing vassalage and hereditary jurisdictions." The relation between Wandering Willie and his master in the old days, however emotionally satisfying to contemplate, also represented a "feudal yoke." Here again the ambivalence of Scott's attitude toward past and present reveals itself.

"Wandering Willie's Tale" is of course closely linked with the main theme of the novel. A brilliantly told story of the relation between a violent old feudal landlord and his piper and tenant, with enough of the supernatural brought in to give it the air of an old Scottish folk tale yet enough shrewd and humorous realism to make it also a *critical* piece about master-servant relations in old Scotland, it occupies a central position in the story. The piper was Wandering Willie's grandfather, and the lairds concerned were ancestors of Darsie Latimer and his uncle Redgauntlet—Sir Robert Redgauntlet and his son. In telling the tale to Darsie (who, as the heir of the Redgauntlets is, though neither of them know it at this stage, Wandering Willie's master if the feudal pattern is to be preserved), Willie is acting as a minstrel to his lord; yet he is but a wandering minstrel, picked up by chance by Darsie in his aimless travels. The tale involves the violence of the Scottish heroic past, but that violence is in the telling filtered through a shrewd and unromantic mind. It is also, of course, a perfect piece of story-telling in itself, a model of how to tell a tale dealing with the supernatural (allowing alternative, natural explanations, if the reader wishes to accept them, for all but one or two details), the perfect counterpart in prose, from the point of view of technique though not of content, of Burns's "Tam o' Shanter."

The language of the tale is a racy late eighteenth-century Scots. The tradition of Scots literary prose was quite dead by the eighteenth century; there had been a revival of Scots poetry, but the novel came too late to rescue Scots prose. All the great prose writers of eighteenth-century Scotland wrote in standard English, and some—like David Hume—had their manuscripts looked over by an English friend to be purged of "Scotticisms." Scots had long ceased to be a literary language with literary norms of its own and had degenerated into a series of regional dialects. The only way in which Scots could now be effectively used in literature was through dialogue, and Scott made the most of his opportunity here. The dialogue of his "low" characters — always so much livelier and more convincing than that of his formal heroes and heroines — contains some of the finest Scots of the century. "Wandering Willie's Tale," being an oral tale put into the mouth of a wandering minstrel, is told in a racy spoken Scots. It was a device to enable Scott to use more Scots in his novel than he would otherwise have found possible. For it never occurred to him to endeavor to restore a literary Scots prose by a deliberate conflation of dialects and standard English (as in some degree Burns did with Scots verse) and write his novels in that idiom. When Scott speaks in his own person in the novels he uses standard English, except for an occasional "Scotticism" of which he was unaware. After all, he aimed at an English audience.

The main defect of *Redgauntlet*, as of so many of Scott's novels, even his greatest, is that he uses the conventional plot patterns available to him to provide the external structure of his story, and these plot patterns are really quite unsuitable to the kind of exploration of the relation between tradition and progress which Scott is carrying out. Green Mantle, for all her autobiographical overtones, is just a nuisance; the love interest is perfunctory and unnecessary, and the theme of the lost and rediscovered heir (though handled here better and more organically than anywhere else in Scott) really otiose. Even a character like Nanty Ewart, the former student of divinity who goes to the dogs after carelessly ruining a girl, comes from the sentimental tradition of the late eighteenth century and has no business in this novel at all. And the Dickensian complications and resolutions of the plot, though done with considerable adroitness, are somewhat mechanical.

The real greatness of *Redgauntlet* lies in its dramatic investigation, through the interrelations of the appropriate characters, of the validity and implications of different attitudes toward Scotland's past and present. Nowhere else is this favorite theme of Scott's presented with such vitality and power. This vitality is felt even in the most ordinary of domestic scenes — those describing the relation between Saunders Fairford and his son, for example, which are genuinely moving in virtue of the fully realized treatment of dialogue and action. Between sober routine and romantic melodrama, between daily domestic and professional life and the flamboyant crisis, between living in the world as it is and living in the world of the obsessed imagination, lies a whole gamut of attitudes and experiences. In creating a story which runs this gamut and explores all the crucial points on it Scott has written a kind of historical novel very different from what the historical novel is generally taken to be. He shows that attitudes toward history and attitudes toward the present depend on one another, and both depend on the character of the man who has the attitude, and that in turn depends in part on environment, which in turn is the product of history. We cannot escape from the past, for it has created us; yet we must escape from the past if we are to live in the real world. And the antiquarian can only write books; he cannot re-enact the past he writes about. And, in a profound sense, that for Scott was a tragic insight.

HISTORY ON THE HUSTINGS: BULWER-LYTTON'S HISTORICAL NOVELS OF POLITICS

Curtis Dahl
WHEATON COLLEGE

"THE mode I have adopted," Edward Bulwer-Lytton boasts in the Preface to the third edition of *Harold*, "has perhaps only this merit, that it is my own, — mine by discovery and mine by labour." He was priding himself on having developed a kind of historical novel different from that of Scott. For he thought Scott, as he had said in an essay "On Art in Fiction," too much of a "property-man" who "conceives a story with the design of telling it as well as he can, but is wholly insensible to the high and true aim of art, which is rather to consider for what objects the story should be told." Scott is deficient in the "highest attributes of art — philosophy and ethics." Though (as Bulwer says in a critique of the then popular religious poet Robert Montgomery) Scott excels in arousing a misty veneration for the antique — in picturing the moonlight on the ruins of Melrose — he is not sufficiently "intellectual." He does not seek to winnow out the truths inherent in history. Indeed, Bulwer says in the Preface to *Harold*, instead of extracting "the main interest of romantic narrative from History itself," Scott merely lends "to ideal personages and to an imaginary fable the additional interest to be derived from historical groupings."

Bulwer, on the other hand, sought to create a kind of historical fiction that would be more historically informative and morally enlightening than even the "succinct accounts" of "mere historians." Romance, he thought, should be an aid to history, not history to romance. The aim should be "to produce the greatest dramatic effect at the least expense of historical truth." Thus he prided himself on having constructed his plots "from the actual events themselves," having consulted "authentic but neglected chronicles," having attempted to make original contributions to historical interpretation, and having used fictional characters or imaginary events only in the interest of enlivening or explaining authentic history. If his novels, he says, are not so picturesque and exciting as Scott's, it is because he has not allowed himself historical license. He has steadfastly sought both the truth of history and the moral and ethical truth that history teaches.

Whether or not Bulwer's boast that he was the first discoverer of the historically accurate, carefully documented, and freshly interpretive historical novel is wholly justified, it is true that his *Rienzi* (1835), *The Last of the Barons* (1843), *Harold* (1848), and to a lesser extent *The Last Days of Pompeii* (1834) popularized if they did not actually inaugurate an erudite genre of historical fiction that was immensely influential in the Victorian period and still flourishes lustily today. Despite the critics' disparagement, his historical novels are the ones most widely reprinted and most frequently read now. His followers in the attempt to popularize history through turning it into fictional form (Kenneth Roberts is a good example) are many. Bulwer's fame as a pioneer in the novel of crime, the novel of social protest, and the utopian novel has too much overshadowed his achievement in historical fiction.

But Bulwer's reshaping of the historical novel of Scott goes further than even he himself boasted. For Bulwer assimilates into historical fiction the tradition, ancient in histories and historical drama, of using the delineation of the past as a thinly disguised but specific political and social criticism of the present. Like Thucydides, Tacitus, Addison, Gibbon, and especially his contemporaries Macaulay and Carlyle, he comments on the political and social problems of his own day through his analysis of history. His vaunted dramatization of true history and his attempt at original historical interpretation are really of secondary importance, especially since the history is not truly accurate nor the interpretation truly sound. Indeed, Bulwer's frequent perversion of history in order to make it analogous to Victorian conditions is more important than his intended accuracy. What raises his historical novels above the pedestrian historical pastiches of his followers such as Harrison Ainsworth and G. P. R. James is the fact that in them, frequently better than in his novels of modern life, he reveals his thinking on important Victorian questions. Thus Bulwer was right: he had created a new form. At the same time that his close friend Disraeli was introducing the modern political novel, Bulwer was inaugurating the political historical novel.

Two aspects of Bulwer's thought on art and history led him to the creation of this type of historical fiction. In the first place, he held that all art should be moral. It should strive to clothe and express those ideal truths which are the basis of men's lives. Historical writing, whether in fictional or in ordinary form, should teach. It should have ethical content or "moral utility" applicable to the present. Historical writing, he thought, was of particular moral importance because history itself is a moral teacher. If correctly analyzed (hence the urgency of accurate history), it can provide lessons for the present. Secondly, Bulwer believed that though the costumes, characters, scenery, and background of various ages differ, the basic political situations, social groupings, and causative forces remain constant. He who knows modern psychology and modern politics can explain the past by comparison. In his histories and historical novels, then, Bulwer uses an analogical method: he explains history by comparing it to contemporary life. Or that is what he thinks he is doing. Actually, it is truer to say that he explains contemporary life by reading the political and social conditions of his own time into past eras and there commenting on them. In this way he weakens his historicity but provides his readers with an excellent presentation of his views on Victorian England. His historical novels are really better criticism than history. Thus they establish not only the fashion of introducing historical scholarship into fiction but also the technique of using historical fiction as a means of commenting on current social, political, or personal problems—a technique that one finds used, for instance, in such novels as Eliot's *Romola*, Shorthouse's *John Inglesant*, Thackeray's *Henry Esmond*, Reade's *The Cloister and the Hearth*, Morris's *The Dream of John Ball*, and in a large proportion of the historical poetry and drama of the age.

With the possible exception of *The Last Days of Pompeii* any one of Bulwer's major historical novels could illustrate how explicitly Bulwer's historical novels reveal his political views as they appear also in his non-fictional writings and how closely the novels relate to specific political situations in Victorian times. The best example, however, is *The Last of the Barons*. For to anyone familiar with the early portion of Bulwer's political career, with his essays and speeches and pamphlets, or even with his historical works like *Athens, Its Rise and Fall, The Last of the Barons* is obviously a political novel on contemporary issues almost as much as is a novel by Disraeli. The Wars of the Roses fought with falchion and bill on the plains of Barnet or Shrewsbury are really the Wars of Radical,

Whig, and Tory fought with words on the hustings and in St. Stephen's Hall.

Bulwer's largely Tory-Radical political philosophy of 1843 (he had earlier been a Radical-Whig) appears clearly in the novel. The passing of the feudal age with Warwick mirrors just such a painful change as he saw in his own time and describes in *England and the English* as "an era of visible transition," "of the removal of time-worn landmarks, and the breaking up of hereditary elements of society." This "epoch of great iconoclastic reformation" is caused both in the fifteenth and the nineteenth century by the rise to power of the commercial middle class. The Yorkist Edward IV, the trader king, with whom Bulwer has very little sympathy, is maintained in power largely by the London merchants, while Warwick, with whom Bulwer's sympathies lie, relies on his feudal retainers. The conflict, then, is between a grasping court nobility in control of the Crown and supported by a new moneyed class against the agricultural interest and the squirearchy, for Warwick really represents the squires of ancient family. Bulwer, as he did in the House of Commons, supports country interest against the city interest and has no respect for the dissolute and gilded new courtiers like the Woodvilles. With power, he believes, should go social responsibility. The religious aspect of nineteenth-century politics is reflected in the fact that many of the Yorkist citizens and indeed some of the Lancastrian countrymen tend toward Dissent or Lollardry.

As in Victorian England, however, there is a third force — the people — represented by the forces under Robin Hilyard. As usual in his novels and especially in *Rienzi*, Bulwer, although he has every sympathy for reform and the amelioration of the lot of the people, despises mobs and demagogues. To be effective, he believes, the common people must have leaders of good blood, leaders from the aristocracy. The natural combination is that of the Radicals (Hilyard) and the gentry (Warwick) against the courtiers (new Whig aristocrats) and the middle class. Without such leadership the people degenerates into a mob open to the sway of speculative revolutionary demagogues. Yet curiously enough Bulwer cannot really make up his mind about Robin. Robin is much of the good Robin Hood — his story makes us sympathize with him — and yet Warwick, who is the real hero, cannot truly work with him.

Warwick's program for England is an almost exact reflection of that of the Young England Tory-Radicals of Bulwer's day. It opposes bitterly the materialistic influence of the middle class. It asks for reform, but reform which will help the common people, not just the moneyed classes. Though Warwick cooperates with the fifteenth-century Chartist Robin, he insists that the state should have a national program in the interest of all classes. Warwick's foreign policy aims not at commercial advantage but at the honor and protection of England. His party stands for local government as opposed to despotic central administration. The nobles stand as the protectors of the people's liberty against the Crown, especially if the Crown is controlled by a despotic House of Commons. Bulwer believes in the original tripartite constitutional balance among sovereign, peers, and commons. Warwick promises reform of governmental practice and particularly of tax policy, but he wants moderate, conservative, developmental reform rather than reform based on commercial interest alone or on speculative theory. It is the administration more than the institutions that needs alteration. Strong leaders, a working aristocracy, are needed. Bulwer always believes that a wise minority must impose good on the majority, but their authority should spring from the people's love and respect for their personal qualities rather than out of tight governmental organization. As Carlyle was never tired of saying (Bulwer and Carlyle are exceedingly close on many political and social questions), the common man would be benefited by a return to feudal paternalism. In both *Harold* and *The Last of the Barons* Bulwer shows that the lot of the feudal peasant, however rude his life may seem, was far better than that of the modern wage-slave starving in the reeking slums that commerce and industry had built in our squalid cities. In addition to his political reasons, Bulwer was sympathetic to the cause of Warwick and the aristocrats out of family loyalty; his ancestor Sir Robert de Lytton was a Lancastrian and in the novel appears at Barnet among Warwick's staunchest military leaders.

Thus in Bulwer's eyes the climactic Battle of Barnet was a conflict between two ways of life. Though Bulwer admits that he cannot say which way is better, it is obvious that his sympathy, despite his mistrust of the superstitious Catholicism personified by the weak Henry VI, is with the political path represented by Warwick. Had Warwick won, Bulwer imagines, England's political history might have been quite different. England would have been governed by an aristocracy sincerely attached not to the middle classes but to the people, the masses. The despotism of the Crown would have been limited "by the strength of an aristocracy endeared to the agricultural population, owing to that population its powers of defence, with the wants and grievances of that population thoroughly familiar, and willing to satisfy the one and redress the other." The King would have been made merely the first nobleman of the realm.

Had the policy lasted long enough to succeed, the subsequent despotism, which changed a limited into an absolute monarchy under the Tudors, would have been prevented, with all the sanguinary reaction in which the Stuarts were the sufferers. The earl's family, and his own "large father-like heart," had ever been opposed to religious persecution; and timely toleration to the Lollards might have prevented the long-delayed revenge of their posterity, the Puritans. Gradually, perhaps, might the system he represented (of the whole consequences of which he was unconscious) have changed monarchic into aristocratic government, resting, however, upon broad and popular institutions; but no doubt, also, the middle, or rather the commercial class, with all the blessings that attend their power, would have risen much more slowly than when made as they were already, partially under Edward IV., and more systematically under Henry VII., the instrument for destroying feudal aristocracy, and thereby establishing for a long and fearful interval the arbitrary rule of the single tyrant.

But Warwick's policy, Bulwer continues, was not one of patrician prejudice alone. The commercial class raised up by Edward was a strong weapon against feudal nobility but was long impotent against the encroachments of the Crown. Edward was destroying the only group which could strongly oppose him. Thus the earl rightly viewed the middle class "not only as foes to his own order, but as tools for the destruction of the ancient liberties." Edward's victory at Barnet ripened "into Tudor tyranny, the Republican reaction under the Stuarts, the slavery, and the civil war." But on the other hand, Bulwer is forced to admit, it resulted in "the concentration of all the vigour and life of genius into a single and strong government, the graces, the arts, the letters of a polished court, the freedom, the energy, the resources of a commercial population destined to rise above the tyranny at which it had first connived, and give to the emancipated Saxon the markets of the world." Just as in his attitude toward Adam Warner's steam engine, Bulwer despite his Tory conservatism cannot resist the Macaulayan tendency to marvel at the commercial wonders of Victorian England.

Bulwer's political references, however, are far more specific than these revelations of his general political position. *The Last of the Barons* contains analogues to specific political problems of the 1840's. Robin of Redesdale, as has been remarked, is obviously a Chartist, and Bulwer's somewhat sympathetic yet anti-demagogic treatment of him is a reflection of his views on Chartism as they appear in his essays. In the anger of the mob against the wonderful machine of Adam Warner that, they think, will put them out of work, Bulwer is representing the machine-breaking of the Victorian period. Bulwer's defense of Warwick is in part a defense of the House of Lords which was being so bitterly attacked in the controversies over the various Reform Bills. Though Bulwer was elected member of Parliament on a Radical and Reform platform in 1831, like Disraeli he became in the 1840's more conservative and feared the power of the middle class in the reformed House of Commons. One is tempted to see in Warwick the shadow of the Duke of Wellington. The Duke, Bulwer says in *The Siamese Twins*, was safe when he depended on the people, even though the Church and aristocracy combined against him, but fell when he deserted the people and trusted to a cabal. The struggle over the Corn Laws between the agricultural and commercial interests is clearly reflected in the strife over foreign and domestic policy between the merchant king Edward IV and the great landowners under Warwick. This conflict is closely related to the struggle between the supporters of local aristocratic paternalism and of centralized governmental control. Like Disraeli the politician, Bulwer favors the former. Like Disraeli the novelist, he rewrites English history to make it conform to his views.

Similar analyses can be made of *Rienzi*, *Harold*, and even the fragment *Pausanias the Spartan* (posthumously published in 1876). Each reveals both Bulwer's basic, consistently held political beliefs and his comment on the key political issues of the moment. *Rienzi* is a striking statement of Bulwer's contempt for the mob, his dislike of the commercial classes whose hearts are in their purses, and his doubt whether even the great Reform Bill is a universal panacea. In "The History of the Reign of Victoria I" Bulwer quotes the Radical leader Lord Durham as saying that lasting reform must wait for the people to be morally and politically ready to receive it; it cannot be forced but must grow slowly. Rienzi learns this truth at the cost of his life. *Harold* emphasizes the helplessness of democracy against efficient despotism, shows the need for strong leadership, seems to allude in its comments on ecclesiastical matters to the current Victorian controversies over reforming the English and Irish churches, reiterates Bulwer's contempt for the sheeplike multitude, and even attacks the problem of British drunkenness, which Bulwer had discussed in *England and the English*. *Pausanias* is really a fictionalizing of part of *Athens, Its Rise and Fall*. Had it been completed, like the history it would doubtless have dealt with the matters of franchise, opposing classes, and conflicting theories of government that were brought to the fore by the arguments over the various Reform Bills in nineteenth-century England. Like *The Last of the Barons*, all of the novels deal with times of great political crisis. (Note the word "last" in the titles: *The Last Days of Pompeii*; *Rienzi, Last of the Roman Tribunes*; *The Last of the Barons*; and *Harold, Last of the Saxon Kings*; Boabdil in *Leila* is the *last* Moorish king of Granada.) Even *The Last Days of Pompeii*, principally melodramatic or "catastrophic" as it is, reveals many of Bulwer's religious and political biases.

In this new and complex form of historical fiction blending historical scholarship, political criticism, moral edification, theories of historical causation, and the vivid excitement necessary to fiction, Bulwer was faced with a number of serious artistic and intellectual problems that did not so grievously weigh on a less "intellectual" — as Bulwer would say — historical novelist like Scott. He had committed himself to historical accuracy and yet wished to apply the lesson of history to his own age. He wanted to keep his characters warmly individual, and yet through them he wanted to represent abstract moral and political forces. While in no way misrepresenting historical characters or events (which are not always moral), he wished to present a morally instructive narrative. At the same time that he was trying to be severely analytical, he desired to popularize history by making it into an exciting and dramatic story. To be at once scholar, political critic, historical philosopher, moral allegorist, and popular novelist presented difficulties to even so self-confident a man as Edward George Earle Lytton Bulwer-Lytton. His solutions to these problems are interesting not only in relation to his own novels but also to those of other historical novelists of his school. The grand critical question, of course, is whether he was able to unify the diverse and often almost contradictory elements of his type of historical fiction into a coherent work of art. On the answer to that question rests in large part the critical evaluation of the whole genre of historical fiction that Bulwer popularized. Again the best example is *The Last of the Barons*, Bulwer's most tightly woven and carefully thought out historical novel. If he succeeded anywhere, he succeeded here.

Bulwer in *The Last of the Barons* has at least fair artistic success. His disquisitions on history, though they slow the pace, are interesting, and he has skillfully chosen for his subject events of real dramatic action and characters fascinating even without fictional adornment. Warwick's career, like Rienzi's and Edward's, needs little added dramatization. Bulwer, of course, weakens the historicity of his novel by making all his heroes nineteenth-century idealists with Victorian liberal-conservative politics and Victorian concepts of morality. But this weakening of the historical guards Bulwer against the sink of antiquarianism and, as has been shown, gives his novels added point. To his Victorian readers and even to us his characters are more meaningful because they are created in the Victorian image.

His critical, analogical method offers Bulwer great opportunity to seek out the general laws of historical causation. As in his *Athens*, his "Outlines of the Early History of the East," his essays on the French Revolution and Chartism, so in *The Last of the Barons* he frequently analyzes history in terms of the clash of economic and social forces. Agricultural feudalism and commercial despotism struggle in the novel for supremacy. Yet at the same time and in apparent contradiction Bulwer has an almost Carlylean belief in the influence of individual great men. Strong personalities, whether good like those of Warwick and Rienzi and Harold or questionable like those of Richard of Gloucester and Cromwell and Napoleon, have great influence on history, at least in their own times. These men are no puppets.

Bulwer's method of reconciling these two theories of historical causation is his semi-allegorical characterization. Each of his major characters is representative of a political or social force. Just as Warwick represents the ancient squirearchy of his own and Victorian times, Edward IV stands for the monarchical as against the feudal ideal. The trading classes who support the new (Whig?) nobility are personified in Alwyn, as the feudal retainer is personified in Marmaduke Neville. Adam Warner represents the new science; Friar Bungey the old superstition. Henry VI is the embodiment of narrow medieval piety. Thus each of the characters can at the same time be influential as an individual and yet help portray the action of forces larger than himself. Unfortunately this technique leads to a weakening of the characters' individual personalities. At times, indeed, Bulwer introduces an overt conflict of sympathies. Whenever the reader becomes vitally interested in a character, that character turns into an abstract force. Whenever the reader follows an abstract force, that force is confused by its being given individual personality. Just as the reader begins to gain sympathy for Alwyn as a person, for instance, Alwyn becomes a symbol for the Trader. The reader is supposed, conflictingly, to sympathize with Alwyn as a man but not as a merchant. Edward himself is to be despised as a dissolute seducer and an autocratic schemer, but he is also a brave king. A similar conflict between a character and the force he represents occurs in the treatment of Marmaduke Neville, Hastings, and Henry VI. The result is that even in *The Last of the Barons* one becomes little interested in any of the characters except Warwick himself, who, Bulwer admitted, was the only one of his heroes that he himself really loved.

The allegory is not only political. It is moral too. Bulwer intends to show the various fates of good and evil men. Yet here he must face the fact that in history good does not always win out. Indeed, in his novels the good hero, the man with whom Bulwer and the readers sympathize, always falls. Brave, chaste Warwick is defeated; saintly Henry VI loses his throne; noble Adam Warner and his pure, loving daughter Sibyll are killed by Bungey and the vile timbrel-girls. On the other hand, lewd, lazy Edward IV conquers; Hastings survives his duplicity; Bungey is triumphant; and the malevolent Richard, Duke of Gloucester ends the novel with the comment that knighthood and chivalry die with Warwick: "Happy, henceforth, he who can plot, and scheme, and fawn, and smile."

Bulwer breaks the force of this seemingly immoral lesson partly by telling the reader of the dire fates which await many of these apparently triumphant men of villainy: Hastings will be executed, Edward's children will be murdered in the Tower, Richard will lose his ill-got crown on Bosworth field. But fundamentally he meets the problem by trying to turn each of his novels, without much warrant in history, into almost Aeschylean tragedy. Each of his great men has a tragic flaw. Rienzi is too proud. Warwick brings upon himself the force of his own curse when he supports the Lancastrians who murdered his father. Harold perjures himself by breaking the sacred pledge he had made to William in Normandy. Each is thus in one sense justly struck down by fate. Sometimes this moral tragedy conflicts slightly with the historical and personal analysis. But, though the various causative factors do not always exactly coincide, Bulwer is skillful at making the tragic flaw at once personal, moral, and representative of an error in political judgment or a betrayal of the political constituency which the character allegorically represents. Warwick's betrayal of Edward, for instance, arises out of his own proud nature, his honorable concern for the chastity of his daughter, and his fidelity to his order of barons; and yet at the same time it is a betrayal of his oath and a desertion to the Lancastrian forces of bigotry and revenge which he at bottom opposes. The tragedy of Sibyll Warner, however, is of another kind and is not so well integrated into the novel's historical or moral structure. She really has no fault — her pure love of deceitful Hastings cannot be called one — and yet with all the mystic supernaturalism that Bulwer so loves (see, for instance, *Zanoni*), Furies in the guise of the tymbesteres relentlessly pursue her from the first scene of the novel to her death in the last. Perhaps, however, this is meant not as personal tragedy but as a moral allegory representing sin's undying hatred of virtue.

Bulwer, wishing to give to the historical novel not only tragic but also philosophic weight, adds to the moral tragedies of Rienzi and Harold and Warwick an interpretation of history according to a general law of change. He propounds the doctrine that only the man who is in accord with his Age, with the *Zeitgeist*, can be successful. Those who are either in advance of their Age (Adam Warner and Rienzi) or behind their Age (Warwick and Harold) are inevitably defeated. Those like Edward IV and William the Conqueror who are Men of their Age triumph. According to this fatalistic view of history, individual merit, individual capacity, and individual morality mean little. Men are tossed on the wave of Time. This doctrine, though it does not oppose Bulwer's political allegory and though like Fate in Greek drama it can be reconciled to personal tragedy, interferes with his moral thesis and weakens his social criticism. This is an artistic weakness. But Bulwer attempts to reconcile his historical fatalism with his morality and desire for reform by postulating that history slowly but inevitably moves on toward good. Progress, though it destroys those who oppose it and those who seek to hasten it, though it seems to raise evil men to power, will eventually in some unseen future result in betterment for mankind. The individual suffers so that the many may sometime profit. For Bulwer, "Locksley Hall Sixty Years After" has no happy conclusion.

Thus despite Bulwer's strenuous, clever, and amazingly successful efforts, *The Last of the Barons* and the other historical novels are not wholly self-consistent. Element clashes with element. To some extent political theory and Victorian morality distort history; history cramps plot and characterization; fatalism undermines moral and political allegory; allegory weakens individuality; the love interest interferes with the theory of historical causation; and a wish to popularize history causes history to be made falsely melodramatic. Yet, even after this lack of complete control has been admitted, Bulwer's artistry deserves considerable praise. Though he has not tied every thread securely to every other thread, his general pattern is on the whole satisfactory and susceptible to effective elaboration. Its many facets add to its interest. Though his style is somewhat stilted, though his explanations are often wordy, and though few of his characters vividly live, he provides exciting action, colorful tableaux, instructive historical insights, stimulating political comment, and considerable poignant pathos. His pioneering of his new form of political historical fiction can be said to have been in general successful — more successful, indeed, than Disraeli's creation of the modern political novel with its extended exposition and its lengthy, undramatic political dialogue.

Paradoxically, Bulwer, the man who wanted to "intellectualize" the historical novel of Scott, fails on the intellectual side. His focus is never clear. He does not know exactly what he wants to say. The moral and intellectual lesson — that which he was most eager to add to historical fiction — fails with a correspondent weakening of aesthetic and emotional impact. The fundamental fault is that Bulwer, as even his political career shows, does not know whether he is a Radical, a Whig, or a Tory. Like Cooper and to some extent Scott, he never resolves the conflict in himself between emotional conservatism and intellectual liberalism. Bulwer's great heroes — Warwick, Harold, Rienzi — are reactionaries who seek to stem change or return to the past. (Rienzi is both a reactionary, in that he wishes to revive the ancient glories of Rome, and a liberal, in that he looks forward to the Renaissance in his attempt to destroy the power of the medieval nobility.) His sympathies are with them. Yet Bulwer admits that most really beneficial progress is brought about by strong, unidealistic, practical men well adjusted to their times — men like Edward IV, William the Conqueror, Richelieu, and Napoleon. He believes in Progress but dislikes those who bring it. He holds morality very dear but admits that good ultimately comes out of those who ignore it. He loves liberty but admires strong, almost despotic leaders. He holds that men have moral choice and he values strong personality, but he sees the *Zeitgeist* as the ultimate controlling force. He romanticizes the feudal era as the days of happiness, but he praises the steam engine as the great bearer of civilization. He cannot make up his mind. It is as much this uncertainty of values as any essential fault in his theory of historical fiction that prevents him from writing a truly great novel.

THACKERAY, A NOVELIST BY ACCIDENT

J. Y. T. Greig
UNIVERSITY OF THE WITWATERSRAND

OF THE major Victorian novelists who stood high in reputation with both "the common reader" and the established critic at the beginning of this century, Thackeray seems to have fallen farthest in the fifty-odd years since. Although he has a host of admirers still (of whom I count myself one), their admiration is usually qualified. It is doubtful if "the common reader" often gets to the end of any of his novels except *Vanity Fair*, *Esmond*, and perhaps *Pendennis*; and few even of his admirers would now endorse Trollope's judgments — that Thackeray was "the first of novelists of the day," and *Esmond* "the greatest novel in the English language."

I propose in this essay to consider one of the reasons for this decline in reputation. I will not maintain that it is the only reason, but I believe it is an important one. My contention is that Thackeray was not a born novelist. He took to prose fiction as an afterthought, and never achieved a technique in the art that fully satisfied either himself or the most discerning readers of his own day or since. Dickens, Trollope, George Eliot, and Henry James, whatever incidental blunders they might commit, *were* born novelists; for they were all able for long periods during composition to lose their quotidian selves in the characters and events of their imagined worlds, and thus to suppress for the time being such particular memories of their private lives and such fads and idiosyncrasies of their ways of thought and emotion as were apt to interfere with the illusion they were trying to create. It was not in Thackeray's power to remain very long what Mr. E. M. Forster would call *anonymous*. Again and again, out from the novel would pop the evasive, ill-coordinated, but likeable William Makepeace Thackeray — the familiar and talkative good fellow of the *Punch* table and the Garrick Club. "Old Thack," as Edward Fitzgerald, his faithful friend from Cambridge days, was inclined to grumble, was "always talking so of himself" in the very heart of his novels.

Thackeray turned to prose fiction because he had to make a living. He would rather have been a painter, and said so; but although he could draw enchanting caricatures of himself and others, paint he could not. He would rather have been an essayist, "a preacher without orders," free to discourse amiably or ironically on life in general or on the habits of fellow-Londoners. He would rather have been a historian, and given time and a settled income from another source, like Hallam, he might well have become a distinguished one. But poverty pressed too heavily on him in his early years. To make enough money, he must somehow "take the great stupid public by the ears." He achieved this end by means of *Vanity Fair*, *Pendennis*, and *Esmond*, and having cleared off his heavy debts, he had to continue with prose fiction, even when he wearied of the occupation. Consequently, much that went into his later novels is very dreary. What he delighted in doing in his maturity, and often did superbly, was writing *Roundabout* essays.

Almost from the beginning of his career he could write graceful, sinewy, translucent English; he could be concise and pungent, when the occasion called for it; if his space was limited and he took time to plan, he could tell a story well; and most important of all for a novelist, he could, if he gave his mind to it, endow fictitious characters with life, and enable the reader to know, and not merely know about, them. He had a *daimon*, to whom every now and then he surrendered his discursive mind. Unfortunately, he did not trust his *daimon* often enough. He was always prone to withdraw from his imagined world, and start discoursing on it from without.

It is always dangerous for a novelist to annotate his fiction in this way, since the annotations often shatter the illusion on which everything hangs. The reader's "willing suspension of disbelief for the moment" is interrupted, and if the process is often repeated, may never be resumed. Nothing is more likely to remind the reader that what he is getting from the printed page is only fiction, than frequent disembodied comments by the author.

The embodied comment is quite another matter. It is integral. It subtly but unobtrusively controls the reader's responses. It helps to "manipulate the contents of the reader's mind," to borrow Vernon Lee's phrase. At its best, it becomes so completely fused with other elements in the author's style that the reader is not consciously aware of it as comment. Outstanding examples of this fusion are to be found in the later novels of Henry James, as Mr. H. K. Girling has recently shown in a study of *The Golden Bowl* in the University of California's periodical, *Nineteenth-Century Fiction.*

The result is that "motive and action and significance" are immersed in a consistent medium "through which they are interpreted." Contrasting with this is the disembodied comment often used by Thackeray, which, instead of illuminating and interpreting, blurs and befogs.

In Thackeray's preface, "Before the Curtain," to *Vanity Fair*, he promises that his story will be "brilliantly illuminated with the Author's own candles." This promise he fulfills now and then. The candles are not, like those of the later Henry James, tactfully concealed in the very structure of the novel; they are openly displayed. But they sometimes cast a gleam in the right direction. Speaking of Pitt Crawley the younger as an undergraduate preparing himself for public life, Thackeray remarks:

> But though he had a fine flux of words, and delivered his little voice with great pomposity and pleasure to himself, and never advanced any sentiment or opinion which was not perfectly trite and stale, and supported by a Latin quotation; yet he failed somehow, in spite of a mediocrity which ought to have insured any man a success.

Better, because sharper and more economical, is another comment on the same character:

> He was always thinking of his brother's soul, or of the souls of those who differed with him in opinion: it is a sort of comfort which many of the serious give themselves.

Better still is the quick illumination of the puppy George Osborne and his family: his dear little Amelia, he says to himself, "should take the place in society to which, as his wife, she was entitled."

As a rule the best comments in *Vanity Fair*, whether embodied or disembodied, are directed at characters whom the author does not expect the reader to approve of. Yet he sometimes misfires very painfully. Sir Pitt Crawley the elder is one of his originals. The scene in which the baronet shoulders Becky's trunk and stumps into the decaying town house with it, is one of Thackeray's triumphs. We have good reason to protest, therefore, when later in the book, Thackeray suddenly preaches about him:

> Vanity Fair! Vanity Fair! Here was a man, who could not spell, and did not care to read—who had the habits and the cunning of a boor; whose aim in life was pettifogging; and who never had a taste, or emotion, or enjoyment, but what was sordid and foul. . . .

and so on for a whole paragraph. Another character that Thackeray has delighted in creating is Miss Crawley, sister of the elder Pitt; and yet, when she is ill, he can explode into the homily that begins: "Picture to yourself,

O fair young reader, a worldly, selfish, graceless, thankless, religionless old woman. . . ."

For most readers of today, however, it is when Thackeray is discoursing about his supposed heroine, Amelia, that he becomes most exasperating in his commentary. He simpers or agonizes over her. His favorite epithet for her is *little* — "this little heart," "a little bride's mind," "our poor little creature," her "sweet pretty little foot," for example. As it happened, this simpering was more than some of his staunchest admirers could put up with, while the novel was appearing in monthly parts. They reproved him, and he took their words to heart, virtually deposing Amelia from the post of heroine and promoting Becky to the vacancy. When the story reaches the eve of the Battle of Waterloo, he points the contrast between the two women pretty sharply and, wittingly or unwittingly, much to the advantage of Becky. She keeps all her wits about her, profits by the panic that overtakes many of the English noncombatants in Brussels, and having coolly put her affairs in order, pays a visit to "poor little Emmy." At which point Thackeray makes the significant comment: "If this is a novel without a hero, at least let us lay claim to a heroine." The ambiguity in the word *heroine* must have been intentional.

Of course he could not quite depose Amelia. He was committed to her, and since she was gentle, well intentioned, and obtrusively virtuous, and since the plan he had in mind for the novel was based on a series of contrasts, he had to struggle for the remainder of it to preserve the reader's sympathy for this unhappy young woman. Again and again the struggle forced him into overwriting. He is not content to reveal by situation and significant dialogue how hard the lot of his quondam heroine had become; he has to underline through commentary. Amelia's child becomes her very being. That is convincing enough. But he cannot refrain from generalizing, slipping away from the particular, which is poignant, to flaccid talk about the "raptures of motherly love . . . joys how far higher and lower than reason — blind beautiful devotions which only women's hearts know." To contrive that Amelia must, in the child's interest, surrender him to his Osborne grandfather is an excellent and moving turn in the plot. The fact itself evokes the pity Thackeray is aiming at. But again he blurs the effect by a general comment: "I know few things more affecting than that timorous debasement and self-humiliation of a woman. . . . It is those who injure women who get the most kindness from them — they are born timid and tyrants, and maltreat those who are humblest before them."

Long before he had finished *Vanity Fair* Thackeray knew he had made Amelia too namby-pamby a creature to please readers whose judgment he respected; and it was to compensate for this that he expanded and vitalized the story of Becky further than he had at first intended. For the same reason he began to underline the selfishness of Amelia in her relations with Dobbin.

It is the long discursive story of Becky's struggles to gain a commanding position in London society, culminating in her triumphs at Gaunt House, then ending disastrously when her husband finds her alone with Lord Steyne, which raises *Vanity Fair* to a classic of British fiction. Thackeray seldom, perhaps never, wrote better than in the chapters devoted to this story. The attentive reader will note how seldom in this section of the book Thackeray depends on disembodied comments to help out the narrative, how apt such comments as he does make are, and with what skill and economy he keeps Becky alive and vivid. Here, as in some of the discriminated occasions contrived in *Esmond* to vitalize Beatrix, he trusted his *daimon* and forgot his role of lay preacher.

In Chapter XLI, Becky, back at Queen's Crawley for the funeral of Sir Pitt the elder, takes stock of her position. "It isn't difficult," she tells herself, "to be a country gentleman's wife. I think I could be a good woman if I had five thousand a year. . . . I could pay everybody, if I had but the money. This is what the conjurors here pride themselves upon doing." Every word in this thought-sequence (which runs to some sixteen lines) speaks the essential Becky. The word *conjurors* is brilliant. Becky, we remember, had spent much of her childhood among the riff-raff of the stage.

Yet even here, more's the pity, Thackeray cannot refrain from inserting ten lines of commentary, beginning with the rhetorical question: "And who knows but Becky was right in her speculations?"

Again, the long paragraph on the prudery of Victorian readers that opens Chapter LXIV, though important for literary historians, is evasive, deprecatory, and inept within the story of Becky Sharp. It is difficult to pardon a novelist who hints at the sins of his heroine with a smirking "I could an if I would."

It is pretty clear that in 1853, when Thackeray began upon *The Newcomes*, he was not fully satisfied with his methods of conveying not only belief in his imagined worlds but also the appropriate moral and intellectual attitudes toward them. He thought his best achievement so far was

Esmond, offered as the memoirs of an oldish man who recalled the adventures of his youth. This plan undoubtedly suited Esmond's (and Thackeray's) sensitive and ruminative temperament. It was also apt enough for a novel about life a century and a half ago. Esmond's commentaries arose naturally enough, and though too often long and prosy, did not seriously break the illusion. But would a similar plan suit *The Newcomes*, which was to be a novel of contemporary life?

After some preliminary fumbling, about which Thackeray's letters tell us a little, he decided that at any rate he could employ a narrator, who, without being the hero, would be a fairly prominent character within the novel itself. Young Clive Newcome was to be the hero, but Arthur Pendennis, carried over from the novel written immediately after *Vanity Fair*, should act as narrator and commentator. This decision greatly relieved Thackeray's mind. "I shall be able," he wrote to an American friend, "to talk more at ease than in my own person." If challenged by friends or critics while the novel was appearing in monthly parts, he could always plead that Pendennis was only a fictitious person, and that William Makepeace Thackeray did not necessarily agree with him.

The device worked pretty well, but not perfectly. The Pendennis of the earlier novel had been uncommonly like the younger Thackeray who had written for his life in *Fraser's Magazine* and *Punch*, and many of the public had not hesitated in declaring them to be one and the same person. Now, as it soon appeared, the somewhat older and less flighty Pendennis of *The Newcomes* was still Thackeray, writing with great fluency and often with distinction, but steadily hammering on a theme, the iniquity of the *mariage de convenance*, which his private letters at the time showed to be in the forefront of his mind. Six marriages of this sort occur in *The Newcomes*, and two more are narrowly avoided. In addition, Thackeray, like other novelists who have adopted the plan of an internal narrator — Joseph Conrad comes to mind — was often put to his shifts to account for Pendennis's intimate, sometimes very intimate, acquaintance with what the other characters were thinking, saying, and doing. A narrator who remains strictly anonymous and outside the book is by convention accepted as omniscient; one who plays a part within it is not. Pendennis was accordingly often forced to explain from what source he had derived his information, and not all his explanations were plausible. Once at least, he seemed to disclaim responsibility. "Not always," he confesses, "doth the writer know whither the divine Muse leadeth him." Readers of this novel, and indeed of every other novel of Thackeray's except the remarkably skillful *Esmond*, will admit the truth of this confession. At another point Pendennis ingeniously parries the question, "How do you know all this?" The narrative, he says, "is written maturely and at ease, long after the voyage is over, whereof it recounts the adventures and perils." Then he adds:

I fancy, for my part, that the speeches attributed to Clive, the Colonel, and the rest, are as authentic as the orations in Sallust or Livy, and only implore the truth-loving public to believe that incidents here told, and which passed very probably without witnesses, were either confided to me subsequently as compiler of this biography, or are of such a nature that they must have happened from what happened after.

Later he says:

All this story is told by one, who, if he was not actually present at the circumstances here related, yet had information concerning them, and could supply such a narrative of facts and conversations as is, indeed, not less authentic than the details of other histories.

Whether such explanations really help the reader to remain within the illusion may be doubted. And when the narrator professes to have learned from his wife Laura all the details of the very private conversation between Ethel and Lord Farintosh when she terminated their engagement, the reader is tempted to exclaim: "Fie! 'tis impossible; the proud Ethel would never have repeated a word of that conversation to a living soul."

These are some of the straits to which Thackeray's method has reduced him. If you are determined to have a dummy to protect you from a critical public, you mustn't give him impossible tasks.

A passage in Chapter XLV reminds us at once of Thackeray's perplexities over his two heroines in *Vanity Fair*. Pendennis suddenly exclaims:

I don't think, for my part, at this present stage of the tale, Miss Ethel Newcome occupies a very dignified position. . . . A girl of great beauty, high temper, and strong natural intellect, who submits to be dragged hither and thither in an old grandmother's leash, and in pursuit of a husband who will run away from the couple, such a person, I say, is in a very awkward position as a heroine; and I declare that if I had another ready to my hand (and unless there were extenuating circumstances), Ethel should be deposed at this very sentence. But a novelist must go on with his heroine, as a man with his wife, for better or worse, and to the end.

This leads almost immediately to an explosion on the main theme of the book:

O me! what a confession it is, in the very outset of life and blushing brightness of youth's morning, to own that the aim with which a young girl sets out, and the object of her existence, is to marry a rich man. . . . Bon Dieu! the doctrine with which she begins is that she is to have a wealthy husband; the article of Faith in her catechism is, "I believe in elder sons, and a house in town, and a house in the country."

It is easy to say that this kind of thing was fashionable and accepted in the Victorian Age, and that we do wrong to object merely because it is no longer either fashionable or accepted now. Every student of the Victorian novel knows that Thackeray was not singular in his habit of reminding the reader from time to time that his characters were only puppets whom he could manipulate as he pleased. Trollope does the same thing occasionally—as when in *Dr. Thorne* he discusses whether Mary is really suitable for the role of heroine. Even George Eliot in *Middlemarch* (possibly the greatest novel of the nineteenth century) momentarily smudges the imagined world in which Caleb Garth exists by a reference to the real world in which she deeply admired her own father. But the question is not merely one of fashion. *Ars est celare artem* is true *semper et ubique.* The serious novel (not, of course, the parody or burlesque, which may be art of another kind) depends on a sustained illusion of human life, not on a transcript from real life; and whatever interrupts or shatters the illusion is so far a blunder in art, whether the work dates from 1750 or 1850 or 1950. The novelist born knows this, though he may fall into error now and then. It is because Thackeray falls into error so often that some of us doubt if he *was* a novelist born.

Yet, comparing *The Newcomes* with *Vanity Fair*, we do find that Thackeray has learned to handle commentary more skillfully in the later book. There is still a great deal of it; indeed, too much. But more of it is embodied than in the earlier book.

In Chapter v, Pendennis warns the reader not to be too angry with the Colonel's "two most respectable brothers" for neglecting him while he lived in India. This leads to a very characteristic Thackerayan paragraph, of which a few lines may be quoted:

No people are so ready to give a man a bad name as his own kinsfolk; and having made him that present, they are ever most unwilling to take it back again. . . . If he falls among thieves, the respectable Pharisees of his race turn their heads aside and leave him penniless and bleeding. They clap him on the back kindly enough when he returns, after shipwreck, with money in his pocket.

It may well be that Thackeray's personal experiences in his youth put a little extra sting into the paragraph, and lengthened it unnecessarily, but it is nonetheless relevant to the Newcomes. Farther on in the book the Colonel and his son discover that they have few interests in common; and Pendennis moralizes on this topic, not very profoundly and at too great a length, but not quite irrelevantly. He indulges himself in a much longer disquisition on the imperious Lady Kew and her grandson. Although it consists chiefly of generalities, and so might be regarded as mere padding, it does not seriously impair the illusion. The book contains other homilies, however, longer, little relevant, and therefore distracting, for which it is difficult to find an excuse.

We do find embodied comments, nevertheless — pointed and illuminating. Pendennis can be admirably caustic and penetrating. In the middle of a long dialogue between Barnes Newcome and the Colonel, he briefly remarks: "You see [Barnes] believed that Heaven had made him the Colonel's superior." This, I would say, is an example of the Thackerayan embodied comment at its best.

Again, Thackeray, with the casual prodigality of a man whose store is inexhaustible, has tossed into the novel a wide variety of vivid, knowable, but incidental characters, few of whom were strictly necessary, but many of whom provide welcome relief from some of the rather tiresome principals, like Pendennis and his insufferable wife. No other novel of Thackeray's, I would say, contains so many.

Nor, I would say also, does any other of his books contain so many remarkable discriminated occasions, emerging sharply from long stretches of fluent but often pedestrian passages of narrative. Immediately after the rather fatuous overture, "a farrago of old fables," as Thackeray's imaginary critic calls it not unjustly, we are ushered into the Cave of Harmony, where the old reprobate Costigan grossly offends against the maxim, *Maxima debetur pueris*, and the Colonel in righteous anger shouldered his cane, and "scowling round at the company of scared bacchanalians . . . stalked away, his boy after him." This is a magnificent opening scene, compressed into some half a dozen pages. Every reader familiar with the book will compile his own list of other discriminated occasions that he is glad to recall. Mine would include the first arrival of Lady Ann Newcome and her family at Miss Honeyman's in Brighton; the Colonel's dinner party at which Clive hurls a glass of wine in Barnes Newcome's face; the collapse of Lady Clara Pulleyn in the street at Baden; the elegant war of words between old Lady Kew and the Duchesse d'Ivry; the quarrel, leading to a duel, between Lord Kew and the Gascon; the parting between old Lady Kew and her grandson; the dinner at Miss Honeyman's when Clive and Lord Farintosh maneuver for Ethel's attention; the scene in the Newcomes' London office when the Colonel tells Barnes just what a rascal he is; the brawl between Barnes and Lord Highgate in the street at Newcome; the final scene between Ethel and Lord Farintosh; the incident of Mrs. Mackenzie's packing her trunks; and, greatest achievement of all, the death of the Colonel at Grey Friars.

The last is a miracle. Perhaps, after all, Thackeray *was* a novelist born. If so, why in the name of heaven did he overlay his supreme talent with so many fustian annotations?

A NOTE ON DICKENS' HUMOR

Douglas Bush
HARVARD UNIVERSITY

THE change in the critical view of Dickens during the past generation has been so marked that even the general reader could hardly miss it, and it has now been placed in its historical sequence in George H. Ford's scholarly and lively book, *Dickens and his Readers* (1955). Critics of older generations — both those who gladly surrendered to the magician's spell and those who remained austerely and somewhat snobbishly censorious — were likely to see an unsophisticated, erratic, inspired genius who gave his enormous public what it wanted: crude melodrama, crude pathos, and humanitarian zeal, a world of evil-doing and crime set off against the virtues, sorrows, and joys of the poor, a world of coaches and snug inns and cosy domesticity and good cheer, through which wandered characters of prodigious and eccentric vitality and humor.

The new Dickens has been seen (at least after the first frenzied phase of his career) as a highly conscious and developing artist, a sophisticated molder of symbolic patterns, a savage analyst of society, a half-surrealist creator of the crowded, lonely city, a novelist or novelist-poet to be read as we read Dostoevsky or Kafka or Faulkner. The qualities of the old and the new Dickens cannot be summed up in two sentences, but these headings will serve. The new Dickens has become so well established, in the United States at any rate, that Mario Praz's hostile version of the old Dickens in his *The Hero in Eclipse* (1956) appears as something of an anachronism (like the present essay, except that this is not hostile). The change may be welcome even to those readers of the older or oldest generation who grew up on Dickens. The enchanter of children and of people in their second childhood, who used to invite critics' condescension, has now acquired an artistic stature commensurate with the enjoyment he has always given to the uncritical; what had seemed to be the beer of the populace was really 84-proof brandy. All this is much to the good, and we may hope for more analysis of the potencies and subtleties of Dickens' art.

At the same time it may be hoped that the new criticism of Dickens will not become too severely and solemnly intellectual and analytical. After all, as Mr. Sleary said, "People mutht be amuthed." Some modern critics give the impression of having come to Dickens late in life, perhaps after Dostoevsky, Kafka, and Faulkner (or perhaps after Stendhal, Flaubert, and James), and, however freshly illuminating, do not seem to be very much aware that Dickens is one of the world's greatest humorists — a fact not concealed from that most unexpected of Dickensians, Santayana. Dickens is, to be sure, many other things also, yet the millions who have rejoiced in his comic characters and dialogue may have been wiser than those children of light who either are unresponsive or regard humor as outside the critical pale.

These few pages are not a contribution to criticism; they are — in addition to being a small but cordial tribute to my old friend James Hillhouse (this piece was written before his illness and death) — only reminders of one rich element in some of the greatest comic characters we have. I am thinking of what may be loosely called the instinct for self-dramatization. Since Percy Lubbock's book, at least, it has been a commonplace that Dickens' novelistic technique is "dramatic" (as contrasted with Thackeray's "pictorial" narrative), but the author's dramatic handling of his material is not the same thing as the individual character's dramatizing of himself, though the two can come together. And, while Dickens' devotion to the stage — and the stagey — is a familiar fact, it does not alone explain the frequently theatrical quality of his comic characters' self-dramatization.

Not to refine overmuch, we might say that a character's humor may be unconscious and naïve or conscious and — very probably — ironical, and that either attitude may have a touch of the histrionic. Such combinations are not of course peculiar to Dickens (or to English humor). Thus Chaucer's Miller is consciously giving himself a comic role when he declares, beginning with a high-flown phrase:

> But first I make a protestacioun
> That I am dronke, I knowe it by my soun.

So too when the Pardoner is called on for a tale and, his character being evident, the "gentils" cry out against ribaldry and demand "som moral thyng":

> "I graunte, ywis," quod he, "but I moot thynke
> Upon som honest thyng while that I drynke."

In these simple words the Pardoner suggests that he is capable, with a dubious stimulant, of telling a moral tale, even if it is not his line, that he is amused by the genteel pilgrims' anxiety, and that he enjoys keeping them in suspense.

The self-dramatizing instinct is obvious in Shakespeare's comic characters. The clowns, from the nature of their profession, are continually engaged in a sort of parody of the normal sanity, intelligence, and learning they are not supposed to possess. Falstaff, whether in the tavern or on the battlefield, is so consistently acting a part — the part of Falstaff — that whatever personality he may be imagined to have had has been absorbed into his conscious role. When he stages the little impromptu drama with Prince Hal and acts the part of the royal father and then of the son, he merely steps out of his everyday role into another of slightly heightened exaggeration. Falstaff not only acts in the presence of other people, the exalted as well as his Eastcheap cronies; he acts for the pure love of acting when he has no audience but himself, as in the delivery of his speech on honor.

Even the stiff and sober Malvolio has his high imaginings, when he is beguiled into seeing himself as Olivia's husband. He and the lowly Bottom both belong to the naïve end of the spectrum; in both, self-dramatizing (which is instinctive and habitual with Bottom) is an unconscious revelation of vanity and stupidity — though one character is likeable and the other is not. Neither has any protective irony, and each has a moment of unwitting self-deflation: Malvolio, in his vision of future greatness, stumbles into the thought of his still fingering his steward's chain (which he hastily amends to "some rich jewel"); and Bottom, waking after his experience with the ass's head, stops twice on the brink of admitting what he was and had. Yet each of the two has a measure of half-conscious artistry. Malvolio, in picturing his prospective elevation, speaks — for the delight of his own ear — with a new degree of pomposity; and Bottom, likewise soliloquizing, seeks to do justice to his dream with a garbled version of I Corinthians 2.9: "The eye of man hath not heard, the ear of man hath not seen, man's hand is not able to taste, his tongue to conceive, nor his heart to report what my dream was." Perhaps the most consistent self-dramatizer is the drunken Stephano in *The Tempest*.

It is a question in which category, the naïve or the conscious, to put Barnardine, the obstinate convict in *Measure for Measure*, who speaks only a few lines but is decidedly a personality. Is he displaying only crass obtuseness, or conscious humor, in the face of death? "Friar, not I! I have been drinking hard all night, and I will have more time to prepare me . . . I will not consent to die this day, that's certain . . . Not a word! If you have anything to say to me, come to my ward; for thence will not I to-day."

In exploiting the instinct for self-dramatization Dickens is very much in the tradition. This instinct is not only widespread among his comic characters; it may be their whole existence. These diverse and wonderful individuals have generally two things in common. First, they are very poor in this world's goods and live on the ragged edge, economically and socially; their lives, viewed objectively, are seedy and difficult enough to cause unrelieved depression or despair. Secondly, they have one supreme possession, an overflowing, irrepressible imagination, with its attendant gift of words, which transfigures themselves and their world, which makes their shabby existence a perpetual and exciting drama, and which no amount of painful experience can more than momentarily crush. In Dickens' vision, as in Blake's, all men — or a good many — are poets; and their speeches are the romantic poetry of Cockneydom. This faculty, at its best, seems to be both instinctive and half-conscious; its possessor is being himself and at the same time has a detached enjoyment of himself. Doubtless the psychologists have a word for it.

This mode of comprehension and creation was strong in Dickens from the beginning. Mr. Pickwick is not one of the self-dramatizers — his simplicity and innocence are too complete for that — but his fellow Pickwickians to some degree are, in assuming the roles of lover, poet, and sportsman which they cannot sustain. Jingle, the down-at-heel actor and adventurer, maintains a jaunty buoyancy through his own comic invention and resourcefulness; he is always presenting some other self to the world. Rachael Wardle sees herself as a romantic figure in her belated and short-lived love affairs. Even the fat boy is a conscious dramatic artist in working on the grandmother's feelings — "I wants to make your flesh creep." Sam Weller's self-dramatizing partakes largely of the knowingness of the smart Cockney. His father is a less slick and more primitive philosopher of man and matrimony, but he can also speak of himself with a mixture of complacency and detached irony (we are not quite sure where the division comes):

"I'm a-goin' to leave you, Samivel, my boy, and there's no tellin' ven I shall see you again. Your mother-in-law may ha' been too much for me, or a thousand things may have happened by the time you next hears any news o' the celebrated Mr. Veller o' the Bell Savage. The family name depends wery much upon you, Samivel, and I hope you'll do wot's right by it. Upon all little pints o' breedin' I know I may trust you as vell as if it was my own self. . . ."

Even so might the bearer of an ancient and noble name counsel his heir.

There are endless varieties of comic fantasy, oblique wish-fulfillment. The members of the Crummles troupe support one another in their stagey affectations, which are their unconscious defense against the knowledge that they exist on the lowest level of the profession. The supreme dramatic imagination in this book, however, is Mrs. Nickleby's. In her it takes the form, not of humorous invention, but of naïve reminiscence, since she instinctively evades the troubles of the present by living almost wholly, and blissfully, in the past. (One says "almost wholly" in the past because Mrs. Nickleby becomes, in her own imagination, the attractive heroine of a highly dramatic romance, her admirer being the lunatic next door who throws cucumbers over the wall.) Yet Mrs. Nickleby's flow of reminiscence (she is an early exemplar of the interior monologue) can hardly be called self-centered; rather, her past reflects a general rosy glow. And her recollections, if wayward, rarely lack dramatic particularity:

"Roast pig—let me see. On the day five weeks after you were christened we had a roast—no, that couldn't have been a pig either, because I recollect there were a pair of them to carve, and your poor papa and I could never have thought of sitting down to two pigs; they must have been partridges. Roast pig! I hardly think we ever could have had one, now I come to remember; for your papa could never bear the sight of them in the shops, and used to say that they always put him in mind of very little babies, only the pigs had much fairer complexions; and he had a horror of little babies, too, because he couldn't very well afford any increase to his family, and had a natural dislike to the subject . . ."

There are perhaps four self-dramatizers of superlative quality and consistency. The earliest of the quartet is Dick Swiveller. In his first appearance his taste for flamboyant rhetoric (which is often interlaced with scraps from popular songs) draws from his friend Fred the sour rebuke, "You needn't act the chairman here." But Dick acts at all times. And he is not only dramatic in himself but the cause that drama is in other men, as in the high quarrel with the rival suitor of Miss Wackles, whom Dick is trying to cast off ("Sorry, ma'am! . . . sorry in the possession of a Cheggs!"). He is lending himself to a sordid project, but what he does, or is willing to do, we forget in the joy of what he says. The scene between Dick and the Marchioness has long been recognized as one of the finest examples of Dickens' material and art, a unique blend of realism, romance, comedy, and sentiment that never approaches sentimentality. (If the pair could be imagined in a French novel, they would have a squalid liaison; in a Russian novel, Dick would be a revolutionist intellectual and the Marchioness a girl with a yellow ticket.) The scene in the basement kitchen is the great example of Dick's conscious, comic theatricalism (and goodness of heart):

"Marchioness, your health. You will excuse my wearing my hat, but the palace is damp, and the marble floor is — if I may be allowed the expression — sloppy." . . .

"Ha!" said Mr. Swiveller, with a portentous frown. " 'Tis well. Marchioness! — but no matter. Some wine there. Ho!" He illustrated these melodramatic morsels by handing the tankard to himself with great humility, receiving it haughtily, drinking from it thirstily, and smacking his lips fiercely.

By the way, to inject a bit of scholarship into this paper, is Dick's injunction to the Marchioness as she drinks the purl made from his own recipe — "moderate your transports" — an echo of Wordsworth's Protesilaus rebuking Laodamia, "thy transports moderate"?

In contrast with Mr. Swiveller's many roles, which range from the supposedly jealous lover to the theatrical bandit, the dirty, vulgar, callous, bibulous, and belligerent Mrs. Gamp might seem to be the husky voice of unadulterated nature. Yet the thought of Mrs. Gamp calls up at once that substantial product of her imagination, Mrs. Harris. Mrs. Harris might appear to prove the uniquely dramatic and disinterested creativity of Mrs. Gamp's mind if it were not that Mrs. Harris's chief function is to provide quotable encomiums on Mrs. Gamp. It is true that Mrs. Gamp's imagination is not quite completely circumscribed and self-centered — one of her most famous and breathless passages is the gratuitous account of Mr. Harris's anxieties over the birth of his first child — and Mrs. Harris is so real in her own mind that Mrs. Prig's scepticism causes a violent break between her and her old partner. Yet in her most dazzling flights concerning the life and times of Mrs. Harris, Mrs. Gamp's craving for money and drink can, without the slightest effect on her fancy, intrude the most realistic demands: " 'Mrs. Gamp,' she says in answer, 'if ever there was a sober creetur to be got at eighteenpence a day for working people, and three-

and-six for gentlefolks — night-watching,' " said Mrs. Gamp, with emphasis, " 'being a extra charge — you are that inwallable person.' " Mrs. Gamp's eye being on the main chance, she quotes Mrs. Harris only to impress other people, for the sake of gain or kudos; unlike some other comic characters whose invention stops far short of a Mrs. Harris, she does not carry her dramatic imagining into soliloquies. Dickens' talkers, for that matter, are seldom alone.

Mrs. Nickleby, Mr. Swiveller, and Mrs. Gamp can hardly be said to represent an "idea" in the mind of their creator (unless Mrs. Gamp embodies a sort of early demand for Florence Nightingales), but Mr. and Mrs. Micawber do represent an idea. In addition to being themselves (and to being more or less Mr. and Mrs. John Dickens), they are a dramatic objectification of Dickens' fervent hatred of Malthusianism and Utilitarianism. The pair are unpractical, improvident, polyphiloprogenitive, in every way unfitted for survival in a world of competition; but they are also, in their own peculiar way, above that world. Moreover, in his occasional sober moments, Mr. Micawber has a philosophy, which of course he does not practice; his summary of the relations of income and expenditure to happiness and misery has long been classic. What is more important, at one sober moment he displays — without sentimentality — a depth of feeling and a dignity that we remember through all his troubles and absurdities. Just before one statement of that economic principle, when his censure of procrastination has evoked from his wife a reference to poor papa's maxim, Mr. Micawber pronounces a loyal if limited eulogy over his late father-in-law and continues:

"But he applied that maxim to our marriage, my dear; and that was so far prematurely entered into, in consequence, that I never recovered the expense."

Mr. Micawber looked aside at Mrs. Micawber, and added, "Not that I am sorry for it. Quite the contrary, my love." After which he was grave for a minute or two.

A few paragraphs later, Mrs. Micawber, looking down at David from the top of the coach, sees how small the sharer of their trials is, and beckons him to climb up for a warm and motherly kiss. Because of such moments the Micawbers are not mere figures of fun.

The mental assets of the Micawbers — they have no others — are partly divided. Though both have the resiliency they so greatly need, Mr. Micawber possesses the exuberant dramatic imagination; his wife, it appears, the cool, logical intellect. Mrs. Micawber is much worse off than Mrs. Nickleby, and more acutely aware of her situation, and her frequent glances back to her life with papa and mamma are not a happy escape from the present but a painful contrast. Mrs. Micawber's logical faculty has not altogether extinguished her instinct for self-dramatization; this comes out both in her sincerely theatrical protestations of attachment to her husband and in her tendency to make a public occasion of her own and her family's history: "My papa lived to bail Mr. Micawber several times, and then expired, regretted by a numerous circle." Mr. Micawber is able to live much more buoyantly in the moment and in the future, and his instinct for turning private into public drama is much more richly developed. This instinct is perhaps the armor that keeps him almost invulnerable and almost always happy. If he has nothing else to sustain him, there is his own eloquence. On his lips a chain of rotund clichés lights up the world. His habit of adding a plain statement, by way of translation, to his rolling periods is a sort of concession to the requirements of everyday intercourse (though even these brevities are dramatically rendered), yet his own essential life is lived, as it were, on the platform and the stage. Any audience will do, from little David to his fellow inmates of the debtors' prison or the people assembled for the unmasking of Heep. Whether listening to his own voice, or making flourishes at his throat with a razor, or drinking punch, or leading his family along the Medway with the coal trade in view, Mr. Micawber lives in his imagination, and the slings and arrows of outrageous fortune cannot wound him.

Mr. and Mrs. Micawber seem to be thought of as the last of Dickens' great comic characters, those characters who, by virtue of their dimensions and vitality, have an existence independent of the books in a sort of Platonic heaven. In the later novels, whether because of some lessening of the author's fecundity or because of his seeking a more disciplined organic structure, his comic (and other) characters are nearer life size and their prodigal self-revelations are held in check. Comedy goes on, but the procession no longer includes people who stand out as far larger than life. For instance, Herbert Pocket, Pip's friend, is just such a hopeful and unsuccessful young man "in the City" as the young Micawber would have been; but Herbert is a subdued and relatively normal person. On the other hand, if Mrs. Gamp's Mrs. Harris represents the Cockney dreamworld, what shall we say of that split personality, Mr. Wemmick, who makes such a realistic-fantastic separation between his half-mechanized life in the Newgate world of Mr. Jaggers' office and his human life at Walworth in the minute castle with the drawbridge, the cannon, and the Aged?

We have been recalling a few of the most famous figures in Dickens, mainly the earlier Dickens, but a host of people in all the books — sometimes even nameless people — have in some degree the instinct for dramatizing themselves. At the very beginning of *Pickwick Papers*, Mr. Pickwick's cabman, suspecting the motive behind his passenger's innocent questions about his horse, puts on an act in giving extravagant answers — though at the end of the journey his workaday self is manifested in his appeal to fists. In *Edwin Drood* the drunken Durdles registers, or enlarges, his place in the scheme of things by referring to himself, very favorably, in the third person. A full list of examples between these two chronological poles would run almost into a Dickens dictionary. Perhaps the chief groups of exceptions would be the wholly respectable and the ultra-good characters, who are, often unhappily, their simple selves. The self-dramatizing instinct is especially strong in the multitude of the lower middle and lower class. Their usually drab and commonplace lives do not give scope for their vitality and imagination and they consciously or unconsciously create for themselves a more exciting or glamorous role. Many of them are, by conventional standards, failures, and not at all sublime failures, but ridiculous and pathetic — like Mr. Wopsle, "the celebrated Provincial Amateur of Roscian renown." Such a vision might have invited sentimentality, yet, however ready Dickens was to respond in other areas, he seldom did in this; there is enough realistic detail to disinfect, enough humor to irradiate, such figures. They belong partly to Victorian England, partly to fairyland. George Orwell, who saw truly so much of Dickens, but whose moral boiling-point was rather low, startles us when he pronounces Micawber "a cadging scoundrel"; surely one might as well call Jack the Giant-Killer a homicidal maniac.

It is agreed that Dickens could not deal satisfactorily with love on its common levels, much less with grand passions; yet he could deal, incomparably, with love of the off-beat kind (witness the chapter on the married life of David and his feckless child-wife, which Gissing thought a perfect piece of writing). Dickens could discern a chivalric knight-errant in the soul of an eccentric, frustrated nobody, a divine spark in the wooden Barkis, in the almost equally inarticulate adorer of Florence Dombey, Mr. Toots, in the Walworth side of Mr. Wemmick. Most of these absurd and genuine lovers cast themselves, with varying degrees of consciousness, in romantic roles (even Barkis has his moments of almost wordless drama). The clerks at Mrs. Todgers' boarding-house, roused to new levels of emotion by the disturbing presence of the Pecksniff girls, carry on high feuds with theatrical grandiosity. Mr. Guppy, though his devotion to Esther Summerson does not extinguish his legal prudence ("Half a minute, miss! . . . This has been without prejudice?"), haunts the theatre when she goes there, in a state of woeful dejection, his hair flattened with bear's grease. And along with such lovers must be put the good-hearted Flora Finching, whose coy stream-of-consciousness speeches fail of their effect on Arthur Clennam.

Disappointed lovers are only one category. Countless miscellaneous people have a positive enjoyment in being their dramatic selves (like Betsey Trotwood), or in heightening themselves, playing a bigger role than life has granted them. And the instinct is not limited to the comic. It gives a half-comic note to many villains or near-villains; it animates Squeers and Mantalini, the demonic Quilp and the pious Pecksniff, the windy Chadband and the courtly Turveydrop. Old Krook's playing the part of a Lord Chancellor becomes symbolic satire; Harold Skimpole's role of child-like dilettante ends in base duplicity. (There is no comedy at all in John Jasper's gravitating between the cathedral organ-loft and the opium den.) Indeed the dramatic instinct, which in the Swivellers and Micawbers is pure *joie de vivre*, a sort of comic existentialism, may, in their social superiors, be pure knavery. In all the books, and increasingly in the later ones, most people of the higher levels are acting a part and engaged in some kind of conscious deception.

But that is another story. So too is Dickens' constant endowment of inanimate objects with dramatic life. This has long been recognized as a hallmark of the Dickensian manner in ordinary and incidental description, and of late years it has been more and more recognized as a conscious symbolic device. To mention one of innumerable examples, the casts of the swollen faces of two hanged convicts in Mr. Jaggers' office seem to Pip, every time he calls, to be alive and attentive, and they become in his mind brutal symbols of evil and the law.

This paper, however, has been only a glance at human comedy, and at one quality in that, a quality so self-evident that there is small excuse for talking about it, except the pleasure of doing so.

SELF-HELP AND THE HELPLESS IN *BLEAK HOUSE*

George H. Ford
UNIVERSITY OF ROCHESTER

IN SEEKING the themes of such novels of social criticism as Dickens' *Bleak House* or of Greene's *The Quiet American*, the reader has the task of understanding (if not of sharing) the whole system of values assumed by the novelist. Mr. Greene seems to make the task of understanding a much more difficult one than Dickens does because he obscures from us which of his characters is supposed to be the hero and which the villain. Dickens kindly spares us this difficulty at least; his villains and heroes are quickly identified by our senses. We know when to hiss against Mr. Vholes fingering his pimpled face or against Grandfather Smallweed with his cushion, and when to applaud for John Jarndyce or for Esther Summerson with her "Esther, Esther! Duty, my dear!" Yet even though we are clearly provided with the clues to evaluate the individual heroes and villains in *Bleak House*, there still remains the larger problem of identifying the underlying assumptions upon which the social criticism is based. Who or what is responsible for the plight of the characters in the world of *Bleak House*? Are they presented as free agents or as victims of social forces outside the control of human will? Dickens' assumptions here are not so readily identifiable and have been frequently misrepresented by well-intentioned critics who overlook the complexity of his position.

One way of becoming aware of this complexity is to try to classify Dickens' social criticism as Liberal, Radical, Communistic, Anti-Communistic, Anarchistic, or Conservative. Such classifications produce merely a bewildering variety of labels. And this confusion is not attributable, in Dickens' case, to a lack of historical sense on the part of later readers. Many of his own contemporaries were equally bewildered by his point of departure and could express their bewilderment only by indignantly writing him off as an irresponsible *enfant terrible*. This inapplicability of single labels to Dickens' position has been ably demonstrated by Monroe Engel in his article on Dickens' politics (*PMLA*, December, 1956), an article that sketches in the whole development of Dickens' political views from the evidence of his letters and his contributions to *Household Words*. What follows is confined instead to a single stage of Dickens' development and to a single novel, *Bleak House*, which I have tried to approach in a manner different from that with which it is usually discussed in order to indicate some of its assumptions and its characteristic tensions.

The usual approach to the social criticism of *Bleak House* is to concentrate upon the exposé of Chancery—and with good cause. The great opening chapter and the later sustained development of the atmosphere of fog and rain are so compelling that they may shift our attention away from what is the central concern of this novel, which is not merely to expose Chancery malpractices but to illustrate the nature of true success and failure in modern society. The bunglings of Chancery do indeed affect the lives of most of the characters of this cleverly constructed book, and they provide a central target for the satire. But *Bleak House* is more than a satire just as it is more than a detective story. As Edgar Johnson suggests, it is an anatomy of society.

Of all literary forms it is the novel, according to Lionel Trilling, that is most devoted "to the celebration and investigation of the human will." *Bleak House* is such a novel, but it is essential to note at the outset that there is one assumption concerning the human will throughout this book which accounts for many of the difficulties of understanding it. According to this assumption, a line is drawn in the social structure between those who are helpless and those who are capable of self-help, and the reader is expected to employ somewhat different standards when evaluating those who are above this assumed line and those who are below it. The weak may be exalted in a Dickens novel, as in Christ's parables, but the weak-willed are despised and despicable. In the popular mind, Dickens is sometimes supposed to have devoted all of his attention to those below the line, yet in *Bleak House* almost all of his attention is concentrated upon those above it. The weak, although of less importance, may be considered first.

This vast mass of the population is represented by a few figures such as the wife-beating brickmakers and in particular by Jo, the crossing-sweeper. We get our first glimpse of them in chapter five when Esther, during her morning walk in London, notices some "extraordinary creatures in rags, secretly groping among the swept-out rubbish for pins and other refuse." Such creatures are consistently treated by Dickens as incapable of helping themselves. And because their plight is not of their own making he regards their fate with pity and often with indignation:

> Jo moves on . . . down to Blackfriars Bridge . . . to settle to his repast. And there he sits, munching and gnawing, and looking up at the great Cross on the summit of St. Paul's Cathedral. . . . From the boy's face one might suppose that sacred emblem to be, in his eyes, the crowning confusion of the great, confused city; so golden, so high up, so far out of his reach. There he sits, the sun going down, the river running fast, the crowd flowing by him in two streams — everything moving on to some purpose and to one end — until he is stirred up, and told to 'move on' too.

Dickens really thinks of Jo and his ilk as dependents in the feudal or patriarchal sense. Their lot could be much improved by adequate sanitation and education (the responsibility of the governors such as Boodle who were "born expressly to do it"), and by charity (the responsibility of individuals "to help the weak from failing"), but certainly not by the efforts that the weak ones themselves can make. Self-help, the measuring-stick for men above the demarcation line, is for such beings as Jo a mere luxury. They might rebel like "oxen over-goaded," and from time to time the author follows Carlyle's device in *The French Revolution* of hinting that to ignore our responsibilities toward these poor beings is to court the dangers of revolution. A corrupt and wasteful society may originate a combustion that seems spontaneous but for which there is always cause. But revolution as a *solution*? Not in the mind of the author of *Bleak House*; only in the minds of some of his critics. In fact he really has no solution in the full sense of the word — a deficiency which cannot really prompt many of us to feel superior. He makes it clear that busy-body Mrs. Pardiggle and her religious tracts will not remove the "iron barrier" between the brickmakers and those above them, but Esther's comment goes no further than this negative one: "By whom, or how, it could be removed, we did not know; but we knew that." To know that Mrs. Pardiggle is absurd provides a fine opportunity for small-scale satire but hardly a blueprint for a fresh organization of society in the manner of Marx or Engels. Orwell has noted that Dickens had his greatest difficulty in portraying the unionized workmen of industry. Perhaps the difficulty is attributable to their not quite belonging to either the dependent status or the independent one.

If a kind of determinism operates below the line which divides the helpless dependents from those above it, a different system, which assumes free will, operates for all the others, and hence, as I suggested, a different method of judgment is required of the reader. In discussing this second group of characters, in which the opposition between different social codes is portrayed, it will be helpful to reduce *Bleak House* to the level of a beast-fable, an important level on which much of its action moves. Later the full-scale complexities of Dickens' picture of society can be considered, but the simple fable with its Smilesian concept of self-help must first be established.

From an early period in his career, Dickens was aware of one of the principal conflicts in nineteenth-century England (a conflict to have its counterpart in the struggle between North and South in the United States). The political phase of it, evident in 1832, was important, but as a novelist Dickens was more appropriately interested in its social phase: the conflict between the old easy-going, fun-loving, aristocratic way of life, centered in the country estates, and the new, earnest, hard-working middle-class way of life, with its fierce energies, its fluid structure in which a man of talent and will could rise to eminence by his own efforts as Rouncewell the Ironmaster, son of a housekeeper, rose to the level of factory-manager and bank-owner, a powerful man sought by the electors to run for Parliament.

It would seem that one could readily predict where Dickens' sympathies would lie in this conflict. Himself the grandson of a housekeeper of a country estate, self-made and to a considerable degree self-educated, Dickens seemed to embody all of the preferences and prejudices of the new middle class. Some lines from a play by Bulwer-Lytton, lines which he knew by heart, embody his own story:

> Then did I seek to rise
> Out of the prison of my mean estate;
> And, with such jewels as the exploring mind
> Brings from the caves of knowledge, buy my ransom
> From those twin jailers of the daring heart—
> Low birth and iron fortune.

In *David Copperfield*, when the hero speaks of his "perseverance" and "continuous energy" as "the source of my success," and also of his "habits of punctuality, order, and diligence," Dickens is of course representing his own character and his own faith in the business-like traits recommended by Benjamin Franklin as the foundation for a successful career.

As a fable, *Bleak House* confronts two contrasting types: the dedicated, hard-working self-made professionals on the one hand, and the selfish or weak-willed indolent amateur dabblers on the other. Often this confrontation is provided in pairs. Prince Turveydrop, the dancing-master, "worked for his father twelve hours a day." The father, a fat carry-over of the outmoded Regency code, is a parasite who regrets that England "has not many gentlemen left. We are few. I see nothing to succeed us but a race of weavers."

The Rouncewell brothers also make up a contrasting pair, but here the contrast is different from the others because George, the prodigal son, is redeemed by qualities of heart. He is aware, nevertheless, of his failure. Hoping that he "should rise to be an officer," George has remained "an idle dragooning chap" and by comparison with his successful brother he thinks of himself "not self-made like him, but self-unmade."

Another pairing is presented by Guppy and his indolent friend, Jobling. Guppy, despite his fatuousness and his uncertain accent, is energetic enough to rise in the legal profession. Jobling, who lost his post as law-clerk by getting into debt, had a Micawber-like faith that something would turn up to save him. "I trusted to things coming round," he says. At this point, Dickens himself immediately steps in to pass judgment, and the passage is crucial not only for our impression of the characters but for our understanding of how we are to consider the Chancery muddle itself:

> That very popular trust in flat things coming round! Not in their being beaten round, or worked round, but in their 'coming' round! As though a lunatic should trust in the world's 'coming' triangular!

The difference between Dickens' treatment of the destitute Jo and the destitute Jobling is basic. The one is helpless; the other is capable of choice and can *will* to change his lot. Jobling is like Sir Leicester Dedlock's cousins, whose lack of self-reliance makes them indolent and useless parasites. The "effeminate Exquisites" of the 1820's, the dandies upon whom Turveydrop modeled himself, are largely extinct, says Dickens, but they have these cousins as their successors who, while less conscious of clothes, are equally "languid" and useless. These hangers-on of Sir Leicester's might, however, have served society well. Like Addison in his portrait of Will Wimble, Dickens described the Dedlock cousins as "amiable and sensible, and likely to have done well enough in life if they could have overcome their cousinship." Again the element of choice is assumed.

Another pairing, much more fully portrayed, is provided by Richard

Carstone and Alan Woodcourt. Woodcourt is the ideal character by whom all the others can be measured, and needless to say he must accordingly suffer a lack of interest on the part of readers, especially a later generation of readers with their increased preference for failures or sinners. A hard-working professional, whether on ship or ashore, Woodcourt is whole-heartedly dedicated to his career as a surgeon. And despite the comparative lack of income which may face him in his career (a situation which is vehemently denounced by Boythorn and for which there is considerable evidence in the 1850's), he is sure of success.

Woodcourt's friend, Richard Carstone, is portrayed as charming and seemingly amiable, but he is a drifter. Learning that he cannot acquire a naval commission through patronage he remarks weakly: "I shall have to work my own way. Never mind! Plenty of people have had to do that before now, and have done it." He drifts then into surgery, the law, and the army, in each instance ignoring the Dickensian advice that is put into the mouth of one of Mrs. Bayham Badger's husbands: "If you have only to swab a plank, you should swab it as if Davy Jones were after you." Richard also ignores his guardian's advice that one should "trust in nothing but Providence and your own efforts," and that no one can succeed in a profession "without sincerely meaning it."

To apply the obnoxious term *self-help* to such a conception may seem excessive, but in order to stress the Victorian assumptions of *Bleak House* when the book is examined on this level of the simple fable, it is appropriate to choose a term from Smiles' best seller. Instead of self-help, then, Richard Carstone relies upon his Chancery prospects and dies a failure in every sense of the word. Like Fred Vincy in *Middlemarch* waiting for the death of his Uncle Featherstone, or Pip anticipating his great expectations, Richard fails to measure up to the middle-class standard of self-help. In his case there are some circumstances that could be regarded as extenuating. His guardian treats him indulgently because of the young man's early exposure to the feverish attractions of Jarndyce and Jarndyce, and because of his misfortune in having attended Winchester school, where he has learned Latin verses instead of being prepared for a useful profession. Despite these extenuating circumstances, Richard is presented as a free agent. Even though Dickens does not pursue the problem of free will with the painstaking care displayed by George Eliot, his assumptions about the careers of his characters in *Bleak House* show how fundamentally he was concerned with the same problem. George Eliot's recurring figure to represent her central conception of the human will is of the swimmer or oarsman in the current of circumstance who can elect either to strike out for himself or to drift. The figure applies nicely to Richard Carstone. The muddied waters of Chancery bear him down because he is too deficient in self-help to swim for himself. George Eliot's verdict upon Lydgate's failure in the Middlemarch community would have been endorsed by Dickens: "It always remains true that if we had been greater, circumstances would have been less strong against us." The figures of Miss Flite and Gridley provide a further illuminating contrast here. They too are borne down by a current too strong for them, but they struggle against it, in their fashion, until the end.

George Orwell, in his brilliant and generally sympathetic essay, makes the serious charge that in Dickens' novels there is one "enormous deficiency." Dickens, he says, "has no ideal of *work*. With the doubtful exception of David Copperfield (merely Dickens himself), one cannot point to a single one of his central characters who is primarily interested in his job." If Orwell had had the opportunity to be familiar with *The Dickens World* by Humphry House, we might have been spared his error; for, as House shows, almost everybody in Dickens is identified by his job. Perhaps for such a novel as *Pickwick*, Orwell's objection might have some point, but for *Bleak House* it is absurdly inapplicable. Except for John Jarndyce (to be discussed below) and perhaps Boythorn, virtually all of the characters in *Bleak House* are judged in terms of their occupations and their success or failure in such roles (including the occupation of women, success in which is assumed to consist in affectionate and competent housewifery). One should add that the prospect of securing occupations for a large family of sons may have been partly responsible for Dickens' increased interest in this subject.

Woodcourt and Carstone have been discussed as a pair, but in their case the combination really consists of a threesome. Harold Skimpole, among his various other activities, had been a medical student like these other two young men. In fact he was a qualified practitioner who, like Keats, had abandoned his profession to follow other pursuits, but not, like Keats, to become an artist. Dickens is consistently careful in his representation of Skimpole to stress that the man was a dabbler in music and literature, and nothing more than a dabbler. " 'An artist, sir?' " Sir Leicester asks him. " 'No,' returned Mr. Skimpole. 'A perfectly idle man. A mere amateur.' " For *art* is a sacred word in Dickens' vocabulary. If Skimpole is mercilessly and progressively exposed as the incarnation of the parasite in modern society it is for his indulgent lack of self-help, not for his aesthetic interests. "I have no Will at all," he says cheerfully in explaining why he thinks Jo ought to be evicted. Mr. Micawber, we should remember, although foolishly improvident, was capable of energetic choice and action. Indeed the concept of art for art's sake is applied with favor to any profession which is meaningfully pursued. Richard says enviously to Woodcourt concerning his surgical career: "You can pursue your art for its own sake." Of dedicated artists in the real sense there is no portrait of a professional writer or painter in *Bleak House* to serve as Skimpole's foil, but it is not difficult to supply one if we consider the hard-working and dedicated approach to art embodied in Skimpole's creator. Unlike Thomas Mann, Dickens does not regard the characteristic middle-class traits as *necessarily* opposed to those of the true artist.

As so far considered, then, *Bleak House* could be reduced to the terms of beast-fables such as the story of the grasshopper and the ant or of the spider and the bee. Much of the novel reminds us of a bestiary or, more often we might say, of a termitiary. Great-grandfather Smallweed is likened to a "money-getting species of spider, who spun webs to catch unwary flies." Krook, too, when we first see him, is likened to a spider, and later, more appropriately, to a magpie. Jobling assumes the name of Weevle. The lawyers who live in Tulkinghorn's house "lie like maggots in nuts." As for Skimpole, although the term *grasshopper* is not used, the analogy is ever present when we see him lolling on a sofa, time and again, playing the flute and affirming that "all he asked of society was to let him live." "He didn't at all see why the busy Bee should be proposed as a model for him." With his belief in a "perpetual summer," his lack of interest in preparing for winter, he prefers "the Drone philosophy" like his flabby counterpart, Deportment Turveydrop, who may remind us of a kind of gorgeous beetle. This implicit comparison of Skimpole to a grasshopper is reinforced by many passages explicitly comparing him to a butterfly—another distinctly un-middle-class insect.

Here we seem to have it then: energetic and industrious bees and ants such as Woodcourt, Prince Turveydrop, Mr. Jarndyce, Esther herself, and even Necket (the hard-working debt-collector from Coavinses) show up the follies of lazy drones or butterflies such as Skimpole, Richard Carstone, the elder Turveydrop, and Sir Leicester's cousins. The judgment embodied in the fable is as stern as Browning's contrast between the weak, pleasure-loving Venetians and the soul of the hard-working nineteenth-century scientist:

> "Yours for instance: you know physics, something of geology,
> Mathematics are your pastime; souls shall rise in their degree;
> Butterflies may dread extinction — you'll not die, it cannot be!"

Yet once we have reduced *Bleak House* to the scale of an Aesop fable we become aware of the inadequacy of our basic scheme. It remains valid enough, but it fails to account for the more complex set of values that are assumed in this novel, values which lead to a presentation often reminding us more of Kafka (as I have suggested in another study) than of Aesop. Within the very framework of his images from the insect world, Dickens himself skillfully contrives to establish this complexity. When he introduces us to the Smallweed family, in their grim little den which is furnished with "the hardest of sheet-iron tea-trays," he observes that the Smallweed mind itself is furnished with "a certain small collection of the hardest facts."

> In respect of ideality, reverence, wonder, and other such phrenological attributes, it is no worse off than it used to be. Everything that Mr. Smallweed's grandfather ever put away in his mind was a grub at first, and is a grub at last. In all his life he has never bred a single butterfly.

The counterpointing here is brilliant, for the word *butterfly* is in this context suddenly reversed in value and becomes a term of praise, rich in connotations of art and pleasure. The Smallweeds have the middle-class qualities lacking in Skimpole: they are energetic, hard-working, and eminently capable of self-help. Yet they are certainly portrayed as the most despicable characters in the book. Even the grasshopper is a less reprehensible member of society than the toiling spider which "has discarded all amusements, discountenanced all story-books, fairy tales, fictions, and fables, and banished all levities whatsoever." Without having to turn to *Hard Times* for a full-scale exploitation of this aspect of Dickens' critique of society, we can find in *Bleak House* itself an adequate enrichment of the basic fable.

In *The Protestant Ethic and the Spirit of Capitalism*, Max Weber credits the social criticism of Matthew Arnold with having first demonstrated the connection between the high value placed upon hard work by the middle classes and their Puritan code. Many years before Arnold, from the time of one of his earliest essays, *Sunday Under Three Heads*, Dickens was engaged in a comparable task of disengaging the qualities he admired in his own middle class from those components in the alliance which he despised: the Puritan joylessness, the emphasis upon mere respectability. In *Bleak House*, as we have seen, he does expect us to admire the toilers who follow Carlyle's Victorian exhortation: "Up, up! . . . Work while it is called Today; for the Night cometh, wherein no man can work." But unlike Carlyle, Dickens is not content to recommend hard work as an ascetic discipline. He instinctively turns back, in effect, to the aristocratic way of life, many parts of which he seems to have been repudiating in his basic fable, and uses it to show up the inadequacies of the Puritan ethic.

The kindly treatment of Sir Leicester Dedlock could be cited in this connection. When Sir Leicester chooses to defend his wife, his speech, while somewhat "ludicrous," is characterized by Dickens as "noble . . . gallant . . . honourable, manly, and true." But the more important evaluation of the older code occurs not so much in the kindly treatment of Sir Leicester but in the persistent attacks made upon the Puritanism and mere respectability which the new middle class was imposing like a strait jacket upon all classes of English society. Considered by itself, the old pleasure-seeking principle of the pre-Victorian age (represented, in part, by the guzzlings and other frivolous enjoyments of the Pickwickians) might seem merely irresponsible, but when set beside the new asceticism the principle acquires value by contrast.

In the third chapter of *Bleak House* we are introduced to the gloomy code of hard work as an ascetic discipline by Esther's aunt, Miss Barbary, who advises the child: "Submission, self-denial, diligent work, are the preparations for a life begun with such a shadow upon it." The parting kiss of her maid, Mrs. Rachael, was "like a thaw-drop from the stone porch." The chilling fanaticism of these women has its religious basis, but in the case of Mr. Vholes, the ascetic code has become secularized. Vholes is hard-working, joyless, and "a most respectable man."

> He never misses a chance in his practice; which is a mark of respectability. He never takes any pleasure; which is another mark of respectability. He is reserved and serious, which is another mark of respectability.

When Dickens adds that Vholes is "diligent, persevering, steady, acute in business," we may be reminded of the motto of the Gideons on the title page of every hotel-room Bible: "Diligent in business; fervent in spirit; serving the Lord." Mr. Vholes is not, however, fervent, and he serves not the Lord but his three daughters and his retired father in the Vale of Taunton.

A further illustration of the limitations imposed on the values of industrious self-help is to be found in the ironic picture Dickens gives of the lawyers at Lincoln's Inn who work overtime at night, toiling, he says, "for the entanglement of real estate in meshes of sheep-skin." To which he adds:

> Over which *bee-like* industry, these benefactors of their species linger yet, though office-hours be past; that they may give, for every day, some good account at last.

Once again the image of the toiling insect (which I have italicized) serves as counterpointing. In Dickens' larger fable, it is evident that some species of bees may manufacture gall rather than honey.

Finally, in this same group, we can consider Mrs. Jellyby and Mrs. Pardiggle, a pair of busy bees indeed. Both women are endowed with tireless middle-class energy. "I love hard work," says Mrs. Pardiggle. "I don't know what fatigue is." But her children, and all those upon whom she inflicts her religious tracts, are painfully acquainted with fatigue. Of Borrioboola-Gha, Mrs. Jellyby confesses that "it involves the devotion of all my energies." The dreariness of her home is the price paid for her pointless activity and misdirected effort.

Bleak House thus provides an effective illustration of a thesis suggested by Lionel Trilling in his essay, "Art and Fortune." The novel as a literary type, he says, requires for its "real basis" a kind of society in which there can be displayed "the tension between a middle class and an aristocracy which brings manners into observable relief as the living representation of ideals and the living comment on ideas." And Mr. Trilling adds that to represent this tension adequately, the novelist has to "muster the satirical ambivalence toward both groups which marks the good novel even when it has a social *parti pris*." I have suggested that *Bleak House* can show that Dickens does have his *parti pris*. He has aligned himself with his own class in a manner that sometimes infuriated such feudal-minded Tories as Ruskin, who once damned Dickens as "a pure modernist — a leader of the steam-whistle party *par excellence* — and he had no understanding of any power of antiquity. . . . His hero is essentially the ironmaster." Of *Bleak House* in particular he complained that it was not "tragic, adventurous, or military." But as Ruskin's own enthusiastic response to other phases of Dickens' social criticism can illustrate, especially to Dickens' satire of middle-class hardness, the novelist has certainly provided enough ambivalence to maintain the necessary tensions.

This question of divided allegiance leads back to the division developed at the beginning of the present essay, the division between those capable of self-help and the helpless. Dickens' criticism of the middle class is most severe in this area, for he recognizes that self-help can mean merely selfishness (a selfishness bolstered by Malthusian theories) if the energetic and ambitious are to shun the responsibilities of their newly-gained position in society. The chief of such responsibilities is, of course, to aid the helpless, which means again some reversion to the aristocratic principle of aiding those who are dependent (even if, in practice, the aristocracy had come to neglect their traditional role). Without such responsibilities, the middle-class toiler becomes a bird of prey like Vholes or Smallweed, or like the Leicester Square swindlers, who are described by Dickens as "all with more cruelty in them than was in Nero."

The most obvious form of such help is charity, which is represented in *Bleak House* by John Jarndyce and, in a minor way, by Mr. Snagsby. It is Mr. Jarndyce's largesse that enables such children as the orphaned Charley Necket to survive, and without which help her brother Tom might have become another Jo. Mr. Jarndyce, as I mentioned, is one of the two male characters in this novel whose source of income is never specified. He inherited Bleak House from an uncle, and perhaps he inherited a fortune as well — we are not told. This lack of information makes Mr. Jarndyce seem something of a throwback to Dickens' earlier novels such as *Oliver Twist*, where a kind fairy or rich godfather always arrives to save the hero, and others, thus eliminating the need for self-help. Mr. Jarndyce is, however, discriminating in his extensive benefactions. Despite his indulgence with Skimpole, whom he treats as a creature apart, his aim is to supplement self-help, not to provide substitutes for it. He believes in hard work and is the chief spokesman for professionalism. After describing a medical post in Yorkshire that will "present an opening" for such a man as Alan Woodcourt, he tells Esther:

> I mean, a man whose hopes and aims may sometimes lie (as most men's sometimes do, I dare say) above the ordinary level, but to whom the ordinary level will be high enough after all, if it should prove to be a way of usefulness and good service leading to no other. All generous spirits are ambitious, I suppose; but the ambition that calmly trusts itself to such a road, instead of spasmodically trying to fly over it, is of the kind I care for. It is Woodcourt's kind.

This passage is obviously thematic; the assumed ideal combines the quality of dedicated self-interest with that of social responsibility.

Finally, it is assumed in *Bleak House* that social responsibility involves not only charity (or medical services to the poor) but also the reform of abuses. The first is ultimately conservative in origin; the second is radical, and once again we have a clue to the difficulty in affixing a single label to Dickens' position as a social critic. Nevertheless, the assumption in both instances is that human energy, responsibly directed, can be potent. Richard Carstone likens the contestants in Chancery to pieces moved on a great chessboard, and he complains of "all this wasteful wanton chess-playing" that goes on in the Court. Such an analogy would apply aptly to a novel by Hardy, but in *Bleak House* it is essential to realize that if Chancery is a chess-game, the players (as well as the pieces) are men, not malign divinities or undefined economic forces. Hence the author's indignation when he pictures the slums of Tom-All-Alone's is expressed by a fist shaking not at the sky but at something man-made, something ultimately subject to the control of man's will. A similar conception of purposive energy thus embraces the representation of both the gigantic muddle of Chancery and also the careers of each of the characters.

This attempt to find a unifying principle in *Bleak House* by examining Dickens' assumptions concerning the human will is open to at least two objections, which are closely related. The first is that inasmuch as *Bleak House* has been deeply admired by recent critics, who recommend it to our contemporary tastes for its pictures of a hopeless and irremediable muddle, my analysis may seem perverse in reducing its topicality or modernity. The second is that to admit the potential potency of human will in society is to eliminate the bleakness that we feel pervading the atmosphere of the whole book. I do not think the second objection is sound, and in this case the first is of little consequence. Dickens' assumptions concerning the potential benefits derivable from human energy are not necessarily utopian, and are certainly not incompatible with the bitter tone of his anatomy of society. In his account of society *as it is*, he stresses and makes vivid the power of all the forces operating against the well-intentioned struggle for good: the lazy parasites, the energetic and greedy spiders, the birds of prey, and the whole weight of the dead hand of outmoded customs and accepted stupidities. This is his drama, and the picture is bleak indeed, for even if human will is potent it can never be omnipotent in its struggle against antagonists such as these. And, more specifically, even if Chancery and Tom-All-Alone's could be banished through the efforts of the morally responsible part of society, there would still remain the fact of seemingly helpless poverty.

As a final illustration, we may consider an exchange between the resourceful Inspector Bucket, one of the successful spokesmen for self-help, and Liz, the wife of the drunken brickmaker. Concerning her baby son, Bucket advises the woman: "You train him respectable, and he'll be a comfort to you, and look after you in your old age, you know." But Liz believes that the child might be better off dead. "If I work for him ever so much, and ever so hard," she says, "there's no one to help me." Once again are evident the dramatic tensions which heighten Dickens' whole picture of the conflicting codes of different classes of society, but here it is the helpless who have the last word. Such bleakness may be reduced by the energies of responsible individuals but never completely dissipated by them.

Throughout *Bleak House* there is thus much to substantiate Edmund Wilson's thesis that of all the great Victorians Dickens was "probably the most antagonistic to the Victorian age itself." For this helpful reminder we should be grateful, yet in view of the balancing of opposing codes in *Bleak House*, in which the eminently Victorian concept of will and self-help has an important part, Mr. Wilson's compliment must remain a useful half truth.

FORM AND SUBSTANCE IN THE BRONTË NOVELS

Melvin R. Watson
LOUISIANA STATE UNIVERSITY

FOR over a hundred years now the Brontë sisters have fascinated and puzzled readers, critics, and even some of the general public. No family with literary pretensions, probably, has been more closely examined than Patrick Brontë and his children, and no house more thoroughly sifted than the Haworth parsonage. Doubtless it was inevitable, human curiosity being what it is, that interest should always have been centered on the personality of the sisters, especially Charlotte and Emily, and the origins of those strangely powerful, but very uneven, novels which they produced. That girls from such sheltered environments could write anything with a wide public appeal seemed to need explanation, and explanations have been plentiful. The favorite one has been to interpret all the novels autobiographically — to see Charlotte in all her heroines; to see her Brussels experiences in *The Professor* and *Villette*; to see her dream fantasy of the powerful male in Edward Rochester and Robert Moore; to see Emily projected in both Catherine and Heathcliff of *Wuthering Heights*; to see poor Branwell as sitting for the portrait of Arthur Huntingdon in *The Tenant of Wildfell Hall.* To contend that this is not the best way to approach the novels is not to deny that all of these girls used their limited experiences, their observations, and even their dreams as material — every novelist does — but it is to question the wisdom of using the lives to throw light on the novels at the same time that one is using the novels to throw light on the lives (and this has been done too often in Brontë scholarship). A more recent trend has been to study the novels against the background of the Brontë's web of childhood, those amazing concoctions of pseudo-history, melodrama, and romance which they started writing in childhood, but which some of them continued into young adulthood, and to see, especially in the novels of Charlotte, characters, themes, and incidents carried over into works written for publication. Very likely indeed much can be explained by the influence of these highly fantastic and somewhat chaotic productions of the childish imaginations, but again it is dubious that such an approach will carry us far on the road toward a critical understanding of the novels as works of art. After all the aid that autobiography or formative influence can offer has been gleaned, the novels still remain to be studied as self-contained units of artistic expression.

When one considers the seven novels written by the three sisters, one fact is blindingly clear—only two of them have become established as what we loosely call "classics." Only *Jane Eyre* and *Wuthering Heights* have, at least in our century, been widely reprinted and presumably read, studied in academic courses, and subjected to various kinds of critical analysis. Time has done its winnowing job well, for these two are not only the most exciting and highly charged emotionally; they are also those novels in which form and substance are blended, in which the novelist has successfully, if not perfectly, imposed a form upon materials, however strange and unusual, and in which the artist is the master of her tools. In all the other novels, for one reason or another, and in varying degrees, the form and substance indulge in a tug of war; disparate elements are insufficiently controlled or technical clumsinesses cannot be overlooked or parts seem to exist in and for themselves rather than as necessary units in a preconceived plan.

Wuthering Heights (1847) is unquestionably the greatest of the Brontë novels. The more one studies it, the more remarkable its achievement becomes—and the more difficult the job of assessing it. Yet the fact remains that the form is as consciously and, generally speaking, as artistically worked out as the substance. Though I have written elsewhere of both the theme and the structure of the novel (in *Nineteenth-Century Fiction*, IV, 87–100), I must re-emphasize a few points. Emily Brontë has excluded with a highly refined sense of unity all characters, all incidents, all places that are not completely relevant to her theme, the working out of the hate that has festered in Heathcliff's soul. She has arranged her material with a sure sense of drama. Starting with the early antagonism between Heathcliff and Hindley and the early love between Heathcliff and Cathy, the story moves inexorably through Heathcliff's desire for full revenge on Hindley and the traumatic experience of his discovery that Cathy would be ashamed to marry him. When Heathcliff returns to the moors after his three-year disappearance, the tempo again quickens as tension at Thrushcross Grange mounts to that most passionate of all love scenes from which neither of the lovers really recovers — Cathy going to her death in childbirth, Heathcliff to his revenge on all who have thwarted his love. Emily Brontë's highlighting of significant moments is unerring and her handling of the passage of time remarkable, a considerable achievement since she was working with a sort of double time. And finally, the technique of telling the story, the use of Mr. Lockwood and Ellen Dean, seems the inevitable one. The raw, uncontrolled actions and emotions of Heathcliff and Cathy come to us after being sifted through the sensibilities of two very ordinary people. Certainly this technique helps us to accept the substance and perhaps, as has recently been suggested, to sympathize with the lovers. Obviously, the advantages of the unconventional form completely overbalance the incidental awkwardnesses and the occasional use of time-honored conventions.

In an essay on the Brontës, the two novels published by Anne must be mentioned, but since she never showed any great artistic command over fictional materials, they can be disposed of briefly. *Agnes Grey* (1847) may well have given Charlotte some useful hints for *Jane Eyre* in its straightforward progress and its concentration on psychological analysis of the heroine, but its false start in Chapters II–V, its lack of pointing and emphasis, its failure to achieve the climax which should have occurred in Chapter XVIII, and the coincidences which crowd the last chapters make it the weakest of these first novels.

Though the substance of *The Tenant of Wildfell Hall* (1848) is denser and more interesting than that of *Agnes Grey*, the form is even less satisfactory, for it lacks the directness and unsophisticated ease of the earlier work. Surely few stories have been told with more self-conscious techniques or clumsier devices. From the introductory letter by Gilbert Markham to J. Halford, who turns out to be his brother-in-law (but that makes no difference), with its announcement that Gilbert will rely on a "faded old journal" in recounting his story, through the journal of Helen Graham (included verbatim for forty-eight chapters), to the letters from Helen to her brother Frederick Lawrence, used to reveal necessary information in the later chapters, the difficulties of handling the narrative are apparent. The same lack of craftsmanship appears in the management of the minor characters. All those who will play any role in the story must be mentioned at the earliest opportunity; so Chapter I and Chapter XVI (the beginning of Helen Graham's journal) resemble roll calls. Nor can any character once mentioned be left undisposed of; hence parts of two late chapters (XLVIII and L) are devoted to meting out just deserts to all the functionaries. But the greatest structural flaw is that there are two stories which are combined only in the most casual manner. Gilbert's story of himself, of his circle, and of his wooing and finally winning Helen Graham is, despite considerable contortions toward the end, well-handled. The suspense that Helen Graham creates is natural enough, the actions of the Millwards and the Wilsons are believable, and even Gilbert is convincing (until his romanticized nobility on learning that Helen is an heiress). But the account of Helen's experiences with Arthur Huntingdon and his circle of friends is straight melodrama, regardless of who sat for the portrait of Arthur. Had Anne been able to reduce Helen's account of her trials to a chapter or two, she would not have had a full-length novel, but she would have had a more consistent and better unified work of art — and a more convincing heroine.

Since Charlotte Brontë is the only one of the three sisters who was given the opportunity to develop her craft, she deserves to be considered at greater length. During the course of over a half-dozen years she produced four complete novels and the fragment of a fifth; yet there is no development in her artistry. The first to appear is by far the most satisfying structurally; in the others, parts may be praised and there may be even a firmer realism at work, but the writer has not succeeded completely in planning and controlling her material.

Doubtless not too much emphasis should be put on *The Professor* (1857) since Charlotte refused to publish it after the success of *Jane Eyre* and it appeared only posthumously, but she did write it for publication and gave up her attempts to find a publisher only when Smith, Elder and Company expressed interest in any other work she had. Not to dwell on the clumsy letter convention with which the novel opens, perhaps the biggest difficulty with *The Professor* is the succession of false scents. The first six chapters with their English setting accomplish nothing so far as the story as a whole is concerned except to get William Crimsworth to Brussels and to introduce Yorke Hunsden, who is clearly an extraneous element. He appears again only toward the end, and his round with Frances Henri in the next to last chapter only delays the ending unnecessarily. When Crimsworth gets to Brussels, the novel starts off on the other false scent of the Pelet-Reuter-Crimsworth triangle. At the end of another six chapters after Crimsworth discovers, by what can be described only as eavesdropping, that Reuter and Pelet are engaged, the author starts the second triangle of Reuter, Crimsworth, and Frances Henri. The last six chapters make a restless attempt to tie all the parts together. The emphasis, obviously, is on the Crimsworth-Henri theme, but the relationship with M. Pelet is retraced in Chapter XX and his marriage to Mlle. Reuter mentioned in XXII. Yorke Hunsden is reintroduced in order to provide useless information about the failure of Crimsworth's brother, and a new character, M. Vandenhuten, is created just to provide "the professor" with a real professorship so that he can declare his love to Mlle. Henri.

When one examines the structure of *The Professor*, he gets the distinct impression that Charlotte was essentially improvising, as she had certainly done in her childhood fiction. On the surface, there is a fine balance among the various parts, but they do not grow out of each other. Instead, each section works up to a climax, which represents enough of a dead end to necessitate a fresh start. This is especially evident in the middle of the book with the introduction of the little seamstress. Seldom has a heroine been more unobtrusively brought onto the stage; seldom in a novel has the reader been less sure about the identity of the heroine. Actually, so wraith-like is Mlle. Henri even at the end of the novel that most, I suspect, would remember Mlle. Reuter before Frances Henri. *The Professor* has interesting parallels with the later *Villette*, both in characters and structure, but it is far from a satisfactorily coherent work of art.

How to explain the artistic success of *Jane Eyre* (1847) after the failure of *The Professor* is not easy. It was presumably begun as soon as the first novel was sent off on its round of visits to the publishers, and hence there would not necessarily be any great increase in maturity. I doubt that Charlotte could have learned anything from *Wuthering Heights* though she might have picked up some pointers from *Agnes Grey*. The explanation may be simply that she thought through the entire novel before she started writing, as she probably didn't with *The Professor*, so that she could prepare for and work toward climaxes as she did not in her first attempt. Regardless of the reason, there is a skill shown here that appears in none of her other novels.

The over-all structure of *Jane Eyre*, in the first place, is functional. The first and the third sections contrast not only with each other but with the much longer and more dramatic second part. Jane's experiences first with the Reeds and then much later with the Rivers family are related to and influenced by her family, especially her Uncle John. The first section concentrates on the formation of her character and her trials in an ever-widening environment. After a few strategically chosen incidents, which reveal the characters of the Reeds and of Jane, and the introduction of the Reverend Mr. Brocklehurst, Jane is quickly projected into the larger world of Lowood School. Her early months at Lowood, emphasizing her friendship for Helen Burns, do much to strengthen her character and make her into the person revealed at Thornfield. Helen Burns, I must confess, has never impressed me much, but she fulfills her main function of transferring her stoicism to Jane and of warning her against her natural impulsiveness. This part is neatly rounded off in Chapter x, which tells of the reasons for her leaving Lowood after eight years, her obtaining the position at Thornfield, and the visit from Bessie, who brings her up to date on the Reeds and imparts the crucial information of her uncle's visit to Gateshead Hall seven years earlier on his way to Madeira. Though this section, quite rightly, works up to no strong climax (the rest of the novel will be stormy and climactic enough), there has been a steady progress and preparation in general terms for what is to come.

As highly charged and even improbable as parts of the middle section are, the story is managed with great skill. Everything works toward the grand climax of the wedding between Jane and Rochester when she learns the awful truth of the secret of Thornfield Hall. Though Jane seems more than a little naïve in accepting explanations and not asking embarrassing questions (the reasons given for her behavior are not always convincing), her gradual falling in love with Rochester, the mystery in the house and the slow revelation of the master's character create genuine suspense, as melodramatic as the material may be upon examination. The key events are strategically located: Jane hears the strange laugh upon her arrival and associates it with Grace Poole. In Chapter xv she rescues Rochester from the burning bed. Two chapters later she overhears the servants talking and concludes that a mystery is being concealed from her. Then in Chapter xx she visits the third-floor dungeon where Mason has been knifed and bitten. Finally, in Chapter xxv she awakens one night shortly before her wedding day to see the strange woman trying on and then ripping her veil.

The development of Jane's knowledge of Rochester and her regard for him is as carefully managed. From his introduction in Chapter xii, each succeeding chapter adds something until xvi, in which Jane confesses her deep regard for him. Thereafter the important incidents are spaced: the scene with the gypsy in XIX, the proposal in XXIII, and the attempted marriage in XXVI. Almost exactly in the middle of this section, just after the next to highest climax, the return trip to Gateshead Hall is dealt with. This change makes a fine emotional break and also reveals necessary information about Uncle John Eyre, which will be used soon.

Though the eight chapters dealing with Jane and the Rivers family lack the exciting quality of the middle section, still they are skillfully planned, despite the melodramatic manner in which Jane is precipitated into the Rivers household and the overwhelming coincidence on which they are based. The essential information about Uncle John's death is introduced soon after St. John and his sisters have accepted Jane as one of them, but the secret of their relationship is held back for another three chapters and the discovery is brought about in the most natural manner. The next two chapters (XXXIV and XXXV) build up to the climax of St. John's proposal, Jane's only partial acceptance, his persistence and her being on the verge of succumbing when she hears the supernatural voice. Of course, this strains the bonds of realism, but who now considers *Jane Eyre* a realistic novel? Three more chapters bring the romance to its proper conclusion, now that all obstacles to the union of Rochester and Jane have been removed.

From this brief analysis, it is clear that *Jane Eyre* has what all the other novels of Charlotte Brontë lack—concentration. No one questions after the first page whose story this is. Everything important that happens in the novel has its bearing either direct or indirect and its influence either immediate or eventual on Jane. Almost every incident and character play their part in forming Jane's character, justifying her actions or attitudes, or making us understand and sympathize with her. The four worlds of Gateshead Hall, Lowood School, Thornfield Hall, and the habitation of the Rivers family have Jane at their center insofar as we know them. Obviously too, the proportion of the book seems ideal, for the first part balances fairly exactly the last part (leaving out of account the final chapters on Rochester) and the middle part is almost twice as long. All this seems evidence enough that in *Jane Eyre* a craftsman was at work.

Potentially, *Shirley* (1849) is a better novel than *Jane Eyre*. Set in the early part of the century, played out against the background of international events which affected the economic state of the country, and introducing a serious phase of the Industrial Revolution, *Shirley* has characters and a plot that are often more convincing than the melodramatics of Thornfield Hall and the Byronism of Edward Rochester. Caroline Helstone is in many ways the most attractive of Charlotte Brontë's heroines and many of the minor characters, taken on their own terms, are genuinely interesting. Several scenes at the mill, such as those in Chapters VIII and XIX, arising from Robert Moore's determination to introduce machinery in the weaving industry of the West Riding of Yorkshire, show real dramatic power. Yet it is generally recognized that *Shirley* is actually the weakest of the works which Charlotte herself published, not only because there are false notes and improbable contrivances — these exist in all Brontë fiction — but because the novel never comes together, because insufficient order has been imposed upon the unusually disparate materials.

Perhaps the first and most basic difficulty is with the theme. In Chapter I two big themes are suggested: the religious issue of Dissent versus Establishment and the socio-economic one of frame-breaking. Later we become involved in the personal stories of Caroline Helstone and Shirley Keeldar. The first of these themes is never developed, though it is used occasionally, as when in Chapter VIII, the leader of the frame-breakers turns out to be Moses Barraclough, a Methodist ranter, and when in Chapter XVII the parade for the school feast meets a parade of Dissenters, who are forced to give way. The other three themes make up the body of the book and are connected in various ways, notably through the character of Robert Moore, but they are never successfully blended, largely, I suspect, because Moore is such an unsatisfactory hero. As a manufacturer and businessman, despite his attitude toward the workingman, the reader can understand and even perhaps sympathize with him; but his relationship with the two women can only alienate the reader. Perhaps the trouble is that Charlotte Brontë tried to unite in one person the hard-headed but weakly financed businessman and the romantic lover. No such problem faced her in *Jane Eyre*.

But what about the heroine (or heroines)? The reader is forced to ask the fundamental question, who is the heroine? And the answer is not easy. From the title one would naturally assume it to be Shirley Keeldar, but she is not even introduced until Chapter XI and thereafter there are periods when she is on the sidelines. Her personal story (for the assumed romance between her and Robert Moore turns out to be a red herring) is developed only in the last ten chapters or so, beginning with Chapter XXVI, when Louis Moore, introduced as late as Chapter XXIII after one earlier mention, becomes a main character and her uncle's attempts to marry her off become a matter of some importance. Despite the implicit contradiction of the title and the split in the reader's interest, Caroline would seem to be intended for the heroine. From the time she is introduced in Chapter V she is seldom absent from the stage (and usually her position is near center) until the latter part when Shirley's love life is developed. But more important, wherever possible the story is told from her point of view. She is the only character whose actions and feelings are analyzed, whom we get inside of.

This last characteristic accounts for a good part of the artificiality of the technique. In *Jane Eyre* the first-person point of view had been used consistently and successfully, but in *Shirley*, Charlotte Brontë tried a combination of the omniscient author, which parts of her material required, and the personal point of view. The two are not convincingly blended. Too often one feels that the author is taking unfair advantage of the reader just to maintain suspense. The most obvious example is the handling of Mrs. Pryor. Only if the story were told completely from Caroline's point of view, could the secrecy of her identity until the sentimental moment in Chapter XXIV when she gives Caroline something to live for by giving her a mother be justified. It is striking too that the assumed romance between Shirley and Robert Moore is revealed principally through Caroline's sensibilities and the true romance of Shirley and Louis Moore comes to us largely through Caroline's awareness. The fact seems to be that whenever it suits the writer's convenience or the requirements of the plot, material is presented from Caroline's point of view. Otherwise the impersonal technique is used. The way of telling the story in *Jane Eyre* is surer.

In some ways *Shirley* is a richer novel than *Jane Eyre*. There is more variety of plot and character; yet once again this variety is as much a flaw as a virtue, for some of the material seems not to be used functionally in the novel. Take, for example, the curates, who are introduced with much noise in Chapter I and are carefully disposed of in the last chapter: Donne, Malone, and Sweeting run in and out of the story and Malone even takes some part in the action centered in the mill, but they are really lagniappe. The same may be said of Mrs. Sykes and her three daughters, who do little more than provide part of the crowd at several of the gatherings. Mr. Yorke and his family do at times participate importantly in the action, but the family is principally presented as a group of eccentrics and nothing much is made of the antagonism suggested between Mr. Yorke and the Reverend Mr. Helstone. If this were a novel of manners, there would be more justification for introducing "characters," primarily to fill in the canvas; but since there is no evidence that *Shirley* was intended as a picture of society, these elements provide just one more bit of incompletely assimilated material. The truth is that it would have taken more careful craftsmanship than presumably Charlotte Brontë was capable of to whip all these themes and characters and materials into shape.

The question of autobiography in *Villette* (1853) has received much more attention from writers on the Brontës than its value as a novel. Even granted that Villette is Brussels, that Madame Beck's establishment was copied from the Héger pension, that Héger sat for the portrait of Paul Emmanuel, and that Lucy Snowe is Charlotte Brontë in one of her manifestations, the basic problem still remains: how successfully has the artist transformed fact into fiction, transmuted the raw materials of experience and observation into an orderly and unified picture and interpretation of life? Clearly, she has been more successful here than in *The Professor*, where she was using similar and sometimes identical materials. Lucy Snowe, as unsatisfying as she may be in some respects, is more convincing than William Crimsworth; Madame Beck is a masterpiece compared with M. Pelet; M. Paul Emmanuel is a worthier antagonist than Mlle. Reuter; and the picture of the school is fuller than that in *The Professor*.

Yet there are also unmistakable signs of faulty craftsmanship, of mistaken focusing and emphasis, of poor proportioning. The opening chapters are more functional than parallel ones in *The Professor*, for they establish a group of characters to be used later; but they do little to establish Lucy Snowe at the center of the stage, where she rightfully belongs. Chapters IV–VI serve only to get the heroine, however clumsily, to Villette, where the real action starts in Chapter VII. And yet the *real* action has not started, for clearly the heart of the book is the fascinating, and sometimes frustrating, relationship between Lucy and M. Paul. Though Madame Beck hires Lucy in Chapter VII only on the advice of M. Paul, other matters consume the author's attention and it is only in Chapter XIV that we get any insight into his character. It is even later (in Chapters XIX–XXI) that a positive relationship between the two is suggested and only after Chapter XXVI that the Lucy-Paul thread gets full treatment. After that, except for four chapters, necessary for tying up other threads, the concentration is on M. Paul and closely related matters.

The stories of Ginevra Fanshawe, John Graham Bretton, and Polly Home (de Bassompierre) receive an inordinate amount of attention in the first half of the book. Ginevra, I should say, is expendable. She is ultimately responsible for the appearances of the Nun, who helps to intensify Lucy's emotional instability but who is as much a red herring as the Shirley-Robert Moore thread in *Shirley*. Her only other function is to reveal how essentially unsatisfactory John Graham Bretton is as a potential hero. After she has served this function, which reaches its climax at the concert in Chapter xx, she disappears almost completely until the latter part of the novel, when her elopement with the fop de Hamal serves to clear up the mystery of the Nun. John Graham Bretton, who is called now Graham, then Isidore, again Dr. John, and finally by the full name, as the exigencies of the plot demand, is almost as unsatisfactory a character as William Crimsworth in *The Professor*. At first (in the body of the novel) infatuated with Ginevra and refusing to see the truth about her though he knows she is flirting with de Hamal, he can throw her out of his heart readily when she behaves obnoxiously at the concert. He can be attentive enough to Lucy to raise false hopes in her breast (one admits much wishful thinking on Lucy's part) and then passionately in love with Polly. Actually his most important function for the main plot is to make M. Paul jealous. Perhaps his principal trouble is that he is plot-ridden and he is not strong enough to stand the burden. Polly Home is obviously introduced in the opening chapters just so she can be reintroduced in Chapter xxiii at the appropriate moment to capture John's heart on the rebound. True, this shows a degree of planning; but, when after the brief flurry she appears in only two chapters of the last fifteen, one wonders whether the degree of planning was sufficient to achieve the desired effects.

This point of handling of characters needs to be examined too from a slightly different angle. For short spaces in the novel minor characters are so completely in the spotlight that the reader feels they must be more important than in the end they turn out to be. This is what I would call false emphasis or improper proportioning. The emphasis in the opening chapters on the Brettons and Polly illustrates what I mean. After Chapter iii, the group disappears to reappear only as the plot requires: Dr. John in Chapter x, Mrs. Bretton in Chapter xvi (when Lucy reveals that she recognized Dr. John long ago as her childhood friend but failed, inexplicably, to inform the reader), and Polly not until Chapter xxiii. Then for a while they are near the center of the stage, only to be crowded out by other groups seeking the spotlight. Madame Beck is perhaps even a better illustration. For a number of chapters after her vivid introduction in Chapter VII, she shares the spotlight with Ginevra Fanshawe, but after the description of her fete in Chapter XIV, she is seen almost not at all until Chapter XXXIII, when she starts her machinations to keep Lucy and M. Paul apart. Unlike *Jane Eyre*, where from the very first the reader is sure that the story is Jane's, *Villette* fails to get on the main track until almost half of the novel is over. And unfortunately, one cannot contend convincingly that the first part is significant for Lucy's development since the chapters set in England or Lucy's early experiences in Madame Beck's establishment, or even her reunion with the Brettons and Polly are only casually related to her developing love for M. Paul; only Madame Beck has any real influence on the outcome of that courtship, which is stranger even than Jane's and Mr. Rochester's.

Much has been made by various writers of the contribution to the English novel by the Brontë sisters, and I would be the last to deny them their rightful place in the development of English fiction; but it seems only just to arrive at a proper evaluation of them as novelists. To imply, as some have done, that *Villette* is as important as *Jane Eyre* or that Charlotte is a more significant figure than Emily leads toward, if it does not represent, a distortion of critical values. Whether Emily would have become even surer as an artist had she lived, it is impossible to say; but we possess enough evidence on Charlotte to arrive at a tentative conclusion. Her development as a craftsman was at best uncertain. Yet we can be thankful for the artistic triumphs of *Jane Eyre* and *Wuthering Heights*, which are enough to make any family proud.

CHARLOTTE BRONTË'S 'NEW' GOTHIC

Robert B. Heilman
UNIVERSITY OF WASHINGTON

IN THAT characteristic flight from cliché that may plunge him into the recherché the critic might well start from *The Professor* and discover in it much more than is implied by the usual dismissal of it as Charlotte Brontë's poorest work. He might speculate about Charlotte's singular choice of a male narrator — the value of it, or even the need of it, for her. For through William Crimsworth she lives in Héger, making love to herself as Frances Henri: in this there is a kind of ravenousness, inturning, splitting, and doubling back of feeling. Through Crimsworth she experiences a sudden, vivid, often graceless mastery. But these notes on the possible psychology of the author are critically useful only as a way into the strange tremors of feeling that are present in a formally defective story. Pelet identifies "a fathomless spring of sensibility in thy breast, Crimsworth." If Crimsworth is not a successful character, he is the channel of emotional surges that splash over a conventional tale of love: the author's disquieting presence in the character lends a nervous, off-center vitality. The pathos of liberty is all but excessive (as it is later in Shirley Keeldar and Lucy Snowe): Crimsworth sneers, ". . . I sprang from my bed with other slaves," and rejoices, "Liberty I clasped in my arms . . . her smile and embrace revived my life." The Puritan sentiment (to be exploited partially in Jane Eyre and heavily in Lucy Snowe) becomes tense, rhetorical, fiercely censorious; the self-righteousness punitive and even faintly paranoid. Through the frenetically Protestant Crimsworth and his flair for rebuke Charlotte notes the little sensualities of girl students ("parting her lips, as full as those of a hot-blooded Maroon") and the coquettish yet urgent sexuality of Zoraide Reuter perversely responding to Crimsworth's ostensible yet not total unresponsiveness to her: "When she stole about me with the soft step of a slave, I felt at once barbarous and sensual as a pasha."

Charlotte looks beyond familiar surfaces. In Yorke Hunsden she notes the "incompatibilities of the 'physique' with the 'morale.'" The explosive Byronic castigator has lineaments "small, and even feminine" and "now the mien of a morose bull, and anon that of an arch and mischievous girl." In this version of the popular archetype, "rough exterior but heart of gold," Charlotte brilliantly finds a paradoxical union of love and hate; she sees generosity of spirit sometimes appearing directly but most often translated into antithetical terms that also accommodate opposite motives — into god-like self-indulgence in truth-telling; almost Mephistophelian cynicism; sadism and even murderousness in words.

Charlotte's story is conventional; formally she is for "reason" and "real life"; but her characters keep escaping to glorify "feeling" and "Imagination." Feeling is there in the story — evading repression, in author or in character; ranging from nervous excitement to emotional absorption; often tense and peremptory; sexuality, hate, irrational impulse, grasped, given life, not merely named and pigeonholed. This is Charlotte's version of Gothic: in her later novels an extraordinary thing. In that incredibly eccentric history, *The Gothic Quest*, Montague Summers asserts that the "Gothic novel of sensibility . . . draws its emotionalism and psychology . . . from the work of Samuel Richardson." When this line of descent continues in the Brontës, the vital feeling moves toward an intensity, a freedom, and even an abandon virtually non-existent in historical Gothic and rarely approached in Richardson. From Angria on, Charlotte's women vibrate with passions that the fictional conventions only partly constrict or gloss over — in the center an almost violent devotedness that has in it at once a fire of independence, a spiritual energy, a vivid sexual responsiveness, and, along with this, self-righteousness, a sense of power, sometimes self-pity and envious competitiveness. To an extent the heroines are "unheroined," unsweetened. Into them there has come a new sense of the dark side of feeling and personality.

The Professor ventures a little into the psychic darkness on which *Villette* draws heavily. One night Crimsworth, a victim of hypochondria, hears a voice saying, "In the midst of life we are in death," and he feels "a horror of great darkness." In his boyhood this same "sorceress" drew him "to the very brink of a black, sullen river" and managed to "lure me to her vaulted home of horrors." Charlotte draws on sex images that recall the note of sexuality subtly present in other episodes: ". . . I had entertained her at bed and board . . . she lay with me, . . . taking me entirely to her death-cold bosom, and holding me with arms of bone." The climax is:

"I repulsed her as one would a dreaded and ghastly concubine coming to embitter a husband's heart toward his young bride; . . ." This is Gothic, yet there is an integrity of feeling that greatly deepens the convention.

From childhood terrors to all those mysteriously threatening sights, sounds, and injurious acts that reveal the presence of some malevolent force and that anticipate the holocaust at Thornfield, the traditional Gothic in *Jane Eyre* has often been noted, and as often disparaged. It need not be argued that Charlotte Brontë did not reach the heights while using hand-me-down devices, though a tendency to work through the conventions of fictional art was a strong element in her make-up. This is true of all her novels, but it is no more true than her counter-tendency to modify, most interestingly, these conventions. In both *Villette* and *Jane Eyre* Gothic is used but characteristically is undercut.

Jane Eyre hears a "tragic . . . preternatural . . . laugh," but this is at "high noon" and there is "no circumstance of ghostliness"; Grace Poole, the supposed laugher, is a plain person, than whom no "apparition less romantic or less ghostly could . . . be conceived"; Charlotte apologizes ironically to the "romantic reader" for telling "the plain truth" that Grace generally bears a "pot of porter." Charlotte almost habitually revises "old Gothic," the relatively crude mechanisms of fear, with an infusion of the anti-Gothic. When Mrs. Rochester first tried to destroy Rochester by fire, Jane "baptized" Rochester's bed and heard Rochester "fulminating strange anathemas at finding himself lying in a pool of water." The introduction of comedy as a palliative of straight Gothic occurs on a large scale when almost seventy-five pages are given to the visit of the Ingram-Eshton party to mysterious Thornfield; here Charlotte, as often in her novels, falls into the manner of the Jane Austen whom she despised. When Mrs. Rochester breaks loose again and attacks Mason, the presence of guests lets Charlotte play the nocturnal alarum for at least a touch of comedy: Rochester orders the frantic women not to "pull me down or strangle me"; and "the two dowagers, in vast white wrappers, were bearing down on him like ships in full sail."

The symbolic also modifies the Gothic, for it demands of the reader a more mature and complicated response than the relatively simple thrill or momentary intensity of feeling sought by primitive Gothic. When mad Mrs. Rochester, seen only as "the foul German spectre — the Vampyre," spreads terror at night, that is one thing; when, with the malicious insight that is the paradox of her madness, she tears the wedding veil in two and thus symbolically destroys the planned marriage, that is another thing, far less elementary as art. The midnight blaze that ruins Thornfield becomes more than a shock when it is seen also as the fire of purgation; the grim, almost roadless forest surrounding Ferndean is more than a harrowing stage-set when it is also felt as a symbol of Rochester's closed-in life.

The point is that in various ways Charlotte manages to make the patently Gothic more than a stereotype. But more important is that she instinctively finds new ways to achieve the ends served by old Gothic — the discovery and release of new patterns of feeling, the intensification of feeling. Though only partly unconventional, Jane is nevertheless so portrayed as to evoke new feelings rather than merely exercise old ones. As a girl she is lonely, "passionate," "strange," "like nobody there"; she feels superior, rejects poverty, talks back precociously, tells truths bluntly, enjoys "the strangest sense of freedom," tastes "vengeance"; she experiences a nervous shock which is said to have a lifelong effect, and the doctor says "nerves not in a good state"; she can be "reckless and feverish," "bitter and truculent"; at Thornfield she is restless, given to "bright visions," letting "imagination" picture an existence full of "life, fire, feeling." Thus Charlotte leads away from standardized characterization toward new levels of human reality, and hence from stock responses toward a new kind of passionate engagement.

Charlotte moves toward depth in various ways that have an immediate impact like that of Gothic. Jane's strange, fearful symbolic dreams are not mere thrillers but reflect the tensions of the engagement period, the stress of the wedding-day debate with Rochester, and the longing for Rochester after she has left him. The final Thornfield dream, with its vivid image of a hand coming through a cloud in place of the expected moon, is in the surrealistic vein that appears most sharply in the extraordinary pictures that Jane draws at Thornfield: here Charlotte is plumbing the psyche, not inventing a weird *décor*. Likewise in the telepathy scene, which Charlotte, unlike Defoe in dealing with a similar episode, does her utmost to actualize: "The feeling was not like an electric shock; but it was quite as sharp, as strange, as startling: . . . that inward sensation . . . with all its unspeakable strangeness . . . like an inspiration . . . wondrous shock of feeling. . . ." In her flair for the surreal, in her plunging into feeling that is without status in the ordinary world of the novel, Charlotte discovers a new dimension of Gothic.

She does this most thoroughly in her portrayal of characters and of the relations between them. If in Rochester we see only an Angrian-Byronic hero and a Charlotte wish-fulfillment figure (the two identifications which to some readers seem entirely to place him), we miss what is more significant, the exploration of personality that opens up new areas of feeling in intersexual relationships. Beyond the "grim," the "harsh," the eccentric, the almost histrionically cynical that superficially distinguish Rochester from conventional heroes, there is something almost Lawrentian: Rochester is "neither tall nor graceful"; his eyes can be "dark, irate, and piercing"; his strong features "took my feelings from my own power and fettered them in his." Without using the vocabulary common to us, Charlotte is presenting maleness and physicality, to which Jane responds directly. She is "assimilated" to him by "something in my brain and heart, in my blood and nerves"; she "must love" and "could not unlove" him; the thought of parting from him is "agony." Rochester's oblique amatory maneuvers become almost punitive in the Walter-to-Griselda style and once reduce her to sobbing "convulsively"; at times the love-game borders on a power-game. Jane, who prefers "rudeness" to "flattery," is an instinctive evoker of passion: she learns "the pleasure of vexing and soothing him by turns" and pursues a "system" of working him up "to considerable irritation" and coolly leaving him; when, as a result, his caresses become grimaces, pinches, and tweaks, she records that, sometimes at least, she "decidedly preferred these fierce favors." She reports, "I crushed his hand . . . red with the passionate pressure"; she "could not . . . see God for his creature," and in her devotion Rochester senses "an earnest, religious energy."

Charlotte's remolding of stock feeling reaches a height when she sympathetically portrays Rochester's efforts to make Jane his mistress; here the stereotyped seducer becomes a kind of lost nobleman of passion, and of specifically physical passion: "Every atom of your flesh is as dear to me as my own. . . ." The intensity of the pressure which he puts upon her is matched, not by the fear and revulsion of the popular heroine, but by a responsiveness which she barely masters: "The crisis was perilous; but not without its charm . . ." She is "tortured by a sense of remorse at thus hurting his feelings"; at the moment of decision "a hand of fiery iron grasped my vitals . . . blackness, burning! . . . my intolerable duty"; she leaves in "despair"; and after she has left, "I longed to be his; I panted to return . . ."—and for the victory of principle "I abhorred myself . . . I was hateful in my own eyes." This extraordinary openness to feeling, this escape from the bondage of the trite, continues in the Rivers relationship, which is a structural parallel to the Rochester affair: as in Rochester the old sex villain is seen in a new perspective, so in Rivers the clerical hero is radically refashioned; and Jane's almost accepting a would-be husband is given the aesthetic status of a regrettable yielding to a seducer. Without a remarkable liberation from conventional feeling Charlotte could not fathom the complexity of Rivers — the earnest and dutiful clergyman distraught by a profound inner turmoil of conflicting "drives": sexuality, restlessness, hardness, pride, ambition ("fever in his vitals," "inexorable as death"); the hypnotic, almost inhuman potency of his influence on Jane, who feels "a freezing spell," "an awful charm," an "iron shroud"; the relentlessness, almost the unscrupulousness, of his wooing, the resultant fierce struggle (like that with Rochester), Jane's brilliantly perceptive accusation, ". . . you almost hate me . . . you would kill me. You are killing me now"; and yet her mysterious near-surrender: "I was tempted to cease struggling with him — to rush down the torrent of his will into the gulf of his existence, and there lose my own."

Aside from partial sterilization of banal Gothic by dry factuality and humor, Charlotte goes on to make a much more important — indeed, a radical — revision of the mode: in *Jane Eyre* and in the other novels, as we shall see, that discovery of passion, that rehabilitation of the extra-rational, which is the historical office of Gothic, is no longer oriented in marvelous circumstance but moves deeply into the lesser known realities of human life. This change I describe as the change from "old Gothic" to "new Gothic." The kind of appeal is the same; the fictional method is utterly different.

When Charlotte went on from *Jane Eyre* to *Shirley*, she produced a book that for the student of the Gothic theme is interesting precisely because on the face of things it would be expected to be a barren field. It is the result of Charlotte's one deliberate venture from private intensities into public extensities: Orders in Council, the Luddites, technological unemployment in 1811 and 1812, a social portraiture which develops Charlotte's largest cast of characters. Yet Charlotte cannot keep it a social novel. Unlike Warren, who in the somewhat similar *Night Rider* chose to reflect the historical economic crisis in the private crisis of the hero, Miss Brontë loses interest in the public and slides over into the private.

The formal irregularities of *Shirley* — the stop-and-start, zig-zag movement, plunging periodically into different perspectives—light up the divergent impulses in Charlotte herself: the desire to make a story from observed outer life, and the inability to escape from inner urgencies that with centrifugal force unwind outward into story almost autonomously. Passion alters plan: the story of industrial crisis is repeatedly swarmed over by the love stories. But the ultimate complication is that Charlotte's duality of impulse is reflected not only in the narrative material but in two different ways of telling each part of the story. On the one hand she tells a rather conventional, open, predictable tale; on the other she lets go with a highly charged private sentiency that may subvert the former or at least surround it with an atmosphere of unfamiliarity or positive strangeness: the Gothic impulse.

For Charlotte it is typically the "pattern" versus the "strange." She describes "two pattern young ladies, in pattern attire, with pattern deportment"—a "respectable society" in which "Shirley had the air of a black swan, or a white crow. . . ." When, in singing, Shirley "poured round the passion, force," the young ladies thought this "strange" and concluded: "What was *strange* must be *wrong*; . . ." True, Charlotte's characters live within the established "patterns" of life; but their impulse is to vitalize forms with unpatterned feeling, and Charlotte's to give play to unpatterned feeling in all its forms. She detects the warrior in the Reverend Matthew Helstone; reports that Malone the curate "had energy enough in hate"; describes Shirley weeping without apparent reason; recounts Mrs. Yorke's paranoid "brooding, eternal, immitigable suspicion of all men, things, creeds, and parties"; portrays Hiram Yorke as scornful, stubborn, intolerant of superiors, independent, truculent, benevolent toward inferiors, his virtues surrounding an aggressive *amour propre*.

Shirley is given a vehement, sweeping, uninhibited criticalness of mind; in her highly articulate formulations of incisive thought is released a furious rush of emotional energy. Within the framework of moral principles her ideas and feelings are untrammeled. She vigorously debunks clichés against charity, but against the mob she will defend her property "like a tigress"; to Yorke's face she does a corrosive analysis of his personality; she attacks Milton in a fiery sweeping paean to Eve, the "mother" of "Titans"; in an almost explosive defense of love she attacks ignorant, chilly, refined, embarrassed people who "blaspheme living fire, seraph-brought from a divine altar"; when she insists that she must "*love*" before she marries, her "worldly" Uncle Sympson retorts, "Preposterous stuff! — indecorous — unwomanly!"

Beside the adults who in ways are precocious are the precocious children — the Yorkes who have their parents' free-swinging, uninhibited style of talk; Henry Sympson, having for his older cousin Shirley an attachment that borders on sexual feeling; and most of all Martin Yorke, aged fifteen, to whose excited pursuit of Caroline, almost irrelevant to plot or theme, Charlotte devotes two and a half zestful chapters. Martin is willing to help Caroline see Robert Moore, "her confounded sweetheart," to be near her himself, and he plans to claim a reward "displeasing to Moore"; he thinks of her physical beauties. Once he gets between Robert and Caroline at goodbye time; "he half carried Caroline down the stairs," "wrapped her shawl round her," and wanted to claim a kiss. At the same time he feels "power over her," he wants her to coax him, and he would like "to put her in a passion — to make her cry." Charlotte subtly conveys the sexuality of his quest — a rare feat in the nineteenth-century novel.

In Robert Moore, the unpopular mill-owner, Charlotte finds less social rightness or wrongness than his strength, his masculine appeal; her sympathy, so to speak, is for the underside of his personality. It "agreed with Moore's temperament . . . to be generally hated"; "he liked a silent, sombre, unsafe solitude"; against the vandals his "hate is still running in such a strong current" that he has none left for other objects; he shows "a terrible half" of himself in pursuing rioters with "indefatigable, . . . relentless assiduity"; this "excitement" pleases him; sadistically he likes to "force" magistrates to "betray a certain fear." He is the great lover of the story; he almost breaks Caroline's heart before he marries her, and he even has a subtle impact on Shirley, teasingly communicated, though officially denied, by Charlotte. What Caroline yields to is his "secret power," which affects her "like a spell." Here again Charlotte records, as directly as she can, simple sexual attractiveness. From the problem novel she veers off into "new Gothic"; in old Gothic, her hero would have been a villain.

True to convention, the love stories end happily. But special feelings, a new pathos of love, come through. Louis Moore demands in a woman something "to endure, . . . to reprimand"; love must involve "prickly peril," "a sting now and then"; for him the "young lioness or leopardess" is better than the lamb. There is that peculiarly tense vivacity of talk between lovers (the Jane-Rochester style), who discover a heightened, at times stagey, yet highly communicative rhetoric, drawing now on fantasy, now on moral conviction, verging now on titillating revelation, now on battle; a crafty game of love, flirting with an undefined risk, betraying a withheld avowal, savoring the approach to consummation, as if the erotic energy which in another social order might find a physical outlet were forcing itself into an electric language that is decorous but intimately exploratory. Between Louis Moore, who has "a thirst for freedom," and Shirley, to whom finding love is the Quest for the Bridle (for "a *master* [whom it is] impossible not to love, and very possible to fear"), there is an almost disturbingly taut struggle, a fierce intensification of the duel between Mirabel and Millamant, complex feelings translated into wit, sheer debate, abusiveness of manner, and a variety of skirmishings; Louis, the lover, adopting the stance of power and consciously playing to fright; the pursuit of an elusive prey ending in a virtual parody of "one calling, Child!/And I replied, My Lord"; over all of this a singular air of strained excitement, of the working of underlying emotional forces that at the climax leads to a new frenetic intensification of style in Louis's notebook:

> "Will you let me breathe, and not bewilder me? You must not smile at present. The world swims and changes round me. The sun is a dizzying scarlet blaze, the sky a violet vortex whirling over me."
>
> I am a strong man, but I staggered as I spoke. All creation was exaggerated: colour grew more vivid: motion more rapid; life itself more vital. I hardly saw her for a moment; but I heard her voice—pitilessly sweet. . . . Blent with torment, I experienced rapture.

Nor does Charlotte's flair for "unpatterned feeling" stop here: Shirley, the forceful leader who has already been called "a gentleman" and "captain," languishes under the found bridle of the masterful lover, whom she treats chillily and subjects to "exquisitely provoking" postponements of marriage; he calls her a "pantheress" who "gnaws her chain"; she tells him, "I don't know myself," as if engagement had opened to her eyes a previously undetected facet of her nature. Though "these freaks" continue, she is "fettered" at last; but not before the reader is radically stirred by the felt mysteries of personality. Before Charlotte, no love story tapped such strange depths, no consummation was so like a defeat.

Here Charlotte is probing psychic disturbance and is on the edge of psychosomatic illness. The theme draws her repeatedly. When Caroline thinks Robert doesn't love her, she suffers a long physical decline, described with painful fullness. She "wasted," had a "broken spirit," suffered "intolerable despair," felt the "utter sickness of longing and disappointment," at night found "my mind darker than my hiding-place," had "melancholy dreams," became "what is called nervous," had "fears I never used to have," "an inexpressible weight on my mind," and "strange sufferings," believed at times "that God had turned His face from her" and sank "into the gulf of religious despair." Charlotte divines this: "People never die of love or grief alone; though some die of inherent maladies which the tortures of those passions prematurely force into destructive action." Caroline lingers in illness, has fancies "inscrutable to ordinary attendants," has a hallucination of talking to Robert in the garden. Shirley, having been bitten by a dog which she believes to be mad, becomes seriously ill; psychosomatic illness springs directly from Charlotte's special sensitivity to the neurotic potential in human nature. A complementary awareness, that of the impact of the physical on the psychic, appears when she observes the "terrible depression," the "inexpressible — dark, barren, impotent" state of mind of Robert when he is recovering from a gunshot wound.

To give so much space to a lesser work is justifiable only because some of its contents are of high historico-critical significance. Though *Shirley* is not pulled together formally as well as *Jane Eyre* or even the more sprawling *Villette*, and though the characters are as wholes less fully realized, still it accommodates the widest ranging of an extraordinarily free sensibility. Constantly, in many different directions, it is in flight from the ordinary rational surface of things against which old Gothic was the first rebel in fiction; it abundantly contains and evokes, to adapt Charlotte's own metaphor, "unpatterned feeling." It turns up unexpected elements in personality: resentfulness, malice, love of power; precocities and perversities of response; the multiple tensions of love between highly individualized lovers; psychic disturbances. And in accepting a dark magnetic energy as a central virtue in personality, Charlotte simply reverses the status of men who were the villains in the sentimental and old Gothic modes.

Of the four novels, *Villette* is most heavily saturated with Gothic — with certain of its traditional manifestations (old Gothic), with the undercutting of these that is for Charlotte no less instinctive than the use of them (anti-Gothic), and with an original, intense exploration of feeling that increases the range and depth of fiction (new Gothic).

As in *Jane Eyre*, Charlotte can be skillful in anti-Gothic. When Madame Beck, pussyfooting in espionage, "materializes" in shocking suddenness,

Lucy is made matter-of-fact or indignant rather than thrilled with fright. "No ghost stood beside me . . ." is her characteristic response to a Beck surprise. Once the spy, having "stolen" upon her victims, betrays her unseen presence by a sneeze: Gothic yields to farce. Technically more complex is Charlotte's use of the legend of the nun supposedly buried alive and of the appearances of a visitant taken to be the ghost of the nun: Charlotte coolly distances herself from this by having Lucy dismiss the legend as "romantic rubbish" and by explaining the apparitions as the playful inventions of a giddy lover. True, she keeps the secret long enough to get a few old Gothic thrills from the "ghost," but what she is really up to is using the apparitions in an entirely new way; that is, for responses that lie beyond the simplicities of terror.

First, the apparitions are explained as a product of Lucy's own psychic state, the product, Dr. John suggests, of "long-continued mental conflict." In the history of Gothic this is an important spot, for here we first see the shift from stock explanations and responses to the inner human reality: fiction is slowly discovering the psychic depths known to drama for centuries.

Then, when Lucy next sees the nun, she responds in a way that lies entirely outside fictional convention: "I neither fled nor shrieked . . . . I spoke . . . I stretched out my hand, for I meant to touch her." Not that Lucy is not afraid, but that she is testing herself—an immense change from the expectable elementary response: the *frisson* disappears before the complexer action that betokens a maturing of personality.

Finally, Paul and Lucy both see the spectre and are thus brought closer together: they have had what they call "impressions," and through sharing the ghost they assume a shared sensibility. Paul says, "I was conscious of rapport between you and myself." The rapport is real, though the proof of it is false; the irony of this is a subtle sophistication of Gothic.

The responsiveness, the sensitivity, is the thing; many passages place "feeling" above "seeing" as an avenue of knowledge. Reason must be respected, for it is "vindictive," but at times imagination must be yielded to, like a sexual passion at once feared and desired. There is the summer night when the sedative given by Madame Beck has a strange effect:

> Imagination was roused from her rest, and she came forth impetuous and venturous. With scorn she looked on Matter, her mate—
>
> "Rise!" she said; "Sluggard! this night I will have *my* will; nor shalt thou prevail."

"Look forth and view the night!" was her cry; and when I lifted the heavy blind from the casement close at hand — with her own royal gesture, she showed me a moon supreme, in an element deep and splendid.

. . . She lured me to leave this den and follow her forth into dew, coolness, and glory.

There follows the most magnificent of all Charlotte's nocturnes: that vision of the "moonlit, midnight park," the brilliance of the fete, the strange charm of places and people, recounted in a rhythmical, enchanted style (the "Kubla Khan" mode) which at first reading gives the air of a dream mistaken for reality to what is in fact reality made like a dream. This is a surrealistic, trance-like episode which makes available to fiction a vast new territory and idiom. The surrealistic is, despite Montague Summers, one of the new phases of Gothic, which in its role of liberator of feeling characteristically explores the non-naturalistic: to come up, as here, with a profounder nature, or a nature freshly, even disturbingly, seen.

The surrealism of Lucy's evening is possible only to a special sensitivity, and it is really the creation of this sensitivity, in part pathological, that is at the apex of Charlotte's Gothic. In *The Professor* the tensions in the author's contemplation of her own experience come into play; in *Shirley* various undercurrents of personality push up into the social surfaces of life; in *Jane Eyre* moral feeling is subjected to the remolding pressures of a newly vivid consciousness of the diverse impulses of sexuality; and in *Villette* the feeling responses to existence are pursued into sufferings that edge over into disorder. The psychology of rejection and alienation, first applied to Polly, becomes the key to Lucy, who, finding no catharsis for a sense of desolation, generates a serious inner turmoil. She suffers from "a terrible oppression" and then from "anxiety lying in wait on enjoyment, like a tiger crouched in a jungle . . . his fierce heart panted close against mine; . . . I knew he waited only for sun-down to bound ravenous from his ambush." Depression is fed by the conflict between a loveless routine of life and her longings, which she tried to put down like "Jael to Sisera, driving a nail through their temples"; but this only "transiently stunned" them and "at intervals [they] would turn on the nail with a rebellious wrench: then did the temples bleed, and the brain thrill to its core."

These strains prepare us for the high point in Charlotte's new Gothic — the study of Lucy's emotional collapse and near breakdown when vacation comes and she is left alone at the school with "a poor deformed and imbecile pupil." "My heart almost died within me; . . . My spirits had long been gradually sinking; now that the prop of employment was withdrawn, they went down fast." After three weeks, storms bring on "a deadlier paralysis"; and "my nervous system could hardly support" the daily strain. She wanders in the street: "A goad thrust me on, a fever forbade me to rest; . . ." She observes a "growing illusion" and says, ". . . my nerves are getting overstretched; . . ." She feels that "a malady is growing upon" her mind, and she asks herself, "How shall I keep well?" Then come "a peculiarly agonizing depression"; a nine-days storm: "a strange fever of the nerves and blood"; continuing insomnia, broken only by a terrifying nightmare of alienation. She flees the house, and then comes the climactic event of her going to a church and despite the intensity of her Protestant spirit entering the confessional to find relief.

From now on, overtly or implicitly, hypochondria and anxiety keep coming into the story — the enemies from whose grip Lucy must gradually free herself. At a concert she spotted the King as a fellow-victim of "that strangest spectre, Hypochondria," for on his face she saw its marks, whose meaning, "if I did not *know*, at least I *felt*, . . ." When, after her return to Beck's on a rainy night, things are not going well, a letter from Dr. John is "the ransom from my terror," and its loss drives her almost to frenzy. She describes night as "an unkindly time" when she has strange fancies, doubts, the "horror of calamity." She is aware of her "easily-deranged temperament." Beyond this area of her own self-understanding we see conflicts finding dramatic expression in her almost wild acceptance of Rachel's passionate acting of Phèdre ("a spectacle low, horrible, immoral"), which counterbalances her vehement condemnation of a fleshy nude by Rubens (one of the "materialists"). Paul identifies her, in a figure whose innocence for him is betrayed by the deep, if not wholly conscious, understanding that leads Charlotte to write it: "a young she wild creature, new caught, untamed, viewing with a mixture of fire and fear the first entrance of the breaker in."

There is not room to trace Lucy's recovery, especially in the important phase, the love affair with Paul which is related to our theme by compelling, as do the Jane-Rochester and Louis Moore-Shirley relationships in quite different ways, a radical revision of the feelings exacted by stereotyped romance. What is finally noteworthy is that Charlotte, having chosen in Lucy a heroine with the least durable emotional equipment, with the most conspicuous neurotic element in her temperament, goes on through the history of Lucy's emotional maturing to surmount the need for romantic fulfillment and to develop the aesthetic courage for a final disaster — the only one in her four novels.

Some years ago Edmund Wilson complained of writers of Gothic who "fail to lay hold on the terrors that lie deep in the human soul and that cause man to fear himself" and proposed an anthology of horror stories that probe "psychological caverns" and find "disquieting obsessions." This is precisely the direction in which Charlotte Brontë moved, especially in Lucy Snowe and somewhat also in Caroline Helstone and Shirley Keeldar; this was one aspect of her following human emotions where they took her, into many depths and intensities that as yet hardly had a place in the novel. This was the finest achievement of Gothic.

Gothic is variously defined. In a recent book review Leslie Fiedler implies that Gothic is shoddy mystery-mongering, whereas F. Cudworth Flint defines the Gothic tradition, which he considers "nearly central in American literature," as "a literary exploration of the avenues to death." For Montague Summers, on the other hand, Gothic was the essence of romanticism, and romanticism was the literary expression of supernaturalism. Both these latter definitions, though they are impractically inclusive, have suggestive value. For originally Gothic was one of a number of aesthetic developments which served to breach the "classical" and "rational" order of life and to make possible a kind of response, and a response to a kind of thing, that among the knowing had long been taboo. In the novel it was the function of Gothic to open horizons beyond social patterns, rational decisions, and institutionally approved emotions; in a word, to enlarge the sense of reality and its impact on the human being. It became then a great liberator of feeling. It acknowledged the nonrational — in the world of things and events, occasionally in the realm of the transcendental, ultimately and most persistently in the depths of the human being. (Richardson might have started this, but his sense of inner forces was so overlaid by the moralistic that his followers all ran after him only when he ran the wrong way.) The first Gothic writers took the easy way: the excitement of mysterious scene and happening, which I call old Gothic. Of this Charlotte Brontë made some direct use, while at the same time tending toward humorous modifications (anti-Gothic); but what really counts is its indirect usefulness to her: it released her from the patterns of the novel of society and therefore permitted the flowering of her real talent — the talent for finding and giving dramatic form to impulses and feelings which, because of their depth or mysteriousness or intensity or ambiguity, or of their ignoring or transcending everyday norms of propriety or reason, increase wonderfully the sense of reality in the novel. To note the emergence of this "new Gothic" in Charlotte Brontë is not, I think, to pursue an old mode into dusty corners but rather to identify historically the distinguishing, and distinguished, element in her work.

ELIZABETH CLEGHORN GASKELL

Yvonne ffrench

"I LIKE dearly," wrote Mrs. Gaskell in 1857 to Charles Eliot Norton, "to call up pictures,—and thoughts suggested by so utterly different a life to Manchester. I believe I *am* mediaeval—and *un*-Manchester, and un-American. . . . Now I like a smelling and a singing world. Yes I do. I can't help it. I like Kings and Queens, and nightingales and mignonette and roses. There!"

In such playful moments we catch sight of what Elizabeth Gaskell might have demanded from life had her circumstances been different. These, with her talents and her responsibilities, the weight of her moral background and the sobriety of her forebears precluded much active participation in the world of the senses. By referring to herself as un-American, though her idea of the United States was, as we know, vague indeed, she implied quite clearly that republicanism and puritanism were repugnant to her, and that her sympathies were monarchist, of the old *régime* type; she was even vaguely in sympathy with the Church of Rome, which she had been witnessing in all the splendor of its traditional setting during her radiant visit there in the spring of that year.

Indeed, it is difficult to equate with the influences governing her upbringing as a dissenter with progressive, reforming views, this nostalgia for a vanished medieval heritage which shines so luminously out from much of her work.

In 1857 and, indeed, for many years after, Mrs. Gaskell was celebrated as "the author of *Mary Barton*." It was only later in the century, in fact well after her death, that she became by common consent "the author of *Cranford*." Modern critics, revising their estimate of her work once again in the light of the ninety years which have passed since that time, are inclined to think her most important work was achieved only at the end of her life. They acclaim her as "the author of *Wives and Daughters*."

In considering her life and work it is therefore necessary to separate the social crusader from the creator of the country idyl, and to account for the ascendancy of the latter manner by glancing at the edges of her life.

It had begun uncertainly enough when she was born at Chelsea in 1810, her father, William Stevenson, a former Unitarian minister, having taken unsuccessfully to farming and lost all his money. He had married into the old family of Holland, established in Cheshire for generations, but his wife died when Elizabeth was one year old, and the child was reared by a maternal aunt in the shadow of the old home. There, at Sandlebridge near Knutsford, which reappears under thin disguises throughout her books, Elizabeth Stevenson passed her girlhood among the people she has familiarized in countless stories: the doctors, the farmers, the squires, and the lawyers who, faithfully portrayed, form with irreproachable maiden ladies the backbone of her work. These were the companions of her childhood; her landscape was green with flat, moist pasture, her villages pied with the black and white of plaster and gables. Narrow lanes down which jolted nothing louder than the farmer's cart were shaded by tall elms, and fringed by cumulus clouds. A world of quiet ways and traditional customs, peopled by old-fashioned, slow-thinking, conservative-minded English types: kind aunts, benevolent uncles, and laughing cousins.

This, in the intervals of schooling, had formed her world, until, in 1832, she suddenly fell in love, and married.

It is to the change of circumstances brought about by this marriage to a young Unitarian, William Gaskell, that the early phases of her literary life may be ascribed. Her husband's work lay directly in Manchester where he was assistant minister at a Unitarian chapel. Earnestness and devotion to duty marked all his character, so that an aura of solemnity seems still to surround his memory, in contrast to that of his pretty, gay, devoted wife.

That literary influences had been latent in her from a fairly early age is clear. She had inherited from her father a taste for scholarship, particularly with regard to folklore and topography, for which she had a natural bent. But that all urges to write seriously were stifled, to begin with, by domestic claims is certain. There were one or two early attempts at literary expression. *Blackwood's Magazine* for January 1837 contained a set of verses entitled "Sketches among the Poor," the result of collaboration between the Gaskells in recording the deep sense of pathos which stirred them both at the sight of the patient poverty they lived among, and their recognition of the loyalties that bound together the unhappy and the underprivileged in life. Directly inspired by the poetry of Crabbe, the verses held neither interest nor literary merit. Their value lay in independence of spirit, and the fact that they contained the seed of that desire to take part in the social struggle which lay ahead of the people of Britain.

Another trial at writing, more interesting because more natural to Elizabeth Gaskell herself, had been her contribution, anonymously submitted, to William Howitt, whose *Visits to Remarkable Places* was then being widely read. Howitt had been so impressed with the quality of this topographical sketch recalling Clopton Hall, near Stratford-on-Avon, which she had visited when at school, that he included it in his next volume. On making her acquaintance three years later, he implored Mrs. Gaskell to take up a literary career. Of writing on a professional scale, however, there had been no question during that early period in spite of Howitt's persuasions. The first few years of marriage were absorbed entirely by domestic and parochial duties. Babies were born; money was scarce; above all, the Gaskells lived in Manchester. The Manchester of the 'thirties and 'forties was the chief victim of the early industrial age, and the seat of misery and disease. Poverty led to hunger, hunger to crime. Overcrowding bred filth, squalor, and epidemics. Overproduction at home coincided with an economic depression in the United States; by 1837 half Lancashire was unemployed, and despair was rotting the spirit of the workers. Those in contact with the poor were, in the absence of official aid, to witness horrifying events.

To be surrounded by these conditions, and to have no solution for the problem; to experience the rain, the dirt, the smells, and the epidemics; to see the starved faces and stunted bodies wearing away their ghastly lives in waterlogged dens without hope of effective aid, roused the minister's wife to a sense of passionate indignation. Besides this, she had lost her year-old boy, and personal grief had opened her heart to the daily tragedies surrounding her. In the Manchester of the middle 'forties these were not far to seek. Out of her own depth of feeling came her novel, *Mary Barton* (1848), the first active protest against living conditions in the industrial towns of the Northern Midlands. This is precisely the value and the importance of the book. It is a work less of literary and artistic merit than of missionary zeal. Although previous writers had attempted to tackle the problem, the value of their work had been offset either by their approach or their aims. Mrs. Gaskell was to be the first to achieve an original work of this kind, carrying the imaginative appeal of fiction and having no ulterior motive other than one that was purely humanitarian. Benjamin Disraeli had admittedly tackled the problem in his novel *Sybil*, as had Harriet Martineau in her *Illustrations of Political Economy*; but the one had employed a social theme to serve a political end, and the other had recourse to a means which, however worthily intended, was doomed by its title and its form to lack human interest.

It is not proposed here to discuss the didactic trends in Mrs. Gaskell's novels, nor to examine the little moral issues—those *cas de conscience* for which the French critic Montégut was to rate her so highly. In those of her works which are devoted to the reform of certain social evils, her own self-appointed mission was that of a mediator, and in the first seven years of her literary career she aimed at presenting cases and solving problems that were vexing both sides in the opening round of the clash between capital and labor. In particular she can be seen advocating the Christian ethics which she understood and, indeed, practiced from the depth of her generous and kindly heart. *Mary Barton* is a social novel from first to last. Here, the problems of the working classes are shown against the background of the Chartist movement, the Corn Law troubles, and the tragic consequences of the too rapid expansion in industrial development. Its effect was electric. It stirred a great public conscience to shame that such conditions should exist at all, and established its author among the contemporary writers whose work was to be reckoned with.

Mary Barton was followed by *The Moorland Cottage* (1850), a slight and sentimental story little realized at the time as of significance. Maggie Browne, the heroine, is however of some consequence since she was the direct begetter of Maggie Tulliver, and George Eliot (although the two women seem never to have met) made no attempt to disguise the fact of her debt to Mrs. Gaskell. She deliberately used the brother-and-sister theme from *The Moorland Cottage*, and, hardly altering Maggie's character, placed the two young people in Dorlcote Mill. There, her massive mind recreated them as the Tulliver children, destined to immortality in *The Mill on the Floss.* As creations, although they owe their existence to Mrs. Gaskell, Tom and Maggie Tulliver far outweigh Edward and Maggie Browne in strength, character, and consistency. The children in Mrs. Gaskell's books are often priggish dolls, dressed up to utter pretty, sedate, and unreal sentiments, and it is with almost a sense of shock that one discovers the following dialogue between the children in *The Moorland Cottage*.

In a rare example of rebelliousness, Edward and Maggie Browne discuss their feelings for their dead father and their embarrassment at being taken to weep over his grave each Sunday after church.

"I wish it would always rain on Sundays," said Edward to Maggie, in a garden conference.

"Why?" asked she.

"Because then we bustle out of church, and get home as fast as we can, to save Mamma's crape; and we have not to go and cry over papa."

"I don't cry," said Maggie. "Do you?"

And again:

"Maggie, sometimes I don't think I'm sorry that papa is dead — when I'm naughty, you know; he would have been so angry with me if he had been here; and I think — only sometimes, you know — I'm rather glad he is not."

The next three works dealt with aspects of social problems. *Ruth* (1853) and *Lizzie Leigh* (1855; published first in 1850 in the opening numbers of Dickens' *Household Words*) were concerned with illegitimacy and prostitution and the plea for a more charitable attitude toward the victims of seduction. Then, in 1855 the publication of *North and South* showed Mrs. Gaskell to be able to create in Margaret Hale a finely drawn heroine and to carry the reader along on a stirring industrial theme; this time presenting the case for the employers. It was typical of her role as mediator in any dispute that she was to reply to those critics who had complained that in *Mary Barton* she had done less than justice to the owners. But *North and South* was also to be almost the last of her didactic writings. Happily, because she had done her work as a pioneer. She could now fulfill herself, and turn to that other self which was "*un*-Manchester." From that time on the theme of social reform was abandoned, and her art was directed by that exquisite muse who took possession of her spirit. It is this side of her work, with its particularly English quality and its emphasis on aspects of English life which she understood so well, that will be considered.

The turning point had come in 1853, when she had written a sketch for *Household Words*. It was about life in a village in the Midlands. It had an unusual success, and she was invited to prolong it. She did so. She developed the theme into a series of sketches. In time it became a book, which she called *Cranford*.

Cranford remains the accepted masterpiece of Mrs. Gaskell's literary career, although curiously enough it was the accidental triumph of her genius for improvisation over a certain haphazard, even slipshod, method. When it originally appeared serially, *Cranford* had been limited to the two first chapters, which disposed effectively of the principal characters, and nothing indeed would ever have been heard of the village or its inhabitants again had there not been a general outcry at its early and abrupt end.

Cranford shows the side of Mrs. Gaskell that begins to express a world of mignonette and roses. It fulfills the other side of her nature — the gay, tender, delicate-minded and indulgent side. It brings out all the warmth which had lain for so long stifled beneath the cover of duty, drabness, social problems, and philanthropic urges best left to others. Geraldine Jewsbury, herself astringent and unconventional, had sensed instinctively a lack of realism in Mrs. Gaskell's earlier writing. Perhaps with North Country shrewdness she distrusted the charm which held so many admirers under the spell of Mrs. Gaskell. However this might be, we find her writing to Mrs. Carlyle, "I have a notion that if one could get at the *Mary Barton* that is the kernel of Mrs. Gaskell one would like her, but I have never done so yet."

What she implied by this is open to conjecture. It is permissible to imagine that Miss Jewsbury sensed a fundamental falseness in the author of *Mary Barton*, a lack of integrity in regard to the treatment of her work, and that she instinctively recoiled before the cloying language in which so many of the sentiments are draped. For Mrs. Gaskell's attempts at realism are often immature, and her situations in many instances so improbable that she sometimes fails to convince. The criticism leveled at her by Geraldine Jewsbury is echoed by Charlotte Brontë, who, writing in 1853 to Mrs. Gaskell, tried to clear up this false approach to her literary work. She gave her, politely, a piece of her mind.

> Does no luminous cloud ever come between you and the severe truth, as you know it in your own secret and clear-seeing soul? . . . Are you never tempted to make your characters more amiable than the life, by the inclination to assimilate your thoughts to the thoughts of those who always *feel* kindly, but sometimes fail to *see* justly? Don't answer this question.

Then again, there was Mrs. Carlyle, who found a "moral dullness" in Mrs. Gaskell, a perfectly understandable accusation. This dullness resided in her inability to probe into fundamental human problems and weaknesses unaccompanied by a falsely sentimental glossing-over of facts. *Ruth*, it is true, dealt with a recurring human problem, but its propagandist appeal is spoiled by sentimentality of treatment. And since any exposure in fiction of the harsher side of life must allow the reader a glimpse at least of the truth, however squalid, it is here that Mrs. Gaskell fails to come to terms with the dictates of her art. She, who had never lacked the courage to defend the causes for which she campaigned, compromised again and again by adopting a conventional attitude toward her theme.

Against this, her championship of unpopular causes must stand to her credit, and her charitable, cultivated nature eventually found itself happiest when she abandoned herself to her natural gifts of comfortable, observant, gossipy, and indeed exquisite pictures of the English life which she knew so well, but which has vanished from the modern world forever.

The plan for *Cranford* had already taken form in *Mr. Harrison's Confessions*, written a few months earlier for a women's journal. Here, she had tried out the form of her characters. The two sisters, the Miss Parkinsons, prototypes of the Miss Jenkyns; Miss Horsman, a parallel to Miss Pole; and the country doctor who, modeled on Dr. Peter Holland, Mrs. Gaskell's uncle at Knutsford, is met with again and again in her tales of rural life. He reappears for the last time, brilliantly portrayed, as Mr. Gibson in *Wives and Daughters* (1866).

In *Cranford*, apart from the short preliminary sketch, she initiated the style that would henceforward be associated with her: loving and light, with a tenderness and delicacy always tempered with humor, and in this particular medium she is unrivaled. Lacking the asperity of Jane Austen, as well as the torrential passion and consuming romanticism of Charlotte Brontë, her place is, for purposes of comparison, by the side of George Eliot.

That she stands on a lower rung of the ladder than her great contemporary, she would have been one of the first to admit. Writing to Charles Eliot Norton, whose friendship in middle life she was to value so highly, she observed that it was not worthwhile trying to write while there were such books as *Adam Bede* and *Scenes from Clerical Life*. The magnetic figure of George Eliot, with her bold, searching mind, her powerful grasp of human problems and her philosophical approach to fiction, was nonetheless her natural counterpart in literary form. Their provincial stems, robust dissenting backgrounds, awareness of social trends, and didactic tendencies travel along parallel lines. Essentially complementary, they can be compared as masculine and feminine in their respective art.

The quality which gives *Cranford* its abiding popularity is its charm. That charm lies in its statement of the values of a lost age when a quiet, dignified, though doubtless hum-drum existence went hand in hand with humanity, self-respect, and an acceptance of that station in life to which it had pleased God to call the characters. These were the standards governing ordinary, educated people, among whom the mention of money, let alone its shortage, was a social solecism of the first order. In Mrs. Gaskell's world the country folk in every stage of the social hierarchy know their places. Only the upstart from the industrial centers refuses to keep quietly within bounds. Trade is another unmentionable subject in a universe where neither money, poverty, nor death is even alluded to. And the little snobbish weaknesses are devastatingly introduced. Miss Jenkyns coughs long and loudly so that the Honourable Mrs. Jamieson should not overhear Miss Jessie Brown's naïve admission that her uncle was a shopkeeper.

Respectability triumphs in *Cranford*, and Mrs. Gaskell, irritated by its complacency, yet recognizes its inward strength. She sees through the little pretenses, and longs to get at the truth. "Oh dear! how I wanted facts instead of reflections," says Mary Smith, the observant narrator, epitomizing Mrs. Gaskell's own deep interest in human affairs. Again and again she longs to push aside conventional social views to get at the real story beneath the wrappings. She was a natural storyteller, even when she occasionally confused her details in the headlong rush of her narrative.

Mrs. Gaskell's muse was intensely personal: a muse of charm. And even though *Cranford* has been popularly considered her masterpiece, it remains a minor one, relying for its effects upon the presence of feeling rather than the power of intellect. Humor, poetry, and warmth of heart have combined to make it one of the most lovable works of any English novelist, but it has its limitations, and she was to write better books than this. *Cranford*'s real importance lies in the fact that it is thoroughly representative of Mrs. Gaskell's most attractive work. It represents her Englishness. To say this is not to charge her with insularity; in fact, her very Liberalism embraced every suffering creature on earth, and was a guarantee against such an outlook. Her older characters are frequently exploited as the holders of bigoted or prejudiced views, whether on religion, foreigners, or social problems. They are nonetheless usually converted to her own charitable outlook, which yearned to see the world become more tolerant and more Christian, whether or not this conversion was in character for them. Thus both Squire Hamley in *Wives and Daughters*, who detests Frenchmen and Catholics, and the Vicar of Monkshaven in *Sylvia's Lovers*, who abhors the French and the Dissenters, are allowed redeeming features which preserve them from the worst effects of their die-hard natures.

This particular Englishness, the chief virtue in Elizabeth Gaskell's work, derived from her saturation in folklore and her wise experience of local customs, language, and ways. In company with the Brontës and George Eliot she is one of the first of the English regional novelists, and it is not too much to suggest that *Cranford* is indirectly responsible for the cult of the English village, in its "olde worlde" sense. This can be partly ascribed to a universal wish to share the charmed and protected existence that has vanished from the civilized world. For security in an ordered society is the mainspring of Mrs. Gaskell's own convictions: thus she writes the more willingly upon this theme.

Her views on this are even more explicit in *My Lady Ludlow* (1858), in which well-mannered little treatise on the principles of aristocratic responsibility and privilege she expounds the theories of *noblesse oblige*, presenting a case with the most delicate understanding of what the old ruling oligarchy of the eighteenth century conceived as its duties toward others in humbler walks of life. Trained at the court of George the Third, Lady Ludlow has no patience with modern theories springing from Jacobinism, particularly with regard to education. She can defend her opinions and give sound reasons for them as well. To the young woman who, applying to her for a situation, adds by way of inducement that she can "cast accounts," Lady Ludlow replies, "Go away, wench, you're only fit for trade; you will not suit me for a servant." And giving the girl a Bible she warns her against those principles "which had led the French to cut off their King's and Queen's heads," and engages a girl who is illiterate.

In the interval of novel writing Mrs. Gaskell's social life had developed in step with her own improved circumstances. Fame had brought friends; friends had widened her experience. The curious, half-reticent friendship that had sprung up between Charlotte Brontë and the gregarious, busy, vital Manchester housewife was to have one significant result. Charlotte died in 1855, and Mrs. Gaskell agreed to her relatives' request that she write the official biography.

Although no book was ever more finely conceived or more grandly executed, few biographies of that quality have suffered a more disastrous reception. Errors of judgment, tact, and taste had crept into the text; Mrs. Gaskell, carried away by enthusiasm for her unique theme, had thrown discretion to the winds. Faced by several actions for libel, she was forced to withdraw the first edition and send a public apology to the *Times*. Still, the work remains one of the great classic biographies in the English language. No writer on Charlotte Brontë can afford to ignore it. It was, as Charles Eliot Norton wrote at the time to James Russell Lowell, "almost as much an exhibition of Mrs. Gaskell's character as it was of Miss Brontë's."

Worry and anxiety resulting from her trials over *The Life of Charlotte Brontë* had its effect on her sensitive nervous system, and for the next few years Mrs. Gaskell wrote little except contributions for literary journals and magazines. The surprising ease with which she kept up a flow of short stories is only offset by their frequent unoriginality and lack of quality. She had her public to satisfy and her family to support. To meet the needs of both, compromise was inevitable. Thus her standards were unequal, dipping at times below the level of literature into the current of journalism.

One of her better short stories of this period is *A Dark Night's Work*. The heroine, Ellinor, who resembles Margaret Hale of *North and South*, is a high-spirited creature, though her father is of a type unusual in Mrs. Gaskell's gallery of stock figures. Memories are revived of the carnival in Rome which she had watched there a few years earlier—they form a kaleidoscopic background to Ellinor's meeting with Canon Livingstone—an echo of Mrs. Gaskell's own first meeting with Norton, an impressionable and indelible moment, among the shifting, vivid tumult in the Corso.

Only toward the end of her life, however, was the mastery of technical skill, sought so long and so carefully, to be attained. In 1863, three years before her death, Mrs. Gaskell published *Sylvia's Lovers*; two years later came *Cousin Phillis*. Each in different ways presaged the crowning effort of her life. *Sylvia's Lovers* is in a class by itself, a *tour de force* which, departing from the usual country-life story in which she customarily excelled, yet stands up to every test. Good writing, fine characterization, and superb skill here establish Mrs. Gaskell as a regional novelist of the first order. The book is an achievement both on account of its careful reconstruction of a period—its action is laid at the end of the eighteenth century—and of the now obsolete dialect in which the characters are made to speak. The etymological side of her Northumbrian researches has been dealt with by Professor D. G. Sanders in *Elizabeth Gaskell* (1929), in which the importance of her work in clearing a path through the tangle of obsolete dialect for the benefit of subsequent novelists is made abundantly plain.

Cousin Phillis was published in 1865. This rare and exquisite little study of first love and its deception has never been surpassed in any other story by Mrs. Gaskell. It combines all her tender feeling for the changing moods of the countryside and its quality of Arcadian grace with her warm sympathy for young things in their first innocence, brought face to face with the realities of adult life. Had she written nothing but *Cousin Phillis*, this short and flawless story would contain the essence of her art: the poetry inherent in her own nature, the warmth she felt and radiated toward her fellow-beings, the humor never far from her laughing spirit, the sense of pathos which she knew how to convey, the tragedy which was always present in her experience of life. All the lyricism in her being is found in the pages of *Cousin Phillis*, and it is warmed by her genial outlook, with its quality of diffused radiance that seems to invest the landscape of her mind with the pearly light of pure inspiration.

Toward the end of her life she had come to achieve technical mastery as a writer, and it is the tragedy of her literary career that she was to die suddenly, leaving her last and most accomplished work unfinished. *Wives and Daughters*, commissioned as a serial in 1864, is unquestionably the novel of her career, and it is clear that she was on the threshold of a new period as a writer. In this novel, all her qualities as a chronicler of the English scene have burst into full flower; and the long, well-constructed, intricately-devised, and polished narrative is packed with all the detail of which she was so shrewd an observer. It is a love story, pure and simple, free from the least hint of didacticism or ulterior message. For the first time the religious motive is absent. The story is told as an end in itself, giving the writer every scope for her natural gift of narrative. It is superbly contrived and magnificently handled, treating once again with the types so familiar to her in the life of the countryside in and around Knutsford. This time the town appears as Hollingford, and within its radius can be found a perfectly reasonable, unexaggerated, and well-defined cross section of English country life, from Lord and Lady Cumnor who inhabit The Towers to the Miss Browns who live in the village along with other members of the professional middle class.

There are eight principal characters, all sharply drawn and consistent in type, while two at least achieve a degree of fine characterization that places them high in the scale of creative writing. Clare Gibson, the doctor's wife and former governess at The Towers, is a masterpiece of pretentious affectation — we know on her own evidence that she has always been "a kind of pet with gentlemen," a weakness which has not failed to have its psychological effect on her daughter Cynthia, whose character is a remarkable study in shaded overtones. Molly Gibson, the heroine, has been met with before. She is the spiritual sister of Maggie Browne of *The Moorland Cottage*, a sturdy, clear-eyed, honest, country-bred girl, with a warm heart and an impulsive spirit, foiling the infinitely complicated nature of Cynthia, who, of finer stuff than her dishonest mother, nevertheless inherits some of her disturbing qualities. "It's no use talking," she says to Molly, "I am not good, and I never shall be now. Perhaps I might be a heroine still, but I shall never be a good woman, I know." Both Cynthia and her mother have a quality new to Mrs. Gaskell. They are real creations, with human imperfections. They are original, subtle characters, as different from the *Cranford* ladies, who are easily repeated stock characters, as they are from the pathetically sentimental figures of the early reforming works.

Even so, for the most part Mrs. Gaskell's characters are limited in range and have a way of reappearing in story after story, disguised in only the flimsiest manner. They are usually recognizable from afar, for they are easily identified. Mr.Wilkins (*A Dark Night's Work*) has affinities with Mr. Dudgeon (*The Squire's Story*); Mr. Holman (*Cousin Phillis*) harks back to William Stevenson, Mrs. Gaskell's father, the source of many of her clerical and agricultural characters; while the kinship existing between the Miss Jenkyns, Miss Parkinsons, and Miss Browns is obvious. As with types so with places, incidents, and events, which recur constantly throughout all her work. Certain themes are repeated again and again, drawn from memory or personal experience. The several mysterious disappearances refer to a brother of Mrs. Gaskell's who went to sea and never returned; the frequent ruination of families echoes the financial failure of her father.

This lack of variety in plot and incident is one of her main defects, just as her tendency to select commonplace names reveals poverty of imagination.

Her strength is most noticeable in her inborn sense of narrative. She can carry her reader along with her on the fast current of a story like few other novelists, holding him in suspense for just the necessary time.

Passages of sustained or emotionally dramatic color are consistent with the best of her work, and she can describe atmosphere, or convey crowd excitement in a remarkable degree. Whether in describing the fire at Carson's mill (*Mary Barton*), the carnival (*A Dark Night's Work*), the return of the whaling fleet (*Sylvia's Lovers*), or, in conveying the tense personal conflicts between Thornton and Margaret (*North and South*), she achieves her purpose in dramatic effect by sheer power of description.

In 1862 Manchester once again experienced the effects of a crisis, this time produced by the Civil War in America. Repercussions in the cotton mills led quickly to famine, and relief for the destitute was begun. Mrs. Gaskell was energetic in organizing sewing parties to help the victims, but the exacting work proved too much for her. She strained her heart, and, fearing a physical collapse, invested her savings in a country house, which she might leave to her husband and daughter. Here, on a visit in 1866, she died suddenly while at tea with her family. *Wives and Daughters* lay unfinished on her writing desk, just as Clare is speaking: "And now cover me up close, and let me go to sleep, and dream about my Cynthia and my new shawl. . . ."

TROLLOPE'S *ORLEY FARM*: ARTISTRY *MANQUÉ*

Bradford A. Booth

UNIVERSITY OF CALIFORNIA AT LOS ANGELES

I DO not know that anyone at all sympathetic to the Victorian novel has ever failed to like Trollope's *Orley Farm*. At all events, no unfavorable reaction has been recorded. Trollope thought the plot his best, and when he began to list the well-drawn characters, he could not stop much short of a total roll call. There is not, he says, "a dull page in the book." Such prideful language, so uncommon for Trollope that it is found nowhere else, is almost, if not quite, justified. On this occasion he had, as Henry James saw, an "admirable subject." It is one that not only suited perfectly his own mature temper but gave him a welcome opportunity to skirt certain mid-Victorian clichés and conventions in the design and development of a novel. The result is that *Orley Farm* is one of Trollope's richest and most satisfying books. If, like *The Last Chronicle of Barset*, it fails to attain true greatness, the failure is in large part the measure of his incomplete break with the familiar stereotypes of plotting.

When in 1862 Trollope published *Orley Farm* the Victorian sensation novel was sweeping everything before it. *The Woman in White* had created a taste for melodrama which *Lady Audley's Secret* was currently satisfying. Trollope, of course, cared for neither the premises nor the methods of the sensation novelist, but as a businessman writer, conscious of public demand, he was not above compromises and concessions. These he was able to make very skillfully without abandoning his position as a realist. In *Doctor Thorne* he had indeed come perilously close to giving way to sensationalism in adopting his brother's idea of a good plot, but in *Orley Farm* the danger is minimal. Though there is an ample quota of story interest, the novel is essentially a study of character.

Some years later, when he wrote his *Autobiography*, Trollope expressed fear that he had shown his hand too soon, needlessly sacrificing suspense. The plot, he said, "has the fault of declaring itself, and thus coming to an end too early in the book." It is true that we learn of Lady Mason's guilt very quickly, and at least one critic has suggested that the trial is vulnerable to the "charge of anticlimax." But this is quite to misunderstand Trollope's basic intent. A novel whose interest turns on discovering whether or not a forgery has been committed would be thoroughly un-Trollopian. The question of Lady Mason's guilt is not really at issue, any more than is the question whether or not in *The Last Chronicle* Josiah Crawley stole a cheque for £20. These novels do not have their *raison d'être* in the solving of a mystery. In *Lady Audley's Secret*, however, there is no interest whatever beyond that which may be found in discovering at last that George Talboys was pushed down a well by his wife and left for dead.

Early in *Barchester Towers* Trollope invites the reader to turn to the last chapter, confident that such interest as his novel possesses does not rest on twists of plot. He might have made the same statement on behalf of *Orley Farm*, for again he breaks the Victorian stereotype by deliberately foregoing the interest that attaches to surprise. Lady Mason is guilty; indeed she soon avows her guilt to Sir Peregrine Orme. The power of the novel arises not from the shock of the unexpected, but from the skill with which Trollope explores the tenacity of a woman who will dare all for her son and who will break upon the rack of neither conscience nor the public tribunal. Trollope's main plot, secured and sustained by tensions of its own, needed no help from adventitious maneuverings and manipulations.

Unfortunately, however, Trollope's independence of the tradition does not extend beyond the main plot. In *The Last Chronicle*, which should have been one of the triumphs of the novel, the patiently accumulated effects are scattered by the introduction of three separate sub-plots, only one of which has any relevancy or interest. Collectively they tend to disperse the emotion that gathers sympathetically around the figure of Josiah Crawley, the tragic hero whose fatal flaw is pride of self. In *Orley Farm* one's attention is constantly diverted, by a series of minor characters and issues, from the only matter of importance, the wretchedness of Lady Mason, the tragic heroine whose fatal flaw is ambition for her son. It is not germane to the issue that we should be made intimate with the economy of Groby Park, the legal reformations of Von Bauhr, or the marital hesitancies of John Kenneby. All this is egregious make-weight, as are the four chapters describing the Christmas festivities at Harley Street, Noningsby, Groby Park, and Great St. Helens.

A splinter of plot which calls for fuller comment is the episode (and its many ramifications) of Mr. Moulder, Mr. Kantwise, and the commercial gentlemen of the Bull Inn. The Victorian stereotype demanded that a somber story be offset by a certain amount of high jinks. Trollope does not always oblige, but here, having pulled pretty heavily on the tragic bow, he let fly a shower of arrows from a lighter weapon. The tyrannical Mr. Moulder, baiting Samuel Dockwrath over the wine bill, and entertaining his dinner guests with affecting recollections of his father's early apoplexy, is a lively sketch, as is Mr. Kantwise, the traveling salesman for the Iron Furniture Co., specializing in designs of the Louis Quatorze pattern. Trollope was pleased with what he had done ("Mr. Moulder carves his turkey admirably, and Mr. Kantwise sells his tables and chairs with spirit"), and indeed Dickensian ghosts are raised in a very substantial form. But the pungent air of warehouse and pub which clings to these amusing vulgarians has offended some delicate critical sensibilities. George Eliot, who thought Trollope "admirable in the presentation of even average life and character," wrote Sara Hennell that she liked *Orley Farm* very much, "with the exception of such parts as I have read about Moulder & Co." She does not much further the cause of realism when she adds, "he [Trollope] is so thoroughly wholesome-minded that one delights in seeing his books lie about to be read."

More important than the clutch of commercial gentlemen and their relatives, who in no way forward any issue of importance, are the Staveleys and the Furnivals. Madeline Staveley, together with her suitors Felix Graham and Peregrine Orme, represents Trollope's reluctant acquiescence in the stereotype of the Victorian love story. There is no doubt a large measure of irony in Trollope's statement that Madeline "shall, to many of my readers, be the most interesting personage in this story." The heroine, he had acknowledged earlier, must "by a certain fixed law be young and marriageable." Lady Mason, of course, could not qualify. Yet in the final chapter, as he bids farewell to Lady Mason, he admits, "as we do so the chief interest of our tale will end." Clearly, therefore, the love story is for those who must have it, not for Anthony Trollope.

The participants in this sentimental drama act out another Victorian cliché. Felix Graham is represented as a brilliant young lawyer who writes for the literary reviews. But his family is unknown, he has no funds, he is ugly, and he has contracted a quixotic engagement with the unimaginative daughter of a sniveling alcoholic. These things mean nothing to

Madeline, who, burning with true love, rejects the addresses of Peregrine Orme, a suitable young man and her mother's favorite. Felix is the familiar Trollopian hero who with no other gift than mother wit triumphs over his more favored rival. As for Madeline, she is the apotheosis of the Victorian heroine: demure and self-effacing, yet warm and loyal. Unfortunately, however, she is dull. But the self-seeking Sophia Furnival, set up as foil to Madeline, is lively and amusing. By his allegiance to the formula Trollope very nearly forfeits sympathy for his sweet but rather colorless heroine. Sophia's father, as Lady Mason's chief legal adviser, has his necessary place in the general framework, but his domestic misunderstandings and the intrusions of the officious Miss Biggs are the most obvious filler. In such a novel as *Orley Farm*, which is the story of Lady Mason, nothing should have been permitted to deflect attention from her bitter problem. But Trollope fractioned his plot in deference to the Victorian stereotype of the huge, baggy monster. The inexorable demand for three volumes could not be refused, and the temper and experience of the reading public, still largely feminine and clerical, did not permit the close situational studies through which James imposed order on chaos.

As a realist and anti-sensationalist, Trollope cared so little for details of plotting that he appears to have relied not on design but on the inspiration of the moment to carry him over difficulties. Even in so extraordinary a circumstance as the stealing of the Eustace diamonds there seems to have been no forethought. It is significant that the fragmentary outlines from which Trollope worked when engaged on a novel consist only of thumbnail sketches of the characters. Once launched, they were expected to create by the expression of their own personalities such movement of the plot as might be required. Uncommitted by necessities of plotting, Trollope was free to let his characters develop naturally, and to bend in response to the pressure of people and events. Indeed, his own attitude toward them remained flexible. One of the most extraordinary confessions in fiction must be Trollope's admission in the last pages of *Orley Farm* that in the telling of his story his concept of his central character had undergone a radical change.

Trollope's concern in *Orley Farm*, and in others of his most thoughtful novels, is not with what happens but with its effect upon the individuals most directly involved. Thus, in *The Warden–Barchester Towers* (it is useful to think of them as a single novel) Trollope interests himself in the analysis of a situation: the effect upon Septimus Harding, a man of impeccable honor, of the suggestion that his tenure of a sinecure is ethically indefensible. In *The Last Chronicle* it is the effect upon the Reverend Josiah Crawley, a man of stern, almost forbidding, rectitude, of the charge that he has stolen a sizable cheque. In *Orley Farm* it is the effect upon Lady Mason, an essentially good, if misguided, woman, of the growing certainty that she has ruined not only her own life but, more importantly, that of her son.

The three characters just named are, in my opinion, the best that Trollope created. By "best" I mean, of course, not the most colorful or most amusing or most ingratiating, but those through whom he got beneath the topsoil of superficial manners to the bedrock of fundamental human emotions. It should be noted that one is an old man and the other two are middle-aged. When Trollope broke through the stereotype love story, he did his most significant writing. It is quite possible, of course, to probe deeply into man's basic responses through the study of young love. We learn much of what is fundamental in human nature by observing Elizabeth Bennet's discovery of her lesser self, Maggie Tulliver's lack of perfect self-discipline, Marty South's unwavering devotion in the face of neglect. But Trollope's young people take us into no new areas of self-knowledge, nor is it through them that he tries to enlarge the boundaries of man's sympathies.

Such sharpened perceptions as Trollope can give us of the dignity and the power of life, of its abnegations and renunciations, its terrors and humiliations, come through characters of mature years. The drama of young love did not move him greatly. His own life in this regard seems to have been singularly equable and serene. There is no evidence that he experienced either the ecstasy or the anguish of love. A realist who neither depreciated nor deified women, he wasted no emotion in Shelleyan longing for the unattainable. He preferred a plain girl of common sense to one of supernal beauty who was, to use his favorite adjective, "strong-minded." However wise such views may be, they do not suggest that the possessor will satisfy the taste for romance which largely determined the nature of the mid-Victorian novel. Trollope's observations of what is significant in life simply did not frame themselves in terms of young love.

It should also be remarked that Trollope came to the novel relatively late, with settled, middle-aged views of the decorum of life and of its ultimate values. *Orley Farm* is an early Trollope novel, but it was written in the author's forty-sixth year. In it there is a passage which beautifully exemplifies the harmony and composure of his life at this time, and emphasizes his conviction that while youth is beset with uncertainties and old age with infirmities, middle-age is ripe and golden.

There is great doubt as to what may be the most enviable time of life with a man. I am inclined to think that it is at that period when his children have all been born but have not yet begun to go astray or to vex him with disappointment; when his own pecuniary prospects are settled, and he knows pretty well what his tether will allow him; when the appetite is still good and the digestive organs at their full power; when he has ceased to care as to the length of his girdle, and before the doctor warns him against solid breakfasts and port wine after dinner; when his affectations are over and his infirmities have not yet come upon him; while he can still walk his ten miles, and feel some little pride in being able to do so; while he has still nerve to ride his horse to hounds, and can look with some scorn on the ignorance of younger men who have hardly yet learned that noble art. (Ch. LIX)

These are the sentiments of a man who will not put his heart into a recital of the charms of romantic love but who may illuminate sympathetically and understandingly the psychology of maturity.

Lady Mason, in whom is reflected the intensity with which the older characters are perceived, is one of the triumphs of Trollope's art, and one of the most moving characters of Victorian fiction. She is a forger, and has carried the gnawing secret of her guilt for twenty years, yet she is a good woman. The nature of the circumstances under which the crime was committed are such that only the sternest moralist would turn his face from Lady Mason, and only the most bitterly vindictive would pursue her with retributive justice. Sir Joseph Mason cared little for his wife and nothing for his younger son, for whom he refused to make provision in his will. Lady Mason's act, therefore, in protecting the legitimate rights and interests of her child, enforces rather than violates the equities involved. Trollope further establishes sympathy for his embattled heroine by ranging against her a set of despicable antagonists: Joseph Mason of Groby Park, a shallow man without sensibility, sourly nursing his grievances over the years (Trollope calls him "a bad man in that he could never forget and never forgave"); and Samuel Dockwrath, a prideful country lawyer, narrowly self-seeking, repudiating the friendly instincts of his wife in the pursuit of a petty revenge. The lines of antagonism are well drawn here, and the moral issue is an engaging one.

Ultimately, the law declares Lady Mason "Not Guilty." But there are few, even among outsiders, who do not regard the verdict as a Scottish "Not Proved." The bullying of the skillful Chaffanbrass and the eloquence of Mr. Furnival have carried everything before them. As for the wretched victim, she has not escaped, and the laws of compensation have not been abrogated. The devoted but misguided mother, who has risked all for a son who turns out to be a rather objectionable prig, opinionated and willful, suffers on earth the tortures that are promised the erring in hell. Trollope never loses his firm hold upon character and situation, nor does he fail to engage our sympathies powerfully on behalf of his very human protagonist.

The extent to which Trollope succeeds in immersing his readers in Lady Mason's shattered life is measured by the credibility of the love between her and Sir Peregrine Orme. The relationship between the gallant old gentleman (whose characterization owes something to Colonel Newcome?) and the by no means young widow was fraught artistically with the gravest perils. One false word and the whole structure of this pathetic affair would come tumbling down. The word is not given, and the dignity of the episode is preserved. Though Lady Mason recognizes that the unimpeachable honor of Sir Peregrine's name will provide her with the sheet anchor of support she desperately needs, she cannot at last sacrifice the old man. Instead, she sacrifices herself — and all she has fought for — by confessing. It is not simply a theatrical gesture, it is a total relinquishment, placed on the altar of affection and respect by nobility. The moment of her confession is conceived with great art and executed with a sensitiveness and balance that is quite beyond praise.

Two scenes following upon Lady Mason's confession indicate the power that Trollope has when he meets an emotional situation squarely and the depth of his failure when he avoids it or passes it off conventionally. When Lady Mason leaves Sir Peregrine, knowing that she has sealed her future in the blackness of disgrace and irrevocable misery, she retires to her room at his suggestion and sitting on the bed, her teeth chattering both from the bitter midwinter cold and from nervous exhaustion, casts up the self-abasements of a future irredeemably desolate. The many critics, Victorian and modern, who have charged against Trollope the inability to picture tragedy without shrillness or calculated sentiment, have forgotten this terrible scene. Yet after such an artistic triumph Trollope contrives a moment later that Lady Mason should be visited by Edith Orme, who offers a few words of consolation and forgiveness.

> Many will think that she was wrong to do so, and I fear it must be acknowledged that she was not strong minded. By forgiving her I do not mean that she pronounced absolution for the sin of past years, or that she endeavoured to make the sinner think that she was no worse for her sin. Mrs. Orme was a good churchwoman but not strong, individually, in points of doctrine. All that she left mainly to the woman's conscience and her own dealings with her Saviour, — merely saying a word of salutary counsel as to a certain spiritual pastor who might be of aid. (Ch. XLV)

This is disappointing. Trollope has shirked his task, first by giving us through summary a scene that should have been dramatic, and second, by straddling the moral problem. The truth is, of course, that Trollope had no consistent view of his character. Lady Mason was never intended to be evil, but there is an evident change after her guilt is established that cannot be accounted for solely in terms of the deepening of her nature. The change is in Trollope's attitude toward her. Hester Prynne is shown to have become through her sin more thoughtful, more tolerant, more spiritual. Lady Mason's character, however, is relatively constant. Trollope has led us to a kindlier view because he has himself become more sympathetic.

> I may, perhaps, be thought to owe an apology to my readers in that I have asked their sympathy for a woman who had so sinned as to have placed her beyond the general sympathy of the world at large. If so, I tender my apology, and perhaps feel that I should confess a fault. But as I have told her story that sympathy has grown upon myself till I have learned to forgive her, and to feel that I too could have regarded her as a friend. (Ch. LXXIX)

In the middle of the novel, however, he is not sure of Lady Mason. Consequently, he is careful to take the conventional ethical point of view.

It is highly probable that in the climactic scenes of Lady Mason's agony Trollope's mind reverted, consciously or unconsciously, to another notable moment of retribution. Unique among nineteenth-century novelists for his knowledge of the old drama, Trollope was one of England's keenest amateur students of the Elizabethan and Jacobean theater. He had a first-rate collection of the period's best plays, 257 of which he annotated with critical remarks, still unfortunately unpublished. Among plays he read at least twice is Marlowe's *Doctor Faustus,* which seems to have cut deeply into his mind. Certainly there are more parallels between *Orley Farm* and *Doctor Faustus* than can be accounted for by mere coincidence. This is especially true of the final scenes of the novel, in which one hears palpable and extended echoes of Faustus's last agony and torment.

Both play and novel bring forward centrally a mature person whose essentially noble ambition is carried to criminal lengths: in Faustus the desire for mastery which comes through knowledge, in Lady Mason the world's recognition for her son. In both play and novel the author resorts to a curiously archaic mode of embodying the evil impulse to crime. Marlowe's tragedy is strongly reminiscent of the morality plays which flourished at least half a century before his time, and the bright figure of his Mephistopheles never quite conceals the standard primitive devil beneath. Trollope maintains a running current of stock devil imagery to express not only the evil of Lady Mason's deed but also the inevitability of its disclosure. Her mind runs to such images as that of "the beast [which] had set its foot upon her," and the archfiend is always appearing to her mind in a visible form:

> The black unwelcome guest . . . had ever been present to her; but she had seen it indistinctly, and now and then the power had been hers to close her eyes. Never again could she close them. Nearer to her, and still nearer, the spectre came; and now it sat upon her pillow, and put its claw upon her plate; it pressed her bosom with its fiendish strength, telling her that all was over for her in this world: — ay, and telling her worse even than that. (Ch. LIII)

Just as the forces of evil find in both works a symbolic expression, so do the forces of good: Lady Mason's staunch friend, Mrs. Orme, not less than Faustus's Good Angel, is an almost disembodied voice which cries, "Repent, repent, and be saved." The parallels extend even to small details. Just as the two greatest scenes of *Doctor Faustus* take place in the darkness of night, so do most of the scenes of Lady Mason's crime and punishment. Just as Faustus's impulse to the crime finds culminating expression in the signing of the bond, so Lady Mason's impulse culminates in the signing of the will, and, as Trollope's plot unfolds, we see that Lady Mason, no less than Faustus himself, had signed with her heart's blood. Again, just as "for vaine pleasure of 24 yeares . . . Faustus lost eternall ioy and felicitee," so the period of Lady Mason's vain pleasure covered the same span: "She had lived in this house for some four-and-twenty years." It is significant that this figure rose to Trollope's mind as he was portraying one of the most horrible moments of Lady Mason's suffering, for he elsewhere makes it clear that actually only twenty years had elapsed between her forgery and the confession to her son.

Faustus's torment reaches its height in his unforgettable last speech, which apparently inspired Trollope in his moving portrayal of Lady Mason's almost unendurable agony.

There are [says Trollope] periods in the lives of some of us — I trust but of a few — when with the silent inner voice of suffering we call on the mountains to fall and crush us, and on the earth to gape open and take us in. (Ch. XLV)

Just so had Faustus cried:

> Mountaines and hilles, come, come and fall on me,
> And hide me from the heauy wrath of God.
> No, no.
> Then wil I headlong runne into the earth:
> Earth gape. O no, it wil not harbour me.

And Trollope continues:

When, with an agony of intensity, we wish that our mothers had been barren. In those moments, the poorest and most desolate are objects to us of envy, for their sufferings can be as nothing to our own.

So Faustus:

> This soule should flie from me, and I be changde
> Vnto some brutish beast: al beasts are happy,
> For when they die,
> Their soules are soone dissolud in elements,
> But mine must liue to be plagde in hel:
> Curst be the parents that ingendred me.

(For recognition and development of the *Orley Farm–Doctor Faustus* parallel I am indebted to my colleague Professor Hugh G. Dick of the University of California at Los Angeles.)

The moment toward which the action of *Orley Farm* moves is Lady Mason's trial. Since Trollope shares with Dickens and Wilkie Collins a vital interest in the law, frequently making legal matters of the greatest importance in the resolution of his plots, it may be appropriate here to consider the role of the lawyer in *Orley Farm* and, by way of comparison and contrast, in a few other novels. There are eleven jury trials in Trollope's novels, and, additionally, the interpretation of the law is a basic plot concern in *The Warden*, *Doctor Thorne*, *Is He Popenjoy?*, *Cousin Henry*, and, especially, *Mr. Scarborough's Family*. In none of these do the lawyers carry the burden of the main plot. Either through lack of acquaintance with the legal mind and character (which considering Trollope's experience is not likely) or through a conviction that lawyers do not lend themselves well to the fictional purposes he favored, Trollope does not allow them to become the chief actors in the drama. Unlike his clergymen, they serve, in general, only "to swell a progress, start a scene or two."

One exception to the adjunctive role for the lawyer is the inimitable Mr. Chaffanbrass, who is more sharply conceived than any barrister in Dickens. Much has been written about the transcendent merits of Bardell *v.* Pickwick. To at least one observer the three court appearances of Mr. Chaffanbrass (in *The Three Clerks*, *Orley Farm*, and *Phineas Redux*) are in another and higher echelon of excellence. Trollope's characterization is here more subtle, his humor more pervasive. Chaffanbrass does not escape completely, perhaps, from the stereotype of the shrewd criminal lawyer whose inquisitorial deftness can break down in cross-examination the testimony of the most confident witness, but he is carefully individualized. The slovenly little figure in a rumpled suit, with wig askew, picking his teeth and taking large quantities of snuff remains a memorable characterization. Trollope satisfied himself with the laconic remark, "I do not think that I have cause to be ashamed of him."

There are a few other lawyers, as well, who escape being typed into familiar patterns: Thomas Furnival, dignified defender of Lady Mason, master of direct severity and concealed sarcasm; Samuel Camperdown, aggressive representative of the Eustace interests; Gregory Masters, devoted guardian of the Morton properties; Thomas Toogood, patient adviser to the exasperating Josiah Crawley; and John Grey, harassed attorney for the violent and unpredictable Mr. Scarborough. It might be difficult, however, to add appreciably to this list, even though the lawyers in Trollope's novels number well over one hundred. The frequency of their appearance indicates the delight which Trollope took in introducing them, but the vast majority shade off from indistinct background figures to mere names. These very names—Mr. Allewinde, John Cheekey, Neversay Die, Mr. Gitemthruit, Sir Abraham Haphazard, George Stickatit, *et al.*—make it clear that many, if not most, of the lawyers are conceived as humour characters, exploited for satiric, ironic, or humorous purposes. But the intense seriousness of the *Orley Farm* trial precludes Pickwickian high jinks of the Serjeant Buzfuz variety.

It is clear from several remarks in *Orley Farm* that Trollope was acutely aware of the chicanery of the law and inclined to emphasize what he thought to be a general opportunism and lack of idealism in the profession. Mr. Furnival is represented as defending Lady Mason with eloquence and apparent sincerity:

> And yet as he sat down he knew that she had been guilty! To his ear her guilt had never been confessed; but yet he knew that it was so, and, knowing that, he had been able to speak as though her innocence were a thing of course. That those witnesses had spoken truth he also knew, and yet he had been able to hold them up to the execration of all around them as though they had committed the worst of crimes from the foulest of motives! And more than this, stranger than this, worse than this, — when the legal world knew — as the legal world soon did know — that all this had been so, the legal world found no fault with Mr. Furnival, conceiving that he had done his duty by his client in a manner becoming an English barrister and an English gentleman. (Ch. LXXII)

Earlier Trollope had observed: "I cannot understand how any gentleman can be willing to use his intellect for the propagation of untruth, and to be paid for so using it." Mr. Furnival was, of course, no shyster, but the legal fraternity, by and large, is not attractively presented by Trollope. The unprincipled Hyacinth Keegan, the unspeakable Moylan, the scheming Samuel Dockwrath, the mean-looking Squercum, the grasping Scruby — these are disagreeable people. If it be objected that it is unfair to assume Trollope's judgment of a group on the basis of its renegades, one must answer that among a hundred lawyers there is not one of such large-souled benevolence that he can be taken to one's heart. In *Orley Farm* only Judge Staveley, who does not appear in his legal capacity, and Felix Graham, who is shown to be a frustrated man of letters, are presented sympathetically.

The issues involved in Lady Mason's trial are so grave, and the scenes are described with such patient care, that critics have taken the legal action very seriously. The early reviews were very hard on Trollope for alleged misunderstanding of judicial procedures, and the substance of these attacks was repeated and developed in *Out of Court* (1925), a volume of essays by the distinguished jurist Sir Francis Newbolt, whose caustic remarks have been faithfully repeated by all subsequent critics. In the last few years, however, two American lawyers have come stoutly to Trollope's defense. Henry S. Drinker in "The Lawyers of Anthony Trollope" says, "Numerous strictures on its legal accuracy to the contrary notwithstanding, *Orley Farm* will be found, on careful examination, to be remarkably free from legal mistakes, except for occasional slips in small matters purely technical, such as would naturally be expected and are readily excusable in a novelist." Clement F. Robinson in "Trollope's Jury Trials" studies the proceedings at length and concludes:

Looking at the report of Lady Mason's case as a whole, I should say that it is more accurate than the usual newspaper account of a trial. . . . I am impressed with the few errors that Trollope seems to have made in English procedure, and am inclined to believe that the trial might have taken place in the United States just as Trollope reports it, except in a few minor respects.

Two Harvard law professors, the late Zechariah Chafee, Jr. and John M. Maguire, chose *Orley Farm* as one of ninety books to be read by all law students, recommending it as "a will case with a notable cross-examination."

Orley Farm is a characteristic Victorian novel. Its many-faceted plot is kept more rigorously under control than is traditional, and the tensions of the principal action are maintained with what is, for Trollope, unaccustomed tautness. The problem considered is worthy of a serious artist, and its resolution develops expectancy and invokes pity. If, as I believe, *The Last Chronicle* is a more satisfactory performance, the measure of its superiority must be sought in its leading character. *Orley Farm* fails, in part, because there is no greatness in Lady Mason. Her strength, and it is considerable, is exerted in support of a morally indefensible position. Her moment of renunciation is bitter indeed, but the pity she arouses is tempered by a recognition of her palpable weakness. Josiah Crawley, by contrast, though foundering in his social relationships because of grievous personality faults, has a nobility of soul that makes him a genuinely and impressively tragic figure. But the plot of *The Last Chronicle* is flawed beyond redemption. Each of these two novels, then, has what the other lacks; and Trollope, unable to bring all his powers to a focus in a single novel, left no perfect work of art.

Henry James has told us that a superior novel can be produced only by a fine intelligence, and the point is not likely to be disputed. At this level of criticism, perhaps, the case for Trollope breaks down. He was shrewd, observant, humorous, kindly, tolerant, sympathetic — a man of uncommon common sense; but his mind was not subtle or profoundly creative. That inability to make fine distinctions with which some of his contemporaries charged him was part of a nature not gifted philosophically. The highest reaches of the novel were thus denied him. But still open was a middle ground in which his lively imagination could function effectively. Here, as a home base, he pitched his tent firmly; and striking out across green meadows he wandered into Barsetshire. In *Orley Farm*, still avoiding main-traveled roads, he idled happily among some of the most fascinating people in English fiction.

ANTHONY TROLLOPE: THE PALLISER NOVELS

Arthur Mizener
CORNELL UNIVERSITY

"I should like of all things to see a ghost, and if one would come and have it out with me on the square I think it would add vastly to my interest in life."
Trollope to Kate Field, June 3, 1868

In a well-known passage in the *Autobiography*, Trollope says that he early made up his mind that *Pride and Prejudice* was the best novel in the English language, and if he later discovered in *Ivanhoe* and *Esmond* competitors for that title, his original choice still defines the general character of his sensibility. He did not, however, so much write novels as live with characters, and as a consequence, his powers are best seen in groups of books which deal with the same set of characters. It is customary to consider the Barset novels for this purpose, and there is much to be said for doing so, but the Barset novels come at the beginning of Trollope's career, and there is something also to be said for considering the Palliser novels, which begin with *Can You Forgive Her?*, written in 1864, three years before the last of the Barset novels, and end, five novels and sixteen years later, with *The Duke's Children.* Of the leading characters in these novels Trollope said in the *Autobiography* that "by no amount of description or asseveration could I succeed in making any reader understand how much these characters with their belongings have been to me in my latter life." Characteristically, however, he is not at all sure that this intensity of imagination is not merely a private foible unlikely to be shared by his readers. "Who will read *Can You Forgive Her?*, *Phineas Finn*, *Phineas Redux*, and *The Prime Minister* [*The Duke's Children* is omitted from this list because it was written after the *Autobiography*] consecutively in order that they may understand the characters of the Duke of Omnium, of Plantagenet Palliser, and Lady Glencora? . . . But in the performance of the work I had much gratification. . . ." Perhaps not many people will read these books consecutively; they constitute a large order, something over four thousand pages. But they offer the reader much gratification and are the richest source of evidence for a study of the kind of greatness Trollope had.

It is a kind of greatness that is not so easy to see as it used to be; all Trollope's most evident weaknesses are in those very aspects of the novel that we are now accustomed to scan most attentively and demand the most of. He confessed with almost ostentatious innocence that he scarcely ever knew how a novel was going to end when he started it (he even says of the detective-story plot of *The Eustace Diamonds* that "I had no idea of setting thieves after the bauble till I had got my heroine to bed in the inn at Carlisle"); he had so little interest in the delicate cabinet-making which fascinates artificers of the well-made novel that he hardly ever revised—seldom even read proofs with any care (a bad habit in which the publishers of most modern texts have followed him). What he was prone to boast of was that he never but once (twice including *The Landleaguers*, which was left unfinished at his death) allowed a word of a novel to be printed until it was finished, that he always fulfilled his contracts on the dot, that if his career had any interest it was as an example "of the opening which a literary career offers to men and women for the earning of their bread."

Trollope was able to talk this way seriously because in those respects in which he was a great novelist he was so easily and naturally one and did so much of the work of imagination when he was not at his writing desk that when he sat down he could clock his two hundred and fifty words every quarter of an hour without diminishing his power, just as Jane Austen could write her novels amid the buzz of conversation in that incredibly tiny drawing room. Moreover, Trollope was, so far as these gifts took him, a novelist of a remarkably pure kind. For better and—in a minor sense—for worse, his gifts were never blurred by elaborate ideas, either about The Form of the Novel or about The Nature of Life. Trollope had a certain number of opinions, or perhaps only prejudices, which were organic outgrowths of his direct observation of experience; but he had no ideas in the proper sense; he never reasoned abstractly with any great success. And, as his remarks in the *Autobiography* on his own books and those of others so often show, he hardly grasped with his abstract intelligence what these books were about. Another part of his mind, however, knew, incomparably, and sometimes we can catch glimpses of that other mind even in his exercises of reason—as when he says of Dickens that "it has been the peculiarity and the marvel of this man's power, that he has invested his puppets with a charm that has enabled him to dispense with human nature." But the wonderful nonratiocinative power of Trollope's mind is everywhere in his novels, which fail only in those respects in which success depends on reasoning.

About his limitations in these respects he always displayed that almost belligerent honesty of his on which critics of his novels have depended very heavily in defining their objections to his work. He thought of a plot as a piece of machinery, something that held together mechanically the incidents and characters, "the most insignificant part of a tale," as he called it frankly. As such it was something he was conscientious about, because he was proud to be a good craftsman, and he was always the first to point out the defects in his plot. He says in a letter to Mary Holmes that he thought *The Last Chronicle of Barset* was the best novel he had ever written, but he does not hesitate in the *Autobiography* to point out the defects of its plot. He confesses that when he became a practiced novelist he "abandoned the effort to think, trusting myself, with the narrowest thread of a plot, to work the matter out when the pen is in my hands," and he is frank to say that "I am not sure that the construction of a perfected plot has been at any period within my power."

But if the structures of his novels are seldom perfected, they are nonetheless a good deal finer than is usually allowed. The dangers of proceeding as he did are, of course, disproportion, lack of economy, and the risk that the story may shift direction as it goes along and find itself encumbered by awkward commitments. Trollope knew the dangers: "[*Phineas Finn*] is all fairly good, except the ending,—as to which till I got to it I had made no provision. As I fully intended to bring my hero again into the world, I was wrong to marry him to a simple pretty Irish girl, who could only be felt as an encumbrance on such return." Other instances are easy enough to point to. For example, in *The Last Chronicle of Barset*, we move naturally enough from our interest in Grace Crawley to Lily Dale and therefore to the old question of Johnny's wooing of Lily and thence to Johnny's battles with Sir Raffle Buffle. But the whole business of Mrs. Dobbs Broughton's domestic life and of her husband's business career is much too detailed for the slight connection it has to the main interest. But the very fact that Trollope usually started with a group of characters and a situation and without a predetermined plot means that he seldom imagined an event until he had fully imagined the movements of thought and feeling in the characters which produced the event; situations are seldom forced on characters by the exigencies of plot in Trollope, and this is a very considerable merit.

But Trollope not only failed to plan his story in detail; he was much addicted to the Victorian custom of starting several stories and running them alternately throughout a book. In this way, as it seems to many theoreticians, he maximized the opportunities for trouble. How are the narrative links between the plots to be established without awkwardness unless they are planned ahead? More important, how are the large meanings of the various plots to be related when Trollope's hit-and-miss method of composition is followed? But it is a fact that Trollope does link his plots and, in his quiet and unsymbolic way, play their meanings off against one another. *The Prime Minister*, for example, has, if not three plots, at least three centers of action. There are the Duke and Duchess of Omnium, with their great houses in Carleton Gardens and at Matching and Gatherum, where the political and social life of the great world is lived. There are the Whartons, in Manchester Square and at Wharton, intermarried with the Fletchers at Longbarns, living their lives of country gentility and legal dignity. There is Ferdinand Lopez, floating commercially and socially from his very temporary flat in Westminster to Sexty Parker's office in Little Tankard Yard and thence to the Progress. They are all interlocked in a hundred ways, by Lopez's marriage to Emily, by the Duchess's taking up Lopez and persuading him to contest Silverbridge, where Arthur Fletcher runs, and so on. Each of these is an independent world with its own integrity, and we know each thoroughly, from inside. But they are nonetheless not only related in hundreds of ways but often parallel in character. Trollope had an extremely sharp eye for social differences; perhaps no English novelist has had a sharper one. But he knew very well that vanity, fear, and lust, unselfishness, courage, and love, are much the same everywhere. It is, for example, perfectly obvious that Abel Wharton and the Duke think and act alike time after time, that Emily and the Duchess fail in similar feminine ways—and so succeed, too, that Lopez having a dinner brought into Manchester Square from Stewam and Sugarscraps in Wigmore Street has his resemblance to the Duchess preparing for her entertainment at Gatherum, and that Emily's horror at the ostentatious falseness of Lopez's dinner is not unlike the Duke's sense that the entertainment at Gatherum is vulgar. It would not be easy to exhaust the parallels of this kind in any good Trollope novel; they are an important part of what the multiple plot structure exists for.

But Trollope was convinced that plot construction was a secondary matter. The main task of the novelist, he thought, was to make "the creations of his brain . . . speaking, moving" and therefore "living, human creatures" for the reader. Though he put his famous remark about Mrs. Proudie in his usual way, almost as if he were making ironic fun of himself for a silly habit, Trollope was telling the main secret of his art when he said in the *Autobiography* that "I have never dissevered myself from Mrs. Proudie, and still live much in company with her ghost." This was ten years after he had written the last word about Mrs. Proudie. As he says in the *Autobiography*, "I have been impregnated with my own creations till it has been my only excitement to sit with the pen in my hand, and drive my team before me at as quick a pace as I could make them travel."

It is easy, much too easy if one wishes to convey the full impressiveness of the achieved thing, to generalize the sources of the kind of understanding Trollope possessed. He was, in the first place, an indefatigable and inexhaustibly fascinated observer; one of his Irish friends once told Escott that Trollope's "close looking into the commonest objects of daily life always reminded her of a woman in a shop examining the materials for a new dress." The figure is admirable, because Trollope's kind of observation is an act of the imagination, charged with the excitement and the delight of the thing apprehended. In a way very characteristic of him, he used what he saw of the commonest objects of daily life modestly and quietly in his novels, with an almost perfect sense of when they were relevant to the wholeness of the reader's vision of the action. That is, he used objects, not for themselves, but as integral parts of the action. He seldom indulged in the vanity of being tricky about how he introduced such objects, but their force can be very subtle. Thus, when Phineas Finn meets Lady Laura above the falls at Loughlinter, Trollope gives us a straightforward description of how he was dressed: "At the present moment he had on his head a Scotch cap with a grouse's feather in it, and he was dressed in a velvet shooting-jacket and dark knickerbockers." But the point of introducing these particulars is not so simple. This is not Trollope telling us what Phineas looked like for the sake of the fact. He goes on, "He was certainly, in this costume, as handsome a man as any woman would wish to see." For a woman is seeing him, a woman who is going to love him all her life, and whose tragedy is that at this moment she does not even suspect that she cannot conquer her love for him and marry prudentially. This image of Phineas, with his beauty and his air of breeding, will haunt

Lady Laura's imagination always; if we are to feel exactly what she felt, we must see exactly what she saw. After Mr. Wharton told Arthur Fletcher that he would probably have to yield to Emily's wish to marry Lopez, Arthur "sat himself down on the river's side and began to pitch stones off the path in among the rocks, among which at that spot the water made its way rapidly." Arthur Fletcher will always remember how the water flowed over those rocks, as Trollope will. "*Barchester Towers*," Trollope once remarked to Arthur Tilley, "was written before you were born. Of course I forget every word of it! But I don't. . . . I always pretend to forget when people talk to me about my own old books. It looks modest. . . . But the writer never forgets." Certainly Trollope did not, because he had always been there before he wrote about it.

Ullathorne Court will be described to us in detail, for it is alive with the innocent passion for blue blood which guides the Squire of St. Ewold's and is his sister's "favorite insanity." But the home of that truly insane man, Mr. Kennedy, will never be more for us than a set of "Ionic columns" through which one passes "to the broad stone terrace before the door," because nothing really lives there. With Trollope's characters we always move through the space defined by their consciousnesses; we "cross from Regent Street through Hanover Square, and [come] out *by the iron gate* into Oxford Street."

This fine imaginative sense of material objects is particularly evident where Trollope wishes to convey emotion, especially if the emotion is artificial or if Trollope, though sympathetic, finds it extravagant. Thus, when the moneylender, Mr. Clarkson, attempts to collect from Phineas on Laurence Fitzgibbon's bill, Phineas says,

> "I can pay no part of that bill, Mr. Clarkson."
> "Pay no part of it!" and Mr. Clarkson, in order that he might the better express his surprise, arrested his hand in the very act of poking his host's fire.

When Mr. Chaffanbrass is accused by Sir Gregory of having "indiscreetly questioned" a witness, he

> would not for a moment admit the indiscretion, but bounced about in his place, tearing his wig almost off his head, and defying everyone in Court. . . . The judge looking over his spectacles said a mild word about the profession at large. Mr. Chaffanbrass, twisting his wig quite on one side, so that it nearly fell on Mr. Sarjeant Birdbott's face, muttered something as to having seen more work done in that Court than any other living

lawyer, let his rank be what it might. When the little affair was over, everybody felt that Sir Gregory had been vanquished.

Like Mr. Clarkson, Mr. Chaffanbrass is putting on an act, though in each case the ultimate motive is quite serious, if less marked by moral dignity than the acted one.

When Tom Spooner proposed to Adelaide Palliser, he first sent back to Spoon Hall for a dark-blue frock-coat and a colored-silk handkerchief and brushed his hair down close to his head. When he proposed, Adelaide stopped short in the path in sheer astonishment and Tom Spooner "stood opposite to her, with his fingers inserted between the closed buttons of his frock-coat." After this Trollope has one of his beautiful, amused analyses of "why she should thus despise Mr. Spooner, while in her heart of hearts she loved Gerald Maule."

All this takes great energy of invention, and it is not the least of Trollope's achievements that he created a host of characters, every one of whom lives a life which Trollope imagined fully and particularized in speech and gesture. About the least of them, he knows exactly the look and the tone, as he does, for instance, of Major Pountney when the Major is so ill-advised as to approach the Duke for his support in Silverbridge.

"I don't know when I have enjoyed myself so much altogether as I have at Gatherum Castle." The Duke bowed and made a little but vain effort to get on. "A splendid pile!" said the Major, stretching his hand gracefully toward the building.

"It is a big house," said the Duke.

Because Trollope was thus fascinated by and involved in the life he saw around him, he had what Mr. Cockshut has called an almost "universal pity." He always understood the workings of the minds of even his worst characters and saw how they justified themselves to themselves. He also always saw how comically self-regarding and therefore illogical even the best of his characters were. "It is amusing," as he once put it, characteristically of himself, "to watch how a passion will grow upon a man. During those two years it was the ambition of my life to cover the country with rural letter-carriers." It was a perfectly respectable ambition and Trollope took real delight in throwing himself into it with all his energy. But no one understood better than he how absurd he must look to the common sense of those who did not share his passion for so deliciously incongruous an object as covering "the country with rural letter-carriers."

This was the characteristic tone of his mind, as we can tell from his letters ("My lecture at Bury went off magnificently. I went there in a carriage with a marquis, who talked to me all the way about the state of his stomach — which was very grand") and by the way he treats his own favorite passions, such as hunting. The great question of Trumpington Wood is a constant concern in the Palliser novels. When Phineas arrives for a visit at Harrington Hall, Lord Chiltern barely has time to greet him because of it.

"Finn, how are you?" said Lord Chiltern, stretching out his left hand. "Glad to have you back again, and congratulate you about the seat. It was put down in red herring, and we found nearly a dozen of them afterwards, — enough to kill half the pack."

When fine points of the hunt are in question, your real devotee understands no other demands on his attention.

"I tell you she didn't. You weren't there, and you can't know. I'm sure it was a vixen by her running. We ought to have killed that fox, my Lord." Then Mrs. Spooner made her obeisance to her hostess. Perhaps she was rather slow in doing this, but the greatness of the subject had been the cause. These are matters so important, that the ordinary civilities of the world should not stand in their way.

Thus it was that Trollope understood how a passion, to say nothing of a habit of life or a fixed set of convictions, will grow on a man. When Trollope recalled his own belligerence with Hill at the Post Office, what he remembered was that

I never scrupled to point out the fatuity of the improper order in the strongest language I could decently employ. I have revelled in these official correspondences, and look back to some of them as among the greatest delights of my life. But I am not sure that they were so delightful to others.

One has only to turn the pages of the Geroulds' *Guide to Trollope* to be reminded of how many hundreds of characters he imagined with this kind of understanding.

But if there is almost universal sympathy in Trollope's imagination, there is also unremitting judgment, so that his sympathetic understanding of men's self-evaluation is always balanced by his clear awareness of how common sense will judge them. There is a delicacy in the ironic balance of these two kinds of perception in his work which it would be hard to exaggerate. It is what makes us understand that so likeable a young man as Silverbridge is limited and, indeed, weak. It is what shows us that so impossible a little man as Major Tifto is touching. When Tifto observes that " 'By George, there's Silverbridge has got his governer to dinner' . . . as though he were announcing some confusion of the heavens and earth" and thereupon, having fortified himself with two glasses of whisky-and-water, engages the Duke in conversation, calling him "my Lord Duke" or "your Grace" a dozen times in as many sentences, we are watching a close, external analysis of social uncertainty. But when Silverbridge, in his embarrassment, says, "Tifto, you are making an ass of yourself," and the little man exclaims in outrage and astonishment, "Making an ass of myself!" we are watching a human being.

The characters Trollope thought of most highly, like Plantagenet Palliser, have some awareness of the distortions of self-judgment. Similarly, a man like Mr. Crawley understands most of his own faults of character, often as he is defeated by them, as he typically is when he tries to tell himself that others have suffered more than he:

Of what sort had been the life of the man who had stood for years on the top of a pillar? But then the man on the pillar had been honoured by all around him. And thus, though he had thought of the man on the pillar to encourage himself by remembering how lamentable had been that man's sufferings, he came to reflect that after all his own sufferings were perhaps keener than those of the man on the pillar.

But it is fundamental with Trollope that even the best men are incapable of seeing themselves with perfect clarity, and one of the finest things he regularly does is to add just a shade of self-deception to otherwise admirable characters. Thus, for instance, Emily Wharton is an intelligent, considerate, honest girl. But there is in her just a touch of overassurance about the rightness of her own judgment. She has no such radical overconfidence as Alice Vavasor; nonetheless, her assurance is enough to lead her, against all advice, into her disastrous marriage with Lopez and — finest of all — to make her cling with just her shade of assurance to her later conviction — an essentially self-regarding conviction — that as Lopez's widow she is not good enough for Arthur Fletcher.

What Trollope took the greatest delight in observing was the way people's egos and self-interest would lead them quite sincerely to find arguments of principle for what passion or willful prejudice made them believe. Even his villains are only extreme cases of self-deception; so Lopez, "to give him his due, . . . did not know that he was a villain [and] conceived that he was grievously wronged by [Emily] in that she adhered to her father rather than to him." The openly comic version of this kind of self-deception is the man wholly absorbed by an obsession, as are Trollope's imperceptive lovers such as Tom Spooner, or Lord Popplecourt, or Dolly Longstaff when he woos Isabel Boncassen, or such people as Reginald Dobbes, to whom the hunting at Crummie-Toddie was everything in life and for whom "the beauty of the world would be over" if a railroad were run through that country. When Silverbridge elects to bring the young Gerald to hunt, "Boys who could not shoot were, he thought, putting themselves forward before their time."

But it is the way such self-deception will overwhelm normally shrewd people when self-interest is powerful that fascinates Trollope most, as when Lady Glencora learns that the old Duke wishes to marry Madam Max and thinks:

And to do this for a thin, black-browed, yellow-visaged woman with ringlets and devil's eyes, and a beard on her upper lip, — a Jewess, — a creature of whose habits of life and manners of thought they all were absolutely ignorant; who drank, possibly; who might have been a forger, for what anyone knew; an adventuress who had found her way into society by her art and perseverance, — and who did not even pretend to have a relation in the world!

All this is, of course, fantastically false or distorted; Madam Max will, indeed, presently become the only intimate friend Lady Glencora ever makes. But at the moment Lady Glencora fears the old Duke will marry Madam Max and perhaps have a son who will stand between the dukedom and her own son.

Characteristically, Trollope shows us the attitude of a character directly and balances it with the judgment of common sense by ironic overtone. Technically, he has two important ways of doing so, and he usually uses them together, as he does in the case of Mr. Spooner's proposal to Adelaide Palliser, which was discussed earlier. The first of these ways is to let us see and hear the character; the second is to offer us a summary of the thoughts which accompany the action. It is vital to Trollope's method that, however close he keeps to the original thoughts of the character, these passages should be given in summary, in his own words, because it is his own words which supply the balancing and ironic judgment of common sense. This is, of course, one of the major devices of Jane Austen's fiction, as the very famous first sentence of *Pride and Prejudice* is enough to show, and it is the reason why it is so disastrously wrong for critics to object out of hand to the intrusion of the novelist in a fiction. Of this method, Trollope was a great master.

The technical achievement of Trollope's novels consists in the right combination of this kind of summary with the direct presentation of action. One can see this technique in operation everywhere in his books; a small instance will illustrate its form. In *The Prime Minister*, Everett Wharton is presented as a pleasant young man who "lacked firmness of purpose."

He certainly was no fool. He had read much, and, though he generally forgot what he read, there were left with him from his readings certain nebulous lights, begotten by other men's thinking, which enabled him to talk on most subjects. It cannot be said of him that he did much thinking for himself; — but he thought that he thought.

When Everett, who naturally imagines himself perfectly equipped to be a member of Parliament, fails to persuade his father to spend the money necessary to elect him, he feels put upon. But when he learns that his friend Ferdinand Lopez is planning to run, he feels himself really injured. Trollope first lets us hear him on the subject:

"Upon my word I can't understand you." [he says to Lopez] "It was only the other day you were arguing in this very room as to the absurdity of a parliamentary career, — pitching into me, by George, like the very mischief, because I had said something in its favor, — and now you are going in for it yourself in some sort of mysterious way that a fellow can't understand." It was quite clear that Everett Wharton thought himself ill-used by his friend's success.

The characteristic touch here is Everett's wonderfully irrational feeling that the greatest offense is Lopez's "going in for it . . . in some sort of mysterious way that a fellow can't understand."

Having let us see and hear Everett, he then summarizes Everett's thoughts for us with his characteristic combination of sympathy and a sense of the absurd way that ego translates its needs into principles:

It was so hard that if a stray seat in Parliament were going a begging, it should be thrown in the way of this man who didn't care for it, and couldn't use it to any good purpose, instead of in his own way. Why should anyone want Ferdinand Lopez to be in Parliament? Ferdinand Lopez had paid no attention to the great political questions of the Commonwealth. He knew nothing of Labor and Capital, of Unions, Strikes, and Lock-outs. But because he was rich, and, by being rich, had made his way among great people, he was to have a seat in Parliament! . . . for the moment there came upon him a doubt whether Ferdinand was so very clever, or so peculiarly gentlemanlike or in any way very remarkable, and almost a conviction that he was very far from being good-looking.

It would be easy to write pages on how much Trollope's imagination has concentrated here, relatively small occasion though it is. It is Everett's weakness that he cannot see through Lopez's outward appearance of gentility and wealth, just as it is Mr. Wharton's weakness to be quite right about Lopez on completely irrational grounds. Lopez has got his chance at a seat by deceiving Lady Glencora as he has Everett and Emily, for he is in fact neither rich nor a gentleman. But if Everett's momentary conviction that he is Lopez's superior is quite right, it is so for reasons that have nothing to do with his judgment. His conviction of his peculiar competence for Parliament is a comic delusion, bred of a simple desire to have what he wants: "It was so hard" that some one else should have what he wanted. Yet Everett is a sympathetic character; Trollope never fails to show us the comic absurdity of such characters, but he never fails, either, to make us feel that we are very like them.

Nearly everything that is important in Trollope's plots is the working out of this kind of understanding — for example, the melodramatic career and ending of Ferdinand Lopez and the ironic but delightful conclusion which establishes Everett as Sir Alrud Wharton's heir. To see this is to measure the amount of self-depreciation in such remarks as Trollope's to Mary Holmes, that "I acknowledge the story of the soi-disant hero, Lopez, and all that has to do with him, to be bad."

It is this, too, that makes the "happy endings" for Trollope's lovers right, for they are, as Miss Brown puts it, "pledges . . . to life, whose demands they have learned to accept, or to their own integrity which events have taught them to honour." But Trollope is always at pains to show them making these pledges within the necessary limits of their natures. How perfectly right in its stupidity and pathos is Mr. Arabin's unfortunate allusion to Mr. Slope when he first attempts to propose to Eleanor Bold, and how rightly imagined are both her knowledge that he loves her and her irritation. How exactly adjusted to every shade of his character is Chiltern's reply when Phineas congratulates him on his engagement to Violet Effingham after his long and impetuous wooing:

"And is it to be in a month, Chiltern?" said Phineas.

"She says so. She arranges everything, — in concert with my father. When I threw up the sponge, I simply asked for a long day. 'A long day, my lord,' I said. But my father and Violet between them refused me any mercy."

"You do not believe him," said Violet.

"Not a word. If I did he would want to see me on the coast of Flanders again, I don't doubt."

How precisely imagined is the moment when the Duchess comes in just as Phineas has proposed to Madam Max and Madam Max allows herself almost the only fling of extravagant gaiety she ever indulges in and says to the Duchess, "I couldn't refuse Mr. Finn a little thing like that." What Trollope said modestly of Mrs. Proudie, that he had a "thorough . . . knowledge of all the little shades of her character," is true of all his characters, and the knowledge is a positive thing, a power of imaginative invention, not simply a negative power of consistency.

Trollope was, to borrow from Sadleir a figure which was also a fact, a clumsy rider who had "hands." He knew his characters intimately and he guided them very delicately. As long as he was telling what one of his fully imagined characters was thinking, he displayed an astonishing insight. Old Trollope, as Froude said in some irritation (Trollope beat him to the punch with a book on Africa), went banging about the world, but he never missed anything and his imagination was always tirelessly at work, so that both the inner and the outer natures of his characters were "clear to me as are the stars on a summer night." A London hostess once said to Trollope, "How do you know what we women say to each other when we get alone in our room?" But Trollope always knew this kind of thing.

Of all the characters Trollope created, the ones he lived with longest and who, as ghosts, had it out with him most on the square were the characters in the five Palliser novels, and especially Plantagenet Palliser and Lady Glencora. He thought Plantagenet Palliser "a very noble gentleman," as indeed he is. Who but a great gentleman could have sacrificed himself as he does when he takes his wife abroad; who could have apologized as he does to Mrs. Finn; who else could have dealt so gallantly at the Beargarden with the embarrassment of his meetings with Tregear and Tifto? Who—for all his stiffness—could have so beautifully expressed his love for his wife, his sons, his daughter? Of Lady Glencora, Trollope said, "She is by no means a perfect lady;—but if she be not all over woman, then I am not able to describe a woman."

It is very wonderful how Trollope can show us what he means by Lady Glencora's being all over woman. She fights her battles against Plantagenet's ignorance of her feelings and his sisters' advice with heroic energy and gets herself firmly fixed in a hopeless muddle of mistaken beliefs that she is not going to give the Pallisers an heir and might therefore just as well run off with Burgo Fitzgerald. She fights Plantagenet with a flouncing outrageousness which is nevertheless essentially right.

"My belief is that [Mrs. Marsham] follows me about to tell you if she thinks that I do wrong."

"Glencora!"

"And that odious baboon [Mr. Bott] with the red bristles does the same thing, only he goes to her because he doesn't dare go to you."

Nor does she ever forget or forgive. Months later, when the word reaches them at Basle of the new elections, Plantagenet says in a melancholy way, "another of my friends in the House has been thrown out."

"Who is that unfortunate?" asked Lady Glencora.

"Mr. Bott," said the unthinking husband.

"Mr. Bott out!" exclaimed Lady Glencora, "Mr. Bott thrown out! I am so glad. Alice, are you not glad? The red-haired man, that used to stand about, you know, at Matching;—he has lost his seat in Parliament. I suppose he'll go and stand about somewhere in Lancashire."

Whenever Plantagenet seeks to remonstrate with her, she says some such thing as, "I don't want to stop you, Plantagenet. Pray, go on. Only it will be so nice to have it over." Plantagenet's reasonableness only strikes her as a disregard of her feelings and makes her more trying.

Alice was glad to find [from Mr. Palliser] that a hundred and fifty thousand female operatives were employed in Paris, while Lady Glencora said it was a great shame, and that they ought all to have husbands. When Mr. Palliser explained that this was impossible, because of the redundancy of the female population, she angered him very much by asserting that she saw a great many men walking about who, she was quite sure, had not wives of their own.

When she becomes pregnant and is otherwise quite happy, she is driven nearly frantic by the solicitude of her ludicrously anxious husband. "I wish I had never told him a word about it," she said afterwards to Alice. "He could never have found it out himself, till this thing was all over."

These are the wife and husband who, after maturing in *Phineas Finn* and *Phineas Redux,* move front stage again in *The Prime Minister*. Lady Glencora, now the Duchess, still has her nimble and often outrageous wit, but she has matured. There is a faint touch almost of hardness about her, and she is still incapable of admitting steadily what she can sometimes see, that what she wants her husband to want is only what she wants. Here the serious aspect of Trollope's irony is at its best. The Duke, with his almost feminine sensitivity and his agonized pride, is always trying to make the Duchess understand his motives,

but he had come to fear that they were and must be ever unintelligible to her. But he credited her with less than her real intelligence. She did understand the nature of his work and his reasons for doing it; and, after her own fashion, did what she conceived to be her own work in endeavouring to create within his bosom a desire for higher things.

After this wonderful movement of self-deception, having sulked briefly because the Duke will not make his own wife Mistress of the Robes, she sets out to solidify the Duke's ministry by entertaining lavishly. It might have worked, for the Duchess has great energy and a good deal of skill. But not being a perfect lady, she cannot resist making ill-timed jokes about the ministry to the assembled company at Gatherum; she will plant her heels about having Sir Orlando to her parties and thus contributes materially to his resignation; she cannot quite resist the temptation to say something to Mr. Sprugeon about Lopez's candidacy, despite the Duke's express commands to the contrary. Even these things might not have been fatal had the Duke had a tougher skin. He is essentially right about the vulgarity of the "assumed and preposterous grandeur [of the entertainment at Gatherum] that was as much within the reach of some rich swindler or of some prosperous haberdasher as of himself," but he is too sensitive about it. He is surely right that the Duchess ought never to have laid him open to Quintus Slide's attack on him about Lopez's candidacy and the payment of five hundred pounds, but he knows that Slide's attack is motivated largely by his refusal to invite Slide to Gatherum and he ought not to take it so to heart. If the Duchess was small-boy vengeful in her treatment of Sir Orlando, the Duke had already snubbed him with full ducal pride when Sir Orlando, at Gatherum, first proposed those four ironclads. And then there gradually creeps over him a pride in his position and a desire to cling to the position of Prime Minister. "He spends one quarter of an hour," as the Duchess says, "in thinking that as he is Prime Minister he will be Prime Minister down to his fingers' ends, and the next in resolving that he never ought to have been Prime Minister at all." For she understands everything about him:

To him a woman, particularly his own woman, is a thing so fine and so precious that the winds of heaven should hardly be allowed to blow upon her [some one ought to analyze Trollope's skill with Shakespearean echoes]. He cannot bear to think that people should even talk of his wife. And yet, Heaven knows, poor fellow, I have given people occasion enough to talk of me. . . . I could never tell him what I felt, — but I felt it.

She never can act with proper decorum because she is always carried away by her energy into asserting the half-truth that she does understand and that he does not, so that when he tries to remonstrate with her about the Lopez episode by saying that, though other men's wives may do foolish things, they never interfere in politics, she says to him with the immediate, almost child-like confidence of her short-run good sense,

"That's all you know about it, Plantagenet. Doesn't everybody know that Mrs. Daubney got Dr. MacFuzlem made a bishop, and that Mrs. Gresham got her husband to make that hazy speech about women's rights, so that nobody should know which way he meant to go? There are others just as bad as me, only I don't think they get blown up so much."

So they go on, loving one another at cross purposes, until even the Duke sees he must resign. But the Duchess, alternating between a conviction that he is being cowardly and an angry feeling that he has been betrayed in a most egregious fashion, cannot see it. When he soothes himself by a long talk with Phineas Finn on the theory of liberalism — one of Trollope's finest statements of his political creed — the Duchess cannot resist attacking him.

"Mr. Warburton has sent three messengers to demand your presence," said the Duchess, "and, as I live by bread, I believe that you and Mr. Finn have been amusing yourselves!"

"We have been talking politics," said the Duke.

"Of course. What other amusement was possible? But what business have you to indulge in idle talk when Mr. Warburton wants you in the library? There has come a box," she said, "big enough to contain the resignations of all the traitors of the party." This was strong language and the Duke frowned. . . .

No wonder she loves him and finds him hopelessly inept in all she counts important; no wonder he loves her and frowns on her.

Then the Duchess, having committed one more indiscretion by condoning the secret engagement of Lady Mary and Frank Tregear (because she remembers how she suffered when she was separated from Burgo Fitzgerald), dies, and the Duke is "as though a man should be suddenly called upon to live without hands or even arms." Like a set of firecrackers, the unsuitable engagements of his children explode around him, inducing the comedy of the Duke's inner struggle between his heroic sense of justice and his pride of rank. Remembering how his own Glencora had been separated from Burgo Fitzgerald, he tries his hand, with pathetic clumsiness, at arranging a marriage for Lady Mary with Lord Popplecourt, that foolish young man with the "good looks of that sort which recommend themselves to pastors and masters, to elders and betters." At the same time, not knowing that Silverbridge has asked Isabel Boncassen to marry him, he happily lectures her on the democracy of English society, pointing out to her the way in which "our peerage is being continually recruited from the ranks of the people." But in the end, because he is a just man, and Frank Tregear is a gentleman and Isabel not only a lady but perfectly suited to Silverbridge in her goodness of nature and even in her somewhat limited intellect, he comes around, and because he is a great gentleman, he comes around with his whole nature: "You shall be my own child, — as dear as my own," he says to Isabel, and we know he means it with all his heart. To be sure, as Silverbridge, with one of those flashes of shrewdness that characterize him, points out, "My belief is that he's almost as much in love with you as I am." For Isabel has her touches of Glencora, so that when the Duke says with his solemn dignity, "I almost forget my own boy's name because the practice has grown up of calling him by a title," Isabel says irrepressibly, "I am going to call him Abraham." More than anything else, perhaps, it is this that makes the Duke give her the ring the Duchess had always worn.

The action Trollope constructs around this central comic conflict is more perfectly integrated and is carried on with more comic energy than any other in the Palliser series, so that the book teems with life. "Have you ever read the novels of Anthony Trollope?" wrote Hawthorne. "They precisely suit my taste, — solid and substantial . . . and just as real as if some giant had hewn a great lump out of the earth and put it under a glass case, with all its inhabitants going about their daily business, and not suspecting that they were being made a show of." Characteristically, Trollope described this remark as "a piece of criticism which was written on me as a novelist by a brother novelist very much greater than myself."

GEORGE ELIOT'S ORIGINALS

Gordon S. Haight
YALE UNIVERSITY

THE passion for realism — as George Eliot defines it, "the faithful representing of commonplace things" — led the Victorians to strive in all the arts for meticulous imitation of original models. With Ruskin's approval the Pre-Raphaelite painters spent whole weeks rendering in photographic detail a brick wall, a weedy bank, or an old wagon. The novelists fell easily into the habit of transcribing particular scenes and characters from life. Though Dickens boasted of Boythorn as "a most exact portrait of Walter Savage Landor," he seemed surprised that Leigh Hunt was hurt by his equally unmistakable caricature as Skimpole, and was embarrassed when Mrs. Seymour Hill, a deformed manicurist, protested against his using her as Miss Mowcher. The emotional force of the early part of *David Copperfield* came largely from the painful memories of his own childhood woven into it. Thackeray too, as Professor Gordon Ray shows in *The Buried Life*, took characters from the members of his own family and others to whom he was bound by emotional ties. Trollope's *The Three Clerks*, Meredith's *Evan Harrington*, and Hardy's *A Pair of Blue Eyes* offer further examples of the practice. Nor was it an exclusively English phenomenon. Tolstoi and Dostoevski, George Sand and Balzac, most of the Continental novelists of the time, drew portraits of people they knew. "In the last analysis," Professor Ray declares, "all fiction is inevitably autobiographical, for no novelist can transcend the limits of his personality and experience."

George Eliot's fiction began with the description of episodes that had occurred in the neighborhood of Nuneaton during her girlhood. The original of Amos Barton, her first hero, was John Gwyther, the curate of her parish of Chilvers Coton, where through years of Sundays she had had ample opportunity to study him; she was seventeen in 1836 when his wife (the Milly Barton of the story) died. Like Amos, Mr. Gwyther also moved regretfully to the North, first to a dreary parish in Sheffield, and then to Fewston, Yorkshire, where he died in 1873. When the first part of "Amos

Barton" appeared in *Blackwood's Magazine* for January 1857, his eldest daughter Emma (the Patty of the story) asked him, "Who in the world could have written this—have you, Papa?" so certain was she that it was an episode from his life. Succeeding installments confirmed the opinion that it must have been written by some one intimate with him. The only person he could suspect was the Reverend William Hutchinson King, a former curate at Nuneaton, who figures in the story as Mr. Ely. And in 1859, when speculation about the identity of George Eliot still ran high, Mr. Gwyther asked Blackwood "to make my kind remembrances to our gratuitous Historian" and assure him that, "now the pain I felt at the first publication is past off—although I thought it unkind and taking a great liberty with a living Character—yet I fully forgive for old acquaintance sake. For we are as assured that I am intended by Amos Barton as I am of the Truth of any Fact soever." His curious letter illustrates the accuracy of George Eliot's description: like Amos's it was "not *very* ungrammatical." Twice Mr. Gwyther wrote "it was him" and then changed the offending pronoun to *he*.

George Eliot at once wrote a note of apology for *Blackwood's* to copy and send him:

> The author of the "Scenes of Clerical Life" and "Adam Bede" begs me to inform you that he is not the Rev. W. H. King, but a much younger person, who wrote "Amos Barton" under the impression that the clergyman whose long past trial suggested the groundwork of the story was no longer living, and that the incidents, not only through the license and necessities of artistic writing, but in consequence of the writer's imperfect knowledge, must have been so varied from the actual facts, that any one who discerned the core of truth must also recognize the large amount of arbitrary, imaginative addition.
>
> But for any annoyance, even though it may have been brief and not well-founded, which the appearance of the story may have caused Mr. Gwyther, the writer is sincerely sorry.

Mr. Gwyther was not the only one to confound the imaginative additions with the core of truth in "Amos Barton." Lists giving a key to all the characters mentioned were soon circulating about Warwickshire. In one or two of the less clearly defined minor figures they show some variation, but on at least a score of names there is complete unanimity. No one near Nuneaton could fail to see Mr. Newdigate in Mr. Oldinport, Mr. Harper in Mr. Farquhar, or Mr. Bellairs and Mr. Hake thinly disguised as Fellowes and Carpe.

For "Mr. Gilfil's Love-Story," the second of the *Scenes of Clerical Life*, George Eliot turned back to a generation she had never known. Sir Christopher Cheverel is based on things she had heard about old Sir Roger Newdigate (1719–1806), founder of the Newdigate Prize at Oxford, whose transformation of Arbury Hall from Elizabethan to magnificent Gothic antedated and in some ways surpassed Horace Walpole's better known alterations at Strawberry Hill. George Eliot had slight childhood recollection of the Reverend Bernard Gilpin Ebdell, the original of Mr. Gilfil, who was presented by the Crown in 1786 and lived on as Vicar of Chilvers Coton till she was nine years old; he had baptized her a week after her birth. His wife Sally Shilton had been (like Caterina) a protégée of Lady Newdigate, and died when George Eliot was only four. The outline of the story had been picked up from local legend, perhaps in the housekeeper's room at Arbury, and embellished with such romantic inventions as Caterina's Italian birth, her love affair with Sir Christopher's nephew and heir, and her early death a few months after marrying the faithful Mr. Gilfil. The original of Caterina lived to enjoy twenty-two years of matrimony.

For the third of the *Scenes*, "Janet's Repentance," George Eliot returned to events within her own memory. Janet Dempster is drawn from Mrs. Nancy Wallington Buchanan, whose mother owned the school in Nuneaton, where George Eliot boarded from 1828 to 1832. The central incident of the tale, the persecution of Mr. Tryan, records an actual experience of the Reverend John Edmund Jones, curate during most of those years at Stockingford (Paddiford) parish, where his earnest Evangelicalism provoked similar disorders. Mr. Tryan's chief tormentor is Janet's drunken husband Lawyer Dempster, who brutally mistreats her too and finally turns her out of doors in her nightdress. This violence is soon followed by his death in delirium tremens after he has been thrown from his carriage and broken his leg. Janet, who had taken to drink and been saved by Mr. Tryan, survives, wealthy and sober, to ease the decline of her rescuer, who soon dies of consumption.

The real facts in the case were somewhat different. When she married James Williams Buchanan in 1825, Nancy Wallington, then a teacher in her mother's school, was thought to have made a good match. Her husband was one of the leading lawyers of Nuneaton, the agent of several insurance companies, a trustee of the Leicester Turnpike Company, a man accustomed to lead — even in such misdirected affairs as ridiculing the innovations the Evangelicals had begun introducing into the Church, which as clerk of Nuneaton parish he felt it was his peculiar responsibility to oppose. There is no evidence that her marriage was particularly unhappy or that, like Janet, Mrs. Buchanan sought relief in the brandy bottle. After the death of Mr. Jones in December 1831 she had two children, one born in 1832, the other in 1834. She continued "in her usual busy style" to take an active part in civic affairs. When Queen Adelaide passed through Nuneaton in 1839 on her royal progress to Warwick Castle, we see Mrs. Buchanan rehearsing the children of the various schools to sing the national anthem in the market place. Soon after this great day she fell ill, and in July 1840 she died. A week later her husband suffered the accident that George Eliot inflicts on Mr. Dempster a decade earlier. The Coventry *Standard* says:

> J. W. Buchanan, Esq., solicitor, of Nuneaton, met with a severe accident last week. While driving towards Coventry, one of the wheels of his carriage came off, near the second milestone, and in dismounting he fell, and the vehicle passed over his legs, one of which sustained a compound fracture, and the other was severely lacerated. Mr. Ball, surgeon, of Foleshill, set the broken limb, and he was removed home, where he lies in a very precarious state. The circumstance is rendered more distressing by the decease of Mrs. Buchanan, who died after a short illness at Margate, on Sunday last. She will be a serious loss to her poorer townsfolk, to whom her kindness and charity were unlimited.

Unlike Lawyer Dempster, Mr. Buchanan recovered and survived his wife for nearly six years.

The blackened portrait of him in "Janet's Repentance" may perhaps be explained by the influence on George Eliot of Maria Lewis (1800?–87), principal governess at Mrs. Wallington's School. An Evangelical of the strictest sort, she inculcated in her impressionable ten-year-old pupil a painful piety that frowned on every kind of worldly amusement and dominated her mind for nearly a decade. Miss Lewis doubtless took the darkest view of Mr. Buchanan's "intemperance," which, in those heavy-drinking days, may have been nothing remarkable, and probably gossiped about his "mistreatment" of her friend and colleague Nancy, whom she later accompanied to Margate and nursed in her last illness. The shadows in the Buchanans' married life were seen at their blackest through Miss Lewis's eyes. In 1831 she was one of the Reverend Mr. Jones's most ardent adherents; and the indignation she felt at the public insults offered him was surely imparted to the trembling Marian Evans, kneeling beside her on a bench at the window to watch the noisy crowd in the street below.

On first reading the manuscript of "Janet's Repentance" John Blackwood protested against the stark realism and urged George Eliot to soften the picture as much as possible.

The story [she replied] so far as regards the *persecution*, is a real bit in the religious history of England that happened about eight-and-twenty years ago. . . . Everything is softened from the fact, so far as art is permitted to soften and yet to remain essentially true. The real town was more vicious than my Milby; the real Dempster was far more disgusting than mine; the real Janet, alas! had a far sadder end than mine, who will melt away from the reader's sight in purity, happiness, and beauty.

Mr. Tryan was recognized as quickly as Amos had been. After the first two numbers appeared in *Blackwood's*, the Reverend William Pitman Jones wrote the editor to say that they alluded to his deceased brother and that he was "utterly at a loss to conceive who could have . . . revived what should have been buried in oblivion." Of the parties alluded to, he added, most, if not all, "have long been in Eternity." John Blackwood sent the note to George Henry Lewes to be passed on to George Eliot, saying: "I hope . . . that our friend has not in his love of reality said anything to identify his story with living characters." George Eliot herself replied:

Mr. Tryan is not a portrait of any clergyman, living or dead. He is an ideal character, but I hope probable enough to resemble more than one evangelical clergyman of his day. If Mr. Jones's deceased brother was like Mr. Tryan, so much the better, for in that case he was made of human nature's finer clay. I think you will agree with me that there are few clergymen who would be depreciated by an identification with Mr. Tryan. But I should rather suppose that the old gentleman, misled by some similarity in outward circumstances, is blind to the discrepancies which must exist where no portrait was intended. As to the rest of my story, so far as its elements were suggested by real persons, those persons have been, to use good Mr. Jones's phrase, "long in Eternity." . . .

I should consider it a fault which would cause me lasting regret, if I had used reality in any other than the legitimate way common to all artists who draw their materials from their observation and experience. It would be a melancholy result of my fictions if I gave *just* cause of annoyance to any good and sensible person. But I suppose there is no perfect safeguard against erroneous impressions or a mistaken susceptibility. We are all apt to forget how little there is about us that is unique, and how very strongly we resemble many other insignificant people who have lived before us.

On the last day of February 1858, Mr. Blackwood was finally told that the mysterious unknown George Eliot, whose stories he had been publishing for more than a year, was really Marian Evans, the Mrs. Lewes he had met several times when calling on Lewes at Richmond. Sensitive to the proprieties, as the editor of a family magazine must be, he agreed that on all accounts it was desirable to keep the secret. However, it was becoming increasingly difficult. Some months before a newspaper on the Isle of Man had attributed the authorship of the *Scenes of Clerical Life* to a certain Joseph Liggins, a baker's son at Nuneaton, who in the absence of other candidates was accepted; and though he would neither affirm nor deny the soft impeachment, he declared that the publishers had never paid him a penny. In May when John Blackwood was smoking his cigar in front of the stand at the Derby, he was accosted by C. N. Newdegate, M. P. for Warwickshire, who told him that the capital series of stories, the Clerical Scenes, were "all about my place and County," and that he knew the author, whose name was Liggins. Blackwood lost no time in sending the fascinating news to George Eliot.

> You were right in believing that I should like to hear Mr. Newdegate's opinion of the Stories [she replied]. His testimony to the spirit in which they are written is really valuable, for I know he deserves the character you give him.
>
> As to details, he seems, from what you say, as likely to be mistaken about them as he is about the authorship; but it is invariably the case that when people discover certain points of coincidence in a fiction with facts that happen to have come to their knowledge, they believe themselves able to furnish a key to the whole. That is amusing enough to the author, who knows from what widely sundered portions of experience—from what a combination of subtle shadowy suggestions with certain actual objects and events, his story has been formed. Certain vague traditions about Sir Roger Newdegate (him of "Newdegate-Prize" celebrity) which I heard when I was a child are woven into the character of Sir Christopher Cheverel, and the house he improved into a charming Gothic place with beautiful ceilings, I know from actual vision—but the rest of "Mr. Gilfil's Love Story" is spun out of the subtlest web of minute observation and inward experience, from my first childish recollections up to recent years. So it is with all the other stories. It would be a very difficult thing for me to furnish a key to them myself. But where there is no exact memory of the past any story with a few remembered points of character or of incident may pass for a history.

To avoid the dangerous ground she had trodden in the *Scenes* George Eliot chose more private materials for her next book. The germ of *Adam Bede* was a story told her by her aunt Mrs. Samuel Evans, a Methodist, who in 1802 at Nottingham had softened the heart of a girl named Mary

Voce, about to be executed for child-murder. They were the originals of Dinah Morris and Hetty Sorrel. The character of Adam was based on what she knew of her father, Robert Evans, who was once a carpenter and later agent for several great estates, including that of the Newdegates at Arbury. Unlike the affairs in the *Scenes*, these were hardly known outside George Eliot's own family, from whom she was now quite alienated. Her illegal union with Lewes so outraged her brother Isaac Evans that he had the family solicitor answer her letter announcing the news and forbade her sister Chrissey to communicate with her.

The phenomenal success of *Adam Bede* in 1859 revived curiosity about George Eliot's identity. Liggins's supporters pressed their claim, publishing indignant letters in the *Times*, which Blackwood and the real George Eliot instantly denounced. A foolish busybody, a Warwickshire magistrate named Bracebridge, a Liggins champion, went scouring about the countryside for the original of Mrs. Poyser and discovered one who resembled her — in nothing but the name. Through Florence Nightingale's father he heard of a daughter of the original Dinah Morris and found himself interviewing a Mrs. Walker, the wife of Nightingale's tailor, who recalled that when George Eliot visited her mother she occupied some hours in writing down Mrs. Evans's experiences from her own lips "and was hardly ever seen in Wirksworth without a notebook and pencil in her hand." Dinah's sermon, Mrs. Walker added, was copied from one of Mrs. Evans's manuscripts. Alas for the truth! both notebook and sermon are as imaginary as George Eliot's visit. By the end of June the secret of George Eliot's identity was beginning to leak out in literary circles; and since *Adam Bede* had sold five printings in as many months and had been universally acclaimed, there was no longer much reason to preserve anonymity. Mr. Bracebridge in Pickwickian fashion continued his researches all summer among George Eliot's Staffordshire cousins. To the irritation caused by his findings, which were obligingly passed on by her friend Charles Bray, we owe George Eliot's best statements about the originals:

One of the scenes in my books that many people have pitched on as peculiarly *true* is the conversation of the clergy at the Clerical Dinner, in *Amos Barton*. It is needless to say, that I was never present at a Clerical Dinner party. Mr. Bracebridge is quite right in saying I was too young to witness and judge, when the events that suggested my stories occurred — the inference of a little wisdom and a little modesty would be, that the events are *not* precisely what happened, as people with dim confused memories imagine them to be, because they see a few particulars which they *do* remember. I've no doubt there are people who think that Dempster really spoke from a window just as I have described—if he did, *I* never heard that he did, and I was a child kneeling on a form at a school-room window at that date.

George Eliot admits that there are two portraits in the *Scenes of Clerical Life*:

first, *Amos Barton*, who however is made a much better man than he really was, and far more unimpeachable in conduct. The affair of the "Countess" was never fully known to me: so far as it *was* known, it is varied from my knowledge of the alleged fact. 2nd *Dempster*, whose original has been dead twenty years or more, (I thought 'Amos' was dead) and was by no means so witty, I imagine, as his representative in "Janet."

But in *Adam Bede*, George Eliot insists, "There is not a single portrait."

I could never have written Adam Bede if I had not learned something of my father's early experience: but no one who knew my father could call Adam a portrait of him—and the course of Adam's life is entirely different from my father's. Again, Dinah and Seth are *not* my aunt and uncle. I knew my aunt and uncle and they were Methodists—my aunt a preacher; and I loved them: so far only they resembled Seth and Dinah. The whole course of the story in Adam Bede—the descriptions of scenery or houses—the characters—the dialogue—*everything* is a combination from widely sundered elements of experience. . . . I remember very well the moment of writing that speech of Mrs. Poyser's in which she says Dinah provokes her because she's "like the statty outside Treddles'on church—a-staring and smiling whether it's fair weather or foul." But I never remember seeing any statue outside any church, that suggested the image. It was the only place where Mrs. Poyser could have seen anything like a statue—that was the reason why the statue was "outside Treddles'on church." Treddleston is *not* Ellastone. Hayslope is, with a difference.

One reader of *Adam Bede*, a Derbyshire woman, thinking she recognized the dialect of the country people she knew in her childhood, was convinced that the book must have been written there. But, George Eliot continues,

I never knew any Derbyshire people, or Staffordshire either, except my father and his brothers. His brothers I never saw so many times as I could count fingers, and my visits to those counties were not more than four or five altogether—none of them for more than a few days. Yet, I imagine, no one will go to the length of saying that the dialect was put in for me.

The suggestion that she had copied Dinah's sermon from notes in her aunt's journal George Eliot repudiates indignantly:

I never knew my aunt *had* a journal — and I hear it with some surprize — incredulity, rather. Some one said they thought Mrs. Poyser's sayings must have been collected for me!! It is happy for me that I never expected any gratification of a personal kind from my authorship. The worst of all this is that it nauseates me — chills me and discourages me in my work.

In a letter to her friend Sara Hennell a few weeks later George Eliot describes her aunt more minutely:

Although I had only heard her spoken of as a strange person, given to a fanatical vehemence of exhortation in private as well as public, I believed that [when she came to visit at Griff in 1839] we should find sympathy between us. She was then an old woman — above sixty — and, I believe, had for a good many years given up preaching. A tiny little woman, with bright, small dark eyes, and hair that had been black, I imagine, but was now grey — a pretty woman in her youth, but of a totally different physical type from Dinah. The difference — as you will believe — was not *simply* physical: no difference is. She was a woman of strong natural excitability, which I know, from the description I have heard my father and half-sister give, prevented her from the exercise of discretion under the promptings of her zeal. But this vehemence was now subdued by age and sickness; she was very gentle and quiet in her manners — very loving — and (what she must have been from the very first) a truly religious soul, in whom the love of God and love of man were fused together. . . .

As to my aunt's conversation, it is a fact, that the only two things of any interest I remember in our lonely sittings and walks, are her telling me one sunny afternoon how she had, with another pious woman, visited an unhappy girl in prison, stayed with her all night, and gone with her to execution, and one or two accounts of supposed miracles in which she believed — among the rest, *the face with the crown of thorns seen in the glass.*

Mrs. Evans was more interested in the work of divine grace than in details of Mary Voce and her unhappy end.

In her account of the prison scenes, I remember no word she uttered — I only remember her tone and manner, and the deep feeling I had under the recital. Of the girl she knew nothing, I believe — or told me nothing — but that she was a common coarse girl, convicted of child-murder. The incident lay in my mind for years on years, as a dead germ, apparently — till time had made my mind a nidus in which it could fructify; it then turned out to be the germ of 'Adam Bede.' . . .

You see how she suggested Dinah; but it is not possible you should see as I do how entirely her individuality differed from Dinah's. How curious it seems to me that people should think Dinah's sermons, prayers, and speeches were *copied* — when they were written with hot tears, as they surged up in my own mind! . . .

As to my aunt's children or grandchildren saying, if they *did* say, that Dinah is a good portrait of my aunt — that is simply the vague easily satisfied notion imperfectly instructed people always have of portraits. It is not surprising that simple men and women without pretension to enlightened discrimination should think a generic resemblance constitutes a portrait, when we see the great public so accustomed to be delighted with *mis*-representations of life and character, which they accept as representations, that they are scandalized when art makes a nearer approach to truth.

Regarding her indebtedness to facts and locale of Staffordshire and Derbyshire, George Eliot continues,

I never remained in either of those counties more than a few days together. . . . The details which I knew as facts and have made use of for my picture were gathered from such imperfect allusion and narrative as I heard from my father, in his occasional talk about old times.

Hayslope, as she had told Mr. Bray, was Ellastone, but "with a difference." That is, Hayslope was rather more like Chilvers Coton. The wonderful background of *Adam Bede* in which contour of land, subtle variation in the foliage, the sounds of domestic animals, as well as the countryman's attachment to the soil and the almost instinctive rites of seed-time and harvest — these were never culled from a notebook kept during a hurried visit to a strange county. They were the recollections of a sensitive mind, turning nostalgically back to the world of childhood from which Marian Evans was now cruelly and unjustly excluded.

The same nostalgic feeling permeates the first two volumes of *The Mill on the Floss* (1860). The flood that ends Maggie Tulliver's life could not take place in Warwickshire, but it was not, as careless readers often think, a crude melodramatic device to extricate the author from an impossible and unforeseen dilemma. The flood was the first thing George Eliot determined about the story. In January 1859 she began to look out accounts of inundations in the *Annual Register*, and in September she and Lewes spent ten days in Dorsetshire searching for a suitable setting. At Radipole near Weymouth they discovered a mill that pleased her so much they tried to rent a laborer's cottage so as to live near it for a week. A few days later they went to Dorchester to see whether the Frome would be an adequate river. Neither Wey nor Frome seemed right for the catastrophic flood she needed, and off they dashed to the north to study the Trent. At Newark, where the Avon joins it, the Trent was hardly deep enough. Farther downstream, however, at Gainsborough, where the Idle flows in, she found just what she wanted for the Floss and the Ripple. On the course that Maggie was to follow they rowed down to the Idle, ascended some way on foot, and then walked back to Gainsborough. There one can still see vestiges of St. Ogg's with its "aged, fluted red roofs and the broad gables of its wharves."

But Dorlcote Mill was never on the Trent or the Idle. The old mill of Marian Evans's childhood at Arbury supplied the few details we are given. More clearly than the mill itself we see the wagoner coming home with a load of grain, his horses

> strong, submissive, meek-eyed beasts . . . looking mild reproach at him from between their blinkers, that he should crack his whip at them in that awful manner as if they needed that hint! See how they stretch their shoulders up the slope towards the bridge, with all the more energy because they are so near home. Look at the grand shaggy feet that seem to grasp the firm earth, at the patient strength of their necks, bowed under the heavy collar, at the mighty muscles of their struggling haunches! I should like well to hear them neigh over their hardly-earned feed of corn, and see them, with their moist necks freed from the harness, dipping their eager nostrils into the muddy pond.

This team was not caught on a two-day excursion in Lincolnshire; they are horses Marian Evans knew well in her childhood, and they shed the gleam of reality on the shadowy mill behind them. The background of the scenes drawn from her own memories has a density of realization not achieved in the third volume. Think of the Round Pool, where Maggie fishes with Tom, framed in with willows and tall reeds with purple plumy tops, and then compare the vaguer, more general views of "the silent, sunny fields and pastures" where she drifts along the river with Stephen Guest. The Round Pool was near Griff House, and the details flashed spontaneously from her memory; the banks of the Trent had to be recalled with conscious effort, perhaps even with the help of map and notebook.

The Mill on the Floss is George Eliot's *David Copperfield*, shot through in the early parts with autobiography. In 1859 her brother Isaac Evans was heard to say that *Adam Bede* had "things in it about my father." One would give a good deal to know what he thought of *The Mill*, which is full of things about *him*. The dead rabbits, the new fishlines, the jagged cropping of Maggie's unruly hair are too real to have been invented, and Tom's harshness toward his misjudged sister must have spoken eloquently against the barrier Isaac's stern rectitude had raised between them. He had all of Tom's proprietary feeling about his sister. More than once in the 1840's, when Marian was living at Coventry with her father, he had called to "school" her about her conduct and her unconventional friends. According to Mrs. Bray he

> thinks that his sister has no chance of getting the one thing needful — i.e. a husband and a settlement, unless she mixes more in society, and complains that since she has known us she has hardly been anywhere else; that Mr. Bray, being only a leader of mobs, can only introduce her to Chartists and Radicals, and that such only will ever fall in love with her if she does not belong to the Church. So his plan is to induce his father to remove to Meriden where being away from us and under the guardianship of her sister she may be brought back to her senses.

Tom Tulliver talks much like Isaac:

> I wished my sister to be a lady, and I would always have taken care of you, as my father desired, until you were well married. But your ideas and mine never accord, and you will not give way. Yet you might have sense enough to see that a brother, who goes out into the world and mixes with men, necessarily knows better what is right and respectable for his sister than she can know herself.

Isaac acted on Tom's high but rigid principles in rejecting Marian after her union with Lewes.

Maggie's love for Philip Wakem also came from a germ in George Eliot's own experience. Her first biographer, knowing only that he was a painter and deformed, suggested as the original François D'Albert-Durade, in whose house at Geneva she had boarded in the winter of 1849. The parallel is not close. D'Albert-Durade was not merely a hunchback; he was a dwarf, "not more than four feet high," whom it is impossible to cast effectively in the love scenes with Maggie in the Red Deeps. But another candidate has lately come to light, another painter, whom Marian Evans met in 1845 at her half-sister's house in Baginton. To Mrs. Bray's letter to her sister Sara Hennell we owe the account of this affair:

> She says she was talking to you about a young artist she was going to meet at Baginton. Well, they did meet and passed two days in each other's company, and she thought him the most interesting young man she had seen and superior to all the rest of mankind; the third morning he made proposals through her brother-in-law Mr. Houghton — saying "she was the most fascinating creature he had ever beheld, that if it were not too presumptuous to hope etc., in short, he seemed desperately smitten and begged permission to write to her. She granted this, and came to us so brimful of happiness; — though she said she had not fallen in love with him yet, but admired his character so much that she was sure she should: the only objection seemed to be that his profession — a picture-restorer

—is not lucrative or over-honourable. We liked his letters to her very much—simple, earnest, unstudied. She refused anything like an engagement on so short an acquaintance, but would have much pleasure to see him as a friend etc. So he came to see her last Wednesday evening, and owing to his great agitation, from youth—or something or other, did not seem to her half so interesting as before, and the next day she made up her mind that she could never love or respect him enough to marry him and that it would involve too great a sacrifice of her mind and pursuits. So she wrote him to break it off—and there it stands now.

Since there is no suggestion of deformity in the young picture-restorer, it is possible that two widely separated sources have combined here. But I believe we are more likely to find the germ of Maggie's love for Philip in the emotional experience of this affair than in her relations with a Swiss dwarf old enough to be her father, whose wife she always affectionately called Maman.

The Dodson sisters—Jane Glegg, Sophy Pullet, and Susan Deane—were immediately recognized about Nuneaton as Mary, Elizabeth, and Anne Pearson, George Eliot's aunts Mrs. John Evarard, Mrs. Richard Johnson, and Mrs. George Garner. There is a portrait of Mrs. Evarard in a lace cap and her best "front" of glossy curls over a handsome face that one sees instantly to be Mrs. Glegg's. Like Maggie, Marian Evans was both "niece and legatee," and the property bequeathed her by a codicil to Mrs. Evarard's will in 1844 was the last item proved in George Eliot's own will. Beneath the touches of caricature her gratitude can be read in Aunt Glegg's rebuke of Tom for admitting the worst of his sister before he was compelled. Clanship was as strong a motive with her as equity in money matters. "If you were not to stand by your 'kin' as long as there was a shred of honour attributable to them, pray what were you to stand by?" Of Aunt Pullet there are fewer traces in George Eliot's biography. Both Mr. and Mrs. Johnson died in 1833, and the few references to them concern prolonged illnesses, which perhaps explain the medicine bottles Mr. Pullet preserved so carefully:

"He won't have one sold. He says it's nothing but right folks should see 'em when I'm gone. They fill two o' the long store-room shelves a'ready—but," she added, beginning to cry a little, "it's well if they ever fill three. I may go before I've made up the dozen o' these last sizes."

The Garners, originals of the Deanes, were more cheerful folk living comfortably at Sole End, the Garum Firs of the novel, and the brief allusions to them in Robert Evans's journal mention family dinners rather than funerals. Their daughter Bessie seems a more likely prototype of Lucy Deane than George Eliot's sister Chrissey, who is traditionally assigned the part.

Chrissey appears in *The Mill on the Floss*, I believe, in the very different guise of Mr. Tulliver's sister Gritty Moss. Christiana Evans, to give her her proper name, was married in 1837 to Edward Clarke, fifth son of Robert Clarke, Esq., of Brooksby Hall, Leicestershire, whose earnings as a country surgeon were never adequate to maintain the family. In January 1842 his father-in-law bought from him for £250 the little house at Attleborough that her uncle John Evarard had bequeathed to Chrissey, his favorite niece, and a few months later lent him £800 more, which, if not repaid, was to be taken out of her share of Mr. Evans's estate. In spite of these measures, by October 1845, shortly after the sixth of his nine children was born, Mr. Clarke was bankrupt. When he died suddenly in December 1852, he left Chrissey with scarcely any resources. Isaac was kind to her, George Eliot said, "though not in a very large way." He allowed her to live in the house, once her own, which he had inherited, but did little to provide for her children. George Eliot shuddered at talk of an orphanage and once considered going with them all to Australia— "to settle them and then come back." Overworked and undernourished, Chrissey came down with tuberculosis, and in 1859, two months after *Adam Bede* appeared, she died. Isaac Evans could hardly have read the chapter describing Mr. Tulliver's visit to his sister Gritty Moss without recalling his own less generous treatment of his late sister Chrissey Clarke.

Edward Clarke appears plainly in *Middlemarch* as Tertius Lydgate, who was not unwilling to have people know that he was better born than the other country doctors and who also had debts of £1000 when bankruptcy threatened him. Several other candidates have been mentioned as originals. Sir Clifford Allbutt differs too widely from Lydgate in birth, education, and medical career, even during his early days at the Leeds Infirmary, to be considered. I find a likelier prototype in Bray's friend Charles Benjamin Nankivell, who studied medicine abroad (M.D., Pisa, 1828) and came to Coventry in 1831 as the first physician at the new Provident Dispensary. But there are many sides to Lydgate, and possibly Nankivell, Allbutt, and Clarke all contributed toward George Eliot's conception of him. By no stretch of the imagination, however, can I accept Oscar Browning's assumption that *he* was "the man from whom in some measure she had drawn the character of Lydgate."

The other character in *Middlemarch* for whom several originals have been proposed is Casaubon. In most cases the resemblance is reduced to the fact that they married much younger wives. On no better ground than this Miss Cobbe suggested the shy, kindly Robert William Mackay, a scholar of real distinction. Sir Sidney Lee had "no doubt" that Casaubon was drawn from Mark Pattison. But how is one to compare the ignorant pedantry of the Key to All Mythologies with the profound and admirable scholarship of the Rector of Lincoln College? The publication of his great *Life of Isaac Casaubon* in 1875, four years after *Middlemarch*, prompted the identification as much as the fact that Mrs. Pattison, like Dorothea, was nearly thirty years younger. John Morley rightly characterizes the suggestion as "an impertinent blunder."

I find a closer parallel to Casaubon in Dr. R. H. Brabant, with whom George Eliot had an unfortunate experience in her youth. Dr. Brabant, the father of her friend Mrs. Charles Hennell, was a pompous and rather foolish gentleman who was engaged for years on a never-finished book that was to dispose forever of the supernatural elements in religion. In 1843, when Marian Evans was invited to visit him in Wiltshire after his daughter's wedding, we are told by a rather malicious gossip that "she knelt at his feet and offered to devote her life to his service." But the story ended there. Mrs. Brabant, a rather formidable old lady, though blind, was well enough aware of her husband's silliness about the ardent young lady reading German and Greek with him, and after a shorter visit than was at first contemplated, arrangements were made for her return to Coventry. When pressed to say from whom she had drawn Casaubon, George Eliot pointed to her own heart. There in the pain and humiliation of this episode lay the venom that gave Casaubon his horrible vividness.

Though no original has been indicated for Mr. Brooke, it is tempting to think that he may owe something to the scatter-brained Mr. Charles Bracebridge, who had also traveled in Greece and gone into a great many things, at one time, you know. It is a mistake to consider his niece Dorothea an autobiographical projection of George Eliot, who resembled her in little more than the common Victorian urge to be useful, and had neither her birth, fortune, nor beauty, and certainly not the lack of humor that caused most of Dorothea's trouble. If, like Alfred Hitchcock, she must appear somewhere in each of her novels, we should look for her rather in Mary Garth, a land agent's daughter, whose earnest desire to do good was combined with prudence, sound common sense, an omnivorous appetite for reading, and the lively sense of humor that is too often forgotten by critics of George Eliot.

Most of the convincing parallels to real persons are found in the early novels. Apart from the historical figures in *Romola* only the heroine herself has been given an original: Mme. Belloc saw in her "an immortal portrait" of the face and bearing of their friend Barbara Leigh Smith, Mme. Bodichon. In *Felix Holt* the dissenter Rufus Lyon was thought by some to resemble Mr. Francis Franklin, the Baptist minister in Coventry, and the Meyrick sisters reminded them of the Hennells. John Churton Collins's statement that George Eliot "made no secret" of having drawn the portrait of Felix from Gerald Massey, though unsupported by evidence, was repeated by Sir Sidney Lee in his article on Massey in the *DNB*. I see a closer resemblance between Felix and John Chapman, who was also the son of a druggist, a student of medicine, and a watchmaker.

Of the later novels *Daniel Deronda* has attracted most hunters of originals with its Jewish characters. There are several claimants for the title role. Leslie Stephen, who gave George Eliot advice about Daniel's life at Cambridge, fancied that she drew some touches from handsome young Edmund Gurney, whom she met there. According to Beatrice Webb, Edward Bond (1844–1920) was said to be the original. And Theodor Herzl's diary for 1895 recounts a conversation in which Col. Albert Goldsmid told him, "I am Daniel Deronda." Born in India and brought up a Christian, Goldsmid went over to Judaism while a lieutenant in the army—and compelled his reluctant wife to follow him. There is nothing to show that George Eliot knew of this. She was acquainted with Phoebe Sarah Marks, later Mrs. Ayrton, the physicist, who was often called the original of Mirah, though she saw no resemblance herself. The original of Mordecai is usually said to be the watchmaker Cohn, described by Lewes as the expounder of Spinoza to the club of students in Red Lion Square in 1836, though both Lewes and George Eliot repeatedly declared the identification entirely wrong. Cohn, in direct contrast to Mordecai, was a "keen dialectition and a highly impressive man, but without any specifically Jewish enthusiasm." For that element of the character a closer comparison might be drawn with George Eliot's friend Emanuel Deutsch of the British Museum, who died in 1873. Klesmer the musician, with his tall thin figure, his great mane of hair floating backward, his well-modeled features, powerful clear-shaven mouth and chin, probably owes something in appearance to Liszt, whom George Eliot had met in Weimar in

1854, when he was living there with his mistress the Princess Caroline Sayn-Wittgenstein; but aside from genius and talent, their characters are not similar.

Gwendolen Harleth is the only one in *Daniel Deronda* whose origin can be documented from George Eliot's papers. At Homburg in 1872, where she watched the gamblers crowded about the table, "The saddest thing to be witnessed," she wrote, "is the play of Miss Leigh, Byron's grand-niece, who is only 26 years old, and completely in the grasp of this mean, money-making demon. It made me cry to see her young fresh face among the hags and brutally stupid men around her." Here is the germ of the opening chapter at Leubronn. It illustrates the change in George Eliot's method since the early novels. "Was she beautiful or not beautiful?" it begins. The question is never answered in the direct way in which Hetty Sorrel's spring-tide charms were described. Gwendolen remains to the end somewhat elusive; we get less external detail and more impression of her mind—her mood, in the Old English sense. It is something like the change that came about in painting between the 1850's, when Landseer was at the peak of his vogue, and the 1870's, when Whistler was painting his Nocturnes.

Except in the *Scenes of Clerical Life*, which are in a sense *romans à clef*, few of George Eliot's characters are modeled closely on real people. They are, as she told Blackwood, "a combination of subtle shadowy suggestions with certain actual objects and events." A list jotted down on the back of a calendar for 1876 shows her turning over in her mind people she had known twenty or thirty years before. There is Dr. B., surgeon's assistant at K[enilworth?]. There is a "widow supporting herself by keeping a school [like Mrs. Wallington]: imperfectly instructed: dominated over by her head teacher [Miss Lewis?]." There are names of acquaintances at Geneva: Mrs. Lock, the Baronne de Ludwigsdorf and her Cousin Rosa, M. Maunoir [the oculist] and Mme. Courier. There are a good many others. Such "widely sundered portions of experience," if she had lived, might have become the germs of another *Middlemarch*.

MIDDLEMARCH, GEORGE ELIOT'S MASTERPIECE

Sumner J. Ferris

UNIVERSITY OF MINNESOTA

GEORGE ELIOT's recent critical popularity, at least since the publication of Virginia Woolf's essay in *The Common Reader*, has been largely the product of a single novel—*Middlemarch. Silas Marner*, *The Mill on the Floss*, and *Adam Bede* have retained and even increased their popularity; and *Felix Holt* and *Daniel Deronda* have lately pleased the wiser sort; but on the whole the *consensus criticorum* has been that *Middlemarch* is George Eliot's best novel. In this essay I shall attempt simply to reiterate and to justify this common opinion by making some observations on the setting and the characterization of *Middlemarch*, and the way that these contribute to its theme. My purpose, then, is threefold: to show how *Middlemarch* is, first, representative of George Eliot's novels in these respects; second, less flawed than any of the others; and third, the most original and carefully executed of them all.

Although it is a critical commonplace to say that George Eliot wrote most effectively when her setting was English provincial life in the early nineteenth century, and that *Middlemarch* is her particular triumph in creating such a setting, it is of a special character in this novel, for all its outward similarity to the others. First of all, *Middlemarch* is not weakened by Eliot's occasional substitution of research for imagination. Inheritance laws, Jewish ritual, and Italy of 1492–98 do not obscure the action of this novel; nor does, say, Wellington make such startlingly casual appearances here as Machiavelli does in *Romola.* Instead, topical references are made quite unobtrusively and almost always in a general way so that the reader is never bored by erudition. The political background is lightly sketched in; and references to Scott, Peel, William IV, and the railroad, as well as the master stroke of Mr. Brooke's nostalgic preference for Smollett, Johnson, and Young ("the poet, you know"), serve to locate the action firmly in one time and at one place, England at the end of the third decade of the nineteenth century. The distance of the action of the novel from the time George Eliot wrote it is not, of course, surprising; for, as Mrs. Tillotson has lately reminded us, the action of the typical Victorian novel was customarily from twenty to forty years in the past: at a time neither wholly familiar nor wholly strange to the Victorian reading public. And yet *Middlemarch* is laid at a curious time, in an age that is almost Victorian. Of none of the rest of George Eliot's novels can this be said: *Adam Bede*, to the Victorian, was set in the late afternoon of an age preceding his own; most of *Scenes of Clerical Life*, *The Mill on the Floss*, and *Silas Marner* might have been laid at almost any time from 40 to 140 years before the publication of *Middlemarch*; the setting of *Daniel Deronda* is inconsequential to its action; and *Felix Holt*, whatever more recent events it might have paralleled, had to do with political concerns that, the Victorian was probably relieved to recall, were at least moribund. But the setting of *Middlemarch* is in a strange middle ground; for 1830 was a transitional year, with the Reform Bill at hand but not yet come and the Regency gone but not yet forgotten, at a time halfway between the Pickwick Club's stagecoaching and Dombey's train trips, in an England no longer Merry but not yet Mechanized.

What is the purpose of this particular setting, then, and what are its effects on the novel? For one thing, by adding to the topicality of *Middlemarch*, it also keeps it from the pastoralism George Eliot was often likely to fall into. *Adam Bede*, in particular, and many of her other novels as well, have a serious moral tone; but they frequently strike the modern reader as sorts of genre paintings, nostalgic evocations of a past that the Victorian reader liked to dream about. *Middlemarch*, on the other hand, by coming closer to the England that the mid-Victorian audience itself knew, had to eschew nostalgia and could substitute for it a more serious — because more topical — kind of study and criticism of society. One need only compare Mr. Irwine of *Adam Bede* with his counterpart, Mr. Farebrother, in *Middlemarch*, to see the difference that the different settings impose on the novels. Both are obviously similar to the Vicar of Wakefield (as Mary Garth reminds us that Mr. Farebrother is); and George Eliot seems equally fond of both, defending the earlier character explicitly and the later implicitly. And although both of them retain their ecclesiastical posts, when Mr. Farebrother fails to get the curacy of the hospital, one feels that the failure was due not so much to Bulstrode and Lydgate as to George Eliot herself. If he had been born thirty years earlier, or if he could have been transplanted to *Adam Bede*, Mr. Farebrother would probably have been given the post and lived out his life playing whist with pensioners; but in the age of pathology and muscular Christianity, the author seems to confess, a more industrious cleric is needed— one who will not, for all the charm he is graced with, have leisure for playing cards.

This, then, is the setting of *Middlemarch*: distant enough to be idyllic but too recent to be pastoral, with holdovers from the easy pace of the eighteenth-century world but with harbingers of a newer and more hurried industrialized one. To go to *Adam Bede* for another example, the Poyser household could be the symbolic center of a novel set in that period, representing the firm and stable world-order and the moral and social certainties that, in the end, would always recur. But its equivalent in *Middlemarch*, the Garth household, is, in terms both of action and of theme, far from the center of its novel: the two main plots have nothing but an incidental connection with it; and certainly the virtues of stability, honesty, and simple good faith that it symbolizes do not triumph at the end of the novel. In fact, although George Eliot says that Caleb Garth is rather an employer of men, himself laboring in his appointed station for duty's sake and not for gain ("It must be remembered that by 'business' Caleb never meant money transactions, but the skilful application of labour"), only a few pages later it is Caleb himself who defends, of all things, the coming of the railroad—the most important expression and tool of the later Industrial Revolution. And Fred Vincy's taking a job would, in almost any of George Eliot's other novels, shock us as much as if Bob Jakin of *The Mill on the Floss* had demanded to be called "Squire." But the difference between the other novels and *Middlemarch* is precisely this, that characters are having to adjust themselves to a new world, not somehow to re-establish the old one for themselves. The earlier novels were largely reconstructions of a static society, rather like the one of Jane Austen's novels; and despite the force that attaches to an image of such a society, *Middlemarch* seems to me to be a more honest novel for the age in which it was written, and to be actually investigating the changes (in social and political structure, for instance) that society did encounter in the decade before Victoria.

The setting of *Middlemarch*, then, is typical of George Eliot only in a certain sense; for on closer investigation it proves to be quite different, original, and significant. Can the same be said of the characters? In characterization, her imagination was, I believe, quantitatively restricted, so that all of the successful characters in her novels fall within a certain narrow range. She could, and often did, depict religious excitation, having experienced it herself, but such real enthusiasm as Savonarola's was quite beyond her comprehension. She knew, oddly enough, what an eighteenth-century vicar or rector was like (or at least what the literary stereotype of him was); but not a single Low Churchman is well portrayed in her novels, and no Broad Churchman or High Churchman at all. She knew bad men and even better, knew misguided men and women; but, like so many of her contemporaries, she tended to confuse wickedness with hypocrisy and sanctimoniousness. And though she knew and depicted good people, she confused virtue with dedication to social service and seems to have had an almost unquestioning faith in the worth of honesty and honor. With such restrictions and, furthermore, with restrictions to certain definite character types, George Eliot rarely fashioned a novel in which all the characters created the effect she wanted them to — in which, that is to say, they were all successful. The extremes of *Romola* can, in kindness, be passed over, but even Adam Bede is something of a prig, a John Ridd with extra unction; Daniel Deronda is a strange combination of religious mystic and do-gooder; and even Eppie is sentimental and melodramatic in her role if not in her person. And yet in spite of all these perils, George Eliot succeeds with her characterization more completely and successfully in *Middlemarch* than she does in any other novel.

The women of the novel are the best and most successful characters in it; and even though some of them conform to well-established types, they are none the worse for it. Mary Garth, for example, despite her unfortunate resemblance to the worst moments of Romola and Dinah Morris, is plain and good and ennobling to Fred Vincy. Her refusal to destroy Featherstone's alternate will is, I admit, somewhat overscrupulous; and although sometimes one wishes that Fred would quote Dorothy Parker to her, her notion that a husband should have a regular source of income is not, perhaps, only a Victorian shibboleth. Whatever she does, moreover, is motivated and natural to her; her ways are never as cryptic as those of her predecessor, Maggie Tulliver. Celia Brooke, too, is a plain character, purposely somewhat simpler than even Mary Garth; but in the space that George Eliot does devote to her, she is depicted neatly and deftly, as an uncomplicated but charming and sincere young girl who likes jewelry, a husband, and children. But if both Mary and Celia are well drawn, Rosamond Vincy, who is shallow where they are simple, is a major achievement. Certainly enough attention is devoted to her in *Middlemarch*; but that she is not developed with any complexity is surely intentional. Yet all that is important to an understanding of her or of the effect she has on Lydgate's career and ambitions is traced in the novel: purpose, passion, and self-deception. She is introduced thus:

Rosamond . . . was rather used to being fallen in love with; but she . . . had remained indifferent and fastidiously critical towards both fresh sprig and faded bachelor. And here was Mr Lydgate suddenly corresponding to her ideal, being altogether foreign to Middlemarch, carrying a certain air of distinction congruous with good family and possessing connections which offered vistas of that middle-class heaven, rank: a man of talent, also, whom it would be especially delightful to enslave: in fact, a man who had touched her nature quite newly, and brought a vivid interest into her life which was better than any fancied 'might-be' such as she was in the habit of opposing to the actual.

She destroys Lydgate's dreams, as much by her thoughtlessness as by her improvidence:

"I was not able [says Lydgate] to pay for all the things we had to get before we were married, and there have been expenses since which I have been obliged to meet. The consequence is, there is a large debt at Brassing. . . . I took pains to keep it from you while you were not well; but now we must think together about it, and you must help me."

"What can *I* do, Tertius?" said Rosamond, turning her eyes on him again. That little speech of four words . . . is capable by varied vocal inflexions of expressing all states of mind from helpless dimness to exhaustive argumentative perception, from the completest self-devoting fellowship to the most neutral aloofness. Rosamond's thin utterance threw into the words "What can *I* do?" as much neutrality as they could hold. They fell like a mortal chill on Lydgate's roused tenderness.

And she is content when his dreams are destroyed:

His acquaintances thought him enviable to have so charming a wife, and nothing happened to shake their opinion. Rosamond never committed a second compromising indiscretion. She simply continued to be mild in her temper, inflexible in her judgment, disposed to admonish her husband, and able to frustrate him by stratagem. As the years went on he opposed her less and less, whence Rosamond concluded that he had learned the value of her opinion; on the other hand, she had a more thorough conviction of his talents now that he gained a good income, and instead of the threatened cage in Bride Street provided one all flowers and gilding, fit for the bird of paradise that she resembled.

"Character is a process and an unfolding," George Eliot says at one point in the novel; but it is the failure of Rosamond Lydgate to change her attitude and, unlike any sympathetic character in the novel, to adapt herself to changing circumstances, that provides not only the flaw in her character but the cause for the failure of one of the potentially strongest people in the novel, her husband Tertius Lydgate. In certain respects, she may be compared with Gwendolen Harleth, who will follow her in *Daniel Deronda*; but, although Gwendolen has a depth of moral response, Rosamond is just as George Eliot had planned her, and exquisite in her shallowness.

But if Rosamond Vincy is unlike any woman that George Eliot had created before, Dorothea Brooke seems, at first, like practically all of the memorable ones. She is like Dinah Morris, Romola, and Eppie in her dedication to a life of either piety, self-abnegation, or altruism; like Gwendolen Harleth, Maggie Tulliver, and Dinah in her strong will; and like Esther Lyon, Maggie, and Romola in her goodness. Yet to say this is just to say that Dorothea has all of the qualities, one or more of which George Eliot usually attributes to the women she wants the reader to sympathize with. The differences between these other characters and Dorothea is, of course, immense; but since others have commented on Dorothea at length before me, I shall make only a few remarks about one aspect of George Eliot's characterization of Dorothea in *Middlemarch*, the attitude the novelist takes toward her heroine.

For the most part, although George Eliot does give all of her women some complexity of character and although most of them are faced with a moral problem whose solution is not easy or simple, the reader is always sure of what attitude to take toward them (or at least what attitude the author intends him to take), since George Eliot always indicates, either explicitly through her own comments or implicitly by her arrangement of the action of the novel, what attitude she herself takes. Dorothea, on the other hand, is presented in an unusual way, at least in the first two thirds of *Middlemarch*, not tendentiously, from the author's point of view, but subjectively, from her own. Consequently, interpretation of her character and — even more important — judgment of her actions is purposely made more difficult than for any other of George Eliot's heroes and heroines.

This kind of point of view was not easy for the omniscient Victorian novelist, who had not yet hit upon the technique of the limited third-person point of view; and in *Middlemarch* George Eliot achieves it only by the most studied neutrality, and through the careful combination and alternation of irony and sympathy. The often-cited "Prelude" to *Middlemarch*, I believe, helps set the tone for much of the rest of the novel: does George Eliot really mean that St. Theresa's "reform of a religious order" was of a satisfactorily epical quality, or that it was just a poor substitute? Is the meaning of this brief parable that St. Theresa was turned back from impracticably romantic adventure by more sensible people, or that even though these dreams were frustrated, some fulfillment of them was possible? From the "Prelude" alone I think it is impossible to tell; for I think that this ambiguity was intentional and that the parable applies to Dorothea, who, like St. Theresa, can be called naïve by one reader and loftily idealistic by another. After all, her ambition to reform the condition of Sir James Chettam's tenants is proper and good, though her failure to see that Sir James is in love with her is stupid. Her faith may be overexercised, but it is sincere. Her preference for plain things and her disdain for jewels is as vain as her sister's preference for both ribbons and jewels, though certainly as natural and perhaps indicative of a finer character. And her mistaking Casaubon for Milton is an error of self-indulgence, but also an error simply of judgment, and as such hardly sinful. And, for that matter, should she have married the only other suitor for her hand, the rather dimwitted Sir James? Exactly how far she is motivated by vanity and how much by a real desire for a "life beyond self," like St. Theresa's, the reader cannot tell—for George Eliot does not tell, does not justify, does not condemn. Consequently the reader, if he wants to judge Dorothea at all, must steer the careful course that George Eliot points out, among amusement, sympathy, understanding, and disapproval.

This portrayal of Dorothea is, consequently, an achievement in several ways. For one thing, if, as seems to have happened, George Eliot drew on her own experiences in order to supply Dorothea's, the distance between the artist and the autobiographical creation is immense, and the skill with which George Eliot avoids the two pitfalls of autobiographical fiction—self-inflation on the one hand and self-deprecation on the other—is astounding. But besides this negative sort of achievement, some positive ones attach to this kind of portraiture. For one thing, although twentieth-century criticism prefers to use "realistic" as a term of description rather than one of approbation, I think it is just and appropriate to say that one of the merits of Dorothea's characterization is that it is realistic, in that it portrays a good person marked with a few flaws. (Though of course that metaphorical black and white are not good colors for literary depiction does not mean, logically, that metaphorical gray and speckled white are better; but this last kind of characterization pleased the Victorians mightily and still has something to be said for it.) Or, if this justification is not sufficient, "The point of view is well handled" can replace the statement "Dorothea is realistic," for this technical consideration, as I have said, concerned George Eliot here as much as it concerned Henry James, the great master of point of view who learned so much — as Mr. Leavis demonstrates — from her. And if James is indebted to Gwendolen Harleth for the suggestion of Isabel Archer, Dorothea Brooke in her sense of dedication and in her vanity may also have played her part in suggesting both James's character and possible techniques for presenting her.

But if Dorothea and the other women of *Middlemarch* are well depicted, the men of the novel are particularly worth scrutiny, for it is in characterization of men that George Eliot is particularly likely to be unsatisfactory. I have already mentioned Adam Bede and Daniel Deronda; the list of failures could be extended to include Felix Holt (who is anything but the radical he is credited with being) and that odd combination of Machiavellian diabolism and human selfishness, Tito Melema (who nevertheless just misses being the equal of Count Fosco). Even Silas Marner, rightly a favorite among George Eliot's readers, is less a person than an allegory — Man made selfish through Betrayal and humanized again by Love. And it is distressing to see where George Eliot fails by not observing Jane Austen's famous discretion in never reporting conversations that occur among men only. The result rarely, but still occasionally, can be as egregious as this passage from *Felix Holt*:

> "Let me go, you scoundrel!" said Harold, fiercely, "Or I'll be the death of you."
>
> "Do," said Jermyn, in a grating voice; "*I am your father.*" . . .
>
> "Leave the room, sir!" the Baronet said to Jermyn, in a voice of imperious scorn. "This is a meeting of gentlemen.
>
> "Come, Harold," he said, in the old friendly voice, "Come away with me."

Here the melodrama is due not only to the situation but to George Eliot's lack of acquaintance with men's probable reactions in such situations.

But although I have taken exception to five major characters, four of whom are eponyms of their novels, the minor male characters of *Middlemarch*, like those of the other novels, are usually successful. Despite the passage I have just quoted, both Jermyn and Harold Transome in *Felix*

Holt are credible, unmelodramatic characters; and so too, for example, are Mr. Irwine, Mr. Tulliver, and Mr. Wakem. In *Middlemarch*, practically the whole male cast (except Mr. Featherstone, a poor copy of old Martin Chuzzlewit) is believably and fully depicted, with varying degrees of elaboration as the part requires. George Eliot's success here is probably due to her recognition, either conscious or unconscious, that she could portray men best by means of a technique approaching that of the caricaturist—that is, by taking one or two prominent characteristics of a man and, by exploring more deeply than widely, letting these characteristics represent the whole man. Thus Mr. Brooke's kindness and his humorous *laus temporis acti* suffice, when sufficiently elaborated, to characterize him; and Sir James's pleasant simple-mindedness, Mr. Farebrother's easy-going piety, and Bulstrode's sanctimoniousness and hypocrisy characterize them.

But although George Eliot attempts to use much the same technique on the three important men who are not minor characters in this novel, Tertius Lydgate, Will Ladislaw, and Mr. Casaubon, they occupy too central a position, it seems to me, for her to handle them all with the same sureness that she does the others. Lydgate, indeed, is drawn with clarity, even in his confusion of motives, means, and ambitions; and if the reader feels any difficulty in understanding his character, the difficulty is in Lydgate's own inconsistencies, not in George Eliot's presentation of them. The real problem lies in resolving the conflicting attitudes that the author herself takes toward the other two, Casaubon and Ladislaw.

For at least half of *Middlemarch*, the reader is at a loss to know whether to think of Ladislaw favorably or unfavorably. When he is first introduced to Dorothea, he is a rather petulant young man:

> Young Ladislaw did not feel it necessary to smile, as if he were charmed with this introduction to his future second cousin and her relatives; but wore rather a pouting air of discontent.

And although George Eliot soon assures the reader that when he laughs a short while later, it is with "the pure enjoyment of comicality, and . . . no mixture of sneering and self-exaltation," he bears out his cousin's description of him as a dilettante when he is later seen in Rome. His thoughts then about Casaubon are scarcely creditable:

> the idea of this dried-up pedant, this elaborator of small explanations about as important as the surplus stock of false antiquities kept in a vendor's back chamber, having first got this adorable young creature to marry

him, and then passing his honeymoon away from her, groping after his mouldy futilities (Will was given to hyperbole)—this sudden picture stirred him with a sort of comic disgust: he was divided between the impulse to laugh aloud and the equally unseasonable impulse to burst into scornful invective.

A short while later, he casually remarks that "'If Mr Casaubon read German, he would save himself a great deal of trouble.'" However just the criticism, though, George Eliot is impelled to counter that "Young Mr Ladislaw was not at all deep himself in German writers; but very little achievement is required in order to pity another man's shortcomings." And by this she diagnoses, and criticizes, Ladislaw's contempt for his cousin (and benefactor) as what it really is: the ignoble emotion of jealousy. And yet, though a certain image of him as a dilettante remains in the rest of the novel, it grows fainter; and though his infatuation and flirtation with Dorothea are not, strictly speaking, morally defensible to George Eliot, he becomes more and more attractive, the former image of him fades, and his sincere love is increasingly contrasted with Casaubon's jealousy and suspicion.

Casaubon presents a similar, and even more perplexing problem, of interpretation of George Eliot's own attitude. Satire, mixed with a moderate amount of pity, is the dominant attitude toward him at first:

With his taper stuck before him he forgot the absence of windows, and in bitter manuscript remarks on other men's notions about the solar deities, he had become indifferent to the sunlight.

His reasons for not wanting Dorothea to marry Ladislaw after his death are sensible ones, for Will, up to this point in the novel, is a rather facile and objectionable young man; and the poignance of Casaubon's realization that he is to die ("Here was a man who now for the first time found himself looking into the eyes of death") and his subsequent concern for Dorothea ("'Come, my dear, come. You are young, and need not to extend your life by watching'") are the most moving passages in the entire novel. But this poignance gives way to Dorothea's own feeling, "a violent shock of repulsion," which as the novel proceeds becomes more and more George Eliot's own reaction. Not a word further of justification is offered for Casaubon after his death; to the author as to Dorothea he is "the dead hand" that keeps Dorothea from happiness. The most startling and convincing proof of this change of attitude comes with Dorothea's bitter rejection of editorial responsibility for Casaubon's Synoptical Tabulation. If George Eliot had seen anything heartless in this — as the reader cannot fail to — she would have commented on it; but instead she says merely that "this little act of Dorothea's may perhaps be smiled at as superstitious."

Although the reason for this curious shifting of affection from Casaubon, who had been granted it, to Ladislaw, who had not — curious in that it is unexplained or insufficiently explained in the action of the novel — is not difficult to diagnose, it points up an element in *Middlemarch* that is of more profound significance than simply George Eliot's methods of characterizing her male characters. I have remarked already that George Eliot was originally concerned with establishing Dorothea's point of view clearly and fully, without intruding her own judgment about her. Similarly, it seems to me, she tried to present the points of view of Casaubon and Ladislaw, but particularly of Casaubon, who, if seen solely from the outside, or solely through Dorothea's disillusioned consciousness, would strike the reader as quite unbearable. But instead, George Eliot ensures, by means of a significant anacoluthon midway through the third book, that Casaubon will be seen on his own terms by the reader:

> One morning, some weeks after her arrival at Lowick, Dorothea — but why always Dorothea? Was her point of view the only possible one with regard to this marriage? I protest against all our interest, all our effort at understanding being given to the young skins that look blooming in spite of trouble; for these too will get faded, and will know the older and more eating griefs which we are helping to neglect. In spite of the blinking eyes and white moles objectionable to Celia, and the want of muscular curve which was morally painful to Sir James, Mr Casaubon had an intense consciousness within him, and was spiritually a-hungered like the rest of us.

If Casaubon is kept from being unbearable by being seen in his own lights, Ladislaw, I suggest, is given a similar, but reverse kind of treatment, so that he will not strain the reader's credulity, or lose the reader's sympathy by seeming to require too much of it. And yet *Middlemarch* is by George Eliot, not by Henry James; and her attempt at this kind of multilateral third-person point of view breaks down, I think, after Casaubon's death, when her subject becomes not the conflicting motives and moods of three characters, Dorothea, Casaubon, and Ladislaw, but the quest by one of them, Dorothea, for happiness and a way to remedy her past mistakes. In several different ways this change of emphasis would have been hard for George Eliot to avoid. One of the themes of *Middlemarch*, as of so many other Victorian novels, is the process of initiation into life of a central character (early in the novel Dorothea is called a "neophyte"), by a series of steps from innocence to disillusionment to experience to happiness; and to the Victorian novelist a central character meant a hero, and a hero meant a happy ending. Furthermore, a multilateral point of view is, by its nature, difficult to handle: except in an intentional *tour de force* like *Point Counter Point*, it is almost impossible for an author to present as many points of view as George Eliot tries to, and yet not choose one character to side with against the others. And lastly, even though George Eliot could be fair to Casaubon during his lifetime, the sympathy won for him is won through her presentation of his own mind: once he is dead, his consciousness vanishes from the novel, and consequently there vanishes the sympathy George Eliot has, until then, shown for him.

But this technical inconsistency not only does not seriously mar *Middlemarch*; it emphasizes its theme and George Eliot's successful carrying out of its theme. Casaubon, in the last passage I have quoted, is "spiritually a-hungered"; and this curious figure is repeated when, in his marriage, he is said to have a "pining hunger" that Dorothea is unable to satisfy. Dorothea too has a "deep longing" for Ladislaw, after her husband's death; in fact, "Her soul thirsted to see him." All of the other characters have similar deep cravings, all the more important for their being relatively unambitious ones. Rosamond wants a husband with money and family; Lydgate wants a hospital and a reputation; Fred Vincy wants a little money and a life of ease; Bulstrode wants power and prestige; Ladislaw wants to marry Dorothea and live happily with her; and Dorothea, at the beginning of the novel, wants her own romantic dreams fulfilled and, at the end, wants only the happiness to which she feels entitled. All of these ambitions are private ones, felt only by the character himself and never communicated; all of them are the result, largely, of vanity and egoism (in varying degrees blameworthy) and even those that are achieved are hard-won.

Middlemarch, then, is a study of society only in a very special way. In most of George Eliot's other novels, society is almost an entity in itself; it posits a norm of social order, virtue, and love, from which characters depart at their peril. In *Middlemarch*, on the other hand, society is shaped by the individual characters, and they do not merely fill appointed stations. The difference between the other novels (especially *Adam Bede* and *Silas Marner*) and *Middlemarch* is the difference between sociological novels and a psychological one; and this difference is, I suspect, the reason for George Eliot's success in characterization in this novel. Felix Holt and Maggie Tulliver are as much symbolic counters as they are people, the one a radical who advocates both reform and moderation and the other a study in two conficting loves. But while both *Felix Holt* and *The Mill on the Floss* had theses to uphold about the way in which the law of social order asserts itself, *Middlemarch* does not. And since the characters in this novel rather determine their own world than are determined by it, extreme care was necessary for George Eliot in depicting them; and, faced with the necessity of creating original figures, instead of ones who would fill obvious, traditional places in society, she recognized the challenge and met it. Except for some of the minor characters, everyone in *Middlemarch* is developed as fully and as originally as his role in the action requires; everyone is given his own psychological development, so that he can take his place not merely as the mortar between the blocks of George Eliot's theme but as part of the foundation from which the meaning will emerge.

The way in which the major characters are presented, from what I have called a multilateral third-person point of view, takes on increased significance, therefore, in the light of the society they form. The characters in most of the other novels are related to one another almost despite themselves: they are either drawn back to their mutual relations in the norm of order, virtue, and love, or suffer for their departure. But the major characters of *Middlemarch*, although their affairs and fates are intertwined, are not related in this way. Each of them — Casaubon, Dorothea, Will, Rosamond, and Lydgate — has his own cravings, different from the others and kept secret from the others, and even from himself perhaps; and these cravings only isolate each of them from the others. The only way to regain any sort of communication, a reciprocal sympathy, is through love like Dorothea's and Will's, or like Fred's and Mary's. But even this is slow and hard-won; not a social solution but a personal one; effective for individual couples, not for society at large. All of *Middlemarch* traces these cravings, these individual fates, and follows the separate points of view of each of the characters, who may be able to establish communication with one another, but never are able to join with them all in a stable, subsuming social order.

The setting of *Middlemarch*, just before the complete industrialization of England, further emphasizes this. The age of bumbling benevolence, simple hearts, and kindness typified by Mr. Brooke, the Garths, and Mr.

Farebrother, is about to give way to one of depersonalized laws and machinery. The economic position, and largesse, of Sir James are about to be superseded by Bulstrode's invested capital and charity hospital. The old order, economic and social, is crumbling; and in the new, impersonal one, where each man's fate is of little concern to his fellows, his ambitions, his cravings, and his hunger are both tragically and ironically distinct. Tragically, in that he is, in part, responsible for them, but cannot escape them, and does not deserve them (not even Will and Dorothea get the happiest of endings). Ironically, in that every man is in the same condition, alone or practically alone. This is a bleak world that George Eliot is prophesying, and that she, in 1870, saw as having begun to appear in 1830: not completely bare, but profoundly empty of all that "spiritual grandeur" that Dorothea, like St. Theresa, dreamt of.

The accomplishment of *Middlemarch* is a peculiarly great one. The novel is unified in theme and diverse and original in character and setting. Not only does none of George Eliot's other novels accomplish so much with so few flaws; none is so tightly integrated a piece of artistry. And none, I know, retains its impact for the twentieth-century reader so strongly. It would have horrified George Eliot to hear this said, but most of her novels seem to us now to treat indifferent subjects with more attention than they deserve, and in an archaic manner. *Middlemarch,* of all of them, retains its appeal for both its subject— naïve hope, disillusionment, and personal triumph—and its manner of execution—complex in its approach but single in its purpose, detached in its tone yet intense in its concern.

CHARLES READE'S *CHRISTIE JOHNSTONE:* A PORTRAIT OF THE ARTIST AS A YOUNG PRE-RAPHAELITE

Wayne Burns

UNIVERSITY OF WASHINGTON

> "We were all reading his jaunty, nervy books, and some of us were questioning whether we ought not to set him above Thackeray and Dickens and George Eliot, *tulli quanti*, so great was the effect that Charles Reade had with our generation. . . . Then it [*Christie Johnstone*] was brilliantly new and surprising; it seemed to be the last word that could be said for the truth in fiction; and it had a spell that held us like an anaesthetic. . . .
>
> A few months ago I was at the old home, and I read that book [*Christie Johnstone*] again, after not looking at it for more than thirty years; and I read it with amazement at its prevailing artistic vulgarity, its prevailing aesthetic error shot here and there with gleams of light, and of the truth that Reade himself was always dimly groping for. The book is written throughout on the verge of realism, with divinations and conjectures across its border, and with lapses into the fool's paradise of romanticism, and an apparent content with its inanity and impossibility."
>
> W. D. Howells, *My Literary Passions*

Christie Johnstone (1853) expresses Charles Reade's own quest for personal and artistic fulfillment. It is his *David Copperfield*, his *Sons and Lovers*, his *Portrait of the Artist as a Young Man*. And while it does not measure up to any of these novels, it is a work of considerable artistic merit, and one that is crucial to an understanding of Reade's artistic development. For in his portrait of the artist as Pre-Raphaelite son and lover can be discerned the fear of self-recognition that caused him, in his later writing, to seek refuge from imagination in fact and social purpose.

Reade began taking notes, with a view to becoming a writer, as early as 1835. Yet for some fourteen years he could not write; the words simply would not come. The earliest version of *Christie Johnstone*, his first original work of any consequence, dates from 1849, when, at the age of thirty-five, he was called home to Ipsden to be reconciled with his dying father. That Reade should begin writing, and as he elsewhere says, "living," just when his father began dying, is fully in keeping with his attitude toward his father. Equally in keeping is his choice of subject: the would-be artist emasculated, as both lover and artist, by the demands of his mother's love — much as he himself had been emasculated by Mrs. Reade's love.

Reade first met and fell in love with the original of his fictional Christie on one of his many trips to Scotland. Then, some time between 1835 and 1839, there was presumably a Scotch marriage, i.e., a kind of marriage oath before witnesses. In any event Reade lived with this girl (whenever his circumstances and his mother permitted) from 1838 or 1839 up to the time of her death in 1848, following the birth of a son who was christened Charles Liston and generally thought to be Reade's godson, until Reade, shortly before his death, recognized him as Charles Liston Reade. Beyond these few facts, little is known about this chapter in Reade's life, though it would appear that his mother played a role similar to that of Mrs. Gatty in *Christie Johnstone*, forcing him to treat his Scottish wife as a mistress, his son as a godson — as a means of preserving his Magdalen Fellowship and as the price of retaining her own love and respect. The novel itself bears out this interpretation, as do Mrs. Reade's actions of a few years later (1851), when her boy was thirty-seven years old, vice-president of Magdalen, and threatened by the charms of a famous actress, Mrs. Stirling, who had come to spend a week with him at Oxford. In Reade's own words (as recounted by John Coleman in his *Charles Reade as I Knew Him*):

> Some good-natured friend wrote to Ipsden that the Vice-Chancellor of Magdalen had been seen trotting about with a play-actress, and next day, just as my fair friend and I were sitting down to lunch in my rooms, the Chatelaine of Ipsden descended upon us. She did not wait for any introduction. It was the first and only time I ever knew the mater to forget herself.
>
> I must do the other lady the justice to say *she* did not — indeed, she never acted so well on the stage as she did on that occasion.
>
> "You are his mother, madam, and he is my friend," she said. "Don't trouble, sir; you are needed here, and I am not. I can find my way."
>
> I drove home with mother that night, and next day (Sunday) we went to church together. When she said "forgive us our trespasses," she clasped my hand. I returned the clasp, and from that time forth the incident was closed.

With due allowance for Coleman's own theatrical propensities, the Oedipal sentimentality he dramatizes may well be authentic — even to the final handclasp. Reade's own letters to and about Mrs. Stirling — one of which

Percy Allen described as "too intimate and passionate for quotation"—show that Reade was in love with Mrs. Stirling or thought he was; that despite a break in their relationship, probably exacerbated if not caused by Mrs. Reade, he was thinking of Mrs. Stirling as well as his Scottish wife when he wrote the last chapter of *Christie Johnstone*. In a letter to Mrs. Baylis, mostly devoted to Mrs. Stirling, he wrote: "C. J. concludes with a panegyric on Marriage (as I understand it). I describe it as Moses might the promised land, all the brighter because I have no hope of ever tasting it. God's will be done!"

By this time, in deference to God's will or his mother's, Reade had given up all hope of marriage—and with it, he believed, all hope of personal fulfillment. And if he had fully accepted God's will, as set forth by his mother, he would long since have given up his hope of becoming a writer, for like so many strict Evangelicals she looked upon the theatre as little short of iniquitous, other forms of writing as at best frivolous. "Immortal beings," she declared, "should not flutter among the trifles of literature. What a field for thought and action are the realities of life, and the certainty of a future state." These admonitions Reade could never accept, yet neither could he reject them outright. He was too much his mother's son. The best he could do, for some fourteen years, was to cherish his reluctant muse as he had cherished his Scottish wife—in fear and doubt and secrecy.

This is why, from the first, he was so neurotically defensive about his writings, why he sank into fits of depression when he could not place his early plays—fits that at times (as on May 7, 1852) obliged him to seek medical aid, first at Malvern, in what would now be called a sanitarium; then, a few months later, at Durham, in what was apparently a rest home—though Reade did not rest: he wrote. On July 20, 1852, he noted in his *Diary*: "I have written three-copy books of 'Peg Woffington,' a novel. I hope to make a decent three-volume novel of it; but whether any one will publish it is another question. If not now, perhaps in three years' time. Literature no doubt is a close borough." Within a matter of days, however, he abandoned these plans entirely, to complete the novel in one volume—a volume which is little more than a narrative version of the play *Masks and Faces* that he had written in collaboration with Tom Taylor.

While Reade no doubt had practical reasons for resorting to this strategy (among others, his anxiety to get on with his play *Gold*) his statements in the novel and *Diary* suggest that his feelings of depression, bordering on despair, had for the time being rendered him incapable of carrying out his original plans. At one point in the epilogue to the novel he speaks in his own person of "this dirty little world"; at another, in commenting on a certain character's death, he adds: "And I who laugh at him, would leave this world today, to be with him; for I am tossing at sea—he is in port." Moreover the same note recurs in the *Diary*, most revealingly perhaps in the entry dated August 3: "My life is very monotonous. . . . No sympathy with my pursuits. I am a most unhappy artist, to have no public and no domestic circle. Praise and sympathy are the breath of our nostrils. . . . It is crushing when no one cares for what we do. . . . I have finished my novel, 'Peg Woffington'; I don't know whether it is good or not. I wish to Heaven I had a housekeeper like Molière. . . . But how purposeless, hopeless, and languid I feel."

Nor was Reade much heartened by the favorable though limited recognition accorded the novel. He had struggled for so long, his fears and doubts went so deep, that when he gained a few shillings and a few critical nods they were no longer enough, particularly when the nods were qualified by doubts concerning "the precise connection between the story and the play." Fully to vindicate himself as man and writer he had to write a novel all his own: a full-length, three-volume novel of social purpose that would enable him to act out his heroic vision of himself as the anti-Carlylean and Baconian and Pre-Raphaelite savior of the Nineteenth Century.

These aims Reade eventually realized, at least to his own satisfaction, in *It Is Never Too Late To Mend* (1856). In 1852, however, he was still too frantic, too anxious for immediate success as a dramatist, to devote his energies to a full-length novel. Indeed it would appear, on the basis of his entries in the *Diary*, that he did not begin serious work on *Christie Johnstone* until December 1852; then, drawing heavily upon an earlier version of "this 'Dramatic Story,' 'Novel' by courtesy," finished it off in a matter of months. In an effort to justify the inclusion of dated elements of social purpose, taken over directly from the earlier version, Reade appended a 'Note' to the novel in which he declared it "a story . . . written three years ago"—a declaration that would appear to be disingenuous, unless the word "story" be taken to mean "dramatic story," for prior to 1852 he always referred to *Christie Johnstone* as a play. In the present context, however, there is no need to insist on this point because, regardless of which came first, the novel or the play, the novel is still (like *Peg Woffington*) a play written in narrative form, i.e., a series of comic and melodramatic scenes filled with social purpose and linked up by a stagey double plot.

In the opening chapter Lord Ipsden, cultured and intelligent, but lackadaisical and bored, is refused by Lady Barbara (a disciple of Carlyle); whereupon he lapses into even greater listlessness than before. At this point an eccentric doctor advises him to acquaint himself with the life and needs of the "lower classes." Following this advice, Ipsden goes to Scotland, does his duty by the lower classes, and becomes something of a Baconian and anti-Carlylean hero when he effects a daring rescue in a storm at sea. In the meantime, Lady Barbara appears in Scotland, becomes disillusioned by the unheroic actions of her Carlylean suitor and eventually learns the true worth of a modern man—nay, a modern hero! They live happily ever after. That is one plot. The other centers on Christie Johnstone, a beautiful, intelligent, and talented Scottish fishwife, and Charles Gatty, a weak but well meaning and gifted English painter imbued with Pre-Raphaelite ideas and ideals. They fall in love, and marriage is in the offing, even though Gatty is penniless and as yet unsuccessful in his work, when Gatty's mother appears on the scene. She dissuades him, and does not relent until Christie saves him from drowning. They also live happily ever after. The two plots are rather mechanically joined by bringing the aristocratic Ipsden into contact with Gatty, Christie, and the lower classes.

For the expression of Reade's "genuine contemporaneous verdicts" on Carlylism and Pre-Raphaelitism (discussed at length in my "Pre-Raphaelitism in Charles Reade's Early Fiction," *PMLA*, LX [1945], 1149–64) this double plot proved reasonably adequate; but for the expression of the titular theme (clearly a fictional version of his own Scotch marriage) its melodramatic grooves were far too arbitrary and divisive. To give his autobiographical experiences artistic meaning he was, at the very least, obliged to dramatize them in such a way as to bring out their essential implications, perhaps by having Ipsden (representing the real Charles Reade) fall in love with the Christie of the novel (representing the real Christie) and battle out the question of marriage with a fictional Mrs. Ipsden (representing the real Mrs. Reade). But this or any similar alternative would have forced Reade into soul-searchings that he could ill afford, especially where his mother was concerned. It was simpler and more reassuring to look into the heart of the theatre and theatrical fiction, where doubts were resolved as they should be — in line with his own daydreams.

This helps to explain why, in the novel itself, he so flagrantly dissipated the artistic potential of his autobiographical materials, scattering them over two plots and using his structure to separate out or eliminate those elements which could not be brought into conformity with his dual purpose. While Ipsden, as his name suggests, is a self-portrait, and Christie represents his Scottish wife, Reade does not permit them any such intimacy as that which led to their real-life struggles with Mrs. Reade. In the novel he leaves Ipsden motherless and separates him from Christie by means of the double plot, permitting them to meet only after he has provided them with suitable mates chosen primarily to illustrate his artistic and social theories. True, Reade includes a mother-son conflict (between Charles Gatty and his mother over Christie) that approximates certain features of his own personal experience, but he presents this conflict so melodramatically that (with the exception of a few scenes, to be discussed presently) it degenerates into a transpontine version of *The Silver Cord* — with Mrs. Gatty, a former servant of the Ipsdens who had married a greengrocer and developed delusions of social grandeur, poisoning her son's mind against that common fishwife, and never relenting until Christie, "in front of three thousand spectators," snatches Gatty from a watery grave.

As this denouement suggests, the entire Christie plot is a projection of Reade's wishes and daydreams expressed through his own variations upon the usual Sensation formulas. The stress he places upon Christie's Amazonian proportions (e.g., her "grand corporeal tract," her "leg with a noble swell"), the way he lauds her man-like abilities in everything from trading to fishing, the reversal of the man-woman roles in the final rescue — these and related features of his presentation tie in with his real-life interest in the androgynous and help to explain his admiration for the beautiful yet physically powerful women he constantly reproduced in his novels. It is almost as if, sensing the female component in his own make-up ("my heart is womanish"), he realized that he was too weak, too Gatty-like, to break with his mother, that if he were to marry, the woman would have to play the man and carry him off — the way Christie carried off her Gatty.

But this is a biographical, not a literary interpretation. In the novel itself, Reade's first concern — in line with his own beliefs, techniques, and anxieties — was to render his individual variations conventionally pure.

Christie's "grand corporeal tract" he was at pains to present as so much Victorian womanhood, Gatty's female helplessness as a Victorian version of the artistic temperament. And for the most part he succeeded, thereby sacrificing the artistic potential of his genuine but aberrant perceptions to his own and his reader's ideals.

So far as Reade knew, however, the novel was conceptually as well as structurally sound. The only shortcomings he could recognize (*Diary*, June 17, 1853) were shortcomings in executive technique: "Busy correcting proofs of 'Christie Johnstone.' Fear there is an excess of dialogue in it. I think I ought to throw some of that into narrative. Mrs. Seymour thinks there is too much criticism in it. I have no doubt there is. These are defects to me which judgment cannot correct. I lack the true oil of Fiction, and I fear she will have to inspire me, as well as reform me. The drowned fisherman's scene was admired by Kinglake and by Tennyson; but I feel how much more a thorough-bred narrator would have made of it." For Reade these remarks are unusually sanguine: they indicate that he had at long last found his Egeria, plus a certain amount of outside praise from the right quarters; also that he felt he was on the way to greater things—if only he could improve his narrative technique and pour "the true oil of Fiction" over his other defects.

Just how he proposed to do this he explained at some length in a typically Readean document—an "Auto-criticism" designed to present "the author's candid notion of what an honest critic would say were he disposed to avoid the minimum alike of praise and blame. . . ." In the guise of "honest critic" Reade begins thus:

"CHRISTIE JOHNSTONE

"A Dramatic Story

The origin of this title appears to be the quantity of pure dialogue in the work.

To those effects in which the drama shines the volume before us makes less pretension than three novels out of four.

Once again the stress on excessive dialogue, to the exclusion of other and more flagrantly melodramatic effects. And his further criticism follows along the same lines. "The author of 'Christie Johnstone,'" he points out, "has not the art of mixing his materials. Hence the compound, with some exceptions is dry and lumpy. This is to be the more regretted as the materials themselves are decidedly good. . . ." What the author needs, he goes on to explain, is "A supple and changeable style . . . but above all, some warmth of imagination: this it is which clothes incidents with those glowing details that make them vivid and interesting. . . !"

While it may seem that Reade is here probing a bit deeper, his words are deceptive unless one bears in mind his addiction to Sensation. For example, in criticizing "the drowned fisherman's scene," he implies that the episode, though made up of good materials, is not handled so as to bring out all possible sentiment and suspense. Yet, in point of fact, the scene consists of nothing but sentimentality and suspense, culminating in Christie's daring triumph over the village strong man and alcoholic, when she prevents him, by moral and physical force, from entering that den of iniquity, the local pub — thereby saving him "fra the puir mon's enemy, the enemy o' mankind, the cursed, cursed, drink."

If this were an isolated example of Reade's self-criticism, it might be excused on the ground that he had been temporarily misled by Kinglake and Tennyson, who apparently admired Christie's Cambyses' vein. But Reade was equally well pleased with other and even more questionable aspects of the novel — including its impossible climactic action, which he recounts at length, and with undisguised satisfaction:

All Newhaven is watching a swimmer, who, it appears, is in the habit of going out to the roads and back. One spirit, quicker than the rest, compares the time, the tide, and other circumstances, and doubts the swimmer's safety. This is Christie, who throws off her listlessness, and with her brother darts down to the pier, and goes out in a boat amidst the jeers of the others; before, however, she has made her first tack, the whole town has come to her opinion, and it is in front of three thousand spectators that she with difficulty and dexterity saves her lover without discovering his identity, which her brother, who hates him, is anxious to conceal from her.

The feat has been seen by Lord Ipsden and Lady Barbara from the shore; and Mrs. Gatty, the artist's mother, who had learned in the heat of the business that it was her son, has fainted and been carried to Christie Johnstone's house.

Thus a dramatic close is prepared.

Reade's final "thus" underlines what is all too clear: that in the novel as in the play he resorted to the crudest kind of stage directions as a means of working out his melodramatic plot. In the words of Professor E. G. Sutcliffe: "Christie moves forward on stage waves while a well drilled mob shouts encouragement and applause from the front."

The social purpose of the novel Reade also considered good in itself. As "honest critic" he congratulates himself on having a "quick eye for all that is good and clever in the lower classes," on having expressed his observations "covertly and not without plausibility . . ." and on having shown "forbearance" in his arguments. "They who hold his sentiment," he says of himself, "seldom let us go to bed till they have told us that corduroy is virtue, and broadcloth and soap are vice: and we are in some terror lest through hearing this too often we may end our career by believing it." Nevertheless, after stressing all these virtues (plus numerous others), he once again reverts to the author's lack of narrative skill—a lack which he seeks to remedy by having the author "associate himself with one of our authoresses . . . The pair would produce a novel considerably above the average: something we should read with pleasure and lay aside with delight. . . ." This suggestion harks back to his earlier statements about dramatic collaboration, and his never-ending doubts concerning his powers of invention. The difference is that in his dramatic collaborations he looked to Tom Taylor, a writer of some skill and sophistication, whereas the authoresses he apparently had in mind were of the type now represented in *Queens of the Circulating Library*.

However one views this auto-criticism—as a *jeu d'esprit* or as a serious piece of self-analysis—it shows how inadequate, even simple-minded, were Reade's conceptions of narrative art and the creative process, how inept were his specific criticisms and suggested improvements. On the analytic side, all he could do was to measure his own performance, in a most superficial way, against the most naïve Sensation standards. Of his more crucial shortcomings he showed little if any awareness—and that was usually misguided; e.g., his remarks on "warmth of imagination" and "the true oil of Fiction"—though seemingly perceptive—actually tend to reduce imagination to the oil that lubricates the gears of his creaking stage machinery.

Indeed he was so committed to Sensation mechanics that he could neither recognize nor appreciate the more creative aspects of his work—not even those qualities in his realistic presentation of Christie which W. D. Howells praised so highly, and which still hold up remarkably well, in comparison with similar presentations of Dickens and Thackeray. Less timid in sexual matters than these novelists (or for that matter any other novelist of the time) Reade took advantage of the stage traditions governing the treatment of comic and low-life characters to introduce his heroine as a woman of physical as well as moral substance. In the opening scenes, he uncorsets her, literally as well as metaphorically; and if his performance is a trifle self-conscious, not to say bumptious, he at least does not fall into the inverted pornography that too often characterizes such Victorian efforts — most flagrantly perhaps in Thackeray's presentation of Amelia on the eve of Waterloo, when (posing as George) he enters the novel and Amelia's bedroom to give the reader a strip-tease version of his Victorian ideal: "The purple eyelids were fringed and closed, and one round arm, smooth and white, lay outside of the coverlet. Good God! how pure she was. . . ." After this "one round arm," the "noble swell" of Christie's leg appears refreshingly physical — though, as has been pointed out, Reade's ideals of womanhood ultimately obliged him to reduce Christie's physical beauties to the attributes of an ideal pastoral type.

Equally realistic at times, despite the prevailing theatricality of Reade's presentation, are Christie's actions and words — as, for instance, when Ipsden tries to purchase herring from her:

"What is the price?

At this question the poetry died out of Christie Johnstone's face, she gave her companion a rapid look, indiscernible by male eye, and answered, —

"Three a penny sirr; they are no plenty the day," added she, in smooth tones that carried conviction.

(Little liar, they were selling six a penny everywhere.)

Although Reade's interpolated observations may be irritating, Christie's words are realistic enough in themselves — as are those of the widow Rutherford, one of the lesser characters, when Ipsden mentions her troubles:

"Oh! ye need na vex yourself for an auld wife's tears; tears are a blessin', lad, I shall assure ye. Mony's the time I hae prayed for them, and could na hae them. Sit ye doon! sit ye doon! I'll no let ye gang fra my door till I hae thankit ye — but gie me time, gie me time. I canna greet a' the days of the week."

But this anglicized Scots dialect, however brilliant in itself, in no wise strengthens or deepens the dramatic action: for the most part, as the above quotation illustrates, it merely imparts a realistic Scots flavor to the otherwise stock sentiments and reactions of the *dramatis personae*.

Likewise brilliant, though even more stagey, are the stylistic touches through which Reade now and again twists the words and actions of his otherwise conventional characters into meaningful juxtaposition. The widow Rutherford stands upon "the high ground of her low estate"; Ipsden's conversations with Saunders (a comic counterpart of Dickens' Littimer) are on occasion satirically succinct:

"Saunders! do you know what Dr. Aberford means by the lower classes?"
"Perfectly, my lord."
"Are there any about here?"
"I am sorry to say they are everywhere, my lord."
"Get me some" (cigarette).

Saunders, one of the most successful minor characters, not only talks like a literary annual, he has a three-volume novel in the press: ". . . one of those cerberus-leviathans of fiction, so common now; incredible as folio to future ages." All too often, however, these passages of "realism, with divinations and conjectures across its borders," are merely incidental or ornamental. And even when they are functional, as in the treatment of Saunders, their sophisticated effects too often eclipse or negate the artless responses demanded by the narrative action.

The most notable exceptions are the directly autobiographical scenes, particularly those centering upon the Christie-Gatty-Mrs. Gatty relationship. While these scenes too are basically melodramatic, they are enriched by realistic elements—presumably taken directly from Reade's own experience—which make for an intensity analogous to that which Dreiser and Farrell sometimes achieve in their painfully actualistic scenes. Mrs. Gatty's nagging is strikingly effective in this respect, not only in substance and psychology but in style. Of course it must be recognized that she is not an individualized mother. She cannot be compared with such a character as, say, Mrs. Bede of *Adam Bede*, despite a number of superficial resemblances between the two. Mrs. Gatty is rather an Oedipal villainess (a stage version of the relentlessly possessive mother who alternately pets and lacerates her son into masochistic submission) and her self-righteous platitudes and stratagems would be simply irritating, were they not at times so close, in their theatricality, to the Oedipal reality—the climactic scene being that in which Mrs. Gatty, using her platitudes like a priest his catechism, forces Gatty to break with Christie:

"Look at me, Charles; at your mother."
"Yes, mother," said he nervously.
"You must part with her, or kill me."
He started from his seat and began to flutter up and down the room. Poor excitable creature! "Part with her!" cried he; "I shall never be a

painter if I do . . . What is an artist without love? How is he to bear up against his disappointments from within, his mortification from without? the great ideas he has and cannot grasp, and all the forms of ignorance that sting him, from stupid insensibility down to clever, shallow criticism?" . . .

The old woman paused to let his eloquence evaporate.

The pause chilled him; then gently and slowly, but emphatically, she spoke to him thus: —

"Who has kept you on her small means ever since you were ten years and seven months old?"

"You should know, mother, dear mother."

"Answer me, Charles."

"My mother."

"Who has pinched herself in every earthly thing, to make you an immortal painter, and, above all, a gentleman?"

"My mother."

"Who forgave you the little faults of youth, before you could ask pardon?"

"My mother. O mother, I ask pardon now for all the trouble I ever gave the best, the dearest, the tenderest of mothers."

"Who will go home to Newcastle a broken-hearted woman, with the one hope gone that has kept her up in poverty and sorrow so many weary years, if this goes on?"

"Nobody, I hope."

"Yes, Charles: your mother."

"O, mother; you have been always my best friend."

"And am this day."

"Do not be my worst enemy now: it is for me to obey you, but it is for you to think well before you drive me to despair."

And the poor womanish heart leaned his head on the table, and began to sorrow over his hard fate.

Mrs. Gatty soothed him. "It need not be done all in a moment. It must be done kindly but firmly. I will give you as much time as you like."

The melodramatic intensity of this scene, deriving from the calculated deftness with which Mrs. Gatty wields her pieties, is genuinely expressive. It reveals the features behind the veil of Victorian motherhood, and if the features bear a marked resemblance to Mrs. Reade's, they are still so powerful in their Oedipal grossness that they serve to define not merely Gatty's predicament, and Reade's, but that of nearly all the other Victorian sons and lovers.

But one scene can hardly redeem an entire novel, not even when the novel, in certain of its aspects, compares favorably with those of Thackeray and Dickens. For what avail technical virtues and virtuosities when they are used not to explore but to evade the very realities they are pretending to interpret? Reade could not, as one of his critics advised, express what was in "his own heart": there was too much locked up in it—feelings that he could not contemplate, much less write, without calling into question nearly all the rationalizations on which his emotional balance depended. And this was particularly true where his feelings for his mother were concerned. If he now and then became aware of what it meant to be her son—a querulous, loveless, middle-aged bachelor—he never permitted that awareness to develop into full realization. He could not acknowledge his condition, or its primary cause, even to himself; as for putting such a mother-son relationship directly into fiction, that was, for Reade, literally unthinkable, and therefore unimaginable. For what he could not think, in good round Baconian terms, he dismissed as "cobwebs" spun from "the depths of a penny a liner's inner consciousness."

Had Reade not been so fearful of "inner consciousness," the autobiographical passages suggest that he might conceivably have broken through his self-imposed restrictions, perhaps to express poetically or fantastically, after the manner of Dickens or the Brontës, what he could not express openly. But Reade could not see this, nor did he want to see it. He had no use whatsoever for fantasy or any other form of indirection which derived from "inner consciousness." He wanted the direct, purposeful truth, "the one great truth" that Gatty and "those boys" held so dear, and that he himself had set about realizing, even before the publication of *Christie Johnstone*, by adapting Gatty's Pre-Raphaelite techniques to the writing of a two-volume documentary novel based on his play *Gold*. "*Christie Johnstone* goes on but slowly," he wrote Mrs. Baylis, "I corrected this day proof sheets up to p. 240. I think there are 100 pages more to come, so fear it will be no fatter a vol. than *Peg Woff*. . . . My two vols. will be a much heavier blow—at least I think so—but Lord, if you knew the trouble and bother of writing a solid work upon my present plan, i.e., verifying everything I say or describe! To write my two vols. I must read twenty, and hunt up men as well as books." And this was only the beginning: Reade continued to "hunt up men as well as books" for the next three years, finally to expand his two volumes into the three volumes of *It Is Never Too Late To Mend* (1856), his first "Matter-of-Fact Romance," his first "great hit," and in his own estimation his first "immortal work."

Thus it was that Reade, emulating his Pre-Raphaelite hero, fulfilled his own heroic vision of himself. For Reade the man, teetering on the brink of despair, this triumph came none too soon. But for Reade the artist it was little short of disastrous, since it confirmed him in the very theories and practices which were most inimical to his art. That he nevertheless continued to write fiction worthy of serious consideration shows how great were the powers he sacrificed to his Victorian ideals.

GEORGE MEREDITH'S *ONE OF OUR CONQUERORS*

Fabian Gudas
LOUISIANA STATE UNIVERSITY

As A novelist George Meredith considered himself an innovator experimenting with new techniques and subject matters. Instead of giving the public "rose-pink" sentimentalism, "dirty drab" realism, or the "blood and glory" novels of action (such was his characterization of certain dominant tendencies in contemporary fiction), he was using the novel as a means for conveying ideas; he was asking his readers to become interested in the thoughts and feelings of his characters rather than in their actions; and he was presenting his materials in a style which required concentration, intellectual agility, and imaginative response if it was to be understood and appreciated.

By introducing the philosopher into fiction, he hoped to give the novelist's art new dignity and power. He found the novel "neither blushless infant nor executive man"; at worst it was a "pasture of idiots, a method for idiotizing the entire population which has taken to reading," and at best the amusement of "boys and girls of both ages in this land." In producing such trifles, contemporary novelists were degrading themselves as artists and evading their responsibilities as human beings. "All right use of life," said Meredith, "is to pave ways for the firmer footing of those who succeed us," and he judged his own work to be of value only as it contributed to this end. The novel, he argued, should become a critic and a guide for men struggling to higher stages of civilized development. As an expression of the comic spirit, it could discipline men through laughter and thus help them to get rid of the follies which are hindering their growth — egoism, social pretension, hypocrisy, artificiality, narrow-mindedness, and sentimentalism. More important, it could be a positive influence, teaching men the criteria of maturity and the necessary process for reaching it. To do this, the novelist must take as his subject matter "the clockwork of the brain" and describe in detail the workings of men's minds as they face difficulties and moral crises which force them to make decisions that will fatefully determine their future growth and happiness.

Meredith published *One of Our Conquerors* in 1891, after *Beauchamp's Career*, *The Egoist*, and *Diana of the Crossways* had won him critical recognition. It is a typical Meredithian novel in every way. In it are found many of Meredith's favorite recommendations for the improvement of English civilization: the emancipation of women, the dissolution of the restrictions of the ancient class structure, the dispersion of wealth, the widening of democratic privileges, the need for tolerance and charity in judging erring men and women. For it Meredith chose a subject which gave him many opportunities for presenting whole chapters of minute psychological analysis. And he wrote it in a style rich in allusion, metaphor, symbol, and other devices for conveying his meaning obliquely.

The protagonist, Victor Radnor, the conqueror of women, society, and the world of finance, belongs to the class of characters whom Meredith called tragic comedians. Meredith had explored the psychology of another member of this genus in a novel, published in 1880, entitled *The Tragic Comedians*. This book is a fictional account of the disastrous love affair between Ferdinand Lassalle, the great Jewish leader of the nineteenth-century German Socialists, and a beautiful but shallow and conceited young woman of the upper social classes. The novel ends with the death of Lassalle in a duel with one of her other suitors. Meredith describes Lassalle as a man "profusely mixed of good and evil, of generous ire and mutinous, of the passion for the future of mankind and vanity of person, magnanimity and sensualism, high judgement, reckless indiscipline, chivalry, savagery, solidity, fragmentariness." Meredith explains Lassalle's tragedy as due to the "dissension" within him between the different sides of his nature, a dissension which he was unable to quell by an act of will guided by an insight into the direction his moral development should take; though he "was getting to purer fires," he allowed the animal in him to run "unchained and bounding" at the end. Rejecting both "fool" and "madman" as terms to convey the final judgment on Lassalle, Meredith calls him a "tragic comedian": "He was neither fool nor madman, nor man to be adored; his last temptation caught him in the season before he had subdued his blood, and amid the multitudinously simple of this world, stamped him a tragic comedian: that is, a grand pretender, a self-deceiver, one of the lividly ludicrous, whom we cannot laugh at, but must contemplate, to distinguish where their character strikes the note of discord with life. . . . The characters of the hosts of men are of the simple order of the comic; not many are of a stature and a complexity calling for the junction of the two Muses to name them."

Victor Radnor, because of his "stature" and "complexity" and the "dissension" within him, is also "one of the lividly ludicrous," though he differs from Lassalle in being closer to "fool" than to "madman." Like Lassalle, he is a "giant," a man gifted with great elemental energy and therefore worthy to be a leader of men — to be a "hero" — once he has disciplined himself. The dissension within his divided or "transitional" personality forces him to be a self-deceiver, and, like Lassalle, he fails in mid-career because he is unable to bring his great natural gifts into a harmonious stability.

Victor is obsessed with a desire to "shine in the sun," or, as his friend Colney Durance, the satiric spirit in the novel, unkindly puts it, he has an "insane itch to be the bobbing cork on the wave of the minute." His extraordinary success in being the "first in everything" is explained by the generosity of nature and circumstance. Nature has given him a superabundance of energy; a remarkable practical intelligence; an exceptional power over persuasive language; and an optimistic temperament which gives his step buoyancy and confidence. His optimism has been justified by his "godmother Fortune" who has pampered him to such an extent that he now has the feeling that he is a man for whom it is impossible to fail: the weather conforms to his wishes; he never gets sick, though he takes no pains to protect himself from the east wind; every pound that he invests comes back to him accompanied by another; and once he even receives a supernatural tap on the elbow which stops him from doing something that would have brought him unpleasantness.

As a result of the beneficence of nature and circumstance, he has become one of the richest of England's financiers. In his early youth, though handicapped by a lack of money, he had dreamed of earning an aristocratic distinction for the Radnor name. A cold-blooded marriage with a rich but middle-aged widow, Mrs. Burman, enabled him to begin a successful business career. Having fallen in love with a young lady companion of his wife, Nataly Dreighton, he deserted Mrs. Burman and lived as man and wife with Nataly. To them a child, Nesta, was born. Unable to secure a divorce because of Mrs. Burman's religious scruples, he had at first resigned himself to living in obscurity; but when he found himself accepted by the family of his business associate, whose wife was a worthy daughter of Mrs. Grundy, he decided that his adultery would not be too serious an obstacle to conquering a world which "he could illumine to give him back splendid reflections." In this estimate he was wrong; for whenever the Radnors became established in a house ostentatious enough to make them vulnerable, mysterious rumors, traced to Mrs. Burman, would begin to circulate, their neighbors would cut them, and they would feel forced to move. The character of Nataly was another obstacle. Because she could not allay her guilt feelings, she was frequently depressed, never felt secure, suffered greatly from the slights of others, and became introverted; it was impossible for her to become a leader in the kinds of social circles desired by Victor. Because he loved her deeply, he did not hesitate to make the necessary changes when he saw that her situation was hurting her; but unable to see the full depths of her agony and driven by his ambition, he bounced back after each failure with a fresh plan for the conquest of society.

The book opens at the moment that Victor is hatching a new project. This time the principal is to be his daughter, a charming, warm, intelligent girl, now arrived at marriageable age and still ignorant of the fact that she is illegitimate. Victor is planning a marriage for her with a member of England's nobility, a marriage which, he hopes, will cover the stigma on his name and remove permanently the obstacle to his social success: "Gossip," he reasons, "flies to a wider circle round the members of a great titled family, is inaudible; or no longer the diphtherian whisper the commonalty hear of the commonalty. . . . One blow and we have silenced our enemy: Nesta's wedding-day has relieved her parents." As a means to help him make such a marriage, he has spent the year before the action of the book begins in secretly building Lakelands, a country house large enough to become the social club for all the best people in England and splendid enough to make even the aristocratic mouth water. As a matter of fact, he has already carefully selected the lucky suitor, a young heir to a title, Dudley Sowerby, whose family has the desirable qualifications of an old and unbesmirched name and a growing indigence. Dudley is a dull, unimaginative young man, but thoroughly well-bred and morally sound.

The plot of the novel is the sequence of steps which Victor takes to implement his scheme, and the book closes with his complete failure when Nesta, after an engagement of some months, refuses to marry Dudley. At the end Victor is characteristically embarking on a new project to put himself in the forefront — he intends to run for Parliament. On the night when he is to give the opening speech of his campaign, Nataly, who has suffered unbearably, dies of a heart attack. Victor's personality breaks to pieces, and his death follows a few months later.

In *One of Our Conquerors*, as in other typically Meredithian novels, the plot is of only secondary importance. Meredith deliberately refuses to set the reader astride "the enchanted horse of the Tale"; instead, he invites him to become interested in mental processes and the development of character. The complications of Victor's life provide him with many opportunities to gain insight into himself; at times he seems on the verge of recognizing that as a man he is a failure, but he persists as Victor Radnor to the end. Nataly achieves some insight into herself and into Victor, but her mental and physical exhaustion makes further growth impossible. Nesta, after merely smelling the apple on the Tree of Knowledge, matures sufficiently to see that a marriage with Dudley would be a serious mistake, although she recognizes that he too has been changing for the better. She falls in love with and eventually marries one of Meredith's "heroes," Dartrey Fenellan.

Commentators on *One of Our Conquerors* have variously designated the fundamental weakness of Victor's character as optimism, egoism, and the inability to free himself from the dominance of his sensations and subconscious fears. It is the assumption of the following analysis that additional light can be thrown on this most complex of all of Meredith's creations by interpreting his character and destiny in terms of another of the key words in the novel — "scheme." The word denotes a careful and intelligent marshaling of means to an end; but in Meredithian usage the end is always a material end, like more money or higher social position; and in all of its uses Meredith insists on its derogatory implications of selfishness, cunning, duplicity, and self-deception.

Victor is a "schemer." He is a man gifted with the most incisive practical intelligence — a "lightning arithmetic for measuring, sounding, and deciding." But he is also a man whose critical and moral intelligence has not yet matured; as a result he has not carefully scrutinized and evaluated the various ends which he has set for himself. *One of Our Conquerors* is the history of the failure of one of his grand schemes — "the scheme of the Lakelands"; and the novel may be read as a study of the effects which scheming has on the schemer and on those around him.

One of the great evils of scheming is that the schemer tends to lose sight of human beings as individuals with their own purposes, desires, and moral needs, and to regard them abstractly as obstacles or as means to his ends. Nataly sees Victor as "guilty of the schemer's error of counting human creatures arithmetically, in the sum, without the estimate of distinctive qualities and value here and there."

In the distant past Victor had classed Mrs. Burman as a means to an end: he had married and deserted her without feeling obliged to recognize her pitiful bid for happiness as a factor in his calculations. She has now become the greatest obstacle to Victor's social success. Though old and sickly, she refuses to divorce Victor or to die; he cannot, therefore, legalize his union with Nataly and wear his white waistcoat proudly, spotless before an applauding world. As an obstacle, Victor regards Mrs. Burman only as a thing to be overcome. Too civilized to arrange for her poisoning, he gives way to hatred and "murderous" thoughts as he eagerly anticipates her expected early death.

The marriage of Nesta to Dudley is the heart of the scheme. Victor realizes that by making this marriage he is probably sacrificing the future happiness of his beloved daughter whose freshness and originality would be stifled by the heaviness of Dudley. He also realizes that he may be contributing to the moral delinquency of Dudley. Since Dudley will have to be told about Nesta's illegitimacy, he will be placed in the position of having to give up principle, narrow and obsolete though it is, in order to secure the Radnor fortune. In spite of the memories of his own past, Victor feels contempt for a young man who could be drawn into marriage by the magnet of gold. Nevertheless, buoyed by the thought that love would justify all (but at the same time guiltily aware of the power of his rhetoric to create love), he subtly plots to make each see the virtues in the other: he flourishes the bait of money and diamonds (from Nesta's "own mine") in front of Dudley's nose; arranges a trip to France to throw the two together in more romantic surroundings; insinuates his own desire in the mind of Nesta; avoids the enlightenment of Dudley until some vague future date; refuses to report the death of Dartrey's wife because he fears that Dartrey, who is a hero to both mother and daughter, might now become a serious rival to Dudley; organizes a charity concert at Lakelands, the brilliant success of which makes his benevolence known in all the right places; sends Nesta off to his relatives, the very moral Duvidney ladies, who live only a few miles from the Sowerby estate and under whose protection Nesta finally does become engaged.

Using the same devices of bribery, evasion, and rhetoric, Victor similarly hurts and corrupts his "allies." Through dinners and other kindnesses he wins Mrs. Burman's clergyman, lawyer, doctor, and butler over to his side to use what influence they can either to make her agree to a divorce or to prevent her from exposing him further. He permits the Reverend Mr. Barmby to become a suitor for Nesta's hand though he is certain that Nesta will never have him; Barmby is thus placed in a cruel and ridiculous position because of Victor's fear that a negative answer would deprive his circle of the clergyman and the moral atmosphere which he has contributed to it. Victor even allows himself to succumb to the wiles of Lady Halley, the lone entitled gentlewoman of his set, who, when her hand is held, is much more eager to help him with his social aspirations and use her connection with Dudley's family for the promotion of Victor's scheme.

The greatest sufferer from Victor's scheming is Nataly. Self-effacing by nature and from long habit, she raises no protest to Victor's scheming in spite of her clear insight that the end pursued is worthless and in spite of her moral repugnance to the means being used. Having silently become an accomplice to Victor, she is overcome with guilt feelings. Bent on his scheme, Victor can no longer see realities; he cannot read her or correctly estimate the intensity of the pain she is suffering; he cannot see that every move he makes is another shot in her weakened heart. To himself and others he accuses her of lacking courage, he is annoyed by her becoming an obstacle to the scheme through passive resistance, and he places all the blame for her pain on the dying Mrs. Burman.

The worst effects of scheming are on the schemer himself. "Observe," comments the author on Victor, "how fatefully he who has a scheme is the engine of it; he is no longer the man of his tastes or of his principles; he is on a line of rails for a terminus; and he may cast languishing eyes across waysides to right and left, he has doomed himself to proceed, with a self-devouring hunger for the half desired; probably manhood gone at the embrace of it. This may be or not, but Nature has decreed to him the forfeit of pleasure." Because of the exigencies of his scheme, the schemer can no longer live in terms of his "tastes" or "principles"; he forfeits "pleasure" and suffers the loss of "manhood." The loss of wayside pleasures is disturbing, but the loss of manhood is the loss of life itself.

What are the pleasures which Victor is sacrificing for the sake of his scheme? From the very beginning of the book, Meredith stresses the fact that Victor is a man who delights in simple things, even in the ordinary sights and sounds of the city or country. Nataly says that "the aim of his life was at the giving and taking of simple enjoyment." Nesta is another witness to this characteristic: "He baffled her perusal of a man of power by the simpleness of his enjoyment of small things coming in his way;—the lighted shops, the crowd, emergence from the crowd, or the meeting near mid-winter of a soft warm wind along the Embankment, and dark Thames magnificently coroneted over his grimy flow." Frequently throughout the book we see Victor in the midst of such enjoyments: his pleasure at the sight of the "lemon butterfly in a dell of sunshine"; his love of food, wine, and music; his enjoyment of the little novelties of an excursion to the Continent; his vivid memories of the peaks, valleys, and rills of the Alpine country. Meredith is himself moved to the following comment as he watches Victor listening to music: "Eyes had been given this man to spy the pleasures and reveal the joy of his pasture on them: gateways to the sunny within, issues to all the outer Edens."

Because of the time, energy, and machinations which his scheming involves, Victor is forced to deprive himself of many of these pleasures. At times he feels their loss so keenly that the reward to be gained by the success of the scheme seems to him ludicrously inadequate. Such a moment of doubt occurs just after Dudley finally asks him for permission to court Nesta. The picture of Dudley as the husband of Nesta revolts him; Nesta deserves a better fate than to become the mother of "Philistine babies" (and make him the grandfather of Philistine babies). "Why be scheming?" he asks himself, especially when the end gained is only a "dry stick." And to gain this end he has suffered "perpetual agitations and perversions of his natural tastes." He conjures up a picture of a "nurse-like," "mother-nightcap" world which kindly tolerates the "heroic breakers of its rough-cast laws" as long as they do not make themselves conspicuous. Such a world would have allowed him, in spite of his adultery, "the choice of ways he liked best"; these he has now "incomprehensibly forfeited" by embarking on the scheme of the Lakelands. But such doubts do not last long with Victor: "Lakelands had him fast, and this young Dudley was the kernel of Lakelands."

The irony is that he could have enjoyed his simple pleasures in peace all his life. His picture of a tolerant world is concretely reflected in Mrs. Burman, who never acted against him except when she decided that he was "flaunting" his sin. Had Victor, like the adulterous lovers in Meredith's *Lord Ormont and His Aminta*, been content to live in obscurity, the world would have passed him by; but he would still have had the choice of ways he liked best, and many of the causes of Nataly's heartache would have been removed.

That he was sacrificing his pleasures was obvious to Victor; but that his scheming was preventing the development of his manhood is an insight which he never fully grasped. Near the beginning of the novel Meredith says, "Victor had yet to learn, that the man with a material object in aim, is the man of his object; and the nearer to his mark, often the farther is he from a sober self; he is more the arrow of his bow than bow to his arrow. This we pay for scheming: and success is costly; we find we have pledged the better half of ourselves to clutch it; not to be redeemed with the whole handful of our prize!" Victor's scheming is preventing the evolution of a "sober self" because the good that is in his nature is perverted by being used for unworthy ends, and the moral peccadilloes which his scheming makes necessary must be rationalized in order that his guilt feelings might be repressed. He thus becomes a hypocrite and a self-deceiver.

Victor is no Iago or Volpone. In many ways he is an admirable man: he loves truth; he has a sensitive conscience; he loves his family; he is generous, openhanded, hospitable, benevolent. But all these impulses are set awry by his scheming. On occasion Victor dreams of endowing all-night coffee saloons for rich and poor and of making munificent gifts to the nation of public parks and institutes of art; but in these dreams the most prominent object to his mind's eye is the gilt tablet on which the donor's name is inscribed in perpetual recognition and honor; thus these gifts would be but bribes to "coat a sensitive name." The most striking example of the perversion of his instincts for hospitality and benevolence is the charity concert at Lakelands. He arranges the affair on the grandest possible scale and invites lord and cobbler and half of London. Knowing well the thin persuasiveness of mere music for getting people to buy tickets for the benefit of the poor and knowing well the powerful appeal of the bait of bread and circuses, he plans entertainment for unapologizing low-brow and would-be high-brow and feeds all the guests from tables spread with mountainous provisions. Everyone leaves the concert fully satisfied and morally aglow for having contributed his mite to the poor. The whole affair is an orgy of hypocrisy. And Victor, the perpetrator of it, achieves his aim: he finds himself rocketing to a height of popularity he had never known before. Thus his benevolence, used for an unworthy end, stiffens into a mask. Far from realizing that in gaining such a success he has pledged the better half of himself, Victor at times like these feels that he is "himself," that he can clearly distinguish his "identity," and that he stands "whole and sound."

Scheming also requires him to act in ways that do not meet the approval of his conscience. Not only is the evil act in itself a degenerative influence, but it also imposes the necessity of finding a morally acceptable or at least a pragmatic justification for the act, a process which inevitably leads to self-deception. Just as the schemer no longer can see a situation as it really is, so he also no longer knows himself. Meredith points up the operation of this principle in Victor's justification for his marriage to Mrs. Burman: "Colney Durance accused him of entering into bonds with somebody's grandmother for the simple sake of browsing on her thousands: a picture of himself too abhorrent to Victor to permit of any sort of acceptance. Consequently he struck away to the other extreme of those who have a choice in mixed motives: he protested that compassion had been the cause of it. Looking at the circumstance now, he could see, allowing for human frailty—perhaps a wish to join the ranks of the wealthy—compassion for the woman as the principal motive." Late in the novel he begins to feel guilty because his love affair with Lady Halley is growing warmer. This leads him to "examine the poor value of his aim" which ties him to such "contemptible means." He must rationalize his actions. It is true that her small soft hand is "agreeable to fondle," but it is also true that she is leading him to a pit. Why take this foolish risk? Lady Halley is a means for making his ravishing dream of being a conqueror of a glittering society come true. Since, like in war, "we must pay for our allies," this growing intimacy is no cause for his feeling despondent or guilty, especially when his heart is true to Nataly.

The possibility of Victor's moral development is dramatized by his pursuit of his "Idea." In the first chapter of the book he falls flat on his back as he is crossing London Bridge—a fall rich in symbolic implications. Soon after this fall, he is granted a vision of an Idea which, as he says later, would "cleanse all degradations." The Idea is luminous, splendid, convincing. But Victor loses it almost immediately after its first flash. Throughout the novel he finds himself on the verge of grasping the Idea, or he grasps part of it, or he sees it intellectually but without the visionary force with which it was first attended. Thus Victor cannot quite undergo the transformation which its acceptance would require.

Victor's Idea is a revelation of values the direct antithesis to all that he had been scheming for during the past twenty years. Its acceptance would mean an end to his materialistic yearnings: it prescribes self-conquest over the animal; an end to philandering; a contempt for luxury, wealth, and position. It fixes new responsibilities on the rich: "We the wealthy will not exist to pamper flesh, but we live for the promotion of brotherhood." Finally, it envisions a "society based on the logical concrete of humane considerateness" and condemns the manipulation of people for selfish ends or even for the purposes of some Utilitarian ethic. A hint from the author perhaps justifies the reader in extending Victor's perception of the Idea. The metaphysical insight it provides is to regard the Spirit of Life not as a "Merciful Disposer" (that is, a kind of Grand Schemer), who "plays the human figures, to bring about this or that issue," but as an influence "beside us, within us, our breath, if we will; marking on us where at each step we sink to the animal, mount to the divine, we and ours who follow, offspring of body or mind."

To the end Victor cannot quite bring the Idea into complete focus or make it viable. He does, however, emerge a better man: he admits to himself that there had been a "moral fall" in his maintaining the scheme of the Lakelands and in his relations with Lady Halley, and he has grasped important aspects of his Idea. Though he is ready to preach the Idea to others, he cannot see its full application to himself or to his aims in life. He thus fails to pass through his ordeal and remains an unstable, divided personality.

In *One of Our Conquerors* Meredith wished to draw a broad picture of both the virtues and the vices of English life. In this picture Victor Radnor stands with the virtues: it is men like Victor who will help to regenerate an England grown fat and lazy like a "drear menagerie Lion." Meredith puts into the mouth of Colney Durance his own oft-repeated criticisms of English civilization, some of the flavor of which may be caught in Colney's description of the Duvidney ladies: "They were England herself; the squat old woman she has become by reason of her overlapping numbers of the comfortable fund-holder annuitants: a vast body of passives and negatives, living by precept, according to rules of precedent, and supposing themselves to be righteously guided because of their continuing undisturbed." But Meredith refuses to allow the pessimist to have the last word: "Colney could not or would not praise our modern adventurous, experimental, heroic, tramping active, as opposed to yonder pursy passives and negatives." There is hope because England still produces men of action and strength like Victor Radnor: "We have in Strength a hero, if a malefactor; whose muscles shall haul him up to the light he will prove worthy of, when that divinity has shown him his uncleanness." Furthermore, the Celtic element in the English people (Victor has Welsh blood) is an assurance that even the "taste for elegance, and for spiritual utterance, for Song, nay, for Ideas, is there among them." In the first chapter of *One of Our Conquerors* Victor suffered a symbolic fall on London Bridge; the book ends without his having been able to cross over to firm ground. But Dudley transformed himself, Nesta matured, and it was Meredith's hope that England too would successfully pass through its age of transition.

HARDY'S MAJOR FICTION

John Holloway
CAMBRIDGE UNIVERSITY

THE deepening and harshening pessimism of Hardy's later novels has been stressed often enough in the past. All that need be done here is to remind readers of how it is usually located in two particular aspects of his work: first, his "philosophical" asides ("the President of the Immortals, in Aeschylean phrase, had ended his sport with Tess" will be enough in illustration of this familiar story; the phrase itself will need re-examination later); and second, his apparently growing preoccupation with problems of marriage. One should perhaps add that to see this second issue as the product of difficulties in Hardy's own married life is very uninformative. Much more to the point are the divorce cases (the Parnell case being the best known) which became national sensations in the later 1880's and early 1890's; and besides this, the important influence of Ibsen, at least in the case of *Jude the Obscure*.

Recent criticism of Hardy has also emphasized something else: a special part of his connection with the southwest of England. An earlier generation of writers on Hardy underestimated this. Amiably if innocently equipped with haversack and large-scale map, they cycled over Wessex and noted Hardy's faithful geography, or his intimate and affectionate knowledge of rural occupations and customs. More recently, the stress has fallen on Hardy as one who registered the impact upon rural England of a great historical change, which went to the very roots of life. One cause of this was the swift and decisive decline in British agriculture which followed almost instantaneously on the completion of the railroad links to the American Middle West in about 1870. The other, less spectacular but in the long run much more far-reaching, was the industrial revolution in agriculture. This was progressing steadily in the later years of the century, and has even now far from completed its radical transforming work. As symbol of this second force, one might take a pair of incidents from Hardy's own work. In *The Mayor of Casterbridge* (1886) the new mechanical seed-drill which is to replace the methods in use since the time of the Anglo-Saxons is for sale in the market-place. Someone has still to buy and use it. In *Tess of the D'Urbervilles*, only five years later, the mechanical harvester dominates and controls the whole scene of the corn-stacking (Chapter 48) and reduces the tired, dazed human beings who serve it to mere automatons. The contrast is no proof of how rural life was changing; but as an illustration it is vivid.

Modern criticism of fiction often seems at its weakest in trying (or failing) to consider the forces in a book which unify it from beginning to end. This weakness is perhaps the result of a certain uneasiness which (for reasons obvious enough) often shows itself when the critic turns his attention to the plot. Yet such attention is necessary if the pervasive unifying drives of the work are to be located; and certainly the full seriousness and import of Hardy's major novels will be concealed from the reader who fails to apprehend their plots: plots, that is, not as mere summarizable sequences of events, but as the central unifying and significating forces of the books. These I hope now to approach.

The first step in that approach is not difficult, for it is taken simply by combining the two more or less familiar points from which this discussion started; by seeing Hardy's deepening and harshening gloom as not a mere self-ingraining philosophical bias, but rather as something in most intimate relation to his vision of the passing of the old rhythmic order of rural England. Once the novels are seen from this point of view, they suggest a surprising development in Hardy's thought. They suggest not just a growing preoccupation with the rural problem, nor even a growing sense that an earlier way of life was inevitably vanishing. They suggest something more disquieting: a gathering realization that that earlier way did not possess the inner resources upon which to make a real fight for its existence. The old order was not just a less powerful mode of life than the new, but ultimately helpless before it through inner defect.

When one is arguing that a thought or an attitude comes increasingly into focus in a writer's work, it is always easy to claim too much and hide too much; yet in the present case the change looks convincingly steady. *The Return of the Native* (1878) has a half-tragic ending in its present form; and Hardy's original intention seems to have been to have made it more tragic rather than less so. Yet throughout the book, the stress falls on the revitalizing power of rural life, and on how its vitality is intrinsically greater than that of modernity. Eustacia and Wildeve, and at first Clym too, are alienated from it: indeed, this very alienation lies behind their ostensible successes (the marriages, for example). But because of the alienation, the successes are ill-placed and precarious, they are the successes of those who have lost the soundness, the inner strength, the power to choose and to achieve wisely which belongs to men whose life is in harmony with their world. By contrast, Venn the reddleman suffers reverses, but they do not impair his integrity; his vitality runs submerged, but it runs with the tide of life. The gambling scene on the heath is fantastic enough, but it tellingly conveys this. Moreover, the whole rural ambience can ultimately assert a greater vitality than the city life from which Clym has come. As he gives himself to it, he is regenerated from a basic source. By the end, Egdon has triumphed, even if on its own stern terms. The renegades have been destroyed or won over: even if Venn had never married Thomasin, the faithful would have been in possession. The novel resolves in an assertion of the old order, its regenerative austerity, its rewarding unrewardingness.

The next novel is very different. Henchard is the only major figure in *The Mayor of Casterbridge* (1886) who stands integrally for the traditional qualities. Farfrae is an agriculturalist, but of the new kind: he prospers by chemistry, machinery, and bookkeeping and elementary economics. His traditional songs are partly a social accomplishment, neither sincere nor insincere; his kindliness and even his amorousness are conventional. Henchard's daughter Elizabeth-Jane is turning into a cultivated young lady (I would sooner overrate than underrate Hardy's own educatedness, but I cannot help seeing something of importance in his seeming assurance here that education could without loss be self-education). Lucetta is entirely *déraciné*. On these premises, contrast with *The Return of the Native* is vivid. From beginning to end Henchard's course is downward. Whenever his older way of life meets the new, it is defeated. Step by step, he comes to work for the man whom he once employed, and in the end he feels himself driven away to his death; while those who were once his laborers work the new, harder (and easier) way, for a shilling a week less than they had had from him.

Yet, although this relentless decline of Henchard's is (as we take its meaning) what unifies the book, Henchard still stands above the others in what might be called psychic virtue. In the conventional sense, he is both less moral than they, and more so. He is violent and a liar and in one sense intensely selfish, but his generosity is true magnanimity, and he has reserves of affection and humility that they quite lack. The essential is something else, though: that his whole nature, good or bad, is centered upon a deep source of vital energy. The rich stream of life still issues from life's traditional order. It does not bring success, but it brings greatness and in a sense goodness. Farfrae prospers through *skill* which the new mode of life has impersonally taught him; Henchard is able to struggle on, though defeated, not because of what he has learned but because of what he *is*. He blocks out something like the full contour of the human being.

That Henchard should stand out as a human rather than a man was surely part of Hardy's intention. His lack of interest in "womankind" is stressed more than once, and we are reminded of how Marty South is also in a sense made sexless at the end of *The Woodlanders* (1887). But to turn to *The Woodlanders* is to find that Hardy has now moved further still. Marty South and Giles Winterborne do not display, like Henchard, a defeated strength. On the contrary, they leave the impression of debility. So far as goodness itself goes, they are, to be sure, alone in having contact with it: "you was a good man, and did good things." But the springs of goodness are now no longer the springs of strength. Rather the opposite. Such vitality as there is lies on the other side, in the self-assurance and plausible fluency of Fitzpiers, or the passionate sensuousness of Felice. Grace Melbury has a thwarted contact, anyhow, with the traditional order: but what it does for her is chiefly to make her impassive and acceptant.

In *Tess of the D'Urbervilles* (1891), Hardy moves further. Tess is "a pure woman," admittedly; but this is not the feminine counterpart to Henchard's "A Man of Character." It is not Tess's sexual misadventures which impugn her as a woman of character, and Hardy is indeed at pains to show, in the later part of the book when she resists the now twice-reprobate Alec, that she is comparatively faithful and steadfast. But she has a weakness nearer her center: an alienation, a dreaminess which Hardy depicts unsuccessfully in the ride at night when she tells her young brother that we live on a "blighted" planet (and becomes so engrossed that she causes a fatal injury to the horse), and which he depicts again, this time with brilliant success, at Talbothay's dairy when she tells Dairyman Crick how "our souls can be made to go outside our bodies when we are alive" (Chapters 4 and 18). Again, this incident is nodal in the book, and I must return to it. For the present it is enough to say that its nodality is stressed by Hardy, in that he makes this the moment when Angel Clare first gives Tess any special notice.

This dreamy unreality in Tess is no personal quirk. It results from her heredity, and is reflected in both her parents. Moreover, Hardy is at pains to stress that among country folk, degeneration of an old stock is common enough. The stock is in decline. It seems a positive disparagement of the old order. The contrast with Henchard is revealing. Quietly but clearly, Hardy indicates that in Tess there is something self-destroying. So there was, in a sense, in Henchard. Yet how differently does the stress fall, provided that the reader follows only the contours created by the author!

Tess of the D'Urbervilles also dwells, quite for the first time, upon another unattractive side of rural life. This is what appears in the barrenness and crippling toil of life on the upland farm of Flintcomb-Ash. Hardy links his picture to contemporary agricultural realities — the farm belongs to an absentee landlord — but the essential things which make life hard on it are those which have made the rural life hard since the beginning: stony soil, cold wind, rain, snow, callous masters — things that can be found in the Wakefield *Second Shepherds' Play* as easily as in *Tess*. Should this be in doubt, it may be confirmed from *Jude the Obscure* (1896). In fact, there is something like a parallel here to the double indictment of *Tess*. Jude Fawley is "crazy for books. . . . It runs in our family . . ." Later, when the now adult Jude sees a stone-mason's yard and glimpses for a moment that happiness for him lay only in a life like that, Hardy passes decisive judgment upon bookish tastes in laborers' families. A still clearer parallel with *Tess*, however, is Hardy's insistence in this novel upon the essential harshness of rural life. "How ugly it is here," thinks Jude, as he drives off the rooks from the brown, featureless arable of the upland. This is in part an ironical judgment upon Jude. Hardy is at pains to stress the rich human associations of the scene. Yet some of these associations are themselves associations of human unhappiness; and the whole chapter goes far to endorse Jude's revulsion from the drab landscape and the inevitable greed and callousness of the farmer. Nor are this revulsion, and the inescapable grounds tending to justify it, incidentals. They initiate the whole train of events. Jude's quest for learning is to escape from a life of grinding toil that he could not but wish to escape. And what are the compensations of rurality, as they now appear? Only Arabella, whose work is to wash the innards of the newly slaughtered pig, and whose attractions take their force from brutal humor, coarse sensuality, and a rooted tradition of deceit.

This discussion of the later novels is not by itself, of course, anything like the whole truth about them. It virtually ignores Hardy's rich and intimate contact with the rural tradition in every book before *Jude*, and his profound dependence upon, and loyalty to, its characteristic virtues. It ignores these matters because they have often been discussed elsewhere, and its concentration upon Hardy's growing sense of weakness in the country world must be taken in the context of Hardy criticism as it now stands. Yet it remains true that in these later works the essence of plot, the distinctive trajectory of the narrative, is the steadily developed decline of a protagonist who incarnates the older order, and whose decline is linked, more and more clearly, with an inner misdirection, an inner weakness.

Two of the novels stand out as inviting a closer scrutiny, if we wish to see how this kind of movement lies at the heart of unity and meaning. These are *The Mayor of Casterbridge*, and *Tess of the D'Urbervilles*. *Jude the Obscure* clearly has another kind of concern; and *The Woodlanders*, surprisingly enough, proves largely to have it as well. Indeed, there is a sense in which this novel has a much looser organization than the other late ones. Deep and powerful as its awareness of rural life undoubtedly is (one cannot keep from mind the pictures of Giles spattered all over with his apples and their juice), yet much at the center of this work pursues another concern. Grace's response to Fitzpiers' infidelity, and the gradual rebirth of her affection for him, are not Wessex products. The novel resolves itself by amiably decanting these two characters into the middle-class urban life of the Midlands. The psychological change that we see in Grace is barely connected with Hardy's rural interests; and that, I think, is why the whole episode of their reconciliation is treated with a lightness and even something of a gentle half-ironical detachment that distinguishes the book clearly from *Tess*. At one point Hardy brings the difference out starkly through a metaphor. This occurs when Grace, running swiftly through the wood to meet Fitzpiers, just misses the man-trap (which is in itself, by the way, another scrap of evidence for the view that Hardy was beginning to dwell on the harsher side of country life). Her destiny is to evade, though barely, the issues of life in their brutal sharpness. All the man-trap does is whisk her skirt off: in Hardy's making this the occasion of her being reconciled to Fitzpiers we are to see, I think, that the whole sequence has about it something of the essentially trivial. Tess turns back to Angel over her rush-drawing labor in the snow-laden barn, as she comes to grasp her case, and Angel's, in terms of the plainest, the essential relations between women and men as human animals. We are in a much different world, a world that has not skipped over the waiting man-trap. For these reasons, among others, it is *The Mayor of Casterbridge* and *Tess* that best warrant further questioning. They are the novels which have a single-minded organization along our present line of thought.

The word "theme," now the most hackneyed of clichés in criticism, is also one of its bugbears. An essay, a philosophical discourse, even a collection of different pieces, all these may equally well have a theme, or several themes. The word has no necessary connection even with imaginative literature, let alone with the narrative forms of it, and is therefore a standing temptation to the critic to overlook the whole narrative dimension. But almost always, the narrative trajectory is what makes a novel a novel and what makes any particular novel the novel it is. Only within the framework of this central drive can the real significance of the detail (incident, imagery, metaphor, local contrast) be grasped at all. Examples may be needed here; let us revert to *The Woodlanders.* To connect, say, Giles Winterborne's meeting with Grace while he holds up his apple tree in the market-place merely with "the theme of rural fertility," or Marty South's selling her hair with "the commercial theme," would be grotesquely uninformative. The significance of both these incidents, prominently placed at the outset of the narrative, is that the two characters are made to carry out, at the start, ritual gestures by which they formally (though unwittingly) surrender their essential strength. From this point out, we know what kind of character we are to watch, we are put on the track of the path their lives must take.

A tree also embodies the essential strength of Marty's father. In an aberration from his proper rural life, he wants it cut down. When this is done, he dies. As for Marty's hair, Hardy invests this with almost talismanic virtue. While Felice wears it as her own, her luck prospers. Toward the end of the book, her secret comes out. At once she loses her power over Fitzpiers, and almost immediately after she meets her death. Similarly with the contrast between how Grace meets Winterborne (under the flowering apple tree in his hand) and how she first meets Fitzpiers (he has bought the right to dissect her old nurse's body after she is dead, and Grace goes to buy it back). These meetings are no mere specimens of a theme, but exact pointers to a narrative movement; and they come at the start of the relation and show what its significance is, and what (if pursued) it will bring. For Grace to progress with one is to pursue the forces of life, with the other to pursue those of death. Similarly with the incident where Marty helps Giles to plant the young trees (Chapter 8). This does not merely take up the theme of rural order; it exactly indicates how Marty is Giles's proper strength and counterpart. His trees will flourish if he chooses her to help. When he turns elsewhere, we know what he has done. But all these details have significance within the frame of the basic narrative movement of the book, a movement which, as it takes its shape out of them, reciprocally determines what meaning they shall have.

"From beginning to end," it was suggested above, "Henchard's course is downward. Whenever his older way of life meets the new, it is defeated." It is this narrative movement in the book which embodies Hardy's deepest interests and the essence of his moral insight. But there is more to be said about the exact nature of the struggle and the downward movement, as he envisages it; and it is at this point that such matters as incident and imagery can take their proper and proportionate place in our awareness of the whole work. For it seems that Hardy has employed a single basic metaphor through which to embody the war between Farfrae and Henchard; local incidents and metaphors have their allotted place within it; and in spite of the recurrent suggestion that Henchard (like Old Hamlet) is "a man, take him for all in all," the basic metaphor through which Hardy sees the struggle between Farfrae and him, is that of a struggle between a man and an animal. This begins with the animal in possession of its territory. Henchard arrived on the scene during, as it were, the prehistory of the narrative. Now he is in occupation at Casterbridge. Farfrae is passing through on his way to emigrate. As the novel pursues its course, Farfrae takes possession. It is his rival who thinks to emigrate. But instead he is persuaded to live in his own old home, now occupied by Farfrae; and like an animal, he becomes domesticated. "Henchard had become in a measure broken in, he came to work daily on the home premises like the rest." Later he is likened to a "netted lion," or to a lion whose fangs have been drawn. When he describes how Farfrae, now mayor, as he himself once was, forced him away on the occasion of the royal visit, he says,

". . . how angry he looked. He drove me back as if I were a bull breaking fence. . . ."

Several of the incidents of the book enter into this sustained metaphor. Henchard and Farfrae fighting in the cornstore is, in a sense, animal against man: it is very like the earlier fight in the barn between Henchard and the bull. The parallel extends even to Farfrae's "wrenching Henchard's arm . . . causing him sharp pain, as could be seen from the twitching of his face," and Henchard when he "wrenched the animal's head as if he would snap it off. . . . The premeditated human contrivance of the nose-ring was too cunning for impulsive brute force, and the creature flinched." Finally, at the end of the novel, Henchard crawls away, like a wounded beast, to die in an empty hovel that is more like an animal's hole than a place for men. His final instructions for how he is to be buried are not appropriate for *felo-de-se*: they are appropriate for the burial of an animal.

Henchard's character, moreover, is that of a beast; in the true, not the townee, sense of that word. His immense natural energy, his simplicity, his having no skill of any kind save that of hay-cutting, and his liability to enslavement above all through a disabling, yearning, dog-like need for human affection, all these features of his nature make their contribution. There is no need to remind readers that Henchard is not *simply* an animal. Far from it. At no point does metaphor become literal truth. But it is through this metaphor that we must see the struggle which constitutes the narrative and the unity of the book, and which predominantly defines its significance. Indeed, nothing but awareness of this metaphor will fully bring out the issues between old and new that are involved, or the length to which Hardy pursues them. "My furniture too! Surely he'll buy my body and soul likewise!" Henchard says at one point. (One cannot but—though it is an unhappy touch—see the caged singing-bird which Henchard brings Elizabeth-Jane at the end as a wedding present, and which he leaves behind when he goes away to die, as linking with this idea of his giving up "body and soul" together.) Yet even this is insufficient to bring out the lengths to which Hardy pursues his central conflict. Henchard is more than enslaved, he is *tamed*. That is something far more thoroughgoing. It is the measure of what Hardy sees as at issue.

Tess of the D'Urbervilles also has unity through a total movement; and the nature of this may also largely be grasped through a single metaphor.

It is not the taming of an animal. Rather (at least for a start) it is the hunting of one. Several remarks and incidents in the book make this explicit, notably Tess's letter to her absent husband when he has deserted her: "I must cry out to you in my trouble—I have no one else. . . . if I break down by falling into some dreadful snare, my last state will be worse than my first." So does the night she spends in the wood with the wounded pheasants: strongly reminiscent, of course, of her earlier night in a wood, when she fell into the snare set for her by Alec. Throughout, Tess is harried from place to place at what seems like gradually increasing speed. Even the very start of her relation with Alec is relevant: "the handsome, horsey young buck" drove up early in the morning in his gig to fetch her. At the end, it is especially clear. When the hunt is over, Tess is captured on the sacrificial stone at Stonehenge, the stone where once, like the hart at bay, the victim's throat was slit with the knife. With these things in mind, Hardy's much-abused quotation from Aeschylus ("the President of the Immortals, in Aeschylean phrase, had ended his sport with Tess") takes on a new meaning and aptness.

Yet Tess's career represents more than a hunt. What this is, can again be summed up in a metaphor, one to which we are almost inadvertently led, if we attempt to summarize. That Hardy should have divided his book into "phases" is itself, perhaps, an indication of the field in which his mind was partly working: the word was good nineteenth-century currency in history and natural history, and Carlyle was fond of it. "Phase Three" is entitled "The Rally." In it, Tess strikes out for new country. She leaves the snug and familiar environment of the "Vale of the Little Dairies," surmounts the challenge of barren Egdon Heath which lies across her path, and enters a new territory, the "Vale of the Great Dairies," where life runs upon a basically different pattern. To this she almost completely adapts herself: so much so, that she finds a mate in Angel Clare, and almost succeeds in—there is only one word to use—in germinating. This word is less odd than it seems at first. Hardy lays great stress on the rich, blossoming fertility of Tess's whole environment during this period, and also stresses, discreetly but with great force, her own richly sensuous nubility, her genuine bond, in the truest sense, with the milch cows and the lush blossoms where the fruit is setting.

The rally fails. Tess has to abandon her favorable environment, and is forced on to a harsh upland soil where existence is more difficult. She struggles not at the level of reproduction, but for mere survival. She is resistant, though, and for a long time she does survive. But her strength is shaken when her family is finally driven off the soil; and in the end, what Darwin called sexual selection begins to work contrariwise to natural selection. Tess gives up the struggle. She is driven out of her natural habitat altogether, and goes to live, kept like a pet, with Alec in Sandbourne.

Here, I think, is the second, bigger metaphor, embracing the first, through which Hardy embodies his central fictional movement. The central train of events demands description in Darwinian terms: organism, environment, struggle, adaptation, fertility, survival, resistant — and one more: Hardy has envisaged an individual life at the depth of, and to the length of, the ultimates for a species — establishment at one end, and at the other, extinction.

Many of the incidents in the book bring this total movement into focus. For example, Hardy provides the reader with an index to it by two scenes, one at the beginning and one at the end. In the first, Angel looks back down the road and sees the village girls in white, dancing in springtime on the green: Tess, still integrated with them, stands by the hedge. In the other, he looks back after what he thinks is their final parting, over bare, open countryside and an empty road: "and as he gazed a moving spot intruded on the white vacuity of its perspective. It was a human figure running." It is Tess, now alienated and isolated. Tess and her family take refuge in the family vault (Chapter 52). In terms of the hunt metaphor, they have been run to earth; and this parallels the sleep-walking scene (Chapter 37) when Angel lays Tess in the open tomb: within the larger movement there is a recurrent smaller pattern. Tess at the dairy says that "our souls can be made to go outside our bodies" if we "lie on the grass at night and look straight up at some big bright star." (This is exactly what she does at the end of the book, on her fatal last night on Salisbury Plain.) Meanwhile, Dairyman Crick was balancing his knife and fork together "like the beginning of a gallows." Most striking of all, Hardy reinvites us to register the total movement of Tess's career, in all its integration, by an ingenious and vivid résumé of it, toward the close of the book. He does this through the final days that Tess and Angel spend together — partly a psychological fugue, partly a kind of total recall, partly both. Leaving her sin with Alec behind her, she rejoins Angel, and the rich woodland of the first two days together corresponds to the rich vale of the dairies. The empty manor house they sleep in corresponds to the ancient house where their marriage was so nearly consummated before.

Barren Salisbury Plain corresponds to the uplands of Flintcomb-Ash. The scene at Stonehenge corresponds both to Tess in the vault, and to the moment when she hung on the wayside cross to rest and looked like a sacrificial victim. Her whole tragic life is mirrored in little at its close.

To notice things of this order is to realize, in effect, that Hardy's novels (like many others) need a special mode of reading. The incidents in them which strike us as improbable or strained or grotesque invite (this is not to say that they always deserve) the kind of response that we are accustomed to give, say, to the Dover Cliff scene in *Lear*. Admittedly, Hardy has local failures; but incidents like these are intrinsically at one remove from the probable and the realistic. Almost, it is necessary for them to be unrealistic in order that their other dimension of meaning, their relevance to the larger rhythms of the work, shall transpire. Again and again, it is those larger rhythms which finally expand into the total movement of the novel, transmitting the author's sense of life, the forces that operate through it, the values that chart it out and make it what it is.

From what has so far been said, a new reason may perhaps be advanced as to why Hardy gave up fiction. It is both the strength (because of the integrity that it brought) and the limit of his achievement, to have seen the source of life-creating strength for human beings as connected always with a certain limited context, the traditional rural order. As time passed, he lost confidence in the strength of this order to resist and survive, and in part, even seems more and more to have regarded the element of drabness and harshness in rural life as not a product of change and modernity, but intrinsic. This being so, he had no position to which to retreat. He does not seem ever to have viewed human nature as itself ineradicably vital, as possessing an innate power to transform, from its own resources, its waste land into a fertile one. To say this is not necessarily to make a point against him. He may very well have been right in thinking that the human species, like others, wilts out of its natural habitat and communal order. It is merely to recognize that by the middle 1890's, Hardy's course in fiction had become one that he could neither retrace, nor pursue.

THE SPIRITUAL THEME OF GEORGE GISSING'S *BORN IN EXILE*

Jacob Korg

UNIVERSITY OF WASHINGTON

IN FEBRUARY 1895, George Gissing wrote to Morley Roberts, his friend and future biographer, that he felt his most important contribution as a novelist to have been the depiction of "a class of young men distinctive of our time—well educated, fairly bred, but *without money*." Gissing's practice of using characters like these as heroes in his novels has been interpreted as a symptom of egotism, for he had once been such a young man himself. Actually, however, he had good reason for feeling that the poor young intellectual was a key figure in Victorian society. Educated beyond his station in the newly democratized schools and universities, the young intellectual, though capable of appreciating the culture enjoyed by the leisure classes, was unable to gain access to it himself unless he chose one of two courses: that of finding his way, individually, into a higher social class, or working for a revolution which would make the advantages of leisure available to all. Like Hyacinth Robinson in James's *The Princess Casamassima*, he was compelled, in seeking his own role, to make a crucial decision about society. While most of Gissing's early books were occupied with the various fictional possibilities of this situation, only in his last novel on this theme, *Born in Exile* (1893), did he express the insight that such a judgment of society was not merely a choice of abstract alternatives, but a moral problem involving fundamental questions of right and wrong.

Gissing's firsthand knowledge of the spiritual difficulties of the submerged intellectual began in 1876, when, as an eighteen-year-old student at Owens College in Manchester, he fell in love with a young prostitute, and, to save her from the streets, stole money and personal articles from the common-room used by his fellow-students. An action more out of character for the youthful Gissing can hardly be imagined. The son of a Wakefield chemist, he had been thoroughly indoctrinated with the common lower-middle-class earnestness, sense of responsibility, and admiration for gentility. Though he managed to throw off some of the more repressive influences of his home, and to think for himself in matters of religion, he never lost a gnawing sense of personal duty that drove him to make heroic efforts as a student and as a novelist. A brilliant and industrious schoolboy, he had been admitted to Owens College as a scholarship student on the basis of a remarkable record of prizes and first places in examinations. It seems likely that his repeated thievery was, in his own mind, at least, not a violation of morality, but a gesture of righteous rebellion against the unjust society that had victimized his sweetheart. There was no doubt of Gissing's guilt. He was caught in the act and severely punished by discharge from the College and imprisonment. Relatives of his classmates intervened to have him sent to America, where he stayed for a year before coming to London, a determined enemy of the social order, to marry the young woman for whom he had sacrificed so much, and to begin his career as a novelist.

Gissing's reaction to the new ideas of his time during his years in London suggests that they echoed opinions which he had already formed and which lay behind his behavior at Owens College. He responded eagerly to the philosophic materialism he heard expounded at street-corner meetings and in lecture halls, proclaimed himself a radical, and gave a lecture before a workingmen's club in which he attacked religion by balancing the claims of faith against those of reason. He read Comte, adopted his view that metaphysical questions were unanswerable and therefore irrelevant to human affairs, and joined the small English Positivist Society as a friend of its president, Frederic Harrison. Before long, however, he found these views unsatisfactory, for his native pessimism led him to doubt the effectiveness of active social reform. And although he remained a bitter critic of established conditions to the end of his life, his fear of the changes that science and democracy might bring was greater than his hatred of the superstition and injustice he saw about him.

The novels about poor young men trying to find their way, which Gissing wrote between 1880 and 1893, form a series of explorations, each coming closer to the central issue underlying their situation. Arthur Golding, the protagonist of his first novel *Workers in the Dawn* (1880), has no doubt that he wants to serve his fellow man; the question that occupies him is whether he can serve him best directly, through active political reform, or indirectly, through art. Osmond Waymark of *The*

Unclassed (1884) cynically argues that the artist must be indifferent to questions of social justice, though he cannot escape taking as his natural subject matter the suffering created by industrial poverty. In *New Grub Street* (1891), the novelist Edwin Reardon is the victim, not the judge, of the social order. Industrial civilization rejects the art he offers it, and since he cannot manufacture a product adapted to the demands of the literary market, it calmly eliminates him. These novels, each showing its hero trying to come to terms with society without betraying the claims of his conscience, led by gradual stages to Gissing's most perceptive and most profound analysis of the problem, *Born in Exile*. Its protagonist, Godwin Peak, understands clearly that there is a fundamental opposition between the conventional moral code formed by Christian tradition and the enlightened scientific views he holds. Since he rejects religious belief, he feels that it is logical to reject the moral system based on it as well, for the sake of following a rational, objective morality consistent with scientific truth.

Born in Exile has always been inconspicuous among Gissing's novels. It was unattractive to his contemporaries, and it remains unattractive, for different reasons, today. Most of the novels Gissing wrote before 1888 were enlivened by exceptional social realism and a wide and varied range of interest. They are rich in sub-plots and minor characters that parallel or contrast with the main plot. Though the action usually moves steadily and slowly, held back by Gissing's concern for maintaining an air of reality, there are occasional highly dramatic scenes. *Born in Exile*, however, has almost no action. Its setting is commonplace, its minor elements perfunctory and undeveloped. The plot unwinds through a series of polite and unemotional conversations interspersed with passages of character-analysis. It is reasonably convincing as an example of realism only because its flat narrative style forfeits any other claims. Its one notable fictional feature is the central character, Godwin Peak, a vivid and original personality whose complicated thought-processes are well realized.

Born in Exile was not an easy novel to publish. It was rejected by Smith and Elder, who had been Gissing's regular publishers for about six years. Gissing then entrusted the manuscript to an agent, but it was refused by a number of publishers before being accepted by the firm of Adam and Charles Black at a price that came to only half of what Gissing had originally asked for it. He was particularly anxious and disturbed between June and December, 1891, when the manuscript was traveling from one publisher to another, not only because he was pressed for money, but also because he had hoped that the success of his most recent novel, *New Grub Street*, would create a market for his work. Gissing thought that the reason for the poor reception of *Born in Exile* was not that it was weak, but that the publishers were discouraged by its controversial subject of an atheist's attempt to become a clergyman. Actually, this plot cloaks an even more disquieting theme. In earlier novels of the period that describe a conflict between individuals and society, such as *The Ordeal of Richard Feverel* and *The Mill on the Floss*, the issue is whether or not moral standards can be safely violated. *Born in Exile*, however, questions the moral standards themselves. Gissing's novel is a venture in the direction taken by Butler, Shaw, and Wilde, with the difference that he treats in a sober and conservative manner the conventions they attack in vigorous satire.

The story begins when Godwin Peak is attending a provincial university much like Owens College as a poor and brilliant scholarship student of scientific gifts. Ashamed of his humble family and desperately eager to be a gentleman like his college-mates, Peak suffers intensely from the inferiority of status George Orwell has described as the inevitable lot of a poor boy who goes to school with rich ones. When a Cockney uncle threatens to open a cheap restaurant across from the college with his (and Peak's) name in bold letters on its sign, the boy's pride forces him to give up his academic career without telling his sponsor the real reason. In this way the interruption of Gissing's own college work appears in the novel, heavily disguised. Peak goes to London and grows into a man of complex personality whose moral nihilism is too radical even for his Bohemian friends. "When a man has learned that truth is indeterminable, how is it more moral," he asks, "to go about crying that you don't believe a certain dogma than to concede that the dogma may possibly be true?" He declares that he sees no need to follow any principle but that of being "guided by circumstances as they arise." When a friend argues that happiness can be gained only by following one's convictions, Peak asks, "What if you have no convictions?" The two main tenets of his philosophy are expressed by two Latin mottoes he admires. He argues that the double standard of *Foris ut moris; intus ut libet* is appropriate to a "half-civilised age" like the nineteenth century. On the other hand, he likes the suggestion of the inscription on the clock in Exeter Cathedral, *Pereunt et imputantur*, that one is held responsible for making good use of the vanishing hours.

When he becomes intimate with the well-to-do Exeter family of a former school friend, Buckland Warricombe, Peak's boyhood craving for the amenities of middle-class life and the refinement of middle-class women leads him to put his perverse principles into practice. Feeling justified in his actions by his conviction that "truth is indeterminable," he turns the fact that the Warricombes are confirmed churchgoers into a tool by pretending to undergo a religious conversion and studying for orders. His ultimate ambition is that of marrying Sidwell, one of the daughters of the family, for he has heard that young women like her will accept clergymen as husbands, no matter how poor they may be. He gives up his London life and employment and settles in Exeter as a theological student and friend of the Warricombe family.

Peak's piety arouses the suspicion of Buckland, who cannot believe in the conversion of his atheistic college friend. Buckland's investigations reveal not only that Peak is the author of an anonymous article attacking the Church called "The New Sophistry," but that he coolly discussed the article with his father on one occasion without acknowledging that he had written it. When his deception is laid bare and he is ejected from the Warricombe household, Peak becomes the victim of his own scheme, for his courtship of Sidwell, originally undertaken as a project for fulfilling his social ambitions, has become sincere. He has grown to love her, and now feels that "It was Sidwell or death." A final conversation between the lovers reveals the irony that Peak's orthodox role has made him less attractive to Sidwell, whose ideas have been changing, and that she would have preferred to regard him as the creator of a new order rather than a preserver of the old. Although reconciliation and reunion are implied in the scene where the lovers part, they never meet again, for Peak takes refuge in Germany, and in time the news comes that he has died in his lodgings there. At the end of the novel one of his friends reflects that he has died, as he had lived, in exile.

The disturbing paradox of *Born in Exile* lies in the fact that Peak's hypocritical deception is due, not to lack of moral responsibility, but to uncompromising intellectual honesty. Man's life, seen from a scientific point of view, seems to him to be trivial and futile. This truth presents itself to him most forcibly in a kind of mystic illumination he experiences when, during a walk across the countryside, he sees a number of geologic strata exposed in a quarry, and meditates upon the long ages that produced them. "Escaping from the influences of personality, his imagination wrought back through eras of geologic time, held him in a vision of the infinitely remote, shrivelled into insignificance all but the one fact of inconceivable duration." To the nonentity Peak feels himself to be against the background of the universe revealed by science, life allows no moral grandeur, but only the Benthamite goals which Peak describes as "the achievement of satisfaction and the avoidance of pain." Having learned from his scientific studies the impossibility of ultimate knowledge, he feels that advocating any philosophy of life, even agnosticism, is to claim knowledge inaccessible to man. The only true honesty, Peak feels, is to act according to one's desires, for that is being true to such knowledge as man can have. Thus, his deception, undertaken to gain as much of life's good as possible, is really a moral imperative. "I have been honest," he insists, "inasmuch as I have acted in accordance with my actual belief." Madeleine Cazamian has described Peak's situation by saying, "Il manque à l'honneur vis-à-vis d'autrui, mais non vis-à-vis de lui-même" (*Le Roman et les idées en angleterre*, 1923). It is society and religion that are guilty of dishonesty, for they enforce a moral code based upon mere metaphysical speculation.

In spite of the fact that he has thus deftly succeeded in turning morality inside out, Peak is occasionally attacked by old-fashioned shame and remorse. Only through severe self-discipline can he maintain the strength of his rationalization against the feelings of self-contempt that arise in him. He tells himself that his deception injures no one; that he will be able to do good as a clergyman; and that even if this good is based on a falsehood, it is not worse than other beneficent illusions man is compelled to invent to comfort himself in an unknowable world. Foreseeing that he will eventually have to confess his stratagem to the woman he hopes to marry, he tells himself that he will be able to persuade her to share his views, and that his love will recompense her for the trial she will have to undergo.

"Peak," wrote Gissing to his German friend, Eduard Bertz, "is myself — one phase of myself." The novel is indeed a remarkably candid confession. The details of Peak's sophistical reasoning must have been drawn from his own thoughts at the time of the Owens College episode and from speculations that ran through his mind when he visited the wealthy homes of his pupils, a poor tutor deeply envious of the luxury and refinement he saw. But Gissing does not seem to have been aware of the ideological dimension of his experience, or of the fact that others shared it with him, until he encountered it again and again in European novels. In works by the Russians, Turgenev and Dostoevski; the Frenchman, Paul Bourget;

and the Dane, Jens Peter Jacobsen, he found young heroes intoxicated by the moral freedom offered by materialism, as he himself had once been. He wrote to his sister Ellen that Turgenev's character "Bazaroff" exemplified "the purely *negative* mind, common enough now-a-days in men of thought." The resemblances of these fictional characters to each other and to himself were unmistakable, suggesting that the nihilism of Russia, the Positivism of France, and the agnosticism of England were all forms of the same historical impulse. Through these novels Gissing learned that the moral sophistry of his youth was representative of a general crisis of the European spirit.

In March of 1890, about a year before beginning *Born in Exile*, Gissing reread two novels which had long been familiar to him, Turgenev's *Fathers and Sons* and Jacobsen's *Niels Lyhne*. Bazarov, the hero of the Russian novel, possesses much of Peak's gloomy and unfriendly temperament, and shares many of his beliefs. A nihilist who proclaims that he refuses to accept any principles not based on scientific authority, he speaks of love, tradition, and religion with sarcasm. He denies the existence of principles, declaring that feelings are the only reality. When he contracts a fatal infection through an accident that seems to prove his contention that life and death are purposeless, he prepares himself to go into darkness. The hero of *Niels Lyhne*, a dreamy and imaginative man whose religious faith is shattered by a childhood experience, adopts atheism as a sacred cause, believing that men must realize that they, and not some vague divinity, must bear the responsibility for their actions. However, after the deaths of his wife and son he is unable to hold to his belief, and prays desperately, confessing the power of God. Later he regrets this lapse, and comes to the conclusion that his prayer was a sin against his firm belief that man's ignorance of the ultimate facts of the universe compels him to accept life without falsifying it.

The French author Paul Bourget, who was a favorite of Gissing's, wrote two novels about men who try to make morality over. The protagonist of *Le Disciple* is an admirer of a "French Spencer," a scholar who has put psychology on a positivist basis, showing that human passions are subject to definite laws. In an experiment intended to test the speculations of his teacher, the brilliant young student makes a girl of noble family fall in love with him. When she discovers the motives of his courtship, she commits suicide, and her seducer is shot by her vengeful brother. The elderly scholar whose theories have caused these events wonders whether the responsibility for all this suffering does not really belong to the "truths" he has discovered. The chief character of another Bourget novel, *Un Crime d'amour*, is a wealthy and dissipated idler who seduces the wife of his best friend without really loving her. When the affair is discovered and his mistress offers to sacrifice her marriage to go away with him, the hero is compelled to admit his lack of feeling for her. The effects of this confession upon a sincere and virtuous woman make him realize that his course of action constitutes "a crime of love." In examining the causes of this tragedy, he sees that science, together with misanthropy and debauchery, has destroyed his capacity for feeling and faith.

But perhaps the most striking parallel to *Born in Exile* among contemporary novels, and the one which reveals more of the underlying spiritual conflict than Gissing himself was capable of rendering, is *Crime and Punishment*, a novel to which Gissing was deeply attached. Its hero Raskolnikov commits his dreadful crime to prove that he is capable of independent action. Through it he tries to prove to himself that he possesses the contempt for human beings that enabled Napoleon and other great tyrants to achieve power. In his own mind, as he explains it to Sonia, his crime shows "whether I was a louse like everybody else or a man." Raskolnikov's crime, like the *acte gratuit* of the surrealists, is intended to be an assertion of pure free will, a declaration that man has the power to step off the path of conduct laid out for him by instinct and self-interest. It is the pointlessness of the crime, however, that leads the detective, Porfiry, to the guilty man. He sees that it is "a modern case, an incident of today when the heart of man is troubled . . . when comfort is preached as the aim of life." The criminal, he points out, "murdered two people for a theory," and Raskolnikov was the only one among the suspects who could have had such a motive. Porfiry's analysis of Raskolnikov's crime applies also to Peak's deception, whose ostensible motivation was far less important than the "theory" behind it. To Peak himself his action was a denial that the cosmic order had any moral control over him, a reworking of his destiny with the tool of free will.

Thus, *Born in Exile* emerges as one of a widely-scattered group of novels devoted to a spiritual problem characteristic of the nineteenth century. Such characters as Peak, Raskolnikov, and Bazarov may be regarded as striking anticipatory personifications of Nietzsche's doctrine that man is free to make his own morality, and that prevailing Christian beliefs, which favor the weak and humble, are "bedwarfing." Certainly, the voice of Zarathustra is clearly heard in these novels. The nature of man's heroic destiny, left vague by Nietzsche, was given a definite form in the minds of many people by the philosophy which arose from the general progress of science in the nineteenth century. The special attraction of this philosophy, as it was expressed in such works as Comte's *Cours de philosophie positive* and Ludwig Büchner's *Kraft und Stoff* was the hope it offered that human phenomena could be organized under reliable and incontrovertible principles. "If the Positive Philosophy be anything," said G. H. Lewes in his *Comte's Philosophy of the Sciences* (1871), it is a doctrine capable of embracing all that can regulate Humanity . . ." "Un même déterminisme," asserted Zola in *Le Roman expérimental* (1893), "doit régir la pierre des chemins et le cerveau de l'homme." A condition of the success of scientific study in such fields as government, morals, and ethics was the destruction of the theological and metaphysical ideas which dominated them, though they had long surrendered their hold on the physical sciences. This attack of science on metaphysical tradition, which Comte termed the central intellectual conflict of the nineteenth century, is the real theme of *Born in Exile*.

Godwin Peak and the group of spiritual exiles he exemplifies may be viewed as descendants of the passionate and gloomy heroes of the romantic era. Characters like Werther, Karl Moor of Schiller's *Die Räuber*, and Byron's Manfred had made a place in literature for the spiritual landslides which sometimes take place in the minds of ambitious and imaginative men. Nature seems to have followed art in this instance, and the soul-crisis became a common episode in the biographies of the great. The later nineteenth-century fiction treated these phenomena more analytically as the reflections of general social crises. The actual psychic experiences on which these works were based must have been substantially the same: a feeling of estrangement, an inability to share accepted attitudes, a disturbing emotional anesthesia and indifference to external events. In the novels themselves, these feelings are expressed through an overt repudiation of the external world and its standards, usually in the form of some sudden and unaccountable crime. This pattern of feelings appears in the twentieth century among the French existentialists, who declare that man is cut off from the order of nature and must therefore shape his own destiny without guidance from external authority. They agree with the nineteenth-century opinion that this view of man's relation to the cosmos gives him a new and dangerous freedom. His salvation, according to the existentialists, depends on his ability to recognize fully the "absurdity" of his plight, and to escape, by this awareness, the imprisonment in an alien world to which nature has condemned him. Unfortunately, such attempts to translate this spiritual program into action as we find in *Born in Exile*, *Crime and Punishment*, and Albert Camus's *L'Étranger* win their heroes only transient sensations of freedom and power, before ending in what are, from the conventional point of view, disasters.

Can *Born in Exile* be classed with *Crime and Punishment* as a protest against the characteristic materialism of the nineteenth century, or is it, like *L'Étranger*, a partial apology for the new morality, and a tale of martyrdom? As with most of Gissing's novels, it is difficult to determine exactly what is being asserted. It is not entirely clear, for example, whether Peak is to be regarded as a sympathetic figure. Six months after the novel had been completed, when he was engaged in a last-minute revision, Gissing's attitude toward his protagonist was still so undecided that he recorded in his diary a decision to change his name from "Peak" to "Peek," as though he were not sure whether his character embodied the lofty nobility of the former or the hideous furtiveness of the latter. The fact that the original spelling was restored before publication shows that Gissing did not want to demolish Peak's stature entirely. From Buckland Warricombe's point of view, Peak is little more than a clever bounder seeking to elbow his way into a good family. But Sidwell, who sees more of Peak's mind, feels that he is an innocent victim of social forces. The still greater knowledge of him open to the reader shows that Peak is profoundly contemptuous of himself and all human beings, and that his devotion to barren principle is an expression of satanic pride, but the insight given into the painful feelings of envy and remorse that beset an intelligent man arouses some sympathy for him.

Reference to Gissing's general opinions fails to provide answers to the questions that arise in the novel. Are we to accept Buckland Warricombe's uncritical, yet familiar view that the proprieties are intrinsically sacred, even if their spiritual foundation is dead? Gissing was a vigorous critic of this sort of "hypocrisy," yet in such novels as *Denzil Quarrier* (1892) and in *The Private Papers of Henry Ryecroft* (1903) he finds grounds for defending middle-class convention and Puritanism. He seems to have felt that the proprieties he had been so scornful of in his youth had their value, and that their incompatibility with strict social justice was regrettable. Is Peak's mocking masquerade of religious orthodoxy justified? Gissing's own attitude toward religion varied between indifference and hostility; Peak's fate might be fairly interpreted as a retraction, except for the fact that Gissing remained an unbeliever to the end of his life. While musing on the problems of religious belief in the Ryecroft papers, he wrote, ". . . agnosticism, as a fashion, was far too reasonable to endure," and lamented that religious sentiment might postpone indefinitely "the rationalist millennium."

The moralist and the realist were always at odds in Gissing. *Born in Exile*'s coupling of a strong approach to spiritual problems with an inconclusive treatment of them reflects the rivalry between the moralist's tendency to present his material as an illustration of universal order and the realist's aims of plausibility and objectivity. Like most of Gissing's novels, *Born in Exile* ends by heightening our awareness of moral questions without providing answers to them.

SAMUEL BUTLER AND BLOOMSBURY

William Van O'Connor

UNIVERSITY OF MINNESOTA

SAMUEL BUTLER's attacks on domestic and parental tyrannies as well as his having poked fun at the Ydgrunites and at the congregations attending the Musical Banks all helped to formulate and to define the twentieth-century break with "Victorianism." These are the commonplaces of all handbooks on modern English literature. It is also said that *The Way of All Flesh* (1903) prepared the way for Lytton Strachey's *Eminent Victorians*, his *Queen Victoria*, and the progeny that followed these volumes.

This is not to argue that Butler was the only Victorian who was critical of the mores in which he lived (Meredith, in 1869, three years prior to *Erewhon*, had asked, "Isn't there a scent of damned hypocrisy in all this lisping and vowelled purity of the *Idylls*?"), nor that *The Way of All Flesh* was the sole influence on Strachey and the many others who have worn a sceptical and cold gaze in looking backward at the Victorians.

What I should like to show here is that there are a good many connections between Butler and the Bloomsbury group, those artists and writers who in retrospect can be seen to have helped set the tone of their era. G. B. Shaw borrowed a great deal from Butler and propagandized for him. Lawrence also borrowed from him, even though he left no explicit statement about his having done so. It is also well known that E. M. Forster was an admirer of Butler and was influenced by him. It is not so well known that Butler meant a good deal to many of Forster's Bloomsbury friends.

As Americans we sometimes forget that the English literary world is smaller and more homogeneous than our own, or, to put it more directly, that English writers are more likely to know each other than are American writers. Butler was not a gregarious man, and he did not seek out acquaintances, but upon looking into the matter of his personal relationships one discovers that a number of the literary people whose paths crossed his path were the parents, or in one instance a grandparent, of the men and women who were to become intimates and to be known to the literary world as the Bloomsbury group. By "the Bloomsbury group" I mean, among others, Virginia and Leonard Woolf, Adrian Stephen, Lady and Sir Desmond MacCarthy, E. M. Forster, Lytton Strachey, John Maynard Keynes and Geoffrey Keynes, David Garnett, Francis Birrell, and Clive and Vanessa Bell.

In H. Festing Jones's *Samuel Butler* the name of Leslie Stephen turns up rather frequently. When Butler published *The Fair Haven* (1873) he sent a copy to Charles Darwin, and in the letter of acknowledgment Darwin said he had had lunch with Stephen and they had discussed the book. In his reply Butler says, or seems to say, he also had had a letter from Stephen. (The sentence in which he refers to Stephen is awkwardly expressed, and it is quite possible there was no such letter; Jones does not refer to one.) Some years later when Butler was engaged in his one-sided quarrel with Darwin, Darwin's sons asked Stephen whether they should undertake to answer certain of Butler's accusations. He advised them to say nothing at all, advice which was followed and which helped convince Butler that successful scientists could be very highhanded and overbearing.

Of the two reviews Butler wrote in his entire lifetime, one was of Stephen's *Free-Thinking and Plain-Speaking* (1873). Butler was not much impressed by the book; he said it did not "greatly enlarge the domain of human thought" but it did at least extend the "boundaries [of] licensed utterance." Stephen read the review and commented on it, calling Butler "Our friend Butler (of the Fair Haven)" in a letter to Charles Eliot Norton. There are a couple of other references to Stephen in Jones's biography. The two men were not friends and in fact they seem to have been mutually antipathetic, but the point here is that occasionally their paths crossed. The one thing they held in common was their agnosticism, if Butler's attitude toward belief in the supernatural may properly be labeled agnosticism.

There was a tenuous connection between the Stephen family and the family of Lady MacCarthy (nee Mary Warre-Cornish) through Lady Ritchie (nee Anne Isabella Thackeray). Anne Thackeray Ritchie was the sister of Stephen's first wife, Harriet Marian Thackeray, and she was an aunt by marriage to Mary MacCarthy. Lady Ritchie was an important personage in the life of the Stephen family, and even in the lives of the children of Stephen's second wife, Julia Duckworth. Virginia Woolf mentions her in *A Writer's Diary*, and she was well known to Mrs. Woolf's Bloomsbury friends through her friendship with Lady Strachey. Annie Ritchie, as she was called, wrote novels and was a figure in the literary world. One of her acquaintances was Butler. In Lady MacCarthy's *A Nineteenth-Century Girlhood* (1929) there is this story:

> Her wit was so lightly lambent that often people missed her points. Samuel Butler went to call upon her one day soon after his *Authoress of the Odyssey* (which insists that the book was written by a woman) had been published. He told her he was at work on a book on Shakespeare's sonnets. He was, however, only bewildered at her saying, "Oh, Mr. Butler, do you know my theory about the sonnets? They were written by Anne Hathaway!" It was not she who repeated the story, but the author of *Erewhon*. He never saw that she was laughing at him and used to tell it, shaking his head sadly and saying, "Poor lady, that was a silly thing to say."

This anecdote seems to have had considerable currency in the Bloomsbury group, for it is told in a number of places.

The parents of Desmond MacCarthy made Butler's acquaintance during a holiday in Switzerland. On one occasion Mrs. MacCarthy went out on the hotel porch to call the loitering Desmond (he was ten years old) to lunch, and Butler, fearing she — like all parents, as he saw it — would bully the child, went out with her. Entering with Desmond, he whispered: "I thought I'd better come, with a stranger Mama couldn't be quite so angry." Back in England, the acquaintanceship was maintained, and the young Desmond was regularly taken to visit Butler at his lodgings at Clifford's Inn.

Two other members of the Bloomsbury group, Francis Birrell and David Garnett, also knew of Butler through family connections. Augustine Birrell, the father of Francis, was well known as a writer, although he eventually became even better known as a member of Lord Asquith's cabinet and for the part he played in the question of home rule for Ireland. Birrell wanted to meet Butler, and a meeting was arranged by mutual friends. As recorded both by Jones and by Butler himself, the meeting was not a success. Butler scarcely spoke, and Birrell told an anecdote about a lecture he had given at Sheffield. In Jones's interpretation, Butler was uncommunicative because he did not like being on display, but Birrell tried to be pleasant and agreeable. In his *Notebooks* Butler has left a highly unsympathetic account of Birrell's efforts to be entertaining, or as Butler put it, to show off. The two men seem not to have met again, but after Butler's death Birrell attended one of the Erewhon dinners (organized to pay homage to Butler and to spread his reputation). Birrell was one of the speakers, and he talked about his meeting with Butler. In 1904 Birrell wrote a very favorable review in the *Speaker* of Butler's *Essays on Life, Art and Science*.

Richard Garnett, the grandfather of David Garnett, was Superintendent of the Reading Room at the British Museum, and thereby became friendly with Butler, who did much of his studying and writing there. Garnett reviewed *The Authoress of the Odyssey* for the *Athenaeum*; he obviously did not accept the thesis, but he treated Butler with respect. Butler was an admirer of Garnett's scholarship and of the fanciful wit displayed in his *The Twilight of the Gods*. Butler dedicated *Unconscious Memory* to him. Even so, he liked to tease Garnett, and there are a number of passages in the *Notebooks* in which Butler records his own witticisms at Garnett's expense. In the biography, Jones recorded a number of things Butler had to say about Garnett.

None of the Stracheys is mentioned by Jones as having crossed Butler's path; but Lady Strachey, the mother of Lytton, was on good terms with Anne Ritchie, with the Stephen family, and with Garnett. It would be surprising if she did not hear one or another of them mention him occasionally. There is no evidence that the Keynes family knew Butler, but they were related to the Darwins, and one may assume that they took more than a casual interest in Butler's attacks on Darwin.

This rather long-winded attempt to place Butler in some fairly close relationship with certain of the families of the writers who were to form the Bloomsbury group may seem irrelevant. But one should remember that Butler was not well known to the general public, except as the author of *Erewhon*; whereas he was known to such upper-middle-class intellectual families as these mentioned in this little history. When *The Way of All Flesh* began to exert its influence, the young members of the Bloomsbury group must have found themselves confronted by a "new" writer who had been known to them for a good many years.

In his "My Early Beliefs," a record of his relationship to his Bloomsbury friends and the ideas they shared, John Maynard Keynes emphasizes their debt to Cambridge, where most of them had been students just after the turn of the century. He emphasizes their sense of exhilaration at being free to search out the truth, to cut through sham and hypocrisy, and their freedom to take an ironic view of the Victorian mores. They were subject to the influence of many minds, among them McTaggart, Lowes Dickinson, Russell, and especially G. E. Moore. And to these names, one should add Samuel Butler.

David Garnett says (in a letter to me) that Desmond MacCarthy was very fond of talking about Butler to him, "partly because he knew my family had been acquainted with Butler." And Garnett says he believes Butler "made a much bigger impression on Desmond" than on any other member of the Bloomsbury group. It is very clear from MacCarthy's own reviews and biographical sketches that Butler the man and Butler's ideas had made a great impression on him. In one sketch, he tells how he used to visit him in his rooms in Clifford's Inn. Butler sometimes gave him a copy of one of his books, always with the strict injunction not to read it, and MacCarthy says he was about seventeen before he began to understand Butler's views, especially his intense dislike of overbearingness. "To take advantage of superiority of intellect, or of any other kind of superiority, moral force, knowledge of the world, reputation, wealth, social position, a fine manner, and to use it to browbeat a helpless person, was in his eyes a revolting, unpardonable offence." It is conceivable that this belief of Butler's had an influence on MacCarthy because one member of Bloomsbury, a latecomer and an Oxford man, Raymond Mortimer, has said that MacCarthy greatly distrusted intellectual pride.

MacCarthy's published comments on Butler began in 1908 and continued at fairly regular intervals for the next thirty-odd years. When Mr. Fifield decided to republish most of Butler's volumes, MacCarthy publicized the venture by writing "The Irony of Samuel Butler" for *The Albany Review*. In this he distinguishes between Butler's satire, which is found at its purest form in *The Way of All Flesh*, and his irony, which is at its best in *Erewhon*. He sees Butler's irony arising from inevitable conflicts between logic and common sense, as when he has the two philosophers argue about the rights of animals and the rights of vegetables in *Erewhon*, and the inevitable conflicts one discovers in serving God *and* Mammon.

In 1926, when all but two volumes of the Shrewsbury edition had been published, MacCarthy gave Butler another plug in *The New Statesman*. In 1931 he edited a special Butler issue for *Life and Letters* which included notes of Butler's never before published, plus Butler's own account of his strange relationship with the handsome parasite Pauli.

Butler was quite wrong in his judgment of Pauli's character; but, as MacCarthy points out, in an essay in *Criticism* (1933), Butler was attracted to him because he thought him "a swell." MacCarthy's Bloomsbury friends probably would not have used the term "swell," but they would have understood and sympathized with an observation such as this in the *Notebooks*: "The good swell is the creature toward which all nature has been groaning and travailling together until now. He is an ideal. He shows what may be done in the way of good breeding, health, looks, temper and fortune. He realizes men's dreams of themselves, at any rate vicariously. He preaches the gospel of grace." And they would have applauded his hedonism, about which MacCarthy says: "The happiness of affection between gentle, strong, amorous, beautiful people, among whom there is much kindness and little grief—that was his ideal; and it is one which, translated into terms of everyday life in a complex civilization, admits of no contempt for wealth."

One of MacCarthy's most interesting accounts of Butler was his 1935 BBC talk, "I Know a Man," later printed in *The Listener*. He repeats many of the anecdotes he had written up earlier and adds some new information. He had first read *Erewhon* when he was seventeen, from which one might infer that MacCarthy upon reaching Cambridge talked about Butler with his friends Clive Bell, Woolf, Adrian Stephen, John Maynard Keynes, and E. M. Forster. He gives an example of his father's delight in listening to Butler:

> They laughed a good deal. At that time a Professor was writing to the papers to say that the chatter of monkeys was not meaningless, but that they were conveying ideas to each other. "This," said Mr. Butler, "appears to me to be rash. The monkeys might with good reason conclude that in our magazine and literary and artistic creation we are not chattering idly, but conveying ideas to each other." This amused my father very much. I did not see the joke.

And he gives an amusing account of Butler's manner of shifting from demure propriety to open glee when he heard or said something that struck him as incongruous or ironic:

> His laughter was mostly silent. The corners of his mouth went up in a wide semicircle beneath his beard, his eyes sparkled with mockery, and suddenly before you, instead of the face of a quaintly staid, elderly gentleman mindful of the P's and Q's, was the wild laughing face of an old faun, to whom the fear of giving himself away was obviously a sensation unknown.

(Raymond Mortimer, who succeeded MacCarthy as leading critic of the Sunday *Times*, has written a number of articles about Butler. I have not included him in this discussion because he was a latecomer to the Bloomsbury group, and he did not publish anything about Butler until 1926.)

Mr. and Mrs. Leonard Woolf moved to Clifford's Inn after their marriage in 1912. This means they were living there about ten years after Butler's death. In the first of her *Times Literary Supplement* reviews about Butler (July 21, 1916), Mrs. Woolf refers to his life "in a set of rooms at Clifford's Inn, where he cooked his own breakfast and fetched his own water." She was reviewing *Samuel Butler, Author of Erewhon* by John F. Harris. The long review — it is nearly two full columns — makes it perfectly clear that Mrs. Woolf had given a good deal of thought to Butler's career. In some ways she finds him an inscrutable man. But he did have a consistent point of view. For example, he despised any form of pretence; and, since pretence almost inevitably gets caught up in professionalism (of the minister, the doctor, the professor, or whomever), he despised those people who identified themselves with their profession. Mrs. Woolf relates all this to Butler's view of the Victorian world:

> The Victorian world, to hazard another generalization, was the age of the professional man. The biographies of the time have a depressing similarity; very much overworked, very serious, very joyless, the eminent men appear to us to be. . . . Butler, of course, hated nothing more than the professional spirit; and this may account for the startling freshness of his books. . . .

She does not try to formulate Butler's point of view, but she says that related to it are his "strange, unlaughing" humor, "the peculiar accent and power of his style," "his force of character, his humanity, and his great love of beauty."

In the summer of 1919, Mrs. Woolf wrote a review for the *Times Literary Supplement* of the eleventh impression of *The Way of All Flesh*. She comments on the critical praise it was given in 1903 and on its slowly gaining a wide popularity. This slowness she attributes to Butler's originality: ". . . the public is fundamentally sagacious. It makes up its mind after seven years or so as to what is good for it, and when it has made up its mind it sticks to it with dogged fidelity." She does not believe Butler is a finished or professional novelist: "So, just as Butler himself would have appeared in a crowd of fashionable people, 'The Way of All Flesh' appeared among the season's novels, awkward, opinionated, angular, perverse." Even so, she finds it more "original, more interesting, and more alive" than novels technically superior to it. She also gives Butler credit for opinions that she herself or her own generation somehow think of as new and as their own:

> Then, again, we had fancied that some idea or other was of our own breeding. But here, on the next page, was Butler's original version, from which our seed had blown. . . . The novels that have been fertilized by "The Way of All Flesh" must by this time constitute a large library, with well-known names upon their backs.

Mrs. Woolf was undoubtedly thinking of such novels as *Clayhanger*, *Of Human Bondage*, *A Portrait of the Artist as a Young Man*, *The Longest Journey*, and many of the others that show a sensitive young man, usually an aesthete, struggling against his environment and his family and trying to find his way in a world he finds harsh and insensitive. Probably she was also thinking of some of the ways in which Butler opened windows and let air into some of the stuffier Victorian rooms.

In "Mr. Bennett and Mrs. Brown," she says that in her lifetime she has observed a change in human character. More specifically she means that people in England after 1910 could live a less inhibited, less frustrated existence. She gives as examples the greater freedom allowed to wives, to children, and to servants. "And when human relations change there is at the same time a change in religion, conduct, politics, and literature." To put it bluntly, she is saying that her world has got rid of many of the rigors, solemnities, and pomposities of the Victorian world. It is interesting to observe that she singles out Butler as among the first to record this shift. "The first signs of it are recorded in the books of Samuel Butler, in 'The Way of All Flesh,' in particular. . . ."

Again, in "The Modern Essay," Mrs. Woolf shows her admiration for Butler's forthrightness, his willingness to think his own thoughts, and his ability to put them down directly. She admires Stevenson's prose, for example, but says his consciously beautiful style and verbal decorations cause his subjects on occasion to take on an air of insubstantiality. Butler, on the other hand, wrote as plainly as he could. "And yet obviously Butler is as careful of our pleasure as Stevenson; and to write like oneself and call it not writing is a much harder exercise in style than to write like Addison and call it writing well." Mrs. Woolf's sentences, in her fiction certainly and to a lesser degree in her essays, are consciously wrought and have their own sort of luminous brilliance. If she owed Butler little on this score, she seems to be in his debt on another, that he had helped her generation to believe in the individual's right to pursue his own course unintimidated by the Victorian era's insistence on propriety, on rules, on duties. Mrs. Woolf was convinced that daughters, wives in particular, and women generally had been restricted and frustrated in a hundred-odd ways, and in Butler she had someone asking that everyone, male or female, be allowed greater freedom of movement and expression.

And one may assume that Mrs. Woolf, who looked sceptically at the rituals of church and university and law court, would have admired the sceptical and often irreverent treatment of them in *Erewhon* and elsewhere. She herself frequently satirized the solemnities of the Victorians, nowhere more effectively than in this passage from *Orlando*:

> Stealthily and imperceptibly, none marking the exact day or hour of change, the constitution of England was altered and nobody knew it. Everywhere the effects were felt. The hardy country gentleman, who had sat down gladly to a meal of ale and beef in a room designed, perhaps by the brothers Adam, with classic dignity, now felt chilly. Rugs appeared; beards were grown; trousers were fastened under the instep. The chill which he felt in his legs the country gentleman soon transferred to his house; furniture was muffled; walls and tables were covered; nothing was left bare. . . . But the change did not stop at outward things. . . . The sexes drew further and further apart. No open conversation was tolerated. . . . The life of the average woman was a succession of childbirths. . . . Thus the British Empire came into existence; and thus—for there is no stopping damp; it gets into the inkpot as it gets into the woodwork—sentences swelled, adjectives multiplied, lyrics became epics, and little trifles that had been essays a column long were now encyclopaedias in ten or twenty volumes. . . . Hens laid incessantly eggs of no special tint. . . . The whole sky itself was nothing but a vast feather-bed; and the undistinguished fecundity of the garden, the bedroom, and the hen-roost was copied there.

Mrs. Woolf also has Orlando write this "insipid verse":

> She was so changed, the soft carnation cloud
> Once mantling o'er her cheek like that which eve
> Hangs o'er the sky, glowing with roseat hue,
> Had faded into paleness, broken by
> Bright burning blushes, torches of the tomb.

Reading the above description and this verse one may recall the stuffy world of *The Way of All Flesh*, as well as Butler's jibes at Tennyson. In the *Notebooks* his comment on Tennyson's funeral, for example, sufficiently represents his characteristic tone:

I see they packed the volume of Shakespeare that he had near him when he died in a little tin box and buried it with him. If they had to bury it they should have either not packed it at all, or, at the least, in a box of silver-gilt. But his friends should have taken it out of the bed when they saw the end was near. It was not necessary to emphasize the fact that the ruling passion for posing was strong with him in death. If I am reading, say, *Ally Sloper's Half Holiday* up to my last conscious hours, I trust my friends will take it out and put it in the waste-paper basket when they see I have no further use for it. If, however, they insist on burying it with me, say in an old sardine box, let them do it at their own risk, and may God remember it against them in that day.

One of Butler's pet theses is the importance of money: there are many passages about it in *Erewhon*, *The Way of All Flesh*, and in the *Note-books*. For example, there is this: "A man will feel the loss of money more keenly than the loss of bodily health. . . . Money losses are worst, loss of health is next worst and loss of reputation is a bad third. All other things are amusements provided money, health and good name are untouched." Shaw, of course, made much of this subject, discovering in it a source for many quips, usually at the expense of those who piously insisted that poverty was somehow a virtue. Mrs. Woolf often commented on the pleasant consequences of having five hundred pounds a year (this was the amount that seemed to her necessary for the artist or writer). In *Orlando* we find this:

It is remarkable what a change of temper a fixed income will bring about. No force in the world can take from me my five hundred pounds. Food, house and clothing are mine for ever. Therefore not merely do effort and labor cease, but also hatred and bitterness. I need not hate any man; he cannot hurt me. I need not flatter any man; he has nothing to give me. . . .

And one of Butler's pet aversions, as observed a few paragraphs above, was professionalism, in the family, in the church, or in education. The parent, Butler said over and over again, feels it his duty to impress upon his children his own not-to-be-questioned virtue, his omniscience, and his authority. The clergyman tries to be "a kind of human Sunday," and is led thereby into all sorts of hypocrisies. And the educator, who professes to know, believes he will be undone if he acknowledges there is something he does not know; consequently, he is led into an academicism which is authoritarian, which emphasizes trivia, and, most of all, which avoids issues common to everyday experience. By becoming a professional, in Butler's sense, one assumes an eminent position and does not expect to be questioned or to have to defend his opinions or decisions. All too frequently he exerts his power willfully, without suspicion that he might err.

Mrs. Woolf also satirizes professionalism. In *Mrs. Dalloway*, for example, she ridicules Lady Bruton, who makes her position an instrument of power; Lady Bruton likes to have letters signed by her appear in the *Times*, but correct grammar and appropriate phrasing are beyond her capacities. Without embarrassment or any sense of inadequacy she asks her male acquaintances to write them for her. Clarissa Dalloway ruminates about clergymen whose very positions are a substitute for ability. But Mrs. Woolf's most cutting satire is directed against two doctors, Dr. Holmes and Sir William Bradshaw. Neither man can tolerate anyone's questioning his decisions, and in their willfulness they become responsible for the death of Septimus Warren-Smith. One of Mrs. Woolf's nicest touches is her account of Lady Bradshaw's submission to the will of her husband: "Fifteen years ago she had gone under. It was nothing you could put your finger on; there had been no scene, no snap; only the slow sinking, water-logged, of her will into his." Butler and Mrs. Woolf do not employ exactly the same cast of "professionals," but each is saying essentially the same thing.

A very important point at which Butler's work and Mrs. Woolf's work touch is in their preoccupation with the nature of human identity. Students of Mrs. Woolf's fiction argue about the extent of her indebtedness to the Bergsonian revolt against reason. Clearly enough, her novels do not suggest a primary concern with logic, concepts, or external time; on the contrary, they show us a writer haunted by the indefiniteness of human identity, by the flux of matter and of time — by the mind's being a "luminous envelope." She could well be in Bergson's debt. She could also be in Butler's debt. Throughout the *Notebooks* one finds comments like these:

We have, or at any rate we think we have, a fairly definite idea before us when we talk of matter, but I don't think we ever think we have any definite idea about our own meaning when we talk of mind.

Logic is like the sword — those who appeal to it, shall perish by it.

Memory and forgetfulness are so like life and death — each of these is so much involved with the other, and is so much a process of the other — that as it is almost fair to call death a process of life, and life a process of death, so it is to call memory a process of forgetting, and forgetting a process of memory.

We may say what we will, but Life is, *au fond*, sensual.

Butler's fictional characters do not live in the flux in the same way Mrs. Woolf's do, but there is a situation in *Erewhon* that is strikingly like the situation in Mrs. Woolf's famous story "Solid Objects." In Chapter IV of *Erewhon*, the protagonist found himself in wild, uninhabited country, and he wrote this about it:

> It is a dreadful feeling that of being cut off from all one's kind. I was still full of hope, and built golden castles for myself as soon as I was warmed with food and fire; but I do not believe that any man could long retain his reason in such solitude, unless he had the companionship of animals. One begins doubting one's own identity. I remember deriving comfort from the sight of my blankets, and the sound of my watch ticking — things that seemed to link me to other people. . . .

Butler realized that one's sense of identity or selfhood is greatly strengthened by moving *inside* civilization; its physical objects, its laws, and its beliefs enable us to define or to approach a definition of what we are.

Someone has said that in Victorian literature one reads about haunted houses but that in modern literature the whole world is haunted. In "Solid Objects," the world is haunted, and John, the main character, tries to find a sense of his own reality by collecting certain kinds of solid objects. His career as a politician, even his election to Parliament, does not give him a sufficient sense of being a fixity, of knowing what he is. He collects pieces of glass and metal that are at once mysterious and solid. He is like a person awaking from a nightmare who "turns on the light and lies worshipping the chest of drawers, worshipping solidity, worshipping the impersonal world which is a proof of some existence other than ours." Mrs. Woolf seems to be saying that John's worshipping mysterious solid objects shows our desire, which cannot be satisfied, to have our identity defined by something beyond the ordinary objects in the physical world. The situation in her story is more complicated than that in *Erewhon*, but both writers are dealing with selfhood in relation to objects — documents, watches, or what not — we find around us.

Back of Mrs. Woolf's preoccupation with the nature of human identity are the many nineteenth-century forms of pre-psychoanalytical literature, of Nietzsche, Schopenhauer, Charcot — and of Butler. Ernest A. Baker in his *History of the English Novel: Yesterday* sees Butler as the father of psychological fiction in England:

> As always he insisted that mental phenomena that matter were commonly not those which leave plain traces on the surface, he explored the instincts, the temperamental dispositions, likes and dislikes, obstinate impulses, of

which the individual is not more than half aware. His followers also paid more attention to the unconscious than to the conscious realm of mind and motive; it is there, they believe, that the decisive conflicts are fought out, and insignificant events lead ultimately to failure or success, misery or happiness. . . .

Baker goes on to talk about a character being viewed as a "case," the disposition or bias of novelists toward pathology. It would, he says, be taking too much for granted to call all of the novelists with such interests "Butler's school," but he points out that Butler led the way in such characterizations. If there is a "Butler school," he says, Virginia Woolf is a member of it.

Leonard Woolf (who was greatly interested in psychoanalytical literature) wrote reviews for *The Nation and Athenaeum* of several volumes of the Butler Shrewsbury Edition, published in the early 1920's; he reviewed *Erewhon, The Fair Haven, Alps and Sanctuaries,* as well as C. E. M. Joad's *Samuel Butler.* A short time later he reworked these pieces into an article "Samuel Butler," for a volume entitled *Essays* (1927). Woolf, too, as though repeating his wife's views (or perhaps she was repeating his), traced the relatively slow rise of Butler's reputation; like her, he finds him sometimes angular, perverse, eccentric. "Butler is not, nor ever will become, a popular writer. When time has had the last word with him and given him his final and fossilized place in the strata of literature, he will be less popular and in a lower stratum than he is today. . . . In my own private hierarchy of letters he occupies an extremely high place. His peculiar humour, his dialectic, his precise eccentricities, a certain dryness of mind which seems to convert so many things to a pinch of fine dust — all these qualities happen to appeal very strongly to me personally. But the critic ought sometimes to allow his mind to work undisturbed by his personal likes and dislikes."

Leonard Woolf says that when he was a student at Cambridge, in the early years of the new century, "Butler was one of the writers who meant a great deal to us." One of the books he had read then was *The Fair Haven,* with a full comprehension of its quiet irony, and he singles out this sentence from the preface: "He therefore, to my mother's inexpressible grief, joined the Baptists, and was immersed in a pond near Dorking." Mr. Woolf concludes his evaluation of Butler by saying that he deserves a high place in the history of English society. "For he was a great iconoclast. The end of the nineteenth century was a time of breaking up, the breaking up of images and bonds and creeds and superstitions. In that salutary process of destruction Samuel Butler was one of the earliest and most efficient of pioneers."

The influence of Butler on E. M. Forster has been written about elsewhere, and of course Forster himself has acknowledged his debt, but it will be to the point here to make a summary and perhaps to add a little to what has been already observed.

In "The Legacy of Samuel Butler" (1952) Forster says that the publication of *The Way of All Flesh* "made a great sensation and reawakened interest in *Erewhon*." He also comments on his having attended an Erewhon dinner at which Shaw spoke, on his own friendship with Festing Jones, on MacCarthy's great interest in Butler, on his (Forster's) having read a paper on Butler in 1910, and on his having signed a contract in 1914 to write a book on Butler. In an earlier essay, "A Book That Influenced Me" (1944), Forster gave some of his reasons for admiring *Erewhon*. He says he liked the shyness of its irony, its not offering a frontal attack or providing an all-knowing program. He says he likes Butler's belief in the importance of grace, good temper, good looks, good health, tolerance, intelligence, "and willingness to abandon any moral standard at a pinch." "*Erewhon*," he says, "also influenced me in its technique. I like the idea of fantasy, of muddling up the actual and the impossible until the reader isn't sure which is which, and I have sometimes tried to do it when writing myself."

Butler admired the "swell," but he also had said this: "I suppose an Italian peasant or a Breton, Norman or English fisherman, is about the best thing Nature does in the way of men. . . ." But Butler wanted critical intelligence and reason to operate too. In Gino, from *Where Angels Fear to Tread*, we find Forster admiring Italian spontaneity, but he is also critical of the excesses to which it can lead. In Rickie, from *The Longest Journey*, Forster created a kind of Ernest Pontifex. He is naturally kind and instinctively decent, but he marries a woman, Agnes Pembroke, who is committed to propriety at the expense of kindness or charity, and who is so insensitive that many moral distinctions are beyond her. And her brother, the principal of the school at which Rickie teaches, is at once "overbearing" and a "professional," in Butler's sense of each word. Together the brother and sister destroy Rickie. In *A Room With a View*, Mr. Emerson quotes a sentence from Butler, although not referring to him by name: " 'Life,' wrote a friend of mine, 'is a public performance on the violin, in which you must learn the instrument as you go along.' " Margaret Schlegel, in *Howard's End*, is given things to say that could be from Butler himself:

Isn't the most civilized thing going, the man who has learnt to wear his income properly? The imagination ought to play upon money and realize it vividly, for it's the — second most important thing in the world. . . . Independent thoughts are in nine cases out of ten the result of independent means.

And Margaret learns the art of compromise, that art, as Butler says, "all Nature has been straining and groaning toward for eons"; she loves and marries a Wilcox, who represents public order and material success and who "never bothered over the mysterious or the private." The pure idealists who are at an opposite pole from the Wilcoxes often do not understand how the world runs. Forster is highly sympathetic with the idealists — Helen Schlegel is one — but he presents a case for the Wilcoxes too. And there are many other signs in Forster's fiction, for example his emphasis on "instinctive wisdom," on the falsifications of morality that can arise from stating ethical principles in absolute terms, and on machine civilization, that suggest his indebtedness to Butler.

Probably there is one point of similarity or of alikeness in Butler and Forster that deserves most attention — their anti-dogmatism. On the menu for one of the Erewhon dinners Butler's friends printed a passage from *Life and Habit* which they considered most characteristic of Butler. It begins with this sentence: "Above all things let no unwary reader do me the injustice of believing in *me*." In "What I Believe," which may be, and deservedly so, the best known of Forster's essays, the opening sentence is this: "I do not believe in Belief."

The study of influences is often ridiculed nowadays. E. M. Forster has taken a crack at it himself, saying: "In a history of literature it is usually influences, influences all the way. . . . The critical scene . . . gets cluttered up . . . with pointers, arrows, connecting links, everyone doing something for someone." But, as we have seen, he has written "A Book That Influenced Me" and "The Legacy of Samuel Butler." Influences are most easily studied when they involve paraphrase or direct quotation. With the work of a man like Butler, however, influences and "connections" turn up in odd and curious ways. Strachey apparently did not think of himself as especially indebted to Butler. The following is from a letter he wrote to Virginia Woolf, December 1, 1912:

> I'm reading among other things (a) Un Adolescent, by Dostoievsky—more frantic than any, I think—12 new characters on every page, and the mind quite dazed by the conversations, and (b) the Notebooks of Sam. Butler—have you read them? They are full of amusement, and the man was certainly very intelligent, and writes very well, but he's oddly limited. The Victorian taint, perhaps, was on him too, though to be sure he wore it with a difference. Such an anaesthetic view of life! No swaggering at all—only paradoxes—intellectual acrobatics. One longs for a panache. However, I rather gather from a remark in F. Jones's preface that there are lots of indecent things left out. It's odd how he resembles the author of Hudibras. But I imagine he was ruined by a perverse character. He ought to have written nothing but satire, and he *would* devote himself to the Odyssey and Shakespeare's Sonnets and his rubbishy science and philosophy—which of course nobody could put up with, and so he became a disappointed man and said he was writing for posterity. Can you conceive anyone writing for posterity? or indeed for anyone? or indeed writing at all?

But one cannot read *Eminent Victorians* without seeing Butler laughing silently in the shadows. Again, neither Clive Bell nor David Garnett, although they have read Butler, think of themselves as being especially indebted to him. Yet the varieties of hedonism expressed in Bell's *Civilisation* (there are other matters too that suggest Butler), or in Garnett's *Aspects of Love* are in the Butler line, and it goes without saying that Butler's attacks on Victorian morality and proprieties made it easier for such books to be written.

There is one further and accidental connection which would have amused Butler. Geoffrey Keynes, the brother of John Maynard, helped to arrange the Nonesuch Press edition of *Butleriana* (1932), and he is the co-editor of *Samuel Butler's Notebooks* (1951). Mr. Keynes says he does not think of his work on Butler as having any relationship to his being a part of the Bloomsbury group. But Mr. Garnett points up the irony involved in Keynes becoming Butler's literary executor:

> After Butler's death, Jones took a great liking to a Cambridge man A. T. Bartholomew, who had a bibliographical passion, and made him Butler's literary executor. Bartholomew was a friend and associate of Geoffrey Keynes and when he died he made Geoffrey Butler's literary executor. It thus comes about that a man married to a grand-daughter of Charles Darwin and very proud of the Darwin connection is Butler's executor.

In the same letter, Mr. Garnett says, "Of course we are all indebted to Butler. . . . But it is an influence which pervades a whole generation and is not limited to Bloomsbury." It is not of course limited to Bloomsbury, but our evidence seems to imply that Bloomsbury had a lot to do with popularizing Butler, and with restating, in terms that satisfied the Bloomsbury writers as individuals, views, attitudes, and as it were a tone of voice that are to be found in Butler.

APOLOGY FOR MARLOW

W. Y. Tindall

COLUMBIA UNIVERSITY

THE trouble with Conrad, indeed, the only trouble, says F. R. Leavis, is Marlow. "Heart of Darkness," found good by some good critics, is so generally "marred" by Marlow's adjectives that it sinks into place beside *Lord Jim* among minor works. In "Youth," a "cheap insistence" on glamor makes Conrad seem a Kipling of the South Seas, if not worse. It may be that in *Chance* Conrad-Marlow rises above such "shockingly bad magazine stuff" to a kind of technical respectability, but, save for that, stories in which Marlow figures cannot be counted among the major works: *Nostromo*, *Under Western Eyes*, *The Secret Agent*, and some others in a hierarchy of values, unsupported but proclaimed. Abandoning the "objective correlative" when Marlow is around, Leavis continues, Conrad becomes "intent on making a virtue out of not knowing what he means. The vague and unrealizable, he asserts with a strained impressiveness, is the profoundly and tremendously significant." The trouble with Leavis seems failure to read the text or else to understand it.

It is good to sit down with familiar things again. (I owe a general debt to my seminar in Conrad, Spring, 1957.) Sitting there, let us look again at Marlow to find if years have brought us wisdom or new light. Let Leavis be occasion, not our theme.

Our scrutiny may discover the intention of those works in which Marlow is an element, not the intention of that fallacy at Yale but embodied intention, there in the text and not to be separated from what is often called idea or theme, the intention that elements must serve and critics fix. With the text before us, we may discover or at least accost some values of Marlow as a functioning element and of his stories as organizations of elements. Such matters are puzzling; for when Marlow is there, little is plain. In love with "enigma," he tells "inscrutable" stories.

Other critics besides Leavis have confused Marlow with his creator. When Marlow speaks they think it Conrad; and one must admit some reason for this confusion. As Conrad's other writings prove, Marlow shares some of Conrad's ideas, his moral concerns, and his delight in irony. It requires little critical awareness, however, to discover that Marlow, in spite of monocle and beard (if, indeed, he wears them), is a creature distinct from his creator. Conrad, who appears at the beginning and end and sometimes in the middle of the Marlow books, listens to Marlow and tells us what he tells him. To Conrad, Marlow is the object as Jim or Kurtz seems Marlow's. Marlow may owe something to Conrad's desire for a mask in Yeats's sense of the word, but a mask is a device for achieving impersonality, drama, and distance. No longer subject but object, Marlow has been distanced to the point where Conrad can regard him as another and use him not with the warm concern we devote to ourselves but with aesthetic detachment as an artist should. Marlow is matter to be handled and shaped. Maybe his closest parallel is Stephen Dedalus, who, although resembling his creator in many ways, is nonetheless someone else. Like Stephen, Marlow often exposes his imperfections to the mocking eye.

As Marlow serves the interests of aesthetic distance, so he serves those of realism. Like the impressionists and those who were to employ the stream of consciousness, Conrad seems to have been persuaded for a time that reality, consisting of mental refractions, is subjective. Reality in a Marlow story is in Marlow's head, not somewhere else. Moreover, the "illusion of life" that Conrad admires in the Preface to *The Nigger of the Narcissus* may be improved by a witness's report. Recounted by one who was there or, if not, by one who has received reports from those who were, the story carries a greater air of verisimilitude than an omniscient narrator commands. That, at least, is the theory. Marlow's almost incredible long-windedness might appear to injure this necessary illusion; but as Conrad assures us in the Preface to *Lord Jim*, the length of Marlow's monologue is not so great as it seems, and even if it were, might be excused by cigars, drink, and company. Preface and text alike may persuade us that Marlow was designed for suspending disbelief and establishing verisimilitude. Since, however, these depend upon no particular device or method but upon the success of any, this aspect of Marlow is not central. Marlow as center of reality is.

Conrad seems during this time to have approximated Henry James's ideas of reality. For that reason many critics have traced Marlow's origin to the master, who invented his observer several years before the emergence of Marlow. Seeing him as a development of the Jamesian observer, they have found him a kind of bearded Maisie or a monocled anticipation of Strether. Of their family maybe, Marlow differs nevertheless in so many particulars from his assumed prototype and successor that it is likely he owes Maisie no more than a possible hint. James, looking into the head of his observer, presents a selection of what goes on there. His role is that of interpreter, Conrad's of reporter. Maisie receives impressions which James attends to; Marlow, an amateur philosopher, a compulsive talker, and a kind of artist, considers, colors, and shapes his impressions by himself, while Conrad, aloof, scribbles in his notebook. Maisie's experience is immediate and current, whereas Marlow's, dependent upon memory where it receives further refraction, is distant in time and place. These differences make it clear that if, indifferent to fallacies, we allow genesis, we should look elsewhere for Marlow's.

I think that the idea of Marlow can be traced back to the inner demands of Conrad's work, immediately to *The Nigger of the Narcissus*, of which the Marlow stories seem natural developments — in several ways; but let us limit ourselves for the moment to what Percy Lubbock calls point of view. Since Marlow among other things is an embodied point of view, that limitation is suitable. The story of James Wait and the ship *Narcissus* is told by someone who, like the narrator of the Cyclops episode of *Ulysses*, is nameless and apparently disembodied. No more than a voice, this ghostly attendant employs first person nevertheless: "we" and finally "I." In spite of this long personal ascent from plural to singular, he seems not altogether there. Of and yet apart from the crew whose solidarity is his main concern, he speaks to none, avoids all action, and fails to limit his observations to what is possible. He is present at the interviews of Donkin and Wait and of Wait and the cook although these interviews are without third parties. With equal ease he enters the first mate's head (or else that of the second) to tell us what goes on. He gets around — and as he gets there he anticipates Marlow now and again in his devotion to simile, his moral anxiety, his delight in "enigma," and his surrender to "the fascination of the incomprehensible." It is plain that this concerned yet ghostly voice is an experiment, an unsuccessful experiment perhaps, marking a transition between omniscience and a personified observer. Marlow, developing from this voice, improves it. Equipped with personality, character, limits, attitude, and tone — in a word, with body — Charlie Marlow and his conspiring voice become authentic. More than observant, he not only plays his part in the action but subsumes it, leaving that ancestral voice neither here nor there.

Not Conrad's occasional description, then, but this voice determines Marlow, who, far from Polish, emerges as the Victorian gentleman, the embodiment maybe of Conrad's aspiration. Almost a Colonel Blimp at times, Marlow nevertheless exceeds that caricature in sensibility and complexity. The stiff upper lip conceals the man of feeling and the civilized European. His monocle (if any) might be taken as his image; for rays of light through a single lens are both bent and (if we may pass from the physical to the social sense of this metaphor) distanced. Conrad's monocle, proved by photography, is not, as the wit put it in another connection, a monocle built for two; for Marlow's is singular in every sense. Monocular vision implies ideas, biases, principles, even obsessions. Marlow's are plainly there, changing things. In love with conscious order and light, he detests disorder and darkness. Devoted to duty, fidelity, and prudence as a navigator and master must be, he observes in "Heart of Darkness," at a moment of savage and commercial confusion: "I looked ahead—piloting." As he proceeds, he ruminates in the manner of the popular philosopher on the nature of things. Their nature, we discover, is not altogether different from that observed by Hardy or, indeed, by Conrad—if we may trust his letters. Marlow shares with his creator the all but existentialist conviction that however meaningless and hopeless things are, we must cherish ideals and by their aid change necessary defeat to a kind of futile victory. Such human victories, general defeats, and all things else are mixed and dubious. For this reason too Marlow is obsessed with enigmas and uncertainties. They are part of the nature of things. We can never be sure in this uncertain place, but we must try.

As for attitude: at once cynical and sentimental, Marlow is given to pity and impatience. Maybe his term "romantic" describes him best. Although he fails to define it, this term, as he uses it, seems to include imagination, illusion, anxiety, and concern with self. Marlow has little humor, though he laughs once or twice, as, for example, when Fyne falls down a hole in the dark. If little humor and less wit, there is plenty of irony; and that provides his common tone. Like many ironists, Marlow is committed, *engagé*. All this is apparent enough; but Marlow, changing with the years, reveals new aspects in each story from "Youth" to *Chance*. Whether early, middle, or late, however, and whatever his apparent commitments, Marlow has Marlow in mind.

In "Youth" we have Marlow on Marlow, a congenial theme for this worrier. Here alone among his monologues, subject is plainly one with object and the apparent with the actual. Before an audience composed of Conrad and a variety of bankers, brokers, and directors, Marlow, undescribed but more or less mature, ruminates about himself when young and foolish. As memory searches the past, bringing it to present light, two times, providing tension, center our interest and his own. Marlow's times, simpler than those of Proust's Marcel, may remind us of Eliot's pastness of the past and its presence; for Marlow finds irony in their coincidence— not irony alone, however, but nostalgia and sentiment as well. Most suitably defined at his debut as a sentimental ironist, Marlow makes a point of what he calls "the romance of illusions" and the pleasing folly of "the good old time." His far from tranquil recollections are suitably punctuated. "O youth!" he exclaims, "The strength of it, the faith of it, the imagination of it! . . . Oh, the glamour of youth!" These periodic exclamations compose what Leavis calls Conrad's "cheap insistence" on glamor; but a moment's scrutiny shows that Marlow is speaking, that he is the kind of man who, unwilling to let a thing reveal itself, insists on underlining it. An amateur as yet at telling tales and otherwise imperfect, Marlow is allowed by Conrad to expose himself—in a kind of double exposure. While old Marlow exposes young Marlow to sentimental irony, ironic Conrad, aloof, silent, and listening among men of affairs, lets innocent old Marlow show old Marlow up. The anxious awkwardness and sentimentality that he displays are important; for the nature of Marlow is the theme. What escapes Leavis, detained by an element, is the total structure with its tone, feeling, sense, and intention. We too may dislike Marlow and his manner or method, but we must not blame Conrad for a dramatic revelation of middle-aged nostalgia or the discursive insistency that seems its accomplice. Those thematic exclamations and asides, inseparable from the portrait of Marlow, are the thing itself.

Searching possibilities of Marlow as subject and object, Conrad followed this simple tale with one of greater density or specific gravity, which may be signs or at least metaphors of value. A tale at once complex and ambiguous, "Heart of Darkness" is ostensibly the story of Marlow's quest for Kurtz. Actually Marlow is questing for himself: "The most you can hope," he says, "is some knowledge of yourself." While seeking assurance and knowledge, he exposes himself once more to Conrad's distant eye. But Marlow has developed. Not only a discursive commentator, he has become an imagist as well; and developing in other directions, he has acquired moral concerns. That love of mystery which appears now and again in "Youth," emerges here as one of Marlow's obsessions.

"Image" and "symbol," terms used by Marlow, indicate his new method of presentation — at least in part. By "image," a term he applies to Kurtz and the wild woman, he seems to mean a significant but more or less limited concretion; and by "symbol," a term he applies to skulls on posts, he seems to mean a less definite, more generally suggestive concretion. Rusting machinery in the Belgian wasteland and the gunboat shelling the forest are images in his sense; whereas the enigmatic forest is a symbol. As if familiar with the Preface to *The Nigger of the Narcissus*, Marlow sometimes presents his vision in plastic, sensuous forms that seem designed to "reveal" or "disclose" embodied meaning to an audience that must take these offerings as it can. Conrad's Preface, a symbolist manifesto, is not unlike Yeats's contemporary essay "The Symbolism of Poetry." We have no assurance that Marlow has read Conrad or Yeats on symbolism, but as he tells us in "Youth," he has read Carlyle's *Sartor Resartus* with its famous chapter on symbol, and it seems likely from the text that he knows Baudelaire — as Conrad did. In "Heart of Darkness" Marlow's childish interest in the "delightful mystery" of maps and his consequent journey to the "unknown" suggest Baudelaire's "Le Voyage" as Marlow's dandy at the trading post suggests Baudelaire's ideal man. Comparing his forest to a "temple," Marlow calls to mind the forest of Baudelaire's "Correspondances," which also allows obscure, confusing intimations to emerge.

In the prelude to "Heart of Darkness" Conrad tells us that for Marlow "the meaning of an episode was not inside it like a kernel but outside, enveloping the tale which brought it out only as a glow brings out a haze." This "misty halo" (not unlike the white fog encountered on the Congo) seems to have little in common with the inner truth, lying deep below the surface, that Marlow seeks; but only a difference of metaphor separates these attempts to fix the meaning of symbol. Wherever its meaning lies — whether in halo, fog, or kernel — Marlow's principal symbol, aside from the forest, is the voyage, that, he says in "Youth," seems "ordered for the illustration of life, that might stand for a symbol of existence." His trip up the Congo "seemed to throw a kind of light on everything about me — and into my thoughts." Not "very clear," to be sure, "yet it seemed to throw a kind of light." That Marlow saw his outer adventure as the archetypal embodiment of an inner adventure is clear.

Like Baudelaire, Marlow is seldom content to let his concretions alone. Sometimes he tries to explain them and almost always, driven by anxiety, he anticipates our reaction by stating his own. Marlow, after all, is not early T. S. Eliot. Adjectives and similes, not unlike the eager nouns by which the captain of "The Secret Sharer" tries to fix his delusion, are Marlow's attempts to give his response to halo or kernel and to fix his impression of the images he picks as subjective correlatives. He finds the women knitting black wool "fateful," and the "expressive and puzzling" skulls indicative of moral deficiency. Even the forest is restricted by Marlow's guesses to our primitive, repressed, and hidden desires, below "permitted aspirations." Such discursive limitations, however, are legitimate in this context; for the story is not about knitting women, forests, or even Kurtz, but about Marlow's response to them.

Trying to explain his dark forest, Marlow commonly finds it enigmatic, its darkness properly shrouded in white fog. In this respect Marlow resembles the crew of the *Narcissus*, who, like critics confronted by a text, find Wait, another dark thing, ambiguous. Far from implying certainty, Marlow's comments celebrate uncertainty, as if to support Carlyle's idea of symbol, which conceals as it reveals. The emphasis upon enigma that Leavis finds lamentable is not there to make a virtue of ignorance. Not only the heart of Marlow's darkness, it is also a consequence of his symbolist position. For romantic symbolists there can be no definite conclusions; and however certain Marlow may be about some images, his tale, as listening Conrad says, is "inconclusive."

Imagery of dark and light, by which the voice of the *Narcissus* expresses his uncertainties, is also useful to Marlow. Civilization is light and the forest dark; but darkness and light are always shifting and ambiguous. What seems dark may prove light and what seems light, dark; or else, mixed, they may compose the universal "grayness" that he dreads. Acclaiming light, he faces darkness; but a growing conviction that the darkness of Kurtz and the forest may be his own or that in their internal and external confusion he can no longer tell light from dark is cause for anxiety and a further cause of uncertainty. Howling natives correspond to something within himself; and at the end, still professing light, he is loyal to Kurtz's darkness.

The conflict or confusion of light and dark, inviting irony, allows morality. Marlow's moral position, though seeming plainer than it is, is emphatic. Approving fidelity, duty, discipline, and order, of which rivets, navigation, and light seem symbolic, he abhors dark disorder. Morality involves choice; Marlow's, however, is not between light and dark but between kinds of dark. Forced to choose between "nightmares," that of the rapacious Belgians and that of Kurtz, Marlow chooses the latter; for to him that ultimate exclamation seems "moral victory." Not only proving Kurtz's awareness of his "degradation," his "horror," agreeably corroborating Marlow's own convictions, seems also to imply the "immense darkness" of all things.

As for the ironies: ironic Marlow seems their main and their all but unconscious object. It is ironic that one so vocal should call Kurtz "a voice." There is irony (of which Marlow is also innocent) in his unquestioning acceptance of Kurtz's "horror" as a sign of grace and moral illumination. Marlow's character compels that view of it; but for all we know Kurtz is horrified because his rituals and ivory-gathering have been cut short — or he may be looking at Marlow. The principal irony in Marlow's interview with Kurtz's Intended does not consist, as Leavis thought, in Marlow's attitude toward her or in the discrepancy between her view of Kurtz and the actuality (whatever that is) but rather in the acceptance of darkness by an apostle of light. As Marlow, that apostle, enters the house of this lover of a darkness mistaken for light, darkness enters with him and grows deeper as he talks. His defense of Kurtz out of loyalty to what is perhaps his own mistaken idea of light amounts to defense of darkness and identification with Kurtz. Marlow tells a white lie to keep the Intended in the dark by preserving her light. But even this light is uncertain — as her black dress implies; and Marlow may be right in seeing her momentarily not as a creature of light and of his chivalric expectations but as the wild woman of the Congo. An irony of which Marlow is only half aware is the terrible confusion of light and dark that he reveals within himself. Darkness in white fog seems a fitting symbol.

Chivalric diminution of woman, often attributed to Conrad, is almost peculiar to Marlow. Linda, who tends the lighthouse in the dark bay, and Lena in her black dress, deceiving her man to protect him, are of a larger kind. Even the Haldin girl, also seen through Western eyes, is more nearly human than Marlow's dream of woman. Saved by ambiguity, however, from Marlow's illusion, Kurtz's Intended emerges from it to complete the exposure by standing next to Marlow's notion of her.

As Kurtz and that forest objectify what Marlow fears he has within him, so does Lord Jim. To the great company of paranoiacs, seeking in public the corroboration of private worries and their dramatization, some of Conrad's best people belong, the young captain of "The Secret Sharer" among them. Exceeding him, Marlow finds doubles not only for himself but for others. As he finds doubles for himself in Kurtz and in a variety of savages, and doubles for the Intended in the wild girl and in the girl of the allegorical painting, so he finds (or fears) another double in Jim, and detects one for him in Brown. Captain Brierly affords Marlow intimations of Jim's case and of his own potentialities. That Jim is "one of us" (a broad and ambiguous reference) is the immediate cause of Marlow's concern. Seeking Jim, Marlow seeks himself again.

The case of Marlow as Jim or of Jim as Marlow challenges moral subtlety. Dumb and clearly of the right sort, Jim has a conscience bothered by lost honor — vainly and absurdly bothered, maybe, after society forgets him. Such "exquisite sensibility," shaped not only by the code of British seamen but by that of the middle class, detains Marlow; for he shares it. Jim's heroic death, like Kurtz's "horror," seems an assurance; but even this is imperfect, and Marlow, despairing of finalities among "unanswerable questions," confesses his failure to make the necessary but tenuous distinctions between fact and imagination, truth and illusion. Convinced of the hopelessness of finding truth, Marlow pursues it nevertheless with British fortitude. The results are as inconclusive as he expects, but pleasing enigmas have been encountered in the process. The one thing certain is that Jim is part of Marlow, existing in his memory: "after all it is only through me that he exists for you." Not Jim but what Marlow makes of him is the matter before us.

Evading analysis, Jim's case invites suggestive presentation. To Marlow, equipped for presenting mysteries by objects, Jim himself is "symbolic" and so are his three jumps — one of them, like the unflown flights of Mallarmé's swan, a jump unjumped. But to present his uncertainty, Marlow has recourse again to recurrent imagery of light and dark. Jim in immaculate white against a black coast, "at the heart of a vast enigma," and appropriately under a cloud, embodies Marlow's more definite apprehension. Commonly, however, picking his way in "cross lights," he ends in a "crepuscular" place where he can no longer tell white from black. Images of cloud, veil, fog support this grey confusion as he quests, like Wallace Stevens' guitarist, for "things exactly as they are." Marlow's view of Jim is "like those glimpses through the shifting rents in a thick fog." Though some of Marlow's images are narrowly assigned (the guano island and the ring, for example), most, like the cloven peaks with the moon rising from its grave, are suitably imprecise.

As he tells us of his quest, Marlow pauses to philosophize in his bumbling fashion about the nature of things; but feeling inadequate, he consults Stein, who, however, is less philosophical than oracular, and, like most oracles, enigmatic. This collector of insects uses the butterfly to enlighten and perplex Marlow. A "gorgeous object" on its heap of dirt, captured under fire, Stein's butterfly becomes for Marlow a focal symbol. For us as well its meaning is uncertain; yet it seems somehow to include most of Marlow's concerns and those of Jim. As this lovely thing is Stein's object, so it is Jim's ideal and Marlow's Jim. Sudden challenge, success, reality and dream, dirt and beauty — all things seem embodied here. Maybe "romantic" Jim catches his butterfly at last, but we may wonder if Marlow catches his.

Stein's "destructive element," seeming easier than his butterfly, proves no less difficult. In its context, the "element" refers to dream or romantic illusion; but since this element is the sea and that is commonly an image of reality, the immersion commended by Marlow's philosopher is ambiguous. (Digression: Talking of a man immersed in that element, Stein seems to have provided Eliot with the ending of "Prufrock": "If he tries to climb out into the air . . . he drowns.") Stein fails to tell us, but we may guess, the meaning of "destructive." Marlow's response is the point: feeling enlightened, he remains confused, as Stein significantly walks from lamplight into darkness and back again. Ostensibly discursive, Stein's phrase remains a teasing metaphor; and Marlow's tale, in which Stein is an element of first importance, appears a form for presenting the process, feeling, and result of man's quest for knowledge.

Of the two developments in method here, the first is more elaborate refraction, the second, complexity of structure. Up to the visit to Stein, Marlow's observations, supplemented by those of others, compose the narrative; but as Jim recedes in space, he is also distanced by the intervention of many minds. The results, as memories and fancies trouble fact, are increasing uncertainty and the enlargement of Marlow, who as collector and arranger, becomes more massively the heart of his tale and all we know for sure. As for structure: though Marlow plays with temporal sequence at one point in "Heart of Darkness," it is not until *Lord Jim* that he wins freedom from time.

The "time shift" or the "working backwards and forwards in time" that Conrad and Ford devised together about this time, puts drama, expressiveness, artful juxtaposition, and disclosure ahead of normal order. Ford accounts for such disordering (at the beginning of Part Four of *The Good Soldier*, for example) on grounds of verisimilitude: it is the way a man tells a story—and maybe the way, if a detective, he comes upon its parts. But in "Heart of Darkness" Marlow, speaking of "truth stripped of its cloak of time," implies a more philosophical purpose. Whatever the purpose, the effect is plain. A narrator who scrambles times, finds matter less important than its arranger. No longer itself, moreover, matter becomes things for arrangement, for abstraction. As Picasso rearranged noses, breasts, and eyes to express his idea, so Marlow his less immediate materials.

If Marlow, more than an amateur philosopher, is a kind of artist and if his stories display the artist at work, another meaning of Stein's butterfly is relevant and functional. Stein describes his insect as a thing of accuracy and harmony, balancing colossal forces—as a work of art, in short, created by nature, "the great artist." Among the correspondences offered by that symbol, then, is this: Marlow, not only like a hunter of butterflies, is like their creator. That he fails to see this application of Stein's loaded image is probable; but that Conrad had it in mind and reserved it for development in *Chance* is not unlikely.

Conrad had put Marlow aside for many years before he got around to this. Always experimental and maybe tired of that mask, he tried other ways of presenting vision, among them a return to omniscience in *The Secret Agent*. Three observers, one exposing himself to irony, complicate the general objectivity of *Nostromo*. The effect of these returns to earlier technique is emphasis on things as they are, not on what is made of them. Maybe concern with the world of politics, which Marlow's ruminations could only diminish, accounts for this change. With *Under Western Eyes*, where society is also important, Conrad turned (while writing *Chance*) to an observer, one who is too objective and impersonal, however, to have much in common with Marlow. Whereas he looks in, those Western eyes look out. Why Conrad came back to Marlow in *Chance* is the problem. His interests are moral and philosophical. Here, beyond his depth in a psychological muddle that invites Freud, Marlow seems ill adapted for his apparent role. ("Morbid psychology," said Conrad in a letter of 1908, while writing *Chance*, "is a perfectly legitimate subject for an artist's genius. But not for a moralist.") But Marlow is excellently adapted for what I think his actual role. Apparently more or less indifferent to Flora and Anthony (as we too must be), Conrad centers his interest in Marlow again—this time in another aspect. He is here, I think, to show what he does with this trivial matter, how, in particular, he gives it body and shape, how his creative imagination works. I think that *Chance* is Conrad's portrait of the artist. This seems the only justification for what, unless Marlow's method and construction are central, must be counted tedious. Henry James's praise of *Chance* for doing what requires most doing seems recognition of Conrad and, by dramatic extension, of Marlow as fellow craftsmen.

No longer driven by anxiety about himself, moved now by detached curiosity, a matchmaker's sentiment, and a surviving interest in unjumped jumps, Marlow is concerned for the first time with what he admits is none of his business. Appropriately, he is more distant than ever from his ostensible object, an object so attenuated and transformed by refractions as to make the complex refractions of *Lord Jim* seem elementary. At one point Conrad tells us what Marlow tells him of what Powell has told him of what Franklin has told him of what the Ship-keeper has told him of Flora. Almost never around at critical moments and increasingly indifferent to fact, Marlow calls upon imagination (a faculty he once denied having) for what may have happened. Emphasis, falling no longer on what he makes of a problem, falls now on what he makes. His structure, created by the imagination from almost nothing, is a glittering solid composed of method, an abstraction, like those poems in which Mallarmé elaborately celebrates nothing. Art, despite the Preface to the *Nigger*, is here for art's sake alone. Constructing this autonomous thing, Marlow is uncertain no more. There are no enigmas left; for, having made everything, he knows it. An observer still, he observes what he has made—like that aesthetic god of Stephen Dedalus, paring nails, sitting above his creation, contemplating it. There is nothing more for Marlow.

THE OLD NOVEL AND THE NEW

Martin Steinmann, Jr.
UNIVERSITY OF MINNESOTA

"IN A bird's-eye view of the English novel from Fielding to Ford," says the late Joseph Warren Beach in a chapter of *The Twentieth Century Novel* entitled "Exit Author," "the one thing that will impress you more than any other is the disappearance of the author." The old novel and the new: I deliberately invoke the shade of William Archer so that the error (as I take it) of *The Old Drama and the New*, of exalting (what Archer fancies to be) the disappearance of dramatic conventions, may point a moral. Certainly the disappearance of the author is an important—perhaps the most important—historical fact about the British novel; and I shall have a good deal to say about it. But the tendency in modern criticism to exalt the author's disappearance—we find it in James's prefaces, in Percy Lubbock's *The Craft of Fiction*, in the New Criticism; it is almost a thesis of *The Twentieth Century Novel* (though Beach is aware of its dangers); I have been guilty of it—this tendency is (as I now think) mistaken or at least wants tempering. It is a tendency to persuasively define "novel" in such a way that the only "true" novel is the novel from which the author has disappeared and that the novel in which we feel the author's presence is an impure admixture of history or philosophy or homily with fiction—in such a way, in short, that the old novel is not really a novel at all. In this essay, I shall try to correct this tendency by showing that the disappearance of the author is not the elimination of conventions but the replacement of old conventions with new; and that, though some of the consequences of this disappearance (the splendid dramatizations of states of consciousness, for instance) are gains, others (among them—if I may be permitted a hyperbole surely no greater than "the disappearance of the author"—the disappearance of the reader) are losses. But first I must notice another important historical fact about the British novel and, in doing so, indicate the limitations of my topic.

In the same bird's-eye view of the English novel, we can scarcely fail to see that there are a great many more novels today than there used to be, and a greater variety. Today the novel is the dominant genre of imaginative literature: everyone reads novels; I am tempted to say that everyone writes them. The novel is almost the only genre of economic importance; its only serious rival is the magazine story. Poetry, the dominant genre in a day when novel-writing and novel-reading were not quite respectable, is quite dead as a popular genre. Mr. Eliot has indeed been noticed in *Time*; but we can hardly imagine what it would be like to have a Scott, a Byron, or a Tennyson about, reaching and influencing a large reading public, occupying a position comparable to that of Dr. A. J. Cronin or Mr. Lloyd Douglas or the Reverend Norman Vincent Peale. And Dr. Cronin and Mr. Douglas remind us of how much greater the variety of novels now is.

That more novels should be written and read nowadays is, of course, partly explained by the growth of population and by the spread of popular education and the consequent disproportionate growth of the reading public; but these facts do not directly explain either the dominance of the novel or its great variety. In *Fiction and the Reading Public*, Mrs. Q. D. Leavis argues that they do, however, indirectly explain these phenomena. Of particular relevance here is her argument that the growth of the reading public has split that public into at least three groups — high-brow, middle-brow, and low-brow (as she calls them) — divided (as her names suggest), not on the basis of religion or politics (as in the Restoration), but on the basis of degree of cultivation. Whatever the cause of this split, the fact of the split is apparent enough, and it is surely the chief cause of the great variety. Defoe, Fielding, Jane Austen, Dickens, and Thackeray — in a way these novelists in their times belonged to everyone who read novels; and so did Henry Brooke, Mrs. Radcliffe, and Mrs. Gaskell. There was only one novel-reading public, and every novelist had this public in mind. Today the publics of Dr. Cronin and Joyce are quite discrete (how odd it would be to find that Kingsley Amis reads Faith Baldwin, as Jane Austen did Kitty Cuthbertson, with pleasure), and no novelist has the entire novel-reading public in mind. Indeed, as I shall urge later, though Dr. Cronin surely has a well-defined segment of this public clearly in mind, high-brow novelists such as Joyce and Mrs. Woolf have, or seem to have, no public in mind, not even the small public that they do in fact reach.

A result of this split is, as I have said, a great variety of novels — a greater variety than I can or would even wish to deal with; and I shall deal only with the high-brows — with those novelists who are the subject of serious criticism of the novel and who will, we think, find themselves places in the history of the British novel comparable to those that the major novelists discussed in this volume have found. When I refer to the new novel, I shall mean the work of the former; when I refer to the old, that of the latter. I shall not, of course, undertake a survey of either the new novel or the old; and my generalizations about either novel — especially about the new — should be hedged with more qualifications than I shall have time (or wit) to make. E. M. Forster and Virginia Woolf — Bloomsbury granted — are not really very much alike.

I began by observing, with Beach, that perhaps the most important historical fact about the new novel is the disappearance from it of the author. What precisely can be meant by saying that an author is, or is not, in his novel? The distinction can, I think, be made best in terms of two sorts of convention — conventions of style and conventions of structure — and by reference to the concept of point of view, which also can be explicated best in these terms.

By "style" I mean "selection and ordering of linguistic elements"; by "structure," "selection and ordering of nonlinguistic elements." To study style is to study words and word-orders, vocabulary and syntax; to study structure is to study such elements as plot and character, the things to which the words in certain orders refer. A given style has formal, semantic, and historical characteristics. Formally, the study of style embraces (among other things) that species of figure of speech known as "schemes"; semantically, that known as "tropes"; and, historically, that characteristic of words popularly known as "connotations." In *Lord Jim*, for example, the style of the paragraph (in Chapter 2) describing the embarkation of the pilgrims (not the only style of that novel) is characterized formally by Conrad's use of words averaging 1.43 syllables each, of sentences ranging from six to 72 words in length and averaging 39 words each, of loose sentence structure, of anaphora, and of postpositives; semantically by use of tropes whose vehicles are water; and historically by use of honorific words. On the other hand, the structure of that novel is characterized by, for example, Conrad's selection of Jim, an imaginary being with certain traits, as protagonist; of Marlow as chief narrator; of certain incidents to reveal Jim's character (the failure of nerve on the training ship, the abandonment of the *Patna*, and the flight from Egström & Blake's establishment, for instance); and of a nonchronological order in which to present these incidents. Style and structure, of course, interdepend in many ways. For one thing, we get at the structure only through the language; and, for another, the structure that a writer has in mind — his plan, his outline — influences his language in both obvious and subtle ways. Structure, nevertheless, has some measure of independence; for two works can have roughly the same structure but quite different styles: Shakespeare's *Hamlet* and Charles and Mary Lamb's are such a pair.

Now an author appears in or disappears from his novel — as, indeed, he does everything else — by his selection and management of conventions of style and structure. A novel is a long, fictional narrative. But, to disappear completely from his novel, an author must eliminate the narrative and the narrator and become a dramatist; he must give his novel a dramatic, not a narrative, structure. The drama is a limiting case of the novel (perhaps the autobiography and the essay are others). He must, in other words, eliminate everything except dialogue; when he writes anything that is not within quotation marks, he runs the risk of appearing in his novel — of making his reader conscious of a narrator, of a middleman who stands between the action and the reader.

One way of eliminating everything except dialogue (or, rather, monologue) — a traditional, naïve way, dating back to the birth of the novel — is the structural convention of the first-person narrative — of making one of the characters the narrator and (as it were) putting the entire novel within one set of quotation marks. Thomas Nashe uses this convention in *The Unfortunate Traveller*; Defoe, in *Robinson Crusoe* and *Moll Flanders*; Sterne, in *Tristram Shandy*; Charlotte Brontë, in *Jane Eyre*; Dickens, in *Great Expectations*; Butler (inconsistently), in *The Way of All Flesh*; and in our day (with greater sophistication) Conrad (as we have seen), Hudson, in *Green Mansions*, and Hemingway, in *The Sun Also Rises* and *A Farewell to Arms*. Technically, of course, this convention is purely dramatic; but, unless it is combined with structural conventions of the sort that Conrad uses or stylistic ones of the sort that Hemingway uses, its effect is quite undramatic. It is simply the substitution of one narrator and narrative for another; the author disappears all right, but an imaginary one takes his place. Its aim, however, is verisimilitude (the illusion of autobiography), the realism that in one way or another the novelist has always sought to achieve; and, as we shall notice later, an author's reason for wanting to disappear from his novel, to make it as dramatic as possible, is to achieve a highly refined realism as an end in itself rather than (as in the old novel) a means to something else.

If an author does not want to make one of his characters the narrator (and if he does want a narrative), then he must be his own narrator; and, if he wants to disappear from his novel, he must cast about for other conventions, structural and stylistic, within the third-person narrative. This (with some distinguished exceptions) is what novelists have been doing since the third quarter of the last century. In the third-person narrative in the old novel, the author is everywhere. Structurally, he makes us feel his presence by such conventions as omniscience, exposition, and block characterization; stylistically, by such conventions as the vocative case ("Dear reader"), normative words, persuasive definitions, and panoramic narration. Use of these conventions is characteristic of the point of view of the omniscient author. In novels written from this point of view, we view the action — not from the point of view of one of the characters (as in a first-person narrative or, as we shall see, in some third-person narratives) or from that of the reader or the audience (as in a play) — but from that of the author. And this is the point of view from which the old novel, first-person narratives and epistolary novels apart, and a few new novels are written. In the third-person narrative in most new novels, the author tries to avoid conventions characteristic of this point of view and, in this and more positive ways, to shift the point of view from himself to a character or (in a sense) to the reader.

In a way, of course, every novelist is omniscient in that, having created a world out of his own imagination, he knows everything about this world; in the sense of "omniscient" relevant here, however, he becomes omniscient, not by what he knows, but by what he chooses to tell; and he is said to be omniscient if — not contenting himself with reporting the actions, the appearance, and the speeches of his characters — he chooses to report their inner life, their thoughts and feelings, their states of consciousness, as well. But it is worth noting that omniscience dies hard: we find some new novelists, and distinguished ones at that, keeping it alive — T. F. Powys, for example, and Arnold Bennett, an Edwardian and in many respects an old-fashioned novelist. In Bennett's *Riceyman Steps*, for instance, though his goal, like that of most of his predecessors and successors, is realism (he never wearies, as Virginia Woolf has complained [in "Mr. Bennett and Mrs. Brown"], of giving a complete inventory of every shop, house, square, and pocket that he has occasion to mention) —

and though, like Hardy or Cooper, he makes some pretense of looking at his characters dramatically, from the outside ("a hatless man with a slight limp might have been observed") — he reports the thoughts and the feelings of nearly every character — of Henry Earlforward, the bookseller, for instance, and of his charwoman, Elsie:

> Mr. Earlforward never asked the meaning of life, for he had a lifelong ruling passion. Elsie never asked the meaning of life, for she was dominated by a tremendous instinct to serve. Mr. Earlforward, though a kindly man, had persuaded himself that Elsie would go on charing until she died, . . . and he was well satisfied that this should be so.

This is undramatic because Bennett is (as it were) standing beside his stage and telling us things that we cannot see or hear for ourselves. At best he is coaching us, making inferences from the actions and the speeches of his characters that, were his novel a play, we would if we could have to make for ourselves. Mr. Earlforward's satisfaction with Elsie's calling we might perhaps infer from his actions and speeches, as we make inferences about the inner lives of our friends. But Bennett makes the inference for us; or, rather, being omniscient and therefore having direct access to Mr. Earlforward's inner life, he need make no inferences but simply report. One stylistic mark of omniscience is use of such psychological words as "passion," "kindly," and "satisfied." Such words are not descriptive in the way that "hot," "black," and "thin" are: passion, kindliness, and satisfaction are not directly perceivable qualities. These words have something in common with normative words, discussed later; indeed, some of them ("kindly," for instance) are normative.

With omniscience usually goes exposition (in the sense in which exposition is contrasted with narration, and not in the dramatic sense) — little essays (sometimes growing into whole chapters) in which the author, abandoning for the moment (or a half hour) his action and characters, sets himself up as a psychologist, sociologist, historian, topographer, moralist, or even indeed literary critic, and didactically lectures us on the general principles under which he wishes us to subsume the particulars of his action. In the old novel, such exposition like this passage of "psychological analysis" from *Persuasion* often laces the narration:

> Who can be in doubt of what followed? When any two young people take it into their heads to marry, they are pretty sure by perseverance to carry their point, be they ever so poor, or ever so imprudent, or ever so little likely to be necessary to each other's ultimate comfort. This may be

bad morality to conclude with, but I believe it to be truth; and if such parties succeed, how should a Captain Wentworth and an Anne Elliot, with the advantage of maturity of mind, consciousness of right, and one independent fortune between them, fail of bearing down every opposition?

Presented in this way—but more elaborately (and with Freud hovering over the author's pen)—exposition is found in some new novels (in Proust, to take a Continental example). But much of the time it is presented in the old novel in quite detached blocks, as in the introductory essays in *Tom Jones* and in the essays on evolution and kindred topics in *The Way of All Flesh*, which, though beginning as a first-person narrative by Overton, quickly abandons all pretense of being anything but a third-person omniscient narrative and later, retaining the third person, shifts the point of view to Ernest Pontifex. Whether laced with the narration or presented in blocks, however, such exposition is, far from being dramatic, not even (and by definition) narrative; and the new novel avoids it.

Perhaps the most characteristic species of this exposition is that in which the author assumes the role of moralist. The omniscient author, like God, usually is possessed not only of unlimited information but also of unlimited moral insight. From his point of view, he not only sees but also judges everything. His responsibility to us is not only to tell us everything but also to evaluate everything that he tells us. He lives, not in a physical universe, but in an old-fashioned moral universe in which knowledge of right and wrong is more important than knowledge of facts: he agrees with Dr. Johnson that "Whether we provide for action or conversation, whether we wish to be useful or pleasing, the first requisite is the religious and moral knowledge of right and wrong; . . . we are perpetually moralists, but we are geometricians only by chance" ("Milton," *Lives of the English Poets*). Scott, in a tradition going back at least to the medieval bestiary, appends a *significacio* to *The Heart of Midlothian*:

> This tale will not be told in vain, if it shall be found to illustrate the great truth that guilt, though it may attain temporal splendour, can never confer real happiness; that the evil consequences of our crimes long survive their commission, and, like the ghosts of the murdered, for ever haunt the steps of the malefactor; and that the paths of virtue, though seldom those of worldly greatness, are always those of pleasantness and peace.

Hardy's essays in *The Return of the Native* on the moral constitution of the universe similarly subsume the fates of his ill-starred characters. And the novel of social purpose usually demands large blocks of exposition, as in Reade's *Christie Johnstone* and in Dickens' *Bleak House*, *Hard Times*, and *Little Dorrit* (though *Oliver Twist* and *Nicholas Nickleby*, written before Dickens began to write essays for *Household Words*, show that social purpose can do without much exposition).

The stylistic marks of this species of exposition — normative words and persuasive definitions — can be found not only there but in block characterization (itself a kind of exposition); they are, indeed, the stylistic marks of a didactic tone that pervades most novels written from the omniscient point of view. By "normative word" (as opposed to "descriptive word") I mean "word that does not, or does not only, describe the thing that it denotes, but describes the reaction of its speaker to this thing." In the passage from Scott just quoted, "great," "evil," "malefactor," "virtue," and "greatness" are clear instances of normative words. To say that certain consequences are evil is to describe qualities, not of those consequences, but of our reaction to or evaluation of them. Most — perhaps all — ethical and aesthetic words are normative, and most heatedly argued statements ("Roosevelt was a *great* president") contain at least one normative word. By "persuasive definition" (the term is Charles Stevenson's, in *Ethics and Language*) is meant "statement that takes a common but vague and highly charged word (an honorific or pejorative word) and, by eliminating its vagueness and limiting its denotation but without altering its charge, in effect redefines it in order to persuade people to take a certain attitude toward the things that, as redefined, it denotes." Though a persuasive definition does not look at all like a definition, for it seems to be a statement not about a word but about a thing, its usual stylistic mark — "real" or "true" — makes it easy to identify. The statement in the passage from Scott about "temporal splendour" and "real happiness" is a persuasive definition of "happiness": it limits the denotation of the vague, honorific word "happiness" to the states of mind experienced only by the morally pure and tries to persuade us to view these states (and only these states) with approval.

Block characterization — that is, a complete description of a character upon his first appearance — is undramatic in at least two ways. First, it is, as I have suggested, likely to use normative words as well as descriptive words, to set forth the character's moral as well as his physical qualities; it is, in other words, likely to tell us something about the author as well as about the character, to intrude the author into the description. And, second, it *tells* us about the qualities of the character rather than letting him *exhibit* them in his actions and his speeches as he would in a play or in life itself. It is as though Shakespeare were to enter with Macbeth and Banquo upon their first appearance and, before Macbeth has a chance to say "So foul and fair a day I have not seen," point to him and say, "Here is a man who has much to recommend him (valiant service to his king, for example), who is rightly admired by all for his sterling qualities, but who possesses both the tragic flaw of ambition and a scheming, unscrupulous wife." The dramatic way of characterization is to let the character gradually exhibit his qualities through his actions and speeches with, of course, the help of other characters and their actions and speeches (though the old drama, of course, is sometimes "undramatic" in also using prologues, epilogues, choruses, and, usually in soliloquies, the convention of self-description). This is Conrad's way in many of his most admired novels. Indeed, as Ford Madox Ford shows in *Joseph Conrad: A Personal Remembrance*, the desire to achieve the dramatic, the realistic — to eliminate the author — led both Conrad and Ford to carry this dramatic way of characterization to the extreme of violating the traditional chronological ordering of the action — of letting the reader in on events, not in the order in which they occur, but (as in life) in the order in which an observer (Marlow, say) might well learn about them. But the dramatic way is not the way of the old novel — of Jane Austen, George Eliot, and Trollope; and it is not the way of some old-fashioned new novels — of T. F. Powys, for example. More exactly, it is not the *exclusive* way of these novels. For no author, of old novels or new, relies exclusively upon block characterization as Joseph Hall or Thomas Overbury (say) almost do. Block characterization bears much the relation to actions and speeches that the thesis sentence of an essay bears to the particulars that support it; the actions and the speeches exemplify — testify to the truth of — the block characterization. Like the thesis sentence — and like exposition and normative words — it is a didactic convention.

The novel written from the omniscient point of view — besides being given to omniscience, exposition, and block characterization, normative words and persuasive definitions — is given to panoramic narration as well as scenic. "Panoramic" and "scenic" (note the dramatic derivation of the latter) are Henry James's and Percy Lubbock's contribution to the vocabulary of criticism of the novel. Narration is said to be panoramic if it describes action in general terms, sweeping over large vistas of time in few words; scenic if it describes it in particular ones, presenting a scene as in a play. Panoramic narration, tending as it must to make us conscious of the narrator, is undramatic; for in drama as in life we see only scenes, moments in time, and see the panorama only in retrospect—with the intervention, that is, of our memories or a narrator. Any novel whose action spans any considerable period of time, or whose cast of major characters is large, is, of course, condemned to include much panoramic narration; and, for this reason, the new novel tends to limit both the duration of its action and the number of its characters (compare the fifteen-odd years and the legion of characters in *Vanity Fair* with the single day given largely to Dedalus and the Blooms in *Ulysses*). But panoramic narration, like omniscience, survives in some old-fashioned new novels. In *Sons and Lovers*, for example, more than six months of the life of the Morel family is compressed into a passage of slightly more than 200 words:

He [Paul] drifted away from Miriam imperceptibly, without knowing he was going. Arthur only left the army to be married. The baby was born six months after his wedding. Mrs. Morel got him a job under the firm again, at twenty-one shillings a week. She furnished for him, with the help of Beatrice's mother, a little cottage of two rooms. He was caught now. It did not matter how he kicked and struggled, he was fast. For a time he chafed, was irritable with his young wife, who loved him; he went almost distracted when the baby, which was delicate, cried or gave trouble. He grumbled for hours to his mother. She only said, "Well, my lad, you did it yourself, now you must make the best of it." And then the grit came out in him. He buckled to work, undertook his responsibilities, acknowledged that he belonged to his wife and child, and did make a good best of it. He had never been very closely inbound into the family. Now he was gone altogether.

The months went slowly along. Paul had more or less got into connexion with the Socialist, Suffragette, Unitarian people in Nottingham, owing to his acquaintance with Clara.

Here the omniscient author not only intrudes into the minds of the brothers Paul and Arthur Morel, but also makes an expository remark about Arthur's courage in facing his duty. Lawrence's practice here is comparable to that of Dickens, as shown, for example, in a passage of panorama from *Nicholas Nickleby* (Ch. XXVIII), in which the events of two weeks are compressed into a paragraph of less than 150 words:

That they [Hawk and friends] came at all times and seasons—that they dined there one day, supped the next, dined again on the next, and were constantly to and fro on all—that they made parties to visit public places, and met by accident at lounges—that upon all these occasions Miss Nickleby was exposed to the constant and unremitting persecution of Sir Mulberry Hawk, who now began to feel his character, even in the estimation of his two dependants, involved in the successful reduction of her pride—that she had no intervals of peace or rest, except at those hours when she could sit in her solitary room, and weep over the trials of the day—all these were consequences naturally flowing from the well-laid plans of Sir Mulberry, and their able execution by the auxiliaries, Pyke and Pluck.

And thus for a fortnight matters went on.

And here there is exposition as well, in the statement about the persecution.

The old novel is, we have seen, not indifferent to the dramatic; no novel is. Perhaps the point is that it feels, rightly or wrongly, that the dramatic is not enough. The first chapter of *Pride and Prejudice*, for example, is exclusively scenic—a dialogue between Mr. and Mrs. Bennet that every reader of Jane Austen recalls with delight—exclusively, that is, except for the first two sentences—

It is a truth universally acknowledged, that a single man in possession of a good fortune must be in want of a wife.

However little known the feelings or views of such a man may be on his first entering a neighborhood, this truth is so well fixed in the minds of the surrounding families, that he is considered as the rightful property of some one or other of their daughters.

—the last seventy-five words—

Mr. Bennet was so odd a mixture of quick parts, sarcastic humour, reserve, and caprice, that the experience of three and twenty years had been insufficient to make his wife understand his character. *Her* mind was less difficult to develope. She was a woman of mean understanding, little information, and uncertain temper. When she was discontented, she fancied herself nervous. The business of her life was to get her daughters married; its solace was visiting and news.

—and one or two expository crumbs in between. Jane Austen allows this couple to exhibit their qualities through their speeches; but this, she evidently feels, is insufficient. She must, like an essayist, introduce her scene with generalizations and, when it is over, summarize its particulars with a "thesis sentence" of block characterization.

Trollope, to take another example, often begins a novel and lets it run on for two or three chapters without presenting a single full-blooded scene. In *Doctor Thorne*, for instance, a few scraps of the scenic apart, he gives

over the first chapter, on the Greshams, and the second and the third, on the Thornes, to exposition, block characterization, and panorama. But, as he chummily explains to his reader at the opening of the second, he does this quite deliberately, and with every awareness of its dangers, because (it seems) he believes that the undramatic is as necessary as the dramatic:

> As Dr. Thorne is our hero — or I should rather say my hero, a privilege of selecting for themselves in this respect being left to all my readers — and as Miss Mary Thorne is to be our heroine, a point in which no choice whatsoever is left to any one, it is necessary that they shall be introduced and explained and described in a proper, formal manner. I quite feel that an apology is due for beginning a novel with two long dull chapters full of description. I am perfectly aware of the danger of such a course. In so doing I sin against the golden rule which requires us all to put our best foot foremost, the wisdom of which is fully recognised by novelists, myself among the number. It can hardly be expected that any one will consent to go through with a fiction that offers so little of allurement in its first pages; but twist it as I will I cannot do otherwise. I find that I cannot make poor Mr. Gresham hem and haw and turn himself uneasily in his arm-chair in a natural manner till I have said why he is uneasy. I cannot bring in my doctor speaking his mind freely among the bigwigs till I have explained that it is in accordance with his usual character to do so. This is unartistic on my part, and shows want of imagination as well as want of skill. Whether or not I can atone for these faults by straightforward, simple, plain story-telling — that, indeed, is very doubtful.

Artistry be damned, Trollope says, in an assured tone that sits lightly on an author writing within a well-established set of conventions; first things first: the general must subsume the particular. Or — more exactly — other conventions be damned: for the whole passage shows that Trollope not only cares a good deal about his art but (unlike some of his successors) is anxious to explain its conventions to his reader.

All this — omniscience, exposition, and block characterization; the vocative case, normative words, persuasive definitions, and panoramic narration — the new novel working within the third-person narrative tries to avoid; it tries to avoid these conventions because they are undramatic and hence unrealistic and because its aim, or one of its aims at least, is realism; and it tries to avoid them by shifting the point of view from the omniscient author to one or more of the characters (or, as an impossible metaphor sometimes has it, by limiting or restricting the point of view of the omniscient author). It tries, in a word, to make the author disappear

because he is an unrealistic middleman found on stage neither in drama nor in life. But this is not quite all.

By comparison with the new novel, the old is undramatic and unrealistic. Yet the old novel is in its way realistic enough: it succeeds very well in giving an illusion of life. But, as I have said, realism in the old novel is not an end in itself but a means. Behind it lies not only Aristotle but Horace: it imitates in order to delight, and delights in order to instruct. It is frankly didactic.

In the new novel there are two contrary (if not contradictory) tendencies — one progressive and the other reactionary — sometimes combined in a single novel. One has already been remarked: an extension of the traditional realism, a new realism often sought as an end in itself. The other is a revival of didacticism, a new didacticism. The new realism entails the disappearance of the author; the new didacticism, his furtive reappearance.

The chief manifestation of the new realism is, I have said, the shift of the point of view from the omniscient author to one or more (but one at a time) of his characters within the third-person narrative; and with this shift goes a shift in emphasis from the objective to the subjective — from the action and what a godlike narrator makes of it to what one or more of the characters make of it. In the new realism, not only do we view the action through the eyes and the consciousness of the character; our attention is focused, not upon the action, but upon what the character makes of it, upon his inner life. The subjective — the consciousness of the character — becomes a convention for revealing almost everything revealed about the objective — the action, the setting, the other characters, and so on.

In a sense, of course, this shift to the subjective is undramatic, and undramatic in the way that the omniscient author's revelation of his characters' inner lives is undramatic; for in a play we see (with exceptions already noted) only the objective and must infer the subjective from it. But it is dramatic in that, though we see the subjective, we are made to see it without consciousness of the author's intervention: the author is there all right, arranging everything, but out of sight behind the scenes. "The artist, like the God of the creation, remains within or behind or above his handiwork, invisible, refined out of existence, indifferent, paring his fingernails" — as Stephen's aesthetic, in Joyce's *A Portrait of the Artist as a Young Man*, has it. There is omniscience; but (to hazard an oxy-

moron) it is limited, and it seems to be our omniscience rather than the author's. It is as though there were only one character on stage and we had the gift of X-ray vision so that always before us is his consciousness and through it we see the other characters and the action as he sees them and see also what he makes of them. The point of view is almost ours, that of the reader. This shift to the subjective is an attempt to put us directly in touch with reality, but the reality of the subjective rather than of the objective. There is limited omniscience, but little or nothing other than this to remind us of the omniscient point of view: no exposition, no block characterization, few or no normative words, little or no panoramic narration; or, if there are, they are the character's and not the author's. The organizing principle—the disorganizing principle, perhaps—is the vagaries of the character's consciousness, and not the logic of an omniscient mind analyzing and classifying the data of its imagination.

Such is the new realism. Significant as the differences are among them, it is the method of the later James, of Edith Wharton, of Joyce, of Dorothy Richardson, and of Virginia Woolf. It is the method of such a tidy novel as *The Ambassadors*, which any schoolboy, however much it might bore him, would at a glance recognize as a novel; but it is also the method of such an (apparently) untidy one as *Ulysses*. It is occasionally the method of Dos Passos (in *Manhattan Transfer* and in "The Camera Eye" of *U.S.A.*) and of Faulkner (in *The Sound and the Fury*). In effect, it is much like the method of Conrad in his first-person narratives. It is not really, however, the method of Bennett, Galsworthy, and Lawrence, though they have all felt its touch; and it is certainly not the method of Wells, Forster, T. F. Powys, and (*The Old Man and the Sea* apart) Hemingway. Hemingway, however, in his first-person narratives, almost achieves the purely dramatic (in the more usual sense of "dramatic") by making his narrators report little but dialogue and action, not even their own thoughts, and thus in a way making them disappear. The often-quoted passage in *A Farewell to Arms* about the nastiness of normative words—such words as "sacred," "glorious," and "sacrifice" ("Abstract words such as glory, honor, courage, or hallow were obscene beside the concrete names of villages, the numbers of roads, the names of rivers, the numbers of regiments and the dates.")—is almost an epitome of Hemingway's own dramatic ideal. His narrators, like many modern novelists, have what some of us like to call the modern "sensibility," an attachment to a scientific ideal of objectivity.

The Ambassadors and *Ulysses*, despite their great differences (indeed, because of them), are an instructive pair of examples of the new realism. *The Ambassadors* is, as I have said, a tidy novel. It is written in connected sentences conventionally punctuated. It has a clearly defined, enumerable cast of characters. It has a plot that, though not lively, is easy to follow. And it has a single subject: the awakening of Lambert Strether. *Ulysses*, on the other hand, is in all these respects, and many others, chaos. Its syntax, vocabulary, and punctuation are an affront to the grammarian. It has characters, but it is often hard to say which ones are on stage. It has little plot, and what little it has is well submerged in muddy waters. And it has no single subject; or, if it has, thirty-five years of exegesis have failed to say with certainty what it is. James seems conservative, old-fashioned, traditional; Joyce, outrageously experimental. Yet, for all these differences, both novels instantiate the new realism. From both the author has disappeared. Both are dramatic, scenic third-person narratives written from the point of view, not of their authors, but of their characters; and in both it is not the objective, but the subjective, that counts. In *The Ambassadors*, in an almost unrelieved series of scenes, we see almost everything from the point of view of Strether; we see the doings of the other characters — of Mrs. Newsome, Chad Newsome, Marie de Vionnet, Waymarsh, Maria Gostrey — almost exclusively as they impinge upon Strether's consciousness; and what counts is not their doings, or even Strether's, but what he makes of them. An occasional "our friend" (for "Strether") reminds us that there is an author, and the point of view shifts in the first chapter from Strether to Maria Gostrey to give us what Strether cannot, his physical appearance; but these are about the only sins against the new realism. In *Ulysses*, exclusively scenically, we see everything from the points of view of many characters, though chiefly from those of Dedalus, Bloom, and Mrs. Bloom (the multiplicity of points of view is not germane; for we find this in other novels of James — *The Wings of the Dove*, for example — and what is important is that none of them is the author's); and, even more than in James, what counts — indeed, all that exists — is the consciousnesses of the characters. The chief difference between the novels — and I don't wish to minimize it, for the stream-of-consciousness technique of Joyce is the great technical experiment of the new novel — is that — while in *The Ambassadors* the objective, for all of Strether's consciousness, is always clearly out there, beyond the subjective — it scarcely exists in *Ulysses*: in *Ulysses*, "he said" and "he thought" are nowhere, word and thought literally flow together in one stream, and deed must be inferred from them.

With the new realism often goes the new didacticism — a didacticism that scorns explicit statement, thrives upon indirection, and goes under the name "symbolism." The new novel, like the old novel, often has what used to be called "a moral" and is nowadays called "a theme"; it has some sort of generalization — usually moral — to make about life. But in the new novel, as not in the old, the theme is not the subject of exposition — for the new novel permits no exposition — but is somehow implicit or figured in the narrative or the drama. In other words, the characters and their actions — like those in *Everyman*, *The Faerie Queene*, or *Pilgrim's Progress* (and this is reactionary indeed) — are symbols. But in the new novel, as not in its illustrious allegorical ancestors, it is pretty hard to say just what the values of the symbols are. There is, we have seen, no exposition. And there are few two-dimensional, humour characters and none with allegorical names — no Everyman, no Death; no Red Cross Knight; no Christian; not even a Thwackum, a M'Choakumchild, or a Slope. In short, there is little — little that is obvious at least — to guide the reader in interpreting the allegory. If the new didacticism has been a boon to the little magazines, it has been a bit hard on the common reader (with whom Dr. Johnson rejoiced to concur). If the new novel has — as modern critics sometimes wrongly hold — been more concerned with technique than the old, it has surely been less concerned with the art of rhetoric, of adapting discourse to a given reader for a given purpose; it tends to take a romantic rather than a traditional view of the artist and of his relationship to the reader — viewing literary art as self-expression rather than as communication or persuasion. The complement of "exit author" may well be "exit reader"; if the author disappears, the reader may well disappear, too — in the sense that the author loses sight of him and he must shift for himself. (In another sense, of course, the complement of "exit author" is "enter reader"; the role of the reader who must shift for himself is greater than that of the one who need not.) Happily, however, the ideals of the new realism and the new didacticism are, as we shall see, both unattained and unattainable; and both the author and the reader, shadowy as they may have become, are still with us.

In speaking of didacticism, new or old, however, we must be careful to distinguish between the novel that, like *Ulysses* or *The Ambassadors* or *Mrs. Dalloway* or *Victory*, assumes, exploits, or reaffirms a certain moral code and the novel that, like Godwin's *Caleb Williams* or in our day the novels of Upton Sinclair, has a certain moral code or program as its thesis. The new didacticism, like most of the old, is exemplified in novels of the first sort. And we must be careful also to remember that a given course of events, in life itself or as narrated in a novel, logically entails no single moral or theme; that, if the syllogism of which the moral is the conclusion has (as it were) the course of events as its major premise, it has the observer's or the reader's values as its minor. The reader must bring to the novel either a code of morals, a set of beliefs and attitudes, that roughly corresponds to the novelist's or at least a knowledge of and a disposition to take seriously that code. To put the matter in another way, the novelist must (if he thinks of a reader at all) always assume a reader whose morals or moral knowledge is such that it can cooperate with the novelist in producing the response desired of the reader: it is doubtful that a bright Hottentot or Zulu, however great his facility with English, would ever make much of Edith Wharton's *The Age of Innocence* or even of *Mansfield Park*, let alone *Ulysses* or *To the Lighthouse*. Ironically, the new novel, written in the age in which ethical diversity is greatest, does less than the old to guide the reader.

But, granting that a novelist must have a suitable reader, the fact is, I think, that, though the new realism and the new didacticism are incompatible as ideals, realism cannot, even if it wishes to, escape didacticism; the author cannot, whatever his ideals may be, avoid giving the reader some hints of his beliefs and attitudes. Not even a genre so dramatic, so author-effacing, as the drama itself can escape didacticism. There are at least two reasons why this should be so. For one thing, a particular course of events narrated in a novel, though fictive, symbolizes, by virtue of being similar to, courses of events that are not fictive. Such a course of events is symbolic in the same way that particular events in life itself are symbolic. We always take a particular as an instance of the general, an individual as a member of some class. And similarly, *mutatis mutandis*, with the characters and the setting of a novel: "imaginary characters," David Daiches justly contends,

> . . . always function in some degree as symbols: that is, the characters insofar as they act and are acted upon are represented, through any of a variety of devices, as illuminating more than the behavior of some fortuitously chosen individual. Characters in fiction are always symbols to some extent, and their interest largely derives from this fact. . . . they repre-

sent situations which, though unique in the way they are presented, are not unique in their implications. They become . . . not simply characters taking part in a given action, but characters illuminating, through their "doing and suffering," certain phases of experience. ("Problems for Modern Novelists. I," *Accent*, III, 1943.)

Fiction of whatever kind is incorrigibly and inevitably synecdochic: its fictive particulars symbolize the wholes of which they are imaginary parts or the classes of which they are imaginary members. And, for another thing, a particular in a novel, unlike one in life, always carries with it to some extent those beliefs and attitudes of the author that are relevant to it and, by synecdochic extension, relevant also to similar particulars in life itself; a novel, unlike life, carries its moral or theme with it.

The ways in which it does this are various. Some of the ways of the old novel, which is rich in didactic resources, we have already noted: exposition, humour characters, and allegorical names, for example. The ways of the new novel, which is anxious to avoid either didacticism or, at least, obvious marks of it and is less concerned to guide the reader, are more devious. Its inevitable way, of course, is its structure, the author's selection and ordering of topics. With all the world before him, where to choose, choose the author must; and his choice almost inevitably has moral implications. Even the structure of such a disordered novel as Virginia Woolf's *Mrs. Dalloway*—which, like *Ulysses*, crowds a miscellany of characters and events into less than twenty-four hours—has such implications. Even a very careful reader might, of course, be hard put to it to say just what they are, for structure is the only clue; but, to mention only one thing, Mrs. Woolf's creation and juxtaposition of two worlds—the world of Mrs. Dalloway, a world of well-given parties, and that of people whom Mrs. Dalloway has not met, the world of (among many others) the Septimus Warren-Smith, a world of war, work, neurosis, and suicide—implies a tragic dimension to existence. Another way in which the new novel carries its moral or theme with it, well exemplified in *Ulysses*, is to suggest in one way or another that there is some sort of correspondence, perhaps ironic, between what goes on in the novel and something outside the novel—to suggest, in short, not only that the novel is an allegory but where the key to the allegory lies. The title of *Ulysses* suggests the *Odyssey*; diligence—Stuart Gilbert's if not the common reader's—will discover elaborate correspondences, both stylistic and structural, between the two works; and the veiled comparison of, for example, Bloom with Ulysses implies a moral judgment upon a segment at least of the modern world (comically pronounced, if we are to take Joyce's word for it).

Here I can do no more than briefly speculate about the causes of the new realism and the new didacticism; it is worth noting, however, that, whatever the causes, they seem to have affected not only the new novel but modern literature generally. These two movements, I am inclined to believe, owe their existence or at least bear complex relationships to three related phenomena: the rise of romanticism, the rise of science, and the decline of religion. Behind these two movements probably lie the romantic theory of art as self-expression, which ignores or neglects the reader or the audience; the scientific ideal of objectivity, which (when held by the artist *qua* artist) confuses the roles of science and art (indeed, of life and art); the emergence of psychology as a science, which (in another sense of "objective") shifts the focus of art from the objective to the subjective; and ethical relativism, which makes the artist chary of explicit statement of his values.

When we think of realism, we usually think only of fiction and drama. But this is a mistake. The form and some of the origins of fiction, and the form of drama, predispose these genres toward realism. Fictive discourse often has the superficial form of factual — as in *Secret Memoirs and Manners of Several Persons of Quality*, *A Journal of the Plague Year*, *Pamela*, *The History of Tom Jones, and Evelina* — and, as some of these eighteenth-century titles suggest, has some roots in the factual. It came into being, moreover, when the moral universe was well on the wane; and it has prospered in the physical. And drama, in its use of dialogue and flesh-and-blood actors, has always operated even nearer to the boundary between life and art than fiction has, and far nearer than poetry, which is patently artificial. For these reasons, fiction and drama have been more susceptible than poetry to realism. But realism has altered poetic theory and practice too. As Rosemond Tuve has pointed out (in *Elizabethan and Metaphysical Imagery*), the twentieth century makes two demands on poetry that would never have occurred to sixteenth- and seventeenth- (and, for that matter, eighteenth- and nineteenth-) century poets and readers, to whom "artificial" was a word of praise for a poem, and tropes a common study — demands that probably spring not only (as Miss Tuve surmises) from the modern interest in states of consciousness (that is, psychology) and the modern unwillingness to make assertions about values (due, I might add, to a conviction that such assertions are inappropriate or invalid in a universe that is no longer moral but physical) but also from a modern confusion of the roles of science and art. These two demands both entail uses of sensuous images (comparable, I think, to use of the stream of consciousness in the modern novel) — the first for "the representation of a sensuous experience, or a series of sensuous experiences, without comment or other unmistakable indication from author to reader of value or generalized meaning"; the second for "the accurate representation of the author's emotional experience or state of mind, the communication of that state or experience being regarded as a sufficient aim for a poem (without, for example, further indication by the author of an intended general meaning)." In theory (in the imagist manifestoes and in T. E. Hulme's *Speculations,* for instance), such imagery is neutral in respect of values, of a moral or a theme; it is, in a word, the new realism. In practice (like the stream of consciousness in the novel), it willy-nilly, and however imperfectly, indicates something about the poet's beliefs and attitudes. But, be this as it may, the new realism has in our century pervaded literary art, both in theory and in practice (and the new didacticism, where we find it, is a modest triumph of the artist's literary instincts over his intellectual preoccupations). Indeed, the new realism — and the confusion of science and art, and of life and art, that it encourages — has gone further than this: the housewife who sends fan mail and presents to characters in soap operas — no less than Caroline Spurgeon, who (in *Shakespeare's Imagery and What It Tells Us*) takes Shakespeare's imagery to be an index to his biography — is its minion.

That the ideal of the new realism is an unattained, unattainable, and (it seems to me) undesirable ideal — that the new realism not only cannot escape but needs the new didacticism — is a commonplace nowadays in the criticism of poetry, and perhaps we have the New Criticism to thank that it is; but, as Mark Schorer has complained (in "Technique as Discovery," in *Forms of Modern Fiction*), criticism of the novel lags far behind. Until this century, the novel was not taken seriously enough to get much criticism; but, even now, when it is the dominant genre, the only species of it for which there is anything like a poetic is the new realism, and its poetic is, I have urged, inadequate for that species and, *a fortiori,* for others. The new realism is a set of literary conventions like any other and not the inevitable way of the novelist (or the dramatist or the poet) who knows his business. Like any set of conventions, it imposes limitations: what the new realism gains in one direction — its fine dramatization of the subjective — it loses in others — rapport with the reader, for example, and the kinds of irony (a large topic in itself) that only omniscience permits. But, when the new realism is thought of as a set of conventions, it is sometimes thought of as *the* set of conventions. Even René Wellek and Austin Warren — who, in *Theory of Literature,* which consolidates the critical gains of the century, so label the new realism — go on to discuss motivation as though it were basic to all fiction. We must, I think, conclude that the critic or the reader brought up by the new realism to think of it as an ideal toward which the old novel was bumblingly striving will seriously misread the old novel and, indeed, some of the new. If concern with technique in literature is concern with working within a set of conventions, then the old novel is as much concerned with technique as the new: but with a different technique; and — as almost every essay in this volume testifies — there is abundant evidence, internal and external, of this concern. The reader who goes to Peacock, Dickens, or Emily Brontë — or, for that matter, to T. F. Powys, Lawrence, or Faulkner — equipped only with the poetic of the new realism invites both bewilderment and disappointment.

We need not, of course, choose between the old novel and the new. Neither has displaced the other; both are with us; and we should rejoice that they are. Each has its glories, each its limitations. What we should not do is to take so narrow a view of literary conventions that we are forced to choose between them. Perhaps we need a new *Battle of the Books* to mock both the "critic" (who scorns the old novel) and the "scholar" (who scorns the new).

Index

INDEX

All authors mentioned in the text explicitly by name or implicitly by reference to their works or ideas or influence are listed in the index. All other persons mentioned in the text are listed with a few trivial exceptions; but neither fictional characters nor real persons mentioned only in fictional works (as characters in historical novels, for instance) are listed. All works mentioned in the text explicitly by title or implicitly by allusion to their statements, incidents, characters, or ideas are listed in the index with the exception of a few twentieth-century books and periodical articles. Subheads within entries identify more particularly the subject matter of certain page references (sometimes giving additional information); however, page references amounting to little more than mention of a subject are not subheaded. In addition, topical entries locate discussion of points of style, structure, and literary history. Topics such as characterization, setting, structure, and theme, which pervade the volume, are not listed as main entries (though kinds of theme, for example, are); but they and like broad topics appear as subheads under author and title entries.

Index

Index

Index

Index

Index